Men Don't Love Women Like You:
The Brutal Truth About Dating, Relationships, and How to Go from Placeholder to Game Changer

Ω

Table of Contents

**Dedicated to the first woman I ever loved,
my mother**

Introduction:

a woman once told me how she faked having cancer to get her boyfriend to move in with her. She made a promise to herself that she would be married by 30, and at 29, that was her final Hail Mary. It worked...for two months. Then he left her, still believing she had cancer and all, for another woman. "If cancer couldn't make him stay, then what would have," was the question she asked me. The question I asked myself... *How the fuck did it come to this?*

Over the past six years, I've talked to tens of thousands of women who have sought me out for advice. There aren't too many men with access to such a large and diverse pool of women which I can pull from. Those born in the 60s to those born in the 90s, across all racial backgrounds and socioeconomic classes. I don't need to look at polls or stats; I see firsthand what fails, what works, and what only works for a time. From Sydney to Johannesburg to New York, men play the same games and women look for the same solutions. This is a world where everyone has advice to give on how you should live your life, every pseudo-celebrity tries to make a buck by calling themselves a relationship expert, and every Psych major with an internet connection and webcam claims to be some sort of life coach. It's all bullshit. It's a machine that offers women quick fixes from half-ass therapy, pumps them full of false confidence by using sugary words, and where do they end up? Right back on the dick of a man that doesn't want them. I don't play in that self-help sandbox; I am not the mainstream choice you see on some morning show blowing smoke up your ass. I am the harsh reality that speaks the truth you need to hear to become harder, not the gentle pat on the back that helps you survive another day as a man's doormat.

Men aren't even good at lying. Have you been out lately? Today's males are remarkably idiotic, yet they still manage to get whatever they want by exploiting smart women with those weak lies. Look at the world of compromise that's been allowed. Netflix and Chill is considered a real date. "Hey, are you coming out to the bar tonight?" is courting. "Let me just put the tip in," is poetry. And *Side chick* has become a viable relationship title. Men aren't held accountable for playing games; they are held onto tighter,

1

and a generation of women won't do a damn thing about it but go to war with each other to see whose Instagram picture can attract the cutest loser. All of this empowerment talk, but few women actually live in power. They live in worry of if a guy will call them or not. They buy into lies they know are lies because they imagine a love waiting for them that will be worth the struggle. That weakness makes my stomach turn.

Breaking down the mind games of men and the various dick tactics they use on women is how I give back. Rebuilding self-esteem and giving practical ways to rise above the game has helped thousands, but I still see the same mistakes being made, and now realize I haven't gone hard enough. One woman had a boyfriend who slept with her sister. She took him back, got engaged, and he slept with her cousin. Her only concern was asking me how to keep her current boyfriend happy, so he wouldn't stray like that fiancé. It's amazingly frustrating! What I recognized was that women didn't become angry, they became even more submissive. Despite the manipulative treatment guys put them through, they keep trying to find new ways to win male love. Sure, some develop attitudes, trust issues, and become bitter, but even they aren't angry. Women can't afford to hate men because they believe their future depends on finding a man to love.

Getting a man isn't a success story, the title of girlfriend is like the common cold, leave a girl outside long enough, and she will eventually get it. I rate success on one thing—**Power**. Have I made a woman so powerful that she no longer asks me, "how do I get him to like me," or is she still looking for ways to kneel and roll over for dick's approval? Most don't get to that level of true power. They get a boyfriend who's handsome, wealthy, or even a famous athlete, and run back to me stripped of the confidence I spent so much time trying to build. This book changes that. Comprehend the secrets revealed within, and it will transform you at the core. But as an introduction, I felt a need to bring to the forefront the flaw that keeps you, yes you, stuck where you are—Men don't love women like you.

There is something holding you back; there has always been something holding you back. You don't see it yet, but you will. No matter what relationship advice you try to use or what new teachings you try to embrace, in the end, weak men, damaged men, needy men, flawed men are the only ones that will ever want you, and they won't even love you fully.

The Alpha Males you crush on and make exceptions for, they don't settle for your type. They use you up and push you away. You talk about the same redundant topics and send the same dry texts as every other woman, and when your clothes are on, you are about as exciting as oatmeal. Men don't tell you this, they have to play along for pussy. So they flatter you in the same way they flatter every other woman, and you eat it up just like she did. You catch the same attitude as other women, and a man defuses you with the same "you know I care," tactics she fell for. Everything you do is predictable! The excuse that you're not looking for love, a lie. The excuse that there aren't any good men in your city, a lie. The excuse that your astrological signs don't match up, more bullshit. You don't know how to win, so you hide behind excuses! What are you going to do, wait for men to invent more ways to humble you? Go on, keep hiding behind your attitude, keep promoting that you don't care, but you feel it. Your life is heading towards happily ever settled; another woman that settles for what she could get because she never had the fucking heart to go after what she wanted. *Move in with you but never marry you, get you pregnant then find a way skip out, milk you like a cow for a few years, then replace you with a better version...* is that who you want to be, another failed story? Another old lady that looks back and says, "I wish I would have known better?"

You don't need a hug; you need a kick in the ass. You don't need to be understood; you need to understand. You don't need relationship advice; you need someone to hold your face up to a mirror until you realize that it's all your fault. You made mistakes when you were younger, you kept making mistakes as you grew older, and how did you better yourself each time? You lied. You placed blame on age, you placed blame on friends, you placed blame on parents, you placed blame on men. It's everyone's fault except yours, and here you are again, trying to learn how to do better while clinging on to the notion that nothing is wrong. Lies keep you from crying, but they won't make you any happier. The truth is, if you loved yourself as passionately as you love the idea of a man's validation, you would be unstoppable. You are at a crossroads where you can either follow the truth or swallow the lies, and I am offering you the power to rewrite life itself. This isn't a book; this is that mirror you sent for...

3

Part I
Awaken The Spartan:
Change The Game

Chapter 1:
Typical Bitch, Typical Results

hat makes you so damn special? If you were to sit across from a man on a first date, corner booth, wine flowing, your eyes locked on one another, and he asked you that simple question, what would be your unrehearsed response? Maybe you would lift your head high and read off a list of your academic achievements, your bachelor's in this or your master's in that. Perhaps you would skip the schooling, and start with your career. Name-drop that it's a Fortune 500 company or boast about how many times you've been promoted in a short period. Maybe you're the type that doesn't have any external credentials you can list as amazing, so you use the oldest trick in the book: compare yourself to other women to demonstrate how rare of a catch you are. You have your own car and your own place—you're not like the next bitch. You have your own money and you don't have to ask a man for anything—you're not like the next bitch. You can cook, you keep yourself well dressed, and you are not the kind of woman who has a name around town...I get it...you are not like the next bitch. When challenged with what makes you special, your answer will always be some form of, "I'm special because I'm not like other women." Do you know who says those exact things? Every other woman!

You are essentially a hamburger. No one is ever surprised to see you on a menu, they expect it. Yet another woman who uses words like, "I'm the type that..." "If that were me, I..." and "These girls today are...," failing to realize that you are emblematic of those same girls you are attempting to distance yourself from. When a man sits and listens to you separate yourself by throwing around those generic qualities, he may nod his head, utter a limp "wow, look at you! I need someone like that on the team," but internally, his eyes are rolling because every man has heard this all before.

Unbeknownst to you, four out of the five things you are claiming as special, other women lay claim to as well. Do you think you are the only educated, independent, loyal, spiritual, female that a man who actually gets out beyond his neighborhood will meet? You're a self-proclaimed, good woman. Spoiler alert, a successful man dates multiple "good women" a month. During a conversation, a man will experience Typical Bitch Date Déjà Vu: *This lawyer across from me is just like that school teacher from last month. She says she's looking for this kind of connection, she says she has this going for her, she was just on some vacation, and she's now saying she's the type that blah fucking blah! Jeez, this bitch is vanilla!* In the end, her job, her income, nor her ownership of property will become a major factor in determining if he actually wants more from her than sex. No matter what this woman lists as unique, he does not feel that she is because he has sat across from women who are just as self-reliant and successful, three times this month.

Men will always play along and act as if you're the most interesting woman in the world. You have a new vagina he hasn't sampled yet, so he's going to flatter you and feign impressed, but I know what's actually going on in his head. While sitting across from you, a man is hearing the same typical responses and the same typical opinions. He can tell that, with maybe a few exceptions, you are exactly like that nurse who he dated for three weeks, slept with, and then got bored with—Yawn! 9 out of 10 women bring the same shit to the table in terms of academics, employment, and domestic abilities. "Where is he ever going to meet a woman who is intelligent and makes over 80k a year?" Everywhere!

The majority of grown ass women are studious and responsible. I've given advice to countless women over the years, psychologists, engineers, actresses, small and large business owners. Do you know what I tell them when they give me lame personality traits like, "Well, I'm loyal and honest," and then tout their yearly income as if that's more important than their personality? Congratulations for doing what you're supposed to do in life...but where is the charisma, the fire, the wit, the aggression, and the personality of a powerful woman to go along with those degrees or job titles? Men don't want these ladies, no matter what they bring to the table, and they don't understand why. Typicals cling on to that first few weeks treatment as proof that a man had real interest, but real interest doesn't peak. If a man sees you as different, as special, then interest will only rise. It levels off with the average woman, because despite her achievements or looks, she comes off as unique as seeing snow in Colorado.

This chapter is about defining who you truly are, not who you think you are based on your own egotistical view of yourself. In your own mind, you may be the greatest woman who has ever lived, but to those who meet you, it's highly likely that you are viewed as merely alright. Some of you may feel a need to skip this part because you don't want to have your feelings hurt. All you have is that defensive voice in your head that screams, "He's not talking about me, I'm not typical." Do not run away from this chapter. This is between you and you, there is no reason to put on a strong front as if you don't have any problems, or that you're different. You're not. There are walls that you've built up to keep your sensitive feelings from being hurt. The pride that tells you that you are stronger than what you are, the ego that tells you that the men who didn't want you were stupid or emotionally unavailable, the cosmetics that make you feel prettier than what you are when you first wake up, the materialistic bullshit you buy to make you feel fancier than other people—All Walls!

I work and have my own. I don't need a man financially. I'm the type of woman mothers love. I'm very caring and nurturing. I would make a great mother and wife, myself. I focus on one man because I'm loyal. I don't hang with a lot of girls or put my business online. I'm not clingy or annoying. I stand by my man no matter what. My ex-boyfriends will tell you that I was the best girlfriend they ever had. I'm not trying to brag but look at me, men are always trying to wife me.

Typical women list typical qualities because they aren't self-aware enough to actually dig down deep and share what truly makes them special. Those qualities may add to your greatness, but none of them are so rare that you should lean on them like a crutch and expect a man to feel privileged to be talking to you. Your career doesn't make you any less boring. Your education can help you add up how many missed calls you've left and figure out that he's not calling you back after sex. Your niceness is overrated; tons of women can bring soup to a sick man and listen to him vent about work, maternal chicks grow on trees. Your vagina isn't dipped in gold, and they didn't stop making cute faces after they made yours, so why would a man put up with your dry ass personality after your pretty becomes normal and your pussy expires? All the crap that you think makes you different is T.Y.P.I.C.A.L and I'm going to prove it. You can roll your eyes, you can squirm in your chair, and you can get defensive, but once you're done with those typical reactions, you will be forced to upgrade your mindset. This is not about tearing you down; it's about tearing your false representative down so you can finally set yourself apart from every other woman in this world. Lower your defenses, open your mind, and let's pour gasoline on all of the typical things you think make you, so we can build a stronger you.

YOU ARE NOT YOUR CAREER

Look at how proactive women of all races are in terms of pursuing some form of higher education, and their ability to attain a full-time job. Even those women who were born in poverty, more often than the men from those same backgrounds, will rise to the middle-class through hard work and determination. The majority of women want more out of life, and for the past century, each generation has outshone the last generation in terms of accomplishments. These are beautiful qualities that should be applauded, but the point is, this happens often, which means that men do not see this as unique. There are more responsible women than *Do Nothing Bitches,* despite what you may see on Reality TV shows or Vine videos.

Nevertheless, typical women have this idea that they're the only ones doing it big. This is the root of their false confidence. They didn't stop making successful women when they made you, and men know it. Let's stick with the theme of women who come from humble beginnings and reach some form of middle-class success. Who do they have to compare themselves to in terms of, "Why would a man pick her over me?" A woman who grew up in a working-class family in Flint, Michigan isn't comparing herself to the daughter of a CEO who grew up in Ann Arbor. That wouldn't boost her ego, so she compares herself to those females who originated from the same class and background, to point out her greatness.

Let's pretend that most of the girls who you have known since childhood only did some college or went to a trade school, but you have a degree, that makes you better. That popular girl from high school who you follow on Facebook now has two kids and put on weight, you look better than you did in high school, that makes you better. Those basic bitches on social media who stunt with champagne bottles in the club and blow income tax money on designer bags, you know them in real life. Those birds work part-time and still live with parents or roommates; you have year-round money and your own place, that makes you better. You can sit there and pretend to be humble, and say all the polite things, but the fact is that when asked what makes you better for a man than another woman, you reach for those comparisons. Maybe you have sorority sisters or college roommates who are doing it at your level or higher, but for the most part, those struggling chicks that you are related to, associate with, or constantly hear gossip about, are the women you point to before pointing to yourself. It isn't that CEO's daughter, who just became the youngest executive at her company, you are referring to when you claim to be unique and rare. Your special is only special because you are comparing yourself to the basic women around you, never the most exceptional ones.

Here is what you fail to realize when you let your ego run wild. Men aren't dating from the pool of your friends or associates; they date from an entire sea of women, which is not limited to your background or your environment. Black men, white men, Hispanic men, rich men, poor men, and everything in between, they cross-pollinate in terms of women. They aren't grading on a curve, which means you don't get a cookie for being the first one in your family with a PhD nor do you get a second date because you've overcome the odds your cousins couldn't. The moment you begin that date you're just some woman who went to some school and has some job, and all that matters going forward is your personality type.

Even a woman who doesn't have anything going for herself can spin her circumstances like a politician. "I'm taking night classes; I'm not going to be a waitress forever...I only work at Wal-Mart because it's flexible in terms of giving me time to start and grow my own business." No matter if she's a Bottle Girl at a night club or cashier at Home Depot, she can make herself sound just as impressive as the next woman in terms of ambition.

Men don't look down at women who don't have much. The stereotype of "don't ask for a successful man, if you aren't a successful woman," is unfounded! Look at who men routinely marry, fight over, and chase down. Men are more concerned with a personality type that shows him something different from the last girl he took out. Nevertheless, these Basicas[1] are only a small part of the dating pool for men who aren't in lower-class environments. When men of a certain caliber date, meaning men who are equal or above you in terms of success and education, they aren't running into that many basics; they are running into women who shop where they shop, party where they party, and live where they live. Meaning the women they encounter the most, have the fundamental things that any woman outside of a hood or trailer park would have: <u>Education and Employment</u>.

For a man, meeting a woman with a degree is as common as rain in Seattle. A woman with a full-time job who doesn't live at home is no longer a cause for excitement once a man hits his mid-20s because the average woman tends to flee the nest after college. Your career or job title may be met with some interest if it's something impressive conversation-wise, but in the larger scope, it doesn't matter to a man who has his own career. He's not looking to network with you; he's looking to fuck you! Therefore, the floor your office is on, the hospital you work at, the type of law you practice, isn't going to make him see you as a must-have. Do you know who cares about how much money you make, if you have a new car, and if you own your own place? Users and Playboys! A man who doesn't have a job or who is under-employed needs you. A user doesn't need you for your character or your personality traits, but for those materialistic things, because what you have now, will become what he has later.

If you are trying to impress James the Bouncer/Fitness instructor who only works 20 hours a week, he will be impressed with your degree, your car, your condo, and the fact that you don't need a man for money. James is cute and charismatic, but he doesn't have a pot to piss in, that is until he wins your heart. Once he wins you over, he now has a car, he now has a condo, and he has a walking bank run by an independent woman who doesn't mind "helping out." Wake up!

---

[1] Pet name for a basic bitch. Those generic, hollow, and unoriginal women.

12

A man who has dignity, even if he does make less than you, isn't looking for a sponsor; therefore, all that shit you have is superfluous in his eyes. He wants to know the real you and discover that this real you is not trite. An alpha male is not on the hunt for a breadwinner. Ideally, he wants a partner who can take care of herself and is impressive in her own right, not a spoiled brat with no drive, but ambition is a character trait which is not solely defined by her job title or where she went to school. That means that a woman that works part-time is on equal footing with a woman who owns her own hair salon in the world of dating, as they both will sell themselves as go-getters. The playing field is not rigged because of a job or level of education. Few women want to accept this because their uniqueness is tied to them having made it higher up the career ladder than their pool of peers. A man could give two fucks about the girls you out worked and are more successful than. *Who are you really and how will we get along*? Men won't say they don't care to your face, again, it's "Wow, that's great..." but the proof is in the results. Elite women can and will get passed over for ratchets, Hos, or girls you would consider bums.

You imagine that a man looks for what you look for in a mate; physical appeal, but can bring something to the table. Men aren't wired like women. A man can populate his own table, he isn't hosting a potluck. Guys go on first dates and try to impress women with the same typical things I listed; where they work and what they have because women look for those things. A man is often measured by his success, but if you, as a woman, show up on that date and aren't equal, he doesn't hold it against you. If you don't have your own place, but he does, cool, you can still come over. If you don't have a reliable car, but he does, cool, he can come pick you up. If you don't make much money and can't afford the tip on a $200 dinner, cool, dinner dates aren't going to ruin his monthly budget. Providers do not judge women; takers do. Be proud of your accomplishments, but remember you achieved those things for your self-benefit, not to be more attractive to some guy so he will choose you over the next chick. The most typical move you can make is to parade your success in front of a man as if he's never seen a woman like you before. Trust me; he has seen women doing it just as big as you, if not bigger, so what else can you point to that makes you rare?

YOU ARE NOT WHAT YOU CAN DO FOR A MAN

Basic mothers passed on to their young daughters this idea that the way to a man's heart is through some form of domesticated spoiling. Cooking, cleaning, emotional support, even financial support, are mainstays in the June Cleaver playbook. "No man is going to marry a woman that can't cook," turned out to be as bullshit as the Mayan Calendar. Still, domestic skills, much like careers, are bragged about as if it gives you a leg up on other women. Men play along like, "oh you can cook? Let me come over so you can prove it." He doesn't give a fuck about your recipes, he's baiting you for a house date where you cook, and then he has you as dessert. Your ego confuses a man's spoiled love of being taken care of by a woman with his actual love for that woman. A man's love can't be bribed with those traditional *Kitchen Bitch* skills, but he will always take advantage of what you're naïve enough to give him.

When I was younger, I would ride around during the summer with my uncle who was a renowned ladies man. Every weekend we would stop by this woman's house; I'll call her Ms. May because that's not her name. Ms. May would make these big plates for my Uncle and his henchmen, and he would flirt with her, filling her head up with game that made her blush. Of course, she would play it off as if she knew it was hollow flattery, but I could see by the sparkle in her eye, that it was working. These were not leftovers; they were meals made specifically for him, and with love in hopes of winning my Uncle's heart. One evening we drove off from Ms. May's, and with home-cooked drumstick meat still dangling from his mouth, he looked over to me and said, "That's one simple bitch, right there." I never forgot that moment, and it often repeats in my head every time I see a new generation of "Simple Bitches" attempt to win over a man by being a domestic goddess.

Ask not what you can do for a man, but what a man can do for you. That should be a motto to live by for progressive women, but how many of you actually practice that? When you are face to face with a man who you find attractive, are you allowing him to sell himself while you sit back and observe if he's sincere or full of shit, or do you slip into the habit of trying to sell all the things you bring to a relationship? Typical women talk about what they can do, like a walking floor model, trying to auction themselves off to some dick who hasn't even proven himself worthy. Why are you talking about how well you cook or how some ex-boyfriend's mother loved you? Why are you trying to paint this picture that you are a wife type that just had the misfortune of meeting weak men who couldn't handle your love? Brace for another spoiler alert: We men have heard your pitch before! A woman who is not normal doesn't have to advertise, her results speak for themselves. You have to over-sell because men aren't buying! There is a burning need to be wanted by the men you deem extraordinary, and due to this fire, that weak bitch part of you boils and boils, until it overflows and turns you typical. *Let me show him how I submit, cater, and give him what he wants because through these acts he will realize there aren't too many like me.* Making a man earn you is common sense, but when driven by a fear that the latest Mr. Right will pass you up, you overcompensate. Give him everything for free and watch how you get nothing in return but your time wasted.

YOU ARE NOT YOUR VAGINA

When it comes to sex, let's be honest, those of you that aren't virgins find ways to slide in little clues that point to how skilled you are in the bedroom. You're not trying to seem too nasty, but when the conversation toes that sexual line, you make remarks about how your exes never complained or drop hints about how you lay it down in the bedroom prefaced by some "if/when I have a man..." line to make it seem as if locking you down is the key to some *Fifty Shades of Grey* experience. No matter if you're introverted or extroverted, you know that sex sells, and you play into that. I saw a girl with big lips get offended when a man made a blowjob joke, then ten minutes later, she's making a Snapchat story in front of me, "Guys always say my lips could put in work, but they'll never know." She wasn't offended, she ate it up, and then used it as propaganda to lure in her online guy crush because she wants that image in his head.

For the first time in history, we have women being as sexually competitive as men. You know of the term "penis envy," where a man tries to make up for his shortcomings by buying the biggest car, boat, mansion, you name it, to prove that dick size doesn't matter because he's winning in all other areas. There isn't a vagina envy, but it has become common, especially among millennials, to talk about <u>Good Pussy Vs Bad Pussy</u>. The idea is that certain vaginas feel better than others. This magic box is something a woman is apparently blessed with at birth while others are cursed with vaginas that don't satisfy men. It's an ego play, and unlike things you can measure with your eyes like hair length or deduct through testing like IQ, you can't go to a specialist and come back certified with **Grade A Pussy**, thus any girl can say she has a legendary coochie. This isn't just something ratchet girls on the porch talk about while smoking Newport's. I see educated women also drinking this Kool-Aid. "I know I have good pussy, so sex isn't the reason he's [insert bad behavior]." What happened to cause these females to put so much stock in their vagina being built differently from the next woman? Men happened!

Males are known to promote all kinds of bullshit myths to flatter women and earn points, and the past few generations came up with the concept of *Bomb Pussy, Tight Pussy, Loose Pussy, Weak Pussy*, and used it to either praise the woman they were with or slander a girl who they are no longer with. Vagina quality is propaganda built around the fact that no woman has the power to sample another vagina with a penis to see how it actually feels. Put your finger in it, taste it, grab a toy, but there is no way to experience what a man experiences during vaginal intercourse. This sounds like a harmless ego stroke, but sex is another crutch that props up false confidence. Sex baiting works in terms of *Ho Tactics* or general seduction, because men think with their dicks, making it easy to keep a man's attention before you have sex just by talking about how good you are at it. What happens after you actually bust it open? Does a vagina that was called "best ever" actually get you what you want in terms of love or commitment? Hell no! All vagina is comparable in terms of feeling. If he thrusts, he will cum. It doesn't matter if it's tight from non-use or a bit easier to get in due to active use, if he can maintain an erection he will cum from the in out, in out friction, it's not rocket science. Ooo! You get super wet...so does the next woman when aroused. It's not "super soaker pussy" it's biology.

What really gets men off is the experience of sex. A girl who moans, a girl who talks, a girl who sucks her own breast, a girl who rubs her clitoris, that can upgrade the actual physical feeling, because sex is mental. If any of those things mesh with what a man finds sexually appealing, he will value that experience more than a girl who simply laid there like a corpse bride. The point being, just your vagina spread open, is not a unique force that acts as an emotional magnet where a man falls in love or refuses to leave it. The woman connected to the vagina is what leaves the impression! Even if you end up walking down the aisle, it won't be your vagina that led to his choice, just as it won't be your career, or your ability to cook, those are all false confidence crutches. You claim that he's not going anywhere because your Aquafina is the fountain of youth, but what happened to the last few men you slept with? *Where they at tho*? Not with you! You say that he's going to want to lock you down once he hits it once. Why didn't those other guys lock you down after hitting it multiple times? Your pussy drives men crazy...so crazy that they fall out of love and end up with other women. You had sex with a guy who praised you, would come over late to get some, and even when you broke up, he still came back to hit it. **This is normal male behavior, not evidence of mutant pussy.** Your power isn't in your pussy; it's in the promotion of that pussy. All men are thirsty for sex—fact. To tease him as if he can't handle it, he's not ready, your exes always came fast, or any other sexually dominant idea will drive him into a frenzy. He will do all kinds of romantic things, say all kinds of fake deep words, and tell other people how you're his...that does not mean you have control over him or that you are even special to him.

    I've sampled more than a few boxes and told some tall tales about how great they were during and after sex, so allow me to clear up a man's mindset when you try to play this pussy whip game. Once you give it up, the hype is over. Maybe you're Sasha Grey[2] nasty, but that isn't going to buy you love. I've personally had incredible sex with women who I didn't even bother to see again. They lived up to the hype, but once the lust was gone, I realized that I didn't click with them personality wise. A part of me wanted to hit it again, but I didn't even feel like going through the effort of faking like I was interested just to get a quick nut. As a counter to that, I had extremely boring sex with this girl who was funny and personable, and because I enjoyed her company, she became my girlfriend for a time.

---

[2] Iconic adult film star, notable for going to sexual extremes.

Think about what that means practically. The woman who shines bright in the bedroom doesn't get as far as the woman who shines bright outside of the bedroom. Even boring sex ends in ejaculation, and as a couple you two can always upgrade the freakiness, so why would any man put up with a typical girl for a nut he can reach just as easy elsewhere? He calls you "amazing" because he came, he calls her "wack" because he couldn't maintain a full erection, and needs to place blame for his flaccid penis on someone other than himself. You may mentally stimulate a man to where he wants round after round, but what does that buy you? Not commitment. So what do you get out of saying, "I got that good good," besides attention?

A guy drove miles to have sex with you, don't feel special, other women have that same story. An ex is still trying to hit it even though he's now engaged, don't feel special, other women have that same story. A guy who comes quick each time, a guy who was talking marriage after sex, a guy who wanted to cum in you and have kids, a guy who brags to his friends about you, a guy who wrote poetry about your sugar walls, a guy who cries when he orgasms, a guy who says he's going to leave his girl, a guy who paid your rent afterwards, and the list goes on and on...because it's common. Name something that your vagina had a man doing, and there are thousands of other women that can say, "me too." A so-called "bomb pussy" is extremely common, a bomb personality, now that's the rarity.

YOU ARE NOT YOUR LOOKS

Show Tina Typical a picture of a girl who got married, and her internal reaction would be, superior jealousy, "I look better than that troll, what did she do to get him, suck his dick with ferry dust?" or inferior envy, "She's so pretty, I'm never going to get married." Both are weak bitch reactions that point at various levels of insecurities based on the looks of other women. Not all women are equally pretty, let's not bullshit each other by trying to be nice and politically correct. There are women who you are prettier than, there are women who you are just as pretty as, and there are women who blow you out the water in your own opinion. The great thing about looks is that they are subjective and easy to upgrade, (more on that secret later on) thus, your physical appearance compared to another woman's should never

18

be something that leaves you feeling hopeless or cursed. The problem is, you do feel self-doubt, it's not something that positive thinking has been able to cure. No matter how you look, there is someone in the media or someone in your personal life to remind you that you aren't perfect. This creates a game of cosmetic catch up for weak-minded women who don't realize the fix is in. The beauty industry doesn't solve insecurity; it's actually innovative in the way that it creates new insecurities. Straight hair isn't in, curly is in, adapt bitch. Runway petit is dead, voluptuous is in, adapt bitch. Slanted eyes are the new full lips, adapt bitch. Tastemakers tell people what was disgusting two years before is now sexy, and it leaves insecure women scrambling to keep up.

The cheat code for low self-esteem lays in competing with other women for attention. If you're unhappy with your facial features but have a nice butt, you accentuate that in clothing and lean on swooping bangs to make up for people saying your forehead is too big. If you're unhappy with the build of your body from the chest down but have a doll baby face, you're taking pictures to accentuate cleavage and face, while cropping out the rest. The result is you get attention for things you feel are strong suits, which makes you feel less insecure overall—but not really. This method of self-love is like being a real estate agent that tries to sell an entire house by showing one room. "Look at this living room, it's incredible... The bedrooms are too small, the kitchen is outdated, and the basement is hideous, but this room is amazing!" You're not buying into your own house because with the exception of a few traits, you are unhappy with your reflection. Self-love can't live in that kind of mind.

What do physically insecure people do to promote this idea that they're fine? They attempt to make themselves better at the expense of others. "All my house has is an amazing living room, but look at that house next door; it doesn't even have that going for it." Tearing down what someone else has while promoting what they have, is petty yet effective. This is where male approval becomes more valuable than gold. A woman can throw shade at a rival female, but it's powerless unless a man is there to cosign her superiority. Men know that women can be petty and insecure, and they exploit that. A man will ooh and ahh at you, look at you harder than he looks at your friends, or give compliments that put other women down. Not because you're all that, but because smart men know how to push the buttons of unconfident women. You are open to bullshit male flattery; although transparent, because it helps to temporary plug those holes that you can't fill. It's not just men; it can be other women as well. Those that are built like you or who perceive the same flaws as you aren't rivals, they are sisters in the struggle. Together you can create a cult of fake confidence. *Team Slim, Team Thick, Team Slim Thick, Team Dark, Team Light, Team I Need a Team Because I Don't Feel Pretty Without Outside Validation.* Those bullshit affirmations take one aspect of yourself and shower love on it when you should be loving the entire package!

There will always be women who a man will find just as pretty or prettier than you are. The same way that sex doesn't keep a man; looks will not keep a man. Yes, you should want to look your best, you should be in love with your mirror, but what you shouldn't be is Fake Pretty. Fake Pretty is where your self-image is fragilely built around the opinion of others. You are only feeling yourself so long as someone else is feeling you. This is extremely important because most women I meet are guilty of this hidden disease. To go on a date gassed off your body shape, then to have a man reject you as if that's nothing to him, creates further trauma and widens your insecurity. To have a guy stop calling you and then pop up with a girl who has a body that you won't ever develop naturally, sends your self-esteem crashing down. Women love to over-think, and when rejection happens the first culprit is always, "he didn't like the way I look." You project your internal feelings onto other people when things don't go your way, and the most conscious source of imperfection remains physical looks.

You're hoping that no man sees past your paper-thin confidence, that a guy likes enough of one thing on your body that he doesn't notice those other physical hang-ups that you see as flaws. The moment it doesn't work out you don't ask yourself, "Did our personalities connect in a real way? Was the conversation intriguing? Did I exude confidence?" You go back to how you look because all the shit you talk about being sexy is lip service. **Fake Pretty is tied to male validation; it's an idea that he will want you because you look a certain way.** When you don't get the results you wanted, you pile on more superficial solutions, as if you can somehow become too pretty to be passed up or rejected.

There is no such thing as too pretty to lose! You can't build your confidence around your external presentation; it has to be based on internal beauty. Defensively you can bring up friends or associates who you see winning in terms of men, and say, "That bitch is dumb and boring. You can't tell me it wasn't her looks that lead to her success!" That's the typical response. You don't know what a particular man is looking for or the conversations that are held in private that makes a woman you see as just a body, a must-have to that man. You're assuming that your personality is greater than her personality, but you can't measure her intangibles. You're not getting the same results as her, so you defensively point to perceived advantages such as her looks or the sex she's giving up. Stop trying to make yourself feel better by condemning others through assumptions, and let's be realistic; <u>looks do not lead to long-term success with men</u>. Yes, there can be shallow bias in terms of getting attention easier, but in the larger picture, no matter how attractive you are, it is not a golden ticket to commitment or happiness. There needs to be something behind that face, because when you look at the *Mona Lisa* every day even her magic wears off.

I often get pictures from the women who ask me for advice to emphasize, "I'm not some ugly girl," They think they're in a different boat because they are considered pretty, but if all she has is a look, then she is in that typical boat. We live in a world where makeup can mask bad skin and contour a big nose, where a girl can sew in any texture of hair, where she can enlarge her breasts and ass with the right amount of padding, and any race can tan their way to a golden complexion. Men are spoiled with beauty! *But my body isn't plastic. But I don't need makeup. But this is my real hair.* So? Men don't care about the origin of her beauty, he's trying to see her naked. Being pretty gets you chased after for sex, but is he interested in what you're talking about? Is he listening to you or just imagining you on your back spread eagle? Lust gets you in the door but it doesn't keep you in the house. A typical woman believes all she has to do is get in front of a man, and her looks will do the rest. You would think Sephora sold cover-up for ignorance the way some women blow smoke up their ass. A man is not going to keep you around just because you're a dime. The way you look, another girl looks, and all he has to do is log onto the internet to find one that's comparable. So what makes you special in a world of Kim Kardashians?

21

KILLING BASICA: RESETTING YOUR MIND

You don't want me to be confident in my career, my money, my education, my sex game, or my looks…It doesn't give me an advantage in love so I should just be dumb, broke, ugly, and frigid… If that's what you took away, then this entire chapter has gone over your head. I don't want you to be confident because you have "things" that every other woman can buy or get. I want you to become the type of woman who does things that other women are afraid to do because you aren't held back by typical thoughts. Strip away all the bells and whistles, could you walk across a room filled with beautiful, smart, and successful women, tap a man on the shoulder mid-conversation, and imprint your personality on his brain so you become the only woman on his radar? I don't care what you have or don't have on the surface, what really hooks a man is your internal truth.

This isn't about what you need to do or have in order to make a man want you; this is what you need to become to surpass the normal female mindset. Evolve past that archaic mentality that keeps men in control and women chasing after gimmicks that will help garner his love and appreciation. Spartanhood is enlightenment! When someone asks you what you bring to the table, I want every enlightened woman to be able to lay down her crutches, look a man dead in the eye, and say with conviction, "I am the fucking table!" This isn't a playbook for certain women; this is a reprogramming manual for all women willing to kill ego and embrace truth. I don't care if you're rich or poor, book smart or street savvy, built like Jessica Rabbit or built like Sponge Bob Squarepants, if you're a virgin or a freak in the sheets. I'm going to prove how easy it is to reverse your fortune, be it how to meet men, how to date men, or how to regain control in a relationship. **Typical Bitches get Typical Results. Extraordinary Women get Extraordinary Results.** You don't become extraordinary by feeding your ego lies or piling on at a cosmetics counter; you become extraordinary by rejecting weak bitch thoughts and awakening your inner Spartan.

Chapter 2:
He Loves You but He's Not in Love

a man will only fuck you over if you let him. The key being "let him," but so many women refuse to take responsibility. Their egos paint this picture that they fell for a man who had no warning signs, who was a master manipulator, and that they were merely an unsuspecting victim in his dishonest game. If you think a man can gain mental power over a woman without her giving it, you're either delusional or stupid. You control who gains access to your heart, but the first step is preventing these bums from gaining access to your ears. The counter to this will be the defensive cry of, "If men would be honest, we wouldn't have this problem." If people didn't like cocaine, there wouldn't be cartels. If people didn't steal, there wouldn't be alarm systems. If men were driven by love as opposed to sex, you wouldn't need intelligence. But you do! The reality is that you don't wish a problem away; you take steps to prevent yourself from being victimized. Go write a book about how men shouldn't lie for sex, do you think the average man is going to put his dick away and play nice? Post a social media message about how men are all dogs. Do you think the average woman is going to stop wanting to have that dog's puppies? Go scream from the mountaintop about what's fair and morally right, and see how much the world changes by the time you go on your next date.

Males are winning because they understand what women want to hear, tell it to them, and these girls get open. Women know how men are, no girl that makes it through high school is naïve, yet they continue to fall for the same tricks. The 21st century is a pussy gold rush, where any man who can feign interests can strike gold! The solution isn't to tell the burglar not to rob your house, the solution is to put a fucking lock on your door, and arm yourself with weapons to keep your heart safe from these crooks.

23

How does a man go from being just a guy you find to be handsome visually, to someone you're actually developing feelings for? He tells you a story. How does he reach that next level of sex if you're the type of girl who doesn't sleep around for fun? He does or says things to make you trust him. How does this man get the right to become your boyfriend? He either asks you or claims you without asking, and you choose to go along with that title. Three steps that depend on the same thing in order to move forward at each turn, <u>a woman giving a man access</u>. A man can lie and say that his last girlfriend cheated on him and that he just wants to find someone to trust. If you choose to believe that lie at face value without vetting him, that's your fault. A man can lie and say sex doesn't matter, wait 90 days, 3 dates, or whatever arbitrary rule you came up with to avoid sleeping with guys too fast. If you let him fuck because he waited and put your faith in time spent as opposed to time discovering, you have no one to blame but yourself when he suddenly vanishes. A man can lie and say that he's ready for a relationship, but in reality, he's either comfortable with you as a placeholder or feeling pressured to give you what you want so he can get or keep getting your benefits. If you agree to *that title* without making that man show you *that love*, it's going to be your bad when it crumbles because you didn't question that man's motives and allowed yourself to be claimed. Women have the power to say "no," at every point! A man has to ask permission to take you out, to sleep with you, and even to commit to you. So again, if he fucks you over, you can't blame the person that played you until you look at the person that gave permission.

The majority of women rush into love as if they only get one shot. Your good friend *Fear* is pulling your strings telling you to give that man a date, but not to ask too many questions because he may not like girls who pry. Fear is telling you to have sex with him before you're ready because handsome men these days are going to get it from someone else if you're acting stingy with your kitty cat. Finally, that fear that you won't find another man like the one you barely vetted will make you anxious for a relationship title...*does he really like me...what's he waiting for...is this going to stay a situationship...*That fear transforms from anxiety to joy when he does ask you to be his girlfriend or suddenly starts calling you his girlfriend. You were afraid he didn't want to commit to you, that you were wasting your time, and for him to solidify that you're together doesn't trigger questions like, "Why does he want to be with me? Why do I want to be with him? Do I know enough about him to commit myself? Has he done enough to show me that he's worth committing to?" Instead, you go with the flow. You don't know why you want to be a man's girlfriend other than loneliness, you're just happy someone you like back wants to lock you down. When you break up, and you will eventually break up when you date with a man in full control, you will look back and point the finger at him.

He told you things that made you like his personality, he didn't mention his bad habits or show signs that he would grow bored. No shit! Men aren't in the habit of leading with their worst traits. They hide negatives and amp up positives like any smart person would when trying to win. Most women don't date to learn, they date to be liked. Most women don't have sex because he earns it, they have sex because the combination of hormones, fear of him getting it elsewhere, and the pressure he puts on you in private, becomes enough. Most women rush into a relationship only to find out a man has all kinds of incompatibilities and baggage. These mistakes can all be avoided during the dating stage, but you're so fucking afraid that you will miss out on a once in a lifetime man, that you don't kick the tires and check under the hood before you drive him off the lot!

IN THEORY VS. IN REALITY

What do you really know about men outside of the stereotypes about thinking with their dicks? Dad may have told you that men lie and sweet talk. A brother or male cousin may have shown you via their own mistreatment of girlfriends what men are capable of even when they have a good heart. Maybe your ex-boyfriend, turned platonic guardian angel, has given you a glimpse of how men will do anything for new pussy. You think you know how men are, but you have no idea. You're like that NFL coach who watches footage of the rival team, knows their top plays, and still can't stop them. It's not enough to know about men on a surface area where you make them all into generic cavemen looking to flatter you, fuck you, say they love you, and then dump you. You have to know what the male agenda is, so you can train your mind to be prepared for when the generic becomes

25

an actual individual who you like. Theory remains theory until you put what you know to the test, and that's the problem, the idea of a man versus the actual walking, talking, smiling, physical man is different. I hear, "He was so different from the normal guys I meet," and that's the problem, most of you date the same types, and you've seen most of their tricks...but you become confused when you meet someone who knows how to read you, lead you, and make you think he's different.

All it takes is a guy who has game, who thinks outside the box, or who understands your type better than you understand his type, and you won't know what hit you! Don't let your ego gas you, trust me, you are a type. You have some typical bitch attribute that men look for when plotting to hook a victim. Once a man reads your behavior, he generates your type, and guys who are experts will break you down based on how he broke typical women just like you down in the past. You may not be extremely this way or extremely that way; every woman has shades of various personalities but that's not the same as being unique.

I call this breed of men, *Dicknotists*. They aren't the shy guys or simps[3] who you tend to ignore, they have qualities, physical and character wise, that make them popular with most women. The guys who you crush on the most for whatever reasons, other women crush on too, and they have the confidence to know that despite your resting bitch face, your phone in your hand, or your defensive or sassy attitude, he can have you because he has had other women who act like you. These men are programmed to run through women, and no matter how special you claim to be, all it takes is one phone conversation or date to break you down in his head. Once a Dicknotist figures out that you're a romantic who's playing tough because you have trust issues, he'll adjust his game to exploit your typical ass. If he figures out that you're a relationship girl who just wants to be loved, because Daddy wasn't around, he has a hustle for that as well.

Even when guarded, your flaws still shine through. If you are lonely or bored, the odds are that you will end up telling this man way too much information about your past, and after one date, a long phone conversation, or even a week of texting, he will automatically know how to game you. A

---

[3] A simp refers to a male who is a wimp or pushover, overly nice and regarded as soft.

Dicknotist adjusts his game to become "Mr. I Understand You," and will tell you what you want to hear. You're a victim, people haven't done right by you, poor baby. Then he will share similar real or fabricated stories that bond you, to make it seems as if you're building trust. *He sees my flaws, and still wants me.* Ha! It's all a façade. Most of the men you really want have this Terminator-like ability to read you, push your buttons, and get you sprung. Therefore, if you are going to do battle and end up with your dream guy as opposed to settling for some dork, you have to know how to outsmart the Dicknotists and prove you aren't the normal female.

KNOW THY ENEMY

Why don't men seem to care about love the same way that women care about love? Are they emotionally unavailable as some like to brag, or are they simply hiding their emotions because they're afraid of being hurt? All men are emotionally available, even those that are guarded or went through past heartbreak. Men invented the art of courting, poetry, the love song, and every other sappy concept. Romance was a tool created by men because women have always been regarded as the highest prize he could win! Just a glance from a woman can inspire a man to do all kinds of things that go against his inner logic, no matter how hard or jaded he appears. Every single woman has the power to cast a spell over a man that brings him to his knees. Go research the greatest men throughout history and there will be a correlating woman who had him wrapped around her finger! Women are dangerous creatures, so men developed a way to filter *Lust* from *Love*. If a smart man is going to be brought down and smitten by a woman, she has to be worth it, not just a pretty face, not just a nice girl, not just a nurturer, and not just intelligent, she has to be fucking Cleopatra, a woman worth throwing it all away for without regret. The technique that man cultivated in order to keep typical women away from his heart was the ability to separate women into two categories: <u>Sexual Object & Romantic Interest</u>.

So many women assume that if a man likes the way she looks and wants to have sex, then he must be into her on a deeper level. Why waste time going on dates, spend money, sit for hours on the phone, just for the act of sex, unless he likes you in a real way? A woman will rationalize that

27

there are dozens of other girls that would sleep with him easier, therefore, a man chasing her instead of chasing an easy fuck means there has to be more to his attraction than sex appeal. False. Let's go back to the male power to separate lust from love, the Object from the Romantic Interest. Savvy men don't allow themselves to get close to any woman until she proves that she has something different from the last several women he's dated or slept with no matter how good she looks or how sweet she behaves. To open up too fast is to make the same mistake lesser men make every day when they fall in love with hos, basics, or end up stuck with a baby mama that is nothing more than a bottom bitch[4].

Some of these men made that mistake in the past, others have avoided it, but the genius is that as he goes from boy to man, he perfects this process year after year until it becomes airtight. During high school into college, a male is naïve and open, which is why most men experience heartbreak during this time that smartens them up. He learns to vet girls better by being burned or seeing a friend get burned emotionally. By the time he's in his early to mid-20's he's learned to create a "Representative," a mask he puts on where he can make a woman think that he's letting her in by telling her about his past, present, future ambitions, etc., but in reality, he's not actually opening up at all, it's a fluff story meant to get her to open her box of secrets so he can see if she is more than meets the eye. By the time a man is in his 30's and up, he's perfected the separation game to the point where he knows how to get into a woman's head without her ever truly knowing him on a deep level. Nevertheless, that man is still looking for the same thing every man since the dawn of civilization has hunted for, a woman that is a must-have catch. No matter how good he has become at playing the game, a man is always open to true love! He's dying for a woman who knocks him off his feet, but all he finds is the same old fool's gold of a typical bitch that falls for his mind-fucks. There is no one box you can fit in to become a woman who all men want, nor should you try to fit into such a desperate category. This isn't about how to be for him, this is merely an insight into what is actually going on in the mind of the men you meet who seem guarded. Everyman wants true love but fears the trap of mediocre love.

---

[4] A woman who holds a man down no matter what, but is not fully wanted.

You can't be so prideful to think that the reason you haven't found success is because men simply aren't looking for love these days. The idea of "I'm single because there are no good men left," is basic bitch propaganda fueled by hurt and bitterness. There are good men if by "good," you mean someone looking for a serious and lasting relationship. Wedding facilities aren't going out of business anytime soon. The problem is that men don't want the bullshit that most girls are selling. Men don't want love for love's sake. Love is easy, love is plentiful, and for a man to find a woman to love him for simply being him is as common as seeing a Pumpkin Spice Latte with the name "Becky" on the side of the cup. He was born—his mother loved him. He grew up—his first girlfriend loved him. He's in a situationship[5]—that girl who he won't even commit to loves him. Get the picture? Most women long for someone to love them for real and do anything to prove that, but men routinely achieve that and they have realized after each break-up that love isn't enough to make a man happy. Chris Rock once stated, "Men would rather be happy than comfortable." Truth has never been so clear! Men are greedy; we aim high, even if that means leaving a perfectly comfortable situation where a woman gives us love. A man wants to lock down that girl who he can't find anywhere else. Why? It's a challenge! A man doesn't want to be handed a pretty sword, he wants to pull the one that can't be pulled from the stone, Excalibur...

OF PLACEHOLDERS & GAME CHANGERS

You think you are Excalibur by default. You don't know what other women do or don't do outside of your friends, so again, you rationalize that the way you act is unique because it lands you steady dates or boyfriends. However, this is also misleading because men treat the Objects as if they are Romantic Interests. Despite the bonding, the dating, even the commitment, he still doesn't think of you as *The One*. Why is he suddenly bored, spending more time with his friends than you, breaking his neck to look at other women, or unable to verbalize how he feels about you in a real way? Because you're still stuck in the role of Sexual Object, you've just lasted longer than most.

---

[5] Not a relationship but not a platonic friendship. Purgatory. See: www.Situationship.com

29

A Sexual Object that sticks around becomes what I call a *Placeholder*. You're not there because he's in love with you or actually sees a future, you are there to scratch an itch, to keep him company, in short, you're holding the place of a better woman. You are something to do while he waits for a *Game Changer* to appear. Why is she called a Game Changer? She signifies a change in his life which sends him in another direction. An immature man now wants to settle down. A man, who said he would never marry, suddenly wants to get married. A guy saddled with his own baggage becomes inspired to get over his hang-ups so he can be what that woman needs. All of this is done without a woman asking; it's done simply because she sparks something in him that he had been longing to find his entire life. All men seek a Game Changer...the holy grail among females.

Most men won't tell you that you aren't Game Changer material, they let you assume that you are, in a cowardly act of wanting to maintain comfort until she appears. Even if you're reading this and have a boyfriend, you may just be a placeholder. Hell, I've even met married women who turned out to be placeholders. The signs are always there! He's telling you, but he isn't really showing you love on his own. You feel unappreciated as if he would rather be doing something else. You feel his stress the moment you don't want to do what he wants to do. You think that's what men do in relationships because you've always been a placeholder. You have always had to fuss and fight to get his love, and you assumed that it was how men were...no, you are a placeholder. He cares about you, he does a few nice things, he tells you he loves you, but he isn't in love with you. **Who falls in love with a temp?** Men lie about how much they love you; they fake relationships and treat Pussy as if it's Wifey[6] when they don't actually have to go that far just to get convenient sex or stress-free companionship. Nevertheless, the Achilles heel that brings the average woman down isn't the fact that men lie, it's the fact that women are so consumed with trying to become what a man wants forever that they ignore his lies in hopes they can win him over eventually. No relationship should be built on eventually!

---

[6] Informal way of referring to a man's main woman or actual wife.

"How to tell if he likes you," "What to say to keep him interested," "What color do men like on women," "What does it mean when he says I'm not ready for a relationship..." and the list goes on and on. I look at these Google results, and I'm happy these keywords lead girls to my website, but it tells me that women aren't looking for an edge to become stronger, they're hunting for a gimmick that will make a man love her because she doesn't know how to achieve it naturally. Google can't save you! A man will say he wants a woman that does XYZ but when you give him XYZ he pushes you away like a kid who's handed a bowl of vegetables. You know this to be true. You have experienced the hypocrisy of guys who preach about one quality in a woman then end up with a woman who doesn't have that quality. Which is why you have to stop trying to give a man what he says he wants and stop looking for "secret tricks" to figure out how to hook a man's heart!

So many of you reading this listen to every opinion on "this is what you need to do to get a man," and you try to become all of these basic ass things, only to find out that none of it works! The thing about a Game Changer is that you cannot put her qualities on a list where a man goes on a date, checks those attributes off, and after a week declares her the winner. A Game Changer doesn't stand out because she's doing what men want women to do, she stands out because she doesn't give a fuck about what a man wants her to do. She's confident in her skin, and because she reaches the level of truth where she can project power without running her mouth, a man knows within the first month of dating that she is special. She feels different, talks different, and reacts differently than other women, because she is! The question isn't how to become a man's Game Changer, it's how to become your true self to the point where you have already changed the game because no other female is doing what you're doing 24-7/365!

Spartans are Game Changers by default because they can't be pulled out of a stone by just any man. The key to becoming a true Spartan is what this book will reveal in detail, but first you have to understand the strategy of the opposing team.

Chapter 3:
Dick Lies –
Using a Man's Mind Against Him

men aren't playing with a shot clock. There is no rush to grow up, so to speak. Those males who are well put together emotionally or could be considered Alphas are confident that one day they will find a female that jumps out of the crowd, blows his mind, and makes him want to drop all his other women and settle down. Some call this the one, wifey material, or a soul mate. I call her *The Game Changer*. A man doesn't pressure himself to get married by a certain age nor will he seem concerned with settling down just because he's getting older. He may make claims that he's looking for the right one or say that he's ready to retire from the game, but his actions remain the same. Why? He has faith that she will appear when she appears! Women, in comparison, are tied to a real biological clock in terms of children, those that have a child or aren't worried about being a mom will still feel this pressure internally and externally to find a man by a certain age to settle down with exclusively. This is why the love game is so unbalanced. One side is patient and laid back while the other is literally trying to hit a home run every time they go out because there is a societal push for girls to achieve lasting monogamy.

A man will enjoy the single life and continue to entertain what rival women refer to as hos or sluts because there is no rush! Guilt him all you want about how he's too old to be playing the field and how he is going to be the last of his friends still out on the club scene, but he doesn't give a fuck! A confident man trusts that his Game Changer will eventually come, so he enjoys the ride. Nevertheless, men today, even though they enjoy their freedom, have become jaded and bored with the pool of women.

The average good-looking, well-spoken man or financially thriving man will have dated more frequently and had sex more often than his female counterpart, which means he's had more real-world practice in terms of reading a woman's personality and crafting his own romantic persona. To use a hypothetical, the man who you are most attracted to will have dated 30+ women from various backgrounds over the past two years. All of whom said they were different, yet turned out to be more or less the same as the last. Knowing that these men are exposed to various women at an insane rate, how will he know that you're Wifey or Pussy?

Your ego may tell you that, "I'm a Game Changer, and the right man will know it when he sees me," but does history prove this to be true in terms of your past relationships? Let's not slide back into the placating concept where the man that you're looking for is out there looking for you at this very moment. Instead of wishful thinking, you need to be able to point to real qualities that make you the greatest woman in this universe. The only way a man finds out who a woman truly is and if she is worth giving his all to, is to test each one! <u>All women are Pussy until proven Wifey</u>! Take note that a guy is not looking to disrespect you by not assuming you're exceptional nor is he being misogynistic by not thinking of every woman he potentially dates as a Queen. If a man doesn't set out looking to expose you, then he's opening himself up to be played.

The girl who is cool with Netflix & Chill on the first date. The girl who claims that she waits until she's involved with a man for sex, but sleeps with him as soon as he tries. The girl who gets open off of money after saying she doesn't care about materialistic things. Those women are like the other 30+ he's played that game with over the past few years. He put you to the test to see if you would let him get away with murder, and you did. You didn't know it was a test; you were being nice by not making him take you on a real date. You were showing him that the sexual chemistry was real, by sleeping with him. You do like the idea of a man with money, you only pretended not to so he wouldn't think you were a Ho. Saying that you are different, does not show that you are different. To show is to know, and your actions prove that you bow down to him like every other girl. Sure, he may keep going with the flow and pretend that he loves you. But men don't love women like you. Game Changers get the world dropped at their feet for fear another man will handcuff her before he gets a chance. If you find yourself waiting under the pretense of "we're taking it slow," understand that he's full of shit and you've already been assigned to the placeholder box.

SEX IS EVERYTHING & NOTHING

Saying all a man wants is sex is like saying that all a business owner wants is money. It's true at the basest level, but there is always a larger vision. It's normal for me to receive emails from women who state the following things, "We never even talked about sex...He says he doesn't even want to rush that...If it was only about sex, then why did he not go through with it when he had the chance?" This is where it pays to understand the bigger picture, because you will meet a man who says it's not about sex, acts as if it's not about sex, then you will realize after the fact, it was always about sex. You were used to a man playing checkers in an attempt to get you open, you had no clue how to deal with a man who played chess; that's why you're left confused and frustrated. Let's start by examining what sex means to a man.

If there is no such thing as Kryptonian pussy, then what is the big deal about a vagina that makes men jump through hoops, manipulate, pay, or flat out lie in order to get it from girls they barely know? A man will have a one-night-stand if the conditions are right, so it's not about needing to know her character. A 3rd date ends in sex and it becomes the last date she ever gets, with the guy confessing that he never liked the woman, so it's not about building a bond. A man will sleep with a girl that looks nothing like his preferred Instagram type, so it's not about looks. All the prerequisites that the average woman puts on sex, such as personality, connection, chemistry, even physical attraction, go out of the window with men. There doesn't seem to be any rhyme or reason to whom a man will sleep with if given the green light, but there is... It's not the actual feeling of sticking a penis in and out until he ejaculates, it's the conquest.

Every man who's had sex knows it feels great, but if all a guy was looking for was that euphoric release he would be content with sleeping with one woman for the rest of his life or masturbating multiple times a day like when he was a teenager. A single man will have a *Friend with Benefits* that scratches his itch with no strings attached, but he will still be on the

35

lookout for something new. Even in a relationship, men are notorious for stepping out to taste something new. There are women who speculate, "She's not putting it on him in the bedroom. He needs someone to throw it down on him and he'll be satisfied." All bullshit theories. The hunt for sex has little to do with what a woman is or isn't doing for a man sexually and everything to do with what New Pussy represents—Conquest!

Most of the girls that a man sleeps with, he won't have sex with more than twice, he won't keep a picture of her to show off as a trophy, and at a truly mature age, he won't even feel a need to brag to his friends about that conquest. Only the man and that woman will know what happened, and once they stop talking, it's just a fading memory. Adult sex isn't tied to outside approval the same way a high school or college guy's libido tends to be in terms of notches. The reason a man chases New Pussy as opposed to being content with a vagina he's already had multiple times is the rush of a new experience. Men have been thrill seekers since before they climbed down from the trees. They are hard-wired to chase and then experience the rush of the unknown. Skydiving, mountain climbing, party drugs, fast cars, backpacking through other countries, males need the adrenaline of the undiscovered. You may think of those things I listed as dumb, dangerous, or stupid, but males are wired for the rush.

Sex with a new girl, no matter if he knows her or if she's a stranger, if she's a 5 or a 10 rating in his mind, fulfills a need for adventure that can't be duplicated with something old and familiar. So many of these so-called sex-perts come up with gimmicks to maintain excitement in the bedroom, but they don't realize that men aren't chasing a fresh coat of paint on top of old coochie. New lingerie, still old pussy. New hairstyle, still old pussy. New position, still old pussy. The reason *Ho Tactics* worked so well was because it hit at the heart of a man's self-destructive drive to conquer new pussy. The better the woman was at dangling her brand new box, the more a man chased and tricked to get it. Nevertheless, when you're not looking for a come up, and looking for love, you have to understand that it isn't just a case of men needing a woman nasty enough to tame him, it's an addiction, not with sex but with that adrenaline, knowing this goes a long way.

A man is only as faithful as his options. What that means is that a man with few women who find him attractive is no different from a man who's a famous athlete that thousands of women find attractive, in terms of his lust for something new. Mr. No Options wants to experience the rush of different women, but he behaves himself because there are no serious takers. Money can buy sex, and some men go that route, but for a man who isn't willing to pay a prostitute and doesn't have women threatening to throw it at him for free, he can't act out on that thrill seeking. That fire still burns inside of him, but he is able to manage it better than the athlete, the celebrity, or regular Joe who women find to be "dream guy" attractive. For the record, this isn't something that a man can't control, chasing pussy isn't like breathing air, any man can choose not to chase women. If one tells you it's uncontrollable, he's full of shit. I point this out not to make you see men as horny cavemen, but so you can stop lying to yourself about casting some kind of love spell because you had sex with a man. I want you to understand that all men have a roaring fire that they walk around engulfed in, and a smart woman can use that to her benefit (In a non *Ho Tactics* way) when gaining power over men. We'll dive into this technique later on in the book, after you Spartan Up.

Going back to the opening example of men who tell you that it is not about sex, who claim they are looking to settle down, and who are patient with you... they are exceptions to the rules, right? Wrong. Here is a story to illustrate it. A woman I will call Pretty Eyes had a crush on a guy she went to college with, and a year after they graduated, he finally made a move on her when they ran into each other at a store. Boy Crush admitted that he liked Pretty Eyes but thought she looked down on him. Boy Crush had played ball, run track, and had a reputation like most student athletes. He thought she would be turned off from taking him seriously, so he never pursued. Pretty Eyes didn't care about that, she assumed that he just didn't think she was as pretty as the other girls who were around campus. Both laughed about the miscommunication and they started to date.

Boy Crush ended up over Pretty Eye's apartment on the second date, and things got heavy in terms of kissing. Boy Crush pulled back and said he was in the midst of a vow of celibacy. A friend of his on the track team contacted an STD, and that made him put his own life in perspective.

Since then, Boy Crush decided to abstain from sex until he met the right woman. Pretty Eyes nodded along, but she didn't believe it...until he spent the night and didn't try to do what men typically try to do. Pretty eyes went with the flow, and week after week, it was just make out sessions. To see a man that looked as good as Boy Crush, stop having sex for something noble made Pretty eyes respect his character. They continued to date for another month. Finally, she went down on him. At this point, the two of them began spending the night together. Oral sex happening every night in terms of Pretty Eyes but Boy Crush never engaged...just received because for some reason, her going down wasn't wrong, but him going down broke his vow.

Wait, it gets weirder. Three and a half months in, no sex, mostly house dates where he either got hand jobs, blow jobs, or rim jobs. Yes, Pretty Eyes was eating the groceries. They weren't official but she was treating him to all kinds of benefits that most men never get. Pretty Eyes told me these TMI details to brag. She expressed to me that she felt in control, the aggressor, the dominant force. "I know I'm a Spartan, you should hear him moaning," was even included in the body of her first email. She truly felt that her mouth had turned this guy out. For the first time in her life, Pretty Eyes felt confident because she knew she had a man who she knew wanted her, and it wasn't for sex. Her question to me was how to get Boy Crush to finally have sex. The email had a few holes in it in terms of his personality. For me to really assess a situation I need to know who the man is beyond the generic description of how nice he is and the things he lets you do from behind sexually. She responded to my email four days later with these exact words:

"[Boy Crush Real Name]'s girlfriend came by my apartment. That's right this little bitch has had a girlfriend all this time..."

The story went that Boy Crush didn't want to have sex because he didn't want to use condoms. Apparently, he burned his girlfriend before and wasn't about to make the same mistake again. Thus, he wanted to use Pretty Eyes as New Pussy, but not actually penetrate. Remember, this isn't about the vagina so much as the conquest. This man had managed to create a lie where he not only got head, but got his booty ate, and all he had to do to get her to that point where she was being his oral savior was to play the celibate role for a few months. Boy Crush didn't have to worry about wasting his time because he had in house pussy waiting. His patience and ingenuity allowed him to hit the jackpot in terms of kinky sexual acts where he never even had to go down on her!

The point is that men will play any position they feel will benefit them in the long run because sex is everything, but it's also nothing. If Pretty Eyes didn't want to blow him or if she got pissed off about the lack of sex, Boy Crush wasn't going to lose out on anything. He would most likely have stopped dating her and found another girl to pull the same trick on. Yes, he was willing to risk his relationship, but he knew that his girlfriend would be more upset at Pretty Eyes for being a thirsty ho than at her own boyfriend who could literally say, "but I never fucked her." The closure between the two of them came in the form of a text where Boy Crush called Pretty Eyes, "A halftime Show," meaning she was entertainment nothing more and then went on to talk about how he loved his chick (something probably added on so he could show to his girl to prove Pretty eyes meant nothing). Even with that text as proof that he wasn't ever into her, Pretty Eyes still doesn't believe she was just sex and blames his girlfriend.

This is one of my more extreme email examples but there are normal cases where a man waits for sex using the cover of taking things slow because of not being over an ex, gets sex eventually, and then falls back without ever spelling it out for the woman the same way Boy Crush did. There are others where a man spends money date after date, doesn't get the sex initially, stops talking to the girl, only to have her come running back finally ready to give it up because she felt like he was authentic in retrospect. In both situations, women swear that there had to be more to it because sex didn't seem like an issue. That's the point! Men don't always need to pressure for sex, often the reverse psychology game nets them not only the sex but a woman's trust and loyalty. At the top of I said there is a larger vision. A guy doesn't just want the sex; often times he wants the girlfriend benefits... but in a controlled way.

GIRLFRIEND BENEFITS

Sex with random girls isn't something any man wants to do every week; if it falls in his lap he'll take it as it comes, but in terms of working to get new girl after new girl, few men have the time or energy to continuously play the game that often. New Pussy joy doesn't wear off after one, two, or three sessions, it can last months. The objective is not to only find sex for the night, but to find a girl that can last for a while and give him that consistent girlfriend experience so he doesn't have to go hunting as frequent.

Have you ever thought, "If he didn't really like me he would go call another woman, he's not ugly"? That's a part of this hustle. So many women in typical fashion point to the man she's talking to or dating and then point to the world of women he could have, and then come to the conclusion that if he is continuing to be on her heels that she means more than those other women. I repeat, the short-term goal for men is to experience a new woman; the mid-term goal is to have one or two on the roster that fulfills that thirst for a time. Just because you fit the description of mid-term seat filler, doesn't mean you are his long-term Game Changer. Let go of the egotistical view that a man who won't stop calling you or who always wants to see you is actually into you, until you actually go through the vetting process. The best women to have on a team aren't going to be one night stands, jump-offs, or girls who are traditionally cool with a FWB relationship. Men don't want the bottom of the barrel even when choosing a girl who is only going to be "Something to do for a few months." He wants something that is, at least, entertaining and who he can stomach for those months...maybe even a few years, without getting annoyed.

To be a placeholder means that you're good enough for now, not that you lack complete value. He sees something in you, not a future, but a nice little run where he can get the girlfriend experience without feeling the pressure to actually marry you one day. Dates, Conversation, Fun...it feels so real, and placeholders don't know they are placeholders. They think they're actually connecting with a man because he does give you enough affection to keep you on his team. This isn't a case of being played in a cartoon way, where a man just calls for sex. Again, a placeholder can go on a date and even get a verbal commitment, but that man isn't tied to her.

That placeholder knows that something isn't right no matter how many times she lies to herself and looks for hollow proof that this is real love.

A Spartan would know what to look for and see through this hustle, but normal women tend to believe that if a man does certain things like spend time and money, that he's being sincere. Sex is the root of a man's desire even when he's waiting for that Game Changer, but he also wants a woman he can talk to and have fun with outside of the bedroom, therefore, a man is happy to come away with a placeholder that fits that description. Most women don't realize which role they were playing until it's too late, and he's already in the process of moving on. How could he just leave you? How could he just fall back like he didn't care? How could he try to have sex with someone you were friends with? How could he spend so much time up under you, then let go so easy? Because it was an act! You think you're a Game Changer, but most likely you will turn out to be a placeholder. How do you stop this? We will get into the Spartan way soon, but for now, I want you to understand the mindset.

The older the man, the more strategic. A veteran doesn't always have to play the stereotypical role of, "Come over, I want to see you," and try to fuck the first week he meets you. Time has taught smart men to unwrap a woman slowly because that method nets real girlfriend benefits. You can get a number from a guy next weekend, see that he's already coming off too sexual, and dismiss him. You don't need help with that. It's those men who act as if they want you for which you need to be careful of because by making sex seem like an afterthought you become comfortable sooner. He takes you out, behaves himself, and talks on the phone daily with you both teasing each other that you might misbehave. This is exciting, everyone likes buildup. By the time, you get together for the next date he still behaves himself, but maybe he starts to open up more, making it seem as if you two are experiencing a real mental connection. Sexual chemistry doesn't dissipate because you're only having conversation, that lust bubbles as if under a flame. The more you tease then pull back under the pretense of it being too soon, the more you want the D just as much as he wants the kitty. Within a series of weeks, you are on fire mentally and physically, and even if you have sex, you're already broken in emotionally.

You may not be the kind of girl who does this normally, but you're so comfortable that you will begin to give him girlfriend benefits without even realizing that you've been dicknotized. You are used to the thirst buckets or the smooth players who transparently try to get you open, but your body and mind aren't prepared for a man who's a chess player. From your point of view, you had a real bond; he cared about you, but most likely you were just being groomed for a placeholder position. For a man that can attract a wide range of women, it's always better to hook a woman with value, who has self-respect, and then convert her to that lowly position. Even if you see that you're not what he wants or know that he's not what you want, but are enjoying his company, playing along is a waste of your value. Being a placeholder is not a badge of honor, even if you are up on game, it's still relegating you to Pussy while he continues to wait for Wifey.

THE WAY TO A WOMAN'S HEART IS THROUGH HER EGO

Cheesy pickup lines don't work, but here's the catch; they aren't meant to work. In terms of instantly sweeping a woman off her feet, that is; they're meant to break the ice so a man can start a more personal sales pitch. I've heard more than a few women say something along the lines of, "He said something corny, but he was cute, so I gave him my number," and that's why men don't care about how they come off initially. We're talking about top shelf men, not some dirt ball that screams, "Hey!" across a mall food court or catcalls you while walking down the street. These men know that they're winning or, at least, have qualities that will make you see them as desirable, so their only aim is to get the communication started so they can seal the deal later. Corny line, joke, a random observation, saying you look familiar; it's all part of the game because 90% of women who are approached by attractive men aren't going to shoot him down based on his opening. Women tend to exaggerate who they will and won't talk to, but the reality is they are very generous in terms of giving someone a chance. "He's not really my type," thoughts can still end with that man getting a date, sex, or a relationship down the road. We've all seen examples of this.

What that tells men in general is that the chances of being rejected are much lower than what women claim. Many females talk shallow, but their contact list and the men they've dated prove they aren't shallow. When you put this "I'm open to giving nearly any man a shot if he's nice enough" knowledge in the hands of a Dicknotist who has default good looks he knows he's going to be graded on a curve. In today's social media world, a "You look sexy," from John Q. Lame won't even get a response, but that same comment from someone looking like Chris Hemsworth has a high percentage of getting a response back. Same line from both men, different emotional reaction. It's the perception of what one man represents, be that looks or status, that makes a girl smile as opposed to roll her eyes. Think about your life, there have been men who said things that made your skin crawl, not because of the words, but because it was coming from someone, you didn't like that much. To transfer that to a man you have a crush on, that skin crawl is replaced by a tingle. Men understand their market value! Which means men who know that you're interested also realize that unlike the average Joe, they can easily manipulate you by using the one thing women say gets them nowhere—Flattery.

How can a man bond with a woman really fast so he can skip all the time-consuming bullshit? Stroke her ego through flattery. This is so simple, yet so many women don't realize that it's happening while entangled with a guy they actually like. Let's put a lady on a dinner date with a handsome man who has a good job and nice manners. He's already a better catch than most women are used to, so instead of looking to pick him apart, she is simply looking to impress him. Why do you want to seem impressive? Because you realize that the dating pool sucks! You are sick of the bar/club scene, tired of trying to find a match online, and given the last few dates you've been on you know that this man has attributes that aren't the norm: Money, Looks, No Children (which means no baby mama), and he's not being snobbish or condescending as if he knows he's hot shit. These things are considered high market value because they are qualities in a man you won't come across every day in most cities.

A man knows his market value because he observes how women react to him. A chess player will do the smartest thing any man can do on a date—he will shut the fuck up and let the woman talk. Go back to the typical bitch achievements. This man will listen to you talk about what makes you different, listen to your back-story in terms of family and boyfriends, and he will be there to chime in with flattery. By the end of the date, he's telling you that you're a strong woman because you went through blah blah blah, that you're different from most because you did blah blah blah, and finally he'll remark about how he's been dying to meet someone like you. In your mind, listing your achievements and your history impressed that man. Showing your credentials made him not only realize that you're special, but admit it, and that boosts your self-esteem. Did you ever stop to question if this man says the same exact things to every woman who talks way too much on a date? No. You ate it up.

Women don't question compliments that come indirectly and point to real things she's doing. Unlike some random kiss-ass comment about your body or eyes, positive words that pat you on the back or rebuts an insecurity is better said as a counterattack. No one listens to your sage advice in your real life, but on a date, this man asks your opinion and then remarks that you're brilliant because he didn't think of that. That's an effective compliment that is directed at a confidence hole that he's sniffed out. My cousin Jesse and I were hanging with this girl who he was trying to get with, and she was complaining about her neighbor only having a car because she claimed someone's kid on her tax return. My cousin was an expert ratchet whisperer from a young age, and he told this girl that the fact that she was planning to go get her GED was the reason why she was better than the rest of the girls in Park Heights. He claimed she "wanted more out of life," and her ratchet ass ate that affirmation up like ranch sunflower seeds. When dealing with women of any class, the same rules apply because most are chained to ego. It's not about giving physical praise, women get that all the time, it's about assessing her insecurity and licking that wound.

There are two women whom Dicknotists eat alive: <u>Women with trust issues & women who have been single for long periods of time</u>. A woman who's been cheated on, rejected, or heartbroken, will tell herself it was the man, but they don't believe that. You would think a man would get annoyed having to prove that he wasn't like the last dude, but chess players love this challenge. It's actually easier to hustle a woman with trust issues because she's looking for a reason to prove that it wasn't her taste it men, but that specific man who missed out on how great she was and then did her wrong. When you've been hurt, the best medicine is retribution with a new man. Although she's nervous about trusting a man again, her ego wants to prove there's nothing wrong with her. A smart man won't try to win her trust like a basic boy would, by proclaiming he's different from the rest; he will simply rebuild her faith in herself as someone who has been a hapless victim. A Dicknotist is on her side as a cheerleader, not as someone trying to convince her he's different, that's the genius of his hustle. A woman with trust issues should be on guard, and they are from typical male bullshit, but not this level of slow sneak attack.

Those women who never had a real relationship, those who are divorced and never got back in the game, or haven't seriously dated in ages for whatever reason, are just as vulnerable as those with trust issues. The absence of a positive male force in your life creates a longing. Your family or friends complimenting you gets old, "If I were so great, where's my man?" You need that male force, not in a physical way, but emotionally. A guy who inspires you, who always has kind words about what you're doing, that genuinely feels good, but when life and dating have lowered your self-esteem, it feels even better. Ego strokes become heroin if a man knows how to use it the right way early on. The more versed a man is in saying the right things, the more a woman wants to talk to him, be around him, and share things she normally doesn't talk about until she's in a relationship.

Friends argue, they exercise their opinions, and they only let you vent so they can follow up with their own take. Not a Dicknotist. A Dicknotist knows that you don't want a conversation, you want to express yourself and be told that you're justified in whatever gripe you have. Had an argument with a friend—*she needs to realize how good a friend you are, babe.* Stressful day at work—*fuck those idiots! That place can't operate without you, babe.* Self-doubt about a life choice—*You know I believe in you, I haven't seen you make a wrong move yet, babe.* It's chicken soup for insecure souls!

Let's review. This Dicknotist has succeeded in quickly bonding with you, earning your affection, and has become privy to all kinds of life secrets not because he has earned it through time and revealing himself, but by reading off the oldest cue card in the world: <u>Tell her she's great</u>. Does he really believe that you're Superwoman?

No! He saw a way in, and he's pushing the button that will get him to where he wants to be faster. Why waste a month dating, hours on the phone, constantly having to interview with a woman and answer real questions? Men want to get to the point where they are comfortable, so what better way to accomplish this than to be a shoulder to lean on, an ear to listen, or a mouth to praise? I'm familiar with this hustle because the women who come to me tend to be girls who fell for men too fast, gave away too much emotionally, became addicted to having that man in their lives, and hope I can tell them how to "fix it" to get him back. Their egos are so revved up that they don't realize, even when it falls apart, that it was all a purposeful mind-fuck.

To lose a guy who quickly became your emotional crutch, even a father figure of sorts, will make you do anything to get him back. The sad part is that your entire relationship was not based on your love of him, but of your love of how good he made you feel. He was your drug masquerading as your savior. He had the potential of a boyfriend from the moment you exchanged numbers, he acted as if he was impressed by your life and your mind, he listened intently and learned more and more about you, even the flaws and he didn't run; he *still* saw you as special. Why would he play such a game? I've already covered the why earlier in this chapter. The real question is why did you allow him to infiltrate your mind so quickly? He was always on offense, never on defense, because men know that if you get a woman talking about her, her, her, he'll never have to dig deep. Men know that all women want is to be loved, to be seen as special, and for someone to be in their corner and believe in them. Sadly, most are so blinded by their own pride that they never spot this obvious Dick Tactic.

COMMITMENT ISN'T ALWAYS A COMMITMENT

What makes a man want to stop playing the game and settle down? That's a trick question because settling down doesn't necessitate that he stops playing the game. Even if you aren't seen as a Game Changer, a man will still hibernate in your vagina, giving you all the surface benefits of being his girl, but his heart isn't settled, it's still longing for The One. He will play that boyfriend role, but his effort won't be 100%. You have experienced this or are experiencing it right now, a man who seems distracted, who keeps saying he cares, who claims he will change, but his actions repeatedly prove that he's apathetic. You're confused as to why your "boyfriend" isn't living up to that title. You wonder why he even bothered to enter into the relationship if he was going to act indifferent. You place blame on yourself because you think something had to cause this change. You search for ways to repair the relationship from your side of the ball as if it's all your fault. You're missing out on the easy answer that's right under your nose where your ego dares not look: *He isn't invested in you because you're a Placeholder*!

You are not the permanent solution, just something to tide him over. No matter how good his mask of lies is constructed, the truth peeks through the longer you stay together. Most women are just something to do, the key word being "most" so understand that you may be the rule, not the exception. We discussed the role of the placeholder earlier, but I will remind you that this is not relegated to girls who are FWB, Situationship baes, side chicks, or any other female you can point to as dumb because she's agreeing to a non-exclusive relationship with a man she actually wants to be with monogamously. Men get in relationships with women they don't want every day! The misconception is that you've won because he agreed to the title, not so. Be attentive, because he may still view you as lacking that X-Factor that he needs to actually give his heart to you. I want to dwell on this because despite covering it earlier, I meet so many women hung up on the idea that a man doesn't need to lie or fake a relationship for sex or comfortability because there are so many women willing to provide that without a title. A man that's playing the chess version of Dick Tactics understands there are women who allow a man to get the milk for free because she's thirsty for love, but who wants free milk from low grade cows?

These "It's whatever" girls who consider Netflix and Chill a real date aren't a product of a man having game; they are the product of their own low value. These women are emotionally malleable and filled with holes to be exploited. They want a man to end their loneliness, so they make courting stress free because they don't want to ruin the potential for love by being high maintenance. Girls like this are effortless pussy that any man can get within a matter of weeks, but remember, great men look for challenges! You can't keep feeding a Gladiator a bunch of peasants to slay, he wants to try his hand against a lion. Yes, there are other girls who are easier than you and more accessible, but you must stop assuming it's just about a physical sensation of a vagina. It's the challenge of the conquest and the entertainment of the Girlfriend Experience. Remember this is a game meant to uncover a Queen, so how can a man finally reveal his Game Changer, unless he starts to go for more and more challenging women who have the basic foundation of greatness? Placeholders make good practice because they are half way to Game Changer status, but don't know how to Spartan Up to reach that next level where a man would truly fall in love.

SEEING THROUGH HIS DICK TACTICS

Let's take the average Dicknotist and go through his motions. Let's name him Rick the Dick, and imagine him physically as whatever your type is, don't dirty him up, think of him as your default "He can get it," mental image. Let's add some depth to Rick, he's upper-middle class in terms of income, two years older than you, with no baggage of ex-wives or children from past relationships. At first glance, Rick's market value is high. He dates you right, is respectful of making an effort to be creative, and there is never a question of who will pick up the bill. He listens wonderfully, always asks follow-up questions, and remembers details so you're not constantly repeating yourself. Sexually he's a good flirt, not overt, but not a boy scout. When it comes to his own life, you know what he does, that he's been single for nearly a year, and you have the basics of why he and that last girl didn't work out. You get a skeleton overview of his family life and a few stories about college and childhood, meaning you know enough to say you know him, but you don't know him as deep as he knows you. That's on purpose.

Like most early couples still in the dating stage, you eventually bump heads once over miscommunication, but he doesn't let it drag out nor does he kiss your ass like a pushover. He shows that he can stand up to you, but is also sensitive to your point of view. Rick is doing everything you're taught to look for, and the bond is already there. It hasn't been that long, but it's been long enough for you to have sex, and you're prepared for him to start acting differently...but it never happens. Sex doesn't change him, and you're starting to feel as if this is someone you can actually take seriously. One night you're hanging out, but distracted. Rick reads you, picks up on the abnormal behavior, and asks what's the problem. You play it off, but Rick the Dick already knows the answer. Any time a woman starts acting weird, semi-deep into dating, she's been over thinking the one question all women think when it's going well: *Where is this going?*

Let's go back through these events, but this time, step into Rick's male POV. He spotted you and thought you were pretty, exactly the type that he's into, and he picked up on the vibe that you were someone he would have to work for, not some goofy chick who would be easily impressed by his looks or money. At this point Rick doesn't know if you're Pussy or Wifey, how could he? At the moment of first contact and initial conversation, he's suspending his labels. Assuming that you'll probably be Pussy, but given the way you look and the way you talk, he's hoping for more. The date choice is meant to impress you, to show you that he's a man of quality, he feels a need to overcompensate based on his initial impression of you, as a woman with class.

Skip back for a moment, if Rick talked to you for a few minutes before getting your number or spent hours on the phone before he set up the first date, and automatically decided you were ratchet, basic, ghetto, redneck, or flighty he would adjust his game plan and went a different first date route. You came off as a woman of class, thus, Rick is going to go down the quality path to impress you. Now, on to the actual date.

The first date is all about listening and learning. He's taking mental notes on you, what you react to joke-wise, what topics excite you, and most importantly what you're looking for from a man. Your last boyfriend, your problem with men these days, and your general attitude on why you're single. Rick doesn't have to ask obvious questions; his ears are the canvas and your mouth paints every picture. This Dick will keep the drinks flowing and your mouth moving. He knows half of your insecurities by the time the date is over but still hasn't made up his mind about your potential.

By the second date, Rick's talked to you nearly every day, has had more than a few long late night conversations, and having exposed all of your insecurities as well as your basic character defining traits, he's found a girl to compare you with that he used to date. You're a mix between Angela and Kim, so he's going to push the buttons that he pushed on them to see what works and what doesn't work. At this point, he thinks you have potential; you're smart, fun, and witty, but you're also typical in many ways. Rick doesn't care if he does something to push you away at this point because it's nothing for him to find a new girl to add to the roster, that means unlike you, he's actively testing you without fear of losing you. The misunderstanding that had you two not talking for three days, that wasn't a misunderstanding, Rick set it up to see if you were going to flip out like a bird or handle it like a boss. You didn't pass his test with flying colors, but it was enough to apologize and make it up to you because he realizes he's close to hitting that. Rick is prepared to wait for sex with you; he's not thirsty for a nut. He has an ex-girlfriend that's still open and a bottom bitch to scratch his itch, but he still decides to go for your cookies after the next date, and you give in. Sex is great like most New Pussy tends to be, and at this point he could chuck the deuce, but he's actually enjoying your company.

Rick has to make a choice at this point. He knows that you're not a situationship girl and that your attitude is already changing because you're not used to having sex with a guy who's not your man. Rick loves that you have those standards, and that you won't just let him fuck for free. He doesn't like that you don't speak up about this, that like Angela and Kim, you are content with dropping hints because you don't know how to say what you want. Rick is 70% sure that you're not the girl for him in the long run, but you're good to talk to, and you don't annoy or act clingy like Angela. You're not as smart or wild as Kim, but you have a lot more in common in terms of family and culture, and that's a nice twist. Rick has been gaming you this entire time, not by lying to you, but by remaining emotionally distant. He's wearing a mask because he doesn't want to waste his time opening up his heart to Pussy. Rick sits on the fence in terms of if he should keep kicking it with you or if he should keep looking for what he actually wants. Rick's decision, like most Dicknotist, boils down to three things: <u>Current roster. Season of the year. His current schedule</u>.

Rick has three girls on the team: A chick he's run through dozens of times and is cool with whatever aka the bottom bitch. A girl whom he hasn't slept with that he likes a lot, but is clearly entertaining other men, and not giving Rick time to get in her ear. Finally, Rick has his ex-girlfriend who he can be himself around, who he can share real things with, but he doesn't want her because she has massive daddy issues, and they argue about the same things repeatedly. In terms of the current season, it is late winter, so Rick could wait out and reload his roster in the spring, but that seems too long to wait. Last on the list is Rick's life schedule. He does work a lot, he's not some deadbeat that can hang around chasing tail all the time. It takes time and patience to break a good girl in. So there you are, looking like the best available option. Rick doesn't think you will show him anything to blow his mind going forward, but you're already broken in, he knows what buttons to push and what strings to pull for the most part, and the sex is only going to get nastier and better.

If he chooses to try and situationship you, he knows that you will most likely walk away or give him the passive aggressive treatment until he has to walk away. You are attractive and you have things going for you, so there's also the chance that some new guy or ex-boyfriend could win you back if Rick doesn't commit. Rick isn't into sharing and doesn't want the drama of you trying to make him jealous by using other men like Angela did or have you trying to give him an ultimatum like Kim did. It's better to settle down and hibernate and hope that someone new pops up in the spring or summer. Rick makes a decision that you will be his girlfriend, not based on love, but based on convenience. You won't actually complicate his day to day life, he won't have to do much to keep you happy but listen and maybe do a nice thing once or twice a month, and the pussy gates are open for business... possibly even raw sex sooner than later. You're about to become Rick's chick not because he's infatuated with you, but because you're good enough for now. Welcome to Project Placeholder.

Fast-forward to you and your boo Rick hanging out, and for the first time, he refers to you as his girlfriend to the waiter. You try to play it off, but your brain's on fire. Is he being serious or joking? He does have a habit of playing too much... should you ask or should you just pretend you didn't hear it? Of course he knows you heard it, so maybe he's waiting for you to confirm it. If you don't say anything that could be seen as a rejection, this is crazy... you weren't expecting to hear that tonight. Truthfully, you were thinking about breaking up or, at least, asking him where it was going, but you hadn't decided on what to do yet. Fuck, this is awkward! You're a grown woman feeling like a teenager, so you get a grip and decided to ask, **"So I'm your girlfriend now?"** Say this in an inquisitive slightly sassy way, so as not to seem either excited or turned off by the thought. Rick was waiting for you to take the bait, and you did, now he claims you by telling that you are his woman. Now he follows up with flattery about how great you are, how he's been having the time of his life, and muses about this possibly being something that ends in a family. Hook. Line. Sinker!

Now you're free to drop that defensive guard. All that fear of rejection suddenly lifts off your shoulders, this man is saying that he wants you, respects you, thinks the world of you not because of sex or your looks, but because he got to know your soul. You finally tell Rick how you feel about him, and it's a love fest. For a moment, Rick feels bad. *Damn, this bitch really likes me*...but he reminds himself internally that you and he would never work for long, and just like that girl who he was with nearly a year ago before the Kim and Angela experiments, he knows you'll eventually bore him and he'll grow distant. <u>You're not the kind of woman a man like him loves, you're a placeholder</u>. He deserves something special, something amazing, and while you're a good girl who will one day make some other man a fine wife or baby mama, you will never be his Game Changer...

You and Rick toast to a future that he is already thinking about enjoying with another woman, while you feel overjoyed with reaching the finish line so fast with this "good man" that you've been praying for. In your mind, you did everything right. You went on real dates, you asked about his ex, you asked about his family, you looked for signs that he was mean or an asshole, you waited what you think was long enough for sex, and you didn't pressure him for a relationship—he gave it willingly. If this relationship fails, it won't be because you didn't do your homework...and that's where you're wrong. You dated like a Typical Bitch, not a Spartan.

You didn't vet this man, you didn't test this man, and you didn't question his want to lock you down. No, you were not some basic bitch that allowed a man to fill her head with lies and fuck for the price of a Chipotle burrito; you did something worse, you allowed a man to Trojan Horse himself, not into your vagina, but your heart. Men like Rick, these appealing Dicknotist, they take your pussy, capture your heart, and attain your love without question. In the end, you will waste months if not years of your time as a placeholder, and be left asking, "Why didn't I see through him?"

****

Are you done being a placeholder? Are you finished with these typical results? Are you ready to wake up and start playing the game better than men play it? Or do you want to stay in this comfortable position of vulnerability where you have to hope and pray that the next man you meet is genuine? You don't win at life by remaining the same! You either evolve now or settle for heartbreak after heartbreak until you finally get the hint that it's time to do better. Now or later, you will be forced to grow, and you may as well face your fear and do it today! This mission is not about men; it is about Spartanhood, female superiority, and creating a Queendom of Power where you don't fit into what men want, but where you force them to bow to your needs. You are Excalibur in the flesh, the epitome of a Game Changer, and you have a Universal Force inside of you that guarantees that you will win! The time for mistakes is over. It is time to leave the old you, behind, and become a Spartan.

Book of Spartan

Women are taught to sacrifice, to play nice, to live an altruistic life because a good girl is always rewarded in the end. This is not a virtue; it is propaganda. Submission gets you a ticket to future prosperity that will never manifest. By the time you realize the ticket to success and happiness you have been sold isn't worth the paper it was printed on, it will be too late. Go on, spend a quarter of your life, even half of your life, in the service of others and you will realize you were hustled. You do not manifest your destiny by placing others first! A kingdom built on your back doesn't become your kingdom, it becomes your folly. History does not remember the slaves of Egypt that built the pyramids, they remember the Pharaohs that wielded the power over those laborers. Yet here you are, content with being a worker bee, motivated by some sales pitch that inspires you to work harder for some master than you work for yourself, with this loose promise that one day you will share in his wealth. Altruism is your sin. Selfishness is your savior. Ruthless aggression and self-preservation are not evil. Why aren't females taught these things? Instead of putting themselves first, women are told to be considerate and selfless. From birth, they have been beaten in the head with this notion of "Don't be selfish!" Fuck that. Your mother may have told you to wait your turn like a good girl, but I'm saying cut in front of that other bitch. Club Success is about to hit capacity, and you don't want to be the odd woman out.

Spartans: The strongest women on the planet. They follow no woman. They obey no man. They aren't offended they offend. They don't wait they take. They are the Alpha Females.

Where are the powerful women? Those who refuse to play by those rules and want more out of life than what a man allows her to have? I created a category for such women and labeled them *Spartans*. Much like the Greek warriors who fought against all odds, these women refuse to surrender and curtsy before the status quo.

Being a Spartan is not about being masculine. It is about embracing the full power of being a woman and realizing that men worship what's between your legs and weaker women are infatuated by your control of it. Every female has the tools to regain this power and deprogram herself, but few have the confidence to be unapologetically aggressive and self-serving enough to wield this power. I want you to go deep inside and unearth all of those feelings that you hate to think about...how life hasn't been fair...how you wish you would have made a different choice years ago...how you will never win because the world is working against you. Confront those negative thoughts and take back control of your life. I don't care what happened to you in your past, let go of those feelings of anger due to bias, discrimination, heartbreak, manipulation, and any unfairness. I don't care how you look; close your eyes and let go of those feelings of unattractiveness that keep you self-conscious. I don't care what your perceived social status is, let go of those nagging feelings that you are somehow inferior to the wealthy. You are a woman; you can withstand immeasurable amounts of pain, show unconditional love, and give birth to life. You. Are. The. Shit!

Men kill, wage wars, lie, steal, pay, beg, and betray each other for women. Are you really going to believe the bullshit that you are soft, replaceable, or just a sexual release? You are the most powerful of all human beings! It is time to embrace this fact and shake off the habit and traditions that men have saddled you with in order to keep you obedient and unsure of your place in this world. Take some time to appreciate how important you are in regards to the role you play in this Universe. Spend a moment basking in how potentially great you could be once you had the self-esteem and confidence not to give a fuck. What do you have to fear from a man rejecting you, a woman not liking you, or a group of people judging you? Life is Sparta, a world tailor-made for the strongest women to succeed and ingeniously designed to keep the weakest women in their place.

You are no longer a lamb waiting to be slaughtered, you are the slaughterer. You are a Spartan.

Chapter 4:
Awaken The Spartan Within

"I don't have something you don't; you believe something I don't."
—Jed McKenna

You aren't reading this book by accident. It found you at the perfect time in your life. The old way of thinking, of believing, and of doing has not worked, and it never will work. You are standing on the edge of a paradigm shift, and in order to move forward, you have to leave your defensive shell in the last chapter. You were offended by the idea of being referred to as typical because you have spent a lifetime building your ego up to believe you were special or different from the majority. You were born a certain day—special. Your parents told you a story about something unique you did when you were little—special. Maybe a psychic, teacher, or even a stranger said they saw something great in you—special. If you are so damn special, why are so many other women able to relate to your struggle? "I go through that too," is the glue that keeps you stuck to women all over that world, not because you're special, but because you're making those same mistakes. If you can relate to the same messy situation a woman 200 miles away can relate to, what does that make you? If you can empathize with the stereotype of all men do is lie and cum fast, what does that make you? I can't stress enough how many women I come across looking for my help, from Canada, Germany, the UK, all the way back to the States, and it's the same old song. Your current life is no more special than the average person who also thinks they're "blessed and highly favored." Being special has nothing to do with money, fame, or any egotistical thing someone said about you. Special is defined as better or greater than what is usual. If you can relate to most people, have the same problems, worries, insecurities, and beliefs, how could you possibly be special?

Over the years, you needed ego's fuel in order to keep pushing forward. You needed something to believe in that told you your story would end differently than everyone else's. Some women I've met have bragged to me about how they were an exception to some rule, only to later confess to me that they don't actually believe in themselves the way they pretended. Results don't lie and actions don't hide. You are not an exception to a rule unless you actually shatter that rule when tested in real life. Not in your mind, in real fucking life. You kept piling onto this invention of you as some "chosen one" until your ego became too big to be checked. By labeling you as *Typical*, I checked that ego. Now it's time to open your eyes, so you can finally live up to your true potential.

Why aren't you above the pack? Why are you constantly striving and struggling instead of winning? Why are you lying up at night confused, instead of self-assured? If we are judging by results, you're mediocre and that other woman is remarkable. Yet, there is nothing inside her that isn't buried inside of you. What is really holding you back from being great? Are you the type to create bitter excuses like, "They cheated to get where they are in life," or harmonious excuses like, "My time is coming too..." There is no such thing as cheating at life because life has no rules. Furthermore, your time isn't just going to come because Karma has your back. How do you know Karma has your back? Where's the proof that you are going to win because you are nice? Fuck nice. Your current life is held together by the lies you tell yourself about your role in the universe. In order to not cry about your current situation, you keep telling yourself it will get better because it has to...but the lies aren't sticking as easily as they used to...you don't really believe you're special or chosen. You don't want to think like that, but you do! **What are they doing that I'm not doing**," is a thought that pops into your head, no matter how many times you open your mouth and pretend as if you are fine the way you are. Ego has you believing that your time is going to come. Reality is showing you that isn't true.

Do you want to be a caterpillar that finds joy in crawling and continues to convince itself that it doesn't need wings to be happy, or do you want to wake the fuck up and fly? You have become a bystander in your own life. You wait. You complain. You stress. You pray. Why don't you take action? Because it is easier to think, "I'm a good person; life will reward me for being good, so all I need to do is keep down this path." Everything you believe about life is a sugar coated lie. You have already realized that or else this book wouldn't be in your hands. The age of waiting for things to miraculously fall in place has ended. Defensive lies about how you don't care, how you don't need love, or how you have faith that it will all work out in the end, are done. Life will not work out, and you will fail unless you awake from this dream. Write down today's date, because from this day forward, you will stop letting life control you. From now on, you will control life. If you choose to go down this Spartan path then there will be no reason to lie about how special you are, compare yourself to other women, or brag about bullshit in order to feel bigger than what you actually are. Your petty, typical, basic life has come to an end. The game is about to change because you are about to finally grow wings.

THE AWAKENING

Not all women are created equal, but any woman can rise to surpass her peers, by simply thinking on a higher level. The mystery of greatness has been under your nose your entire life. You have read about the secret used throughout history, laws of power mastered by warlords and entertainers alike, but you still didn't get the hint. Even confronted with this information now, you may not understand what it truly means. Don't play along just so you can make yourself feel smart, because you won't learn shit by pretending. The keyword is THINK. Those that learn to think in a dominant way ascend. Lower level thoughts that cloud your mind such as who likes you and who doesn't like you, lead to insecurities. Insecurities lead to worry. Worry leads to fear. Fear leads to desperation. Desperation leads to typical bitch conformity. *How do I become popular like that person, rich like that person, pretty like that person, respected like that person, tell me what rules to follow and I will follow them because I want people to love me, never want to leave me, and always think I'm wonderful.* Every form of media is in the business of telling you what to do to get things that other women have. Examples of other people who achieved those things are used to reinforce an idea that you need to wear this, eat that, go to this school, follow that doctor's diet tricks or this author's love tips, all so you can acquire what someone else has. The desperate chase for acceptance, popularity, and love leads to life living you, not you living life. It's time to treat the root, not the symptoms.

Insecurity is the root of weakness because it causes your dominant thoughts to be controlled by the fear of not being good enough. How can you be confident in anything you do in life if you fear not ending up with what you want? How can you take chances in life that will catapult you to another level if fear makes you play it safe? How can you express yourself, if you're worried about how you come off and what other people will think of you? Low thinkers have one thing in common; they are slaves to their own insecurities. Women, in particular, fall into these traps the most, a product of living in a male-dominated culture. Told what they can't do, so they don't try. Told what males love, so they conform to those traits. The biggest social conformity is the idea that women have to wait for Mr. Right to come to her. If he doesn't come then she needs to improve her fashion, her looks, tone down her aggression and amp up her submission. Garbage! For centuries, a woman's place has been to wait to be chosen, and you never thought about why that became a tradition? Men have kept you chained to their approval, and you continue to fall for it! *Don't chase boys. Wait for him to come talk to you. Let him call you first. If you can't find a man, pray harder and dab on more makeup.* Tradition is a fancy word for "Stay The Fuck In Your Place." Spartans do not think on that low frequency. You are not born special you must evolve to become special, and that evolution starts with one thought: <u>I Rule This World</u>.

There are Queens and there are peasants. There are those that rule and those that are ruled. For the first time in history, you can choose your hierarchy. Either you can be a Typical Girl who follows the Typical Rules and believes in Typical Concepts created by others, or you can open your eyes and understand that only a ruler gains the power to create and dictate the world they live in. No one has ever told you there is a choice, that there is life outside of the *Matrix*, that the chains in *Plato's Cave* are shackles made of paper. Your life has been presented to you like a Prix fix menu, with one available course of action, do what society tells you to do!

It's time to fearlessly reject the menu, dare to look beyond what's in front of you and realize that you're surrounded by a buffet. Think about your own life for a second. At every step, you were told that life has a blueprint. Adults told you that if you go to school, get good grades, and pick a major or a trade that pays well, you win—financial success. In terms of love, you were told that there is also a formula. Don't be fast, look pretty, wait for the right man to come along, treat him with love and respect, and you will be rewarded with his heart—romantic success. Has life worked out like this blueprint? It hasn't because those people that feed you that stuff are just trying to give you guidance because they themselves have no clue about how to live life without the rules they were given. How can an enslaved mind teach freedom? Read any historical story about success it will undoubtedly show you a person who went against the grain, broke rules, and took a risk that others said was insane or foolish. Everyone has the power to think outside the box, but few do because the traditional blueprint seems like a sure bet, while coloring outside the lines seems like a recipe for failure. All of your life you were told there is a right way and a wrong way. You've lived in the footsteps of wishful thinking, and here you are, face to face with the truth, that if you really want to ascend to the next level, you must think different.

No one is going to reward you for being nice. No man is going to love you just because you love him. There is no Karma that will take you from the back of a line to the front of a line because you happen to be kind hearted. How long have you been alive? How long have you been nice to everyone? How long have you put others first? How long have you given your all, secretly wishing to be rewarded by the universe for your purity? Has it worked? Has playing your position and being selfless actually improved your life? In theory, you should have inherited the earth by now. Look around you, look who is more popular than you are, more successful than you are, and who has found love quicker than you have? The selfish run the world! They don't play by your rules; they play by their own rules because they aren't afraid to think for themselves. The rules of this world are made to keep the peasants in check.

In traditional love and romance, men have held on to this power and operate under a *Master Morality*. Women are to be submissive, humble, hardworking, self-sacrificing, and forgiving. Men are to be dominant, aggressive, managerial, self-advancing, and their ends always justify their means. Who created those attributes? The Master. Who follows the notion of, "that's just how things are, but my time will come..." The Slave! The idea of women as lowly, virtuous, and controllable creatures goes beyond double standards. This mentality has been so deeply embedded in your mind that you accept it as the law of the land. Put a peasant in a cage and tell them they will be damned to hell if they dare step out, and you won't even need a lock to keep them imprisoned. The hell that hangs over women who dare to think different isn't a fiery pit, but a life lived alone and loveless. Follow the rules and it will all work out in the end. Says who? You, the typical women, the selfless girls, the fearful females have been brainwashed into playing by the rules by those that understand there are no rules. You have agreed to be a prisoner because you are too afraid to break the tradition of mental slavery. Enough is enough; it's time for a change.

REFRAME YOUR PAST

Who are you? Right now, you're a typical human being. Just another person whose concepts, morals, and habits were influenced by things experienced during childhood. You are the product of other people's molding, either directly or indirectly. While you believe that you are a unique individual, your mind, your thought process, your "character" is an imitation of others. Your mother, your father, your aunt, your grandmother, your high school bestie, your college sister, or whoever it is that you've been close to at one time or another. Children learn by imitating others. By the time you're an adult you've become an amalgam, and contrary to what your ego says, there are few things that are explicitly you. In short, your past created your current world, thus, the past is the first thing that must be tackled because it's really the only thing holding you back. 90% of the women whom I've given advice to start in the present, then once I get them to open up, they slide backward to reveal that it isn't the current man or the current situation that's casting doubt or creating anxiety, but their upbringing. You can't change your past, but you can reframe it in a way where it no longer affects your day to day attitude, outlook, or decisions.

62

Let's go to the example I call "C+ Karen's Story." This woman, I'll call her Karen, shared a story that when she was younger, she noticed that her father would burst with excitement when her sister would come home from elementary school with good grades. Her father treated them the same generally, but at that moment, Karen felt like her Dad prized her sister because she was "the smart one." Her dad never verbalized this, but Karen saw the pride dripping off him, and it made her envious. At this moment, Karen developed an insecurity that would define her relationships for years to come; a consuming lust for a man's approval. How did Karen, a mediocre student, solve this issue of her father showing favoritism to her sister? She took a marker and started to change the grades on her papers to A's. It worked! The first time Karen did this, her father embraced her the same way he had her sister...but it wasn't the same internally. Little Karen knew that she only achieved her father's love by cheating while the sister did it just by being herself. Nearly 20 years later, Karen came to me in shambles because her relationships with men were built on that same concept, embellishment. C+ Karen felt as if she had to constantly portray herself as top of the line so that men would see her as special because she could never be special on her own. The irony is that when you build your life on lies or act extra to gain approval, the insecurity widens. You're not really A+ you're C+, a big fake ass fraudulent C+. Even if the men buy into your deception, you know who you truly are, and there's no hiding from the truth of self. Some of you can relate to a story like Karen's quest for approval. Sisters or cousins who were loved more than you were because they were smarter, prettier, or had more personality placed a chip on your shoulder. Not a chip that drove you to find your own strength, but one that made you look for other routes to a man's love. Remember, a father is the first man a girl falls in love with, and to be seen as 2nd best by a man who is supposed to love you unconditionally is heartbreaking. So let's start the reframing process with Daddy Issues.

Daddy left mommy. Daddy was home but didn't give you enough attention. Daddy had drinking problems. Daddy played favorites. Daddy started another family...whatever it is that Daddy did in your story that upset you, own it. Admit that you feel a certain way, don't suppress it as if you're good. If you were good, you wouldn't be so damn weak and defensive. Females learn how to play defensive before they learn how to play with Barbie because it's a coping mechanism. Confront your past, soak it in, now dry your eyes, and grow the fuck up. This isn't about feeling sorry for yourself; this is about coming to terms with what is really in your head. You want pity. Your life has been defined by some form of unfairness or lack of love. Be mad! Feel robbed! Understand your anger instead of ignoring your hurt! This level of thinking cuts to the real problem more than looking for someone to say, "Poor thing. You have the right to be guarded, hardened, promiscuous, violent, angry, or depressed." So many women wear masks that they only take off once they find a person to trust. That person they confide in becomes their salvation because they need an outlet. You can't wait for someone to come along and absolve you of your childhood trauma.

Your internal strife can't be held back until you find a friend, mentor, or husband to finally confess to because that person may never come. You must save yourself! Take out a piece of paper, write down your frustration, and let it out. Go into a room and scream until you can't cry anymore. Meditate and place yourself back in your past, and confront it. Check your own baggage by doing any of those internal exercises for as long as you need to do them. Once it's poured out, Spartan up and stop feeling sorry for yourself! Fuck your excuse of a bad childhood. This world doesn't care about what you had to overcome. Tell people your sob story, and then watch them shrug, because you don't get a cookie for surviving trauma. Do you want sympathy or do you want power? If you are ready to take responsibility for your life going forward and not keep pointing backward to make excuses for why you're so broken, then let's rethink your life.

What is a father? What is a mother? What are parents? They are flawed human beings ingrained with their own bias and insecurities. You love them, you look up to them, and you were raised to respect them as if they were gods, but they are fatally human. Let's begin with Dads. They're men. Just because got your mother pregnant, doesn't mean they stopped acting and thinking like the typical male. Some men worship their children unconditionally; the joy of fatherhood transforms them. Other men remain just as inconsistent and petty as they were as teenagers. Having a child doesn't necessarily turn a boy into a man. Maybe he had a baby with a woman he barely liked, the baby doesn't look the way he wanted his child to look, or doesn't act as smart as he would want his child to behave. That disappointment is going to manifest through his behavior. Sure, he may put on a front like, "that's my princess," but he's dialing it in. Daddy may have loved you out of responsibility, not out of a true fatherly bond. It happens.

You are not to blame for the bias of an asshole! Is it your fault that he didn't want you, that he doesn't love everything about you, or that he resents your mother so he resents you? You didn't ask to be born, you couldn't control your physical features, nor did you choose your intelligence or personality at birth. You are what you were meant to be, and that is a beautifully unique creature with endless potential! Are you really going to let some man who was most likely fighting his own insecurities dictate your opinion of yourself for the rest of your life? Your father was not perfect. He was cast in a role where he was *supposed* to be loving and supportive, but that doesn't mean he *knew* how to be that father figure you saw in movies or experienced at your friend's house. Understand that Daddy without the title is just another dude trying to figure out his own shit. Understand that he is not larger than life, that he has weaknesses, and that it wasn't really about you, it was about him! Now forgive him, the same way you forgive any fool. Regret doesn't change the past and neither does anger. Dad was just a confused little boy and life's too short to hate low thinking people.

The same rules apply to your mother. It's always interesting to see a woman idolize their mom and take her word as gospel without ever questioning who she is outside of that role. Just because she was/is, a strong woman doesn't mean she knew what the fuck she was doing raising you or knows what she's doing currently when trying to tell you how to live your life. Think about your father in the terms we just reframed. If your father was a weak and flawed man, ask yourself what kind of woman sleeps with and has children with a weak and flawed man? This is important to delve into, as these days I find myself advising women who are in their opinion "good moms," yet are dealing with self-esteem issues themselves. I tend to say, "Think about how this man is treating you. Would you ever want your daughter or son to know that Mommy is being a basic bitch?" It strikes a chord. Just because a woman becomes a mother doesn't mean she's fully adult and has it all figured out. Women, more than men, tend to be the day to day influencer of what a child grows up to believe, think, and how they ultimately act. If these women today are coming to me in secret for help, imagine how many mothers from the past generations were simply holding it in because there wasn't an anonymous source to go to and confess, "I'm lost, please help!" The well that you're gathering water from in terms of a strong female role model could be tainted. Your mother may sit and give you her opinion on men, tell you the mistakes she made, but is she truly put together or just playing that role?

One woman told me that her mother gives *the* best advice. I asked her to specify, what the best advice she received was, so I could understand why a woman whose mother gives perfect advice was still struggling. When this woman had her wedding called off, her mother told her, "Everything's going to be alright, he just wasn't your soul mate." Think about that. Mom told her that everything was going to be all right because of...what exactly? Mothers, like clergy, are in the habit of just telling you it will be okay, not based on a real reason, but because it sounds nice and positive. Fuck that! It's all ego stroking that keeps you stagnant.

You are special because you're her daughter. Your time is going to come because you're her daughter...that's ego. "God has you, have faith," is the go-to saying for most, but that is not sage wisdom that helps you get to the root of your unhappiness. Again, I ask you to look at your mother like any other woman and ask if she's truly Obi-Wan Kenobi[7] or just another chick that had a kid and is learning on the job with mixed results. A woman who refuses to divorce a loser can be a great mother in terms of nurturing, but that doesn't mean she has any real answers. A woman who divorced her husband and has since taken up with a new man who's just as much as a bum, can be a great mother in terms of supporting your dreams and goals, doesn't mean her opinions of your life choices aren't influenced by her own jaded view of life. A single mother who raised you alone can give you great advice on how to deal with the men she fell for but does she actually know how to advise when a man is from the new school and doesn't play by that 20th century rulebook?

---

[7] Sage Jedi Master, known for his simple yet revealing wisdom.

Alternatively, females compete with other females, and mothers do compete with daughters. Just because she's supposed to be there for you, doesn't mean she's not capable of sabotaging you at the same time. Being your mother doesn't make her enlightened or even good at telling you how to live. You can't hold that against her, however. Just like your father, you have to look at Mom as you look at any female. Understand her mind, forgive her if she led you astray, and going forward take her advice or critique with a grain of salt because her insecurities may still be at play.

No matter who it is that still haunts you from childhood, break them down in your own head or on paper and dismiss them. **No longer give those people, or anything they did, power over you!** What you wanted your life to be at that age was out of your control. Few know how to parent the right way because there is no right way to parent, it's all an experiment where you tell your child what you think sounds right. No matter if they are Janelle from *Team Mom* or Beyoncé, a person can only raise a child the way they understand how to raise a child. You weren't born to the Buddha; you were born to regular people, and regular people don't get most things right. Child rearing is trial and error with the human psyche. You can point the finger in hindsight and say, "You should have done this for me!" What does that really solve? There was nothing you could have done to change that then nor change that now...let go of that baggage; you've spent too many years weighed down.

There are those whose insecurities don't come from the Homefront. Their parents didn't create any conscious or subconscious issues, or they've made peace with parental issues and no longer carry any baggage. Yet other things from the past haunt them in the same manner. That first boyfriend who broke your heart shows up every time you feel yourself getting too close to a new man. That close girlfriend who talked behind your back or betrayed your trust, she made you view all females as conniving backstabbers, now it is hard to let friends into your life. There comes a point where you must stop using your exes, fake friends, or that romantic fling that wasted too much of your time, as an excuse for your current state. People do fucked up things to each other, and most don't pay any price for that. When you let what others did eat at your soul, you're giving them control over your mind.

"It's unfair that he moved on so easy, and I still think of him." This mentality is token weak bitch in its makeup. You must not waste your brain cells or your energy waiting for present to make past right. There isn't some magic force that's going to make him hurt the way you hurt or keep him from moving on because he did you wrong. This idea that God or Karma will punish men who didn't love you is such a petty idea. You want mystical forces to get revenge for you on mean people; you sound like a five-year-old. Blow your nose, pick yourself up, understand the lesson life was trying to teach you and evolve. Stop waiting for the universe to act as your personal hitman, and know that carrying negativity towards others only affects you. There are countless examples of people that caused you pain that you can't shake, and it sticks with you regardless if it was back in grade school twenty years ago or a break-up a year ago. No matter how buried or how fresh the trauma, you have to confront it, understand it, and dismiss it in a healthy way as opposed to suppressing it or feeling sour about the outcome. Those repressed emotions will project out of you as attitude, bitterness, or paranoia, causing you to struggle until the day you die.

Let's move away from the past in terms of specific people and talk about specific feelings. An issue I deal with daily, when giving advice, centers around those women who are gorgeous physically, yet feel ugly because of comments made during their formative years. There is a term called "Glo Up" where a person goes through a physical change and blossoms from Ugly Duckling to Swan. The internet has become a forum for so many women where they can gather remotely and share that story of, "They used to call me ugly, now look at me." It's bittersweet because I know several women who post selfies, have an insane number of men liking their pictures but come to me in secret admitting that they still don't feel pretty. The past still reflects in the mirror because they can't shake the insults or lack of attention that was directly tied to the way they looked. Smiles and glamour shots become yet another mask to hide internal feelings, and no matter how many people compliment the new you, that inward feeling of inadequacy never subsides.

The word "fat" can kill a woman's self-esteem for the rest of her life... if she lets it. A comment as small as, "you've been eating good, I see," is a dagger that a gym membership can't fix. No matter how fit a woman gets, the poison that was injected is rarely cured by simply becoming a new weight. The same can be said of looks in general. Big forehead, crooked teeth, moles, freckles, birthmarks, hair texture, if someone can point it out and use it to make you feel like less of a woman, then that complex will remain until you deal with it mentally, not cosmetically. Little black girls, in particular, may have it the worse in terms of having their looks dragged through the mud relentlessly by fellow black people. Growing up, I saw it firsthand with the "Black as hell, darkness, burnt, African booty scratcher, nappy head..." insults that were thrown at the darker girls in my class starting back in pre-school. I remember sitting with my high school girlfriend and wiping her nose as she told me about how she never felt as pretty as her lighter skinned best friend. Her complexion issues led to all kinds of destructive behavior during the time we were together, and to this day, I continue to hear stories from darker women who can't stop believing that men see their skin as something sexual but not loveable.

Lighter girls or those of mixed race were not free of stereotypical digs about being "white, stuck up, house nigga," and the list goes on. No matter your race or nationality, if you look different, pissy little kids or hateful teens will find a way to single you out in order to make themselves feel better. To be discriminated against as a young girl because you look a certain way which you have no power over is a hard pill to swallow. Much like the father who doesn't think one daughter is as pretty as the next, or that grandmother who favors one grandchild over another because, "she looks like me when I was that age," you can't escape the feeling of not being good enough simply by going through a Glo up. You can use the selfie likes or the "Damn, I'd marry you" thirst as fuel to rebuild your esteem, but it takes more than a few years of praise to make up for a lifetime of slander.

The true Glo up only happens in one part of your body—the mind. Despite whatever trauma you've gone through—you are still standing! Your childhood was your childhood; it was meant to be that way because it was meant to build your character in a unique way. From your first love to your last love, from your best friend to your worst enemy, even being teased about your looks or the way you talked, it was necessary! The up's and downs that made you hate yourself or hate other people served its purpose, and that was to place you right here, right now. You didn't want to struggle, but your current growth was dependent on that struggle! R. Buckminster Fuller said, "There is nothing in a caterpillar that tells you it's going to be a butterfly." The Universe isn't out to fuck you over; its sole purpose is to make you over. You're about to wake up, evolve, and finally, gain the control you always knew you were destined to attain. There is no "If I could only go back," because to go back would mean to change every aspect of yourself. You weren't meant to be "her" you were meant to be you! There is no do-over, there is only do-now! From this moment forward, the past is just a story, a prologue that gave you the foundation of your personality, nothing more, nothing less. Look back with Spartan eyes now. You don't need to hate it, love it, complain about it, or praise it. Your previous life was merely your *Big Bang*, now let's start building your true (Yo)universe.

REWRITE YOURSELF

Who are you? At this point, you should be a blank canvas, not confined to color within the lines of your past self. What does that mean practically? It means it is time to find an identity. When I wrote *Ho Tactics*, something incredible happened. From the women whom I corresponded with, the ones that had the best results did something I didn't foresee. They didn't emulate Maria the Ho, they *became* Maria the Ho. What was only meant to be a combined example of how women that I interviewed, did these things, became an avatar. One girl from Austin Texas told me that after her second time reading that book, she decided enough was enough, and she hit a switch. This woman stared in the mirror and decided that she was no longer Sydney, she was Maria. She colored her hair in a way that felt like sex, dressed in a way that felt like sex, and spent the next week calling herself Maria in her head. It worked! She went out the first week, sized men up, didn't go after any, but flirted with a few dudes that approached her as if she already owned them. There weren't any homeruns her first nights out, but it reinforced that she could talk to men, read them, and actually flirt without feeling stupid or awkward. The concept of *Pussy Power without using Pussy* wasn't something that stayed in her head as a fantasy, she tested it, and as I said in that book, "It does work!"

By the end of the month, she had approached a cute guy and got his number, something that was a breakthrough given that she was deathly shy. A few weeks in, instead of being on his dick and stressing over typical things she used to worry over such as callbacks, *does he like her for real*, etc... Sydney-Maria didn't give a fuck, this guy was just an object, and as a result of her *Hoformation*, he was now chasing her more. She took off Sydney's weakness and tried on Maria's strength. The next few emails I received weren't for advice on how to ask for gifts or about wrinkles that came up, just status reports on how she had this mark wide open. Other women popped up telling me similar things. They didn't merely do what Maria did, they understood the psychology, and they assimilated it into their own mind. I knew there was a way for a woman with this same ingenuity to hit the switch in a Spartan way, but it would require sharing a huge secret...

Confidence is one of those things people pretend they have in theory, yet lack in terms of actual application. They talk big, but when forced to show they aren't typical on a date or in an actual relationship, they fall on their faces. Having someone tell you step by step what to do, helps many women get fast results, it's that habit of following blueprints that I mentioned earlier. Anyone can read a script and win so long as it stays on script, but when the others start to ad-lib, that person who is tied to the script will flounder. It has always disappointed me to see women come back to me at the first sign of a man not acting as she imagined, her confidence out the window like, "He didn't go for that, now what? I knew I couldn't do this, maybe I'm just meant to lose." **That negativity was tied to their past insecurities**. The moment a man went off script and didn't react in a way I listed, they froze like a deer in the headlights. That feeling of being unattractive, the memories of once being rejected, it all came rushing back, and like Peter Pan minus the ferry dust, they came crashing down.

Those women that failed didn't have true confidence. They never believed that they could pull off seducing a man, so they followed my blueprint like a robot, but without understanding the mentality behind Maria they couldn't adapt and conquer. In the Ho game much like the

Spartan life, you will be forced to adapt, not freestyle, adapt—know the difference. Freestyling points to a lack of discipline in girls who think they know it all, but don't know shit. Freestyling never works because you're trying to take a blueprint that is proven and mesh it with that same flawed typical behavior that led you to look for help in the first place.

  To become something stronger is to understand what makes that creation powerful in the first place. Your character knows how to react without being told what to do because you aren't mimicking, you become! It's like actors who tell directors, "My character wouldn't do that," they were just hired to play a part initially but they take it over! Heath Ledger wasn't playing the Joker; by the time that film was complete, it was the Joker *being* the Joker in *The Dark Knight*. You can't just play a part of a Spartan; you must become a Spartan. Now that you're free of your past, it's time to create a new you, one that walks, talks, and thinks like a Spartan.

Chapter 5:
The Spartan Secret

"Reality is merely an illusion, albeit a very persistent one."
—Albert Einstein

Who are you? You are a collection of thoughts creating an experience. You think you look a certain way—that is how you look. You think you act a certain way—that is how you act. You think people either like you or dislike you based on various observations they make about you—that is how people will treat you. Your life is one big concept that you keep repeating to yourself until it feels solid and true. Your body. Your behavior. Other people. It's all a perception of your own creation. The only things that can truly be labeled as real are your thoughts. I don't need you to understand this right now, I just need you to follow the bread crumbs until you're able to understand it later on. This isn't theory this is practical, and if you choose to follow these steps all the way through, there will be direct proof that you are what you think.

The idea of changing your thoughts in order to change your life is easier said than done because your beliefs are hardwired at this point. You can pretend that you understand what Einstein meant when he said life is an illusion, but you can't actually grasp it on a level where you can see past that illusion because you don't fully believe that statement. An illusion is fake, made up, but your life isn't because you live with it each day. Real is real because you can touch it. To say it's an elaborate projection from within goes against everything you have been telling yourself for an entire lifetime. Anytime you smash against the dominant beliefs you have built up for years, the first reaction is to dismiss it as crazy. But after you get over the egotistical idea of whatever you don't believe in must be crazy, your mind does an interesting thing, it actually begins to question itself.

73

Your mind may fight this truth on a surface level, but you know there has always been something deeper than this idea of "seeing is believing," and every night you experience just how unreliable your senses are—in dreams. Remember that dream you had that was similar to your real life, but didn't quite make sense? You kept dreaming, you weren't immediately roused by the lack of believability. No matter if it was a dead relative who was having a conversation with you, a friend who you recognized but was in a different body, or a classmate who you hadn't seen in years that you were having sex with; you bought into the concept to the extent that the dream was able to be played out as if it were real. Your thoughts override the imagined facts of your reality when dreaming, and, even more interesting, they actually create another world that becomes as real as the room you're in right now. If your consciousness is strong enough to create an endless array of worlds and scenarios that feel no different from what you call being "awake," then what determines real?

Throughout your entire life, you used the logic of if you can touch it, smell it, see it, then it's real. However, as proven by your own dreams, that's not true. Your mind can create those sensations even when asleep. You can have sex, hit the lottery, fall, almost die, and in that moment there is nothing telling you that the feelings are only perceived. What's the difference between the dream world and the waking world? One is more constant because you spend more time in that story than the other. From a metaphysical standpoint, you could say life is an extended dream. The most popular phrase used in enlightenment is "wake up" because the dream metaphor is the easiest thing to wrap your mind around. To "wake up" doesn't need to wait until death, you can attain it now. Those that reach this level of understanding realize what life has always been, and all of the fear and anxiety become silly. There is nothing to stress over once you become lucid in your dream. This is the power you are about to tap into.

If you need something more scientific to push you forward, look at quantum physics, zero point field research, or quantum foam tests that demonstrate that virtual particles pop in and out of existence depending on the observer. When not being observed, they remain waves of energy waiting to take shape. "Everything we call real is made of things that cannot be regarded as real," Niels Bohr won a Noble Prize with this information, but you can change your life with it. This book will prove it in terms of results if you choose to accept one thing: The external world is a vibrational force that collapses and then projects what you call life experience, not from that physical brain in your head, not from your "I wish for this, give it to me," ego-driven consciousness, but from your **true self**.

Your first thought may be that you and other people are creating this shared world together, like some group project, but there is only you. You are the observer. Everything is you. To quote quantum physicist John Wheeler, "There is no out there, out there!" It's all inside of you and always has been. Think about all the times you felt a situation was hopeless, and it worked out. As a kid and as an adult, you experienced "Oh shit" moments that you now laugh at, because it ended without you getting in trouble or ended with you getting what you wanted. People call it a miracle or a guardian angel, but once you move away from the supernatural, it is revealed as your true self protecting you from your own stupidity. Any time you make a mistake and don't learn your lesson, it repeats later, teaching you that same lesson that you were supposed to learn earlier. Your life was not created for you to lose. Even when "bad" happens it is actually good because it advances you to either think differently or move differently. Struggle is only struggle because you're attached to primordial thinking. Life's trials are built to wake you up, not to keep you clinging on to your old fearful life view.

Waking up or collapsing the field isn't about doing magic; it's about understanding the engine that's powering your life. Everything in the practical universe, when placed under a microscope is made of energy, that's no secret. What's been hidden is that you are both the plug and the power source. It doesn't matter if you're into metaphysics and embrace the dream metaphor or if you're scientific and buy into the holographic universe model or quantum theory. All that matters is that you open your eyes and stop pretending as if your life is being controlled by chaotic forces outside of you. No matter how you try to slice it, the external world is a concept. Thoughts create reality. Your thoughts.

Spirituality quotes, New Thought ideas, Vision Boards, these things are popping up more and more in your life, and slowly but surely you have been starting to investigate if there is something to the power of the mind.

This isn't an accident. If someone would have told you about a vision board party ten years ago, you may have looked at them like they were crazy or tapping into some devil shit, but your mind has matured, and it's pushing you to take baby steps towards a new view of how life actually works.

I'm not interested in revealing all the answers. That will become your puzzle to piece together. However, I am interested in showing you how to practically put this into practice so you can use it, not next year, not next week, but the moment you finish this book and every day after...

LOOKING GLASS

Rhonda Byrne, the author of *The Secret*, wrote: "All that we are is a result of what we have thought." In response to this claim, a man replied on a message board with an aggressive comment criticizing this idea. Personally, he would never *think* to be in the position of his current financial struggle, only abundance. The "insane" idea of blame the victim for being the victim is controversial, but this is where you have to wipe your ass with controversy and think about what your own dominant thoughts are. **What you want to happen is not what you actually think will happen.** On the surface, people say they want the world and all the good fortune it has to offer, but underneath that surface, they see the world as this big scary place where nothing ever works out because of various injustices or inequalities. Years of thinking that life is out of your control cannot be changed in a day. Proclaiming you want all the money in the world and all the happy experiences you can handle, does not erase the concept of what your life has been built on. The thought that things won't happen in your favor is dominant; when things actually work out, that becomes the exception. You feel happy, you give thanks, you praise, you do all of these things because you don't expect "good fortune" to happen normally. Good things are called blessings, miracles, luck, when in fact if your mind were truly positive, everything from setbacks to achievements would be seen as beneficial because they are all moving you in the same direction—forward!

Think of the time you achieved something remarkable. You looked back to see what you did leading up to that moment which could reveal a reason you deserved to win. You received extra money and pointed to lending money to a friend as the reason it came back to you twofold. You get a promotion at work, and you pointed to how you didn't break when your employer was getting on your nerves, and give thanks because your sacrifice has finally paid off. Your mind is making up bullshit stories to explain abundance. You can't even accept victory without needing to make up an excuse for it. I repeat, in your mind winning is an exception, not a standard. When you're expecting good news or going out for a job, what do you actually think? You feel nervousness, but what do you think? The words "I hope...I pray...I wish...If I'm lucky..." pop into your head. Maybe you wear a lucky charm or look to the sky and ask "please." Why? Because you don't see the world as a giving tree, you see it as a roulette table.

If your conscious self truly thought in a winning way or a forward direction, then why would your mind speak words that denote uncertainty? "Because you never know. I don't want to get my hopes up, assume, and then be disappointed when it doesn't happen." That's the fact I need you to grasp. You hope for success, but your deepest thought is not success; it's fear. The fear of not getting what you want has created the idea that you need to wish, cross your fingers, or ask other people to pray for you because this entire life you live is based on doubting yourself. Few people feel as if they deserve something for nothing, not even you, your thoughts have always been "do this to get that," with a series of obstacles constantly blocking you from winning. The universe isn't going to surprise you with success when you spend 90% of the time expecting failure. Your waking life is the same as your dream state. You don't actively decide what you will dream, your subconscious has already laid it out before you even go to sleep. It's determined by the things that are already on your mind, which you may not even be aware of because you think on *Autopilot*.

Look at your life. You don't think big, you coast. You counter positive thoughts with negative thoughts all day long. You think of something you want, try to hold on to it, then think of reasons why you won't get it, which leads you back to "I hope" or "If I'm lucky." For each forward thought, you have a backward thought. Every hour you fire off more counter thoughts than proactive thoughts because you have built a world where you have to be realistic, humble, or practical. You are afraid to

77

be great, not because you don't want to be great, but because thought after thought reminds you that someone like you can't do it!

You wait until someone else does something remarkable, then motivate yourself to do the same thing. That only lasts a short while, then you lose motivation. Your true self is constantly dropping hints to push you towards your true potential, but you remain scared! Rejection and disappointment have become so embedded in your mind, so you don't try, you simply live life on autopilot. Direct proof that thoughts control reality is found in your everyday life. You hope you can afford to buy something, and that stresses you about money all week. You worry that someone is mad at you, so you dread talking to them all day. You skip out on going to an event because you think other women will be dressed better, so you create a lie to make it seem as if you're not insecure about your body, just too tired to go out. Life controls you when you allow counter thoughts to back you into a corner of mental frustration. Every day you affirm things about yourself that are as true as you choose to believe. Then you buy into these ideas, make them the story of your life, project it out to be played, and the cycle repeats on autopilot.

The problem is your default thoughts are negative, stressful, or doubting. More people have "crazy" dreams than they have dreams where they are relaxing and sipping tea in a mansion. Why? Because your mind is raging with anxiety throughout the day! Thought after thought about how you don't look a certain way are always at war in your mind. Thoughts about how you don't have enough of something make you depressed, bitter, or resentful internally so you keep projecting that externally. Recurring thoughts that people will always see you as less than what you are and there's nothing you can do about it, places a chip on your shoulder and an idea that life isn't fair—so life remains unfair. You don't want to keep living like this; you are sick and tired of being frustrated...and that's why this book is appearing to you at this exact moment. Fearful thoughts project the strongest reality, and the time has come to change that.

GODDESS CONSCIOUSNESS

Every day you wake up and convince yourself that the story of [Insert Your Name] lives on the third rock from the sun, is [Insert Your Age] years old, and has to do XY&Z to have a good and happy life. That your concept of life and your story plays out like a movie every day based on these series of thoughts that you have been thinking since before you can remember. Can you stop in the middle of your movie scene and say, "this is all fake," you could, but you won't because you *think* everyone in that scene will see you as crazy. The reality that you are immersed in has made you fear doing anything other than what's normal because you have already decided the outcome. You don't push someone because they push back. You don't tell someone you like them because they may not like you back. You don't drive fast because you may crash. Even in your dream world, you are still controlled by those same boundaries that you place upon yourself when you're awake. You don't lose your fear in your dream or your sense of worry because you don't know how to live without those limits! Your thoughts, to this point, have been consciously and subconsciously fear based. You don't want to rock the boat of life because you don't want anything "bad" to happen. Therefore, you keep playing out your story just like Ryan plays out the entirety of *Gravity* without taking off her helmet in space and saying to the camera, "This isn't outer space and my name is actually Sandra Bullock." You play your role because you think the role is true self.

You could do anything you want in life right now. You can move to a new city, cut a friend off who annoys you, or go skydiving because it's all just an illusion that goes where you steer it to go. However, it's an illusion that's so convincing that it holds you in check with imagined repercussions. You don't move to a new city because you're afraid you won't find a new job fast enough to pay your new rent. You don't cut your friend off because you don't want a confrontation or to seem mean. You don't go skydiving because your parachute may not open. You are still Ryan in *Gravity* pretending she's an astronaut. Even though it's all a concept, it feels real, so you are going to play it as real until the day you die. This is your red pill moment. You can put this book down and keep playing your role or you can choose to change your reality every day for the rest of your life.

If life is a game, if you're just a character of your own true self thought creation, and this world is one big dreamscape, hologram, or quantum field where you play out various adventures, then how do you go about changing it? By understanding who you are in relation to the rest of the world. You become confident through truth so that there is no fear when you venture out and behave in a different way that will net you different results from what you are used to getting in life. So what is that truth that will make you fearless? **Goddess Consciousness**. Nothing bad will happen because bad no longer exists when you understand that you are being controlled by true self who only wants to live life to the fullest. You won't do anything directly or indirectly to ruin your life, so abandon the idea that this character has the free will to fuck everything up. You have been a slave to over thinking and indecision. Your character was molded from the collection of other women, some weak and some strong, but all who had that one flaw: A need for true love.

You were controlled by this idea that you had to pick the right man, not let go of someone, or take someone back because they were your soul mate. Your movie was playing out like a comedy because your entire way of thinking was built on this lie that there is only ONE person for you, that you have to work hard to keep a man, put up with struggles, speak his love language, and all the other mess that clouded your mind and made you try too hard to appease someone else. You gave away your power so you could follow those dominant thoughts about what love meant, but your true self was always there to make sure you didn't totally destroy your character by chasing pavements. The game is meant to be won, but your thoughts were so focused on losing that you became your own worst enemy. Your character was drifting on autopilot for all those years, and your true self was there to bail you out or to teach you a harsh lesson to get you back on track. Welcome back to the track! This is the moment you let go and let your true self, take over. Everything you want to experience in life, the real shit, not the generic goals you make up to fit in with other people who are still sleeping, will come into focus once you wake up and embrace this.

Two things will become key to this process. The ability to rebrand yourself through thought. This means that from now on the old weak you will begin to fade as you relaunch yourself with a new attitude based on... the second part: The ability to remember who you are. Not who your character is, but who you are—**Goddess Consciousness**. This will build your confidence to new heights, and as your confidence increases so will your results, but it will only work if you remember to remember! You can sit in bed and try to induce a lucid dream by saying, "When I'm sleeping, remember that I'm dreaming so I can have fun in the dream" It won't work. Maybe you'll do it one of the thirty times you attempt it, but you won't remember consistently because your mind is used to resetting itself so that it can be fooled over and over again by the illusion of dominant thoughts. The same way that you read a book that is inspirational or hear a sermon that touches your soul, you feel changed in the moment but not forever. You feel as if you're a different person, vibrating at a higher level... then by the next week, you're back to gossiping about work bullshit and you forget about that mini-awakening. **You are Consciousness playing a role**. That's all you have to know to center yourself in this game.

I want you to avoid the pitfall where you Spartan Up for a week, only to come crashing down full of fear the moment you don't get what you imagined. This isn't a law where you have to bottle up happy thoughts in order to get the world to give you free shit. This isn't some snap your finger and manifest materialism trick as if you're a genie. This isn't about affirming something you don't believe in or being fake-positive all day so you can see quick results. Never lie to yourself in order trick the universe into giving you things that it's already in the process of giving you!

There is a power that goes deeper than visualization techniques or law of attraction synchronicity, and slowly but surely you will come to know it. You will even return to this book, years later, and see the clues you missed. For now, understand that you are not expected to do magic, break the laws of nature, or turn your world into science fiction fantasy, this is about you working within the lines that you created, to get the extraordinary results you were meant to receive. This isn't a race. Do not pressure yourself and push your thoughts into a backward position with hypocritical ideas. You don't need to call out to the universe to help you, give a homeless guy a twenty to get back a hundred, or appease the Karma commission by doing something nice that you don't feel. You are free!

Boomerang thinking, throw it out come back to me, is poisonous. It's like those church women who promise to no longer do something they see as a sin, so they can get blessings going forward. "Lord, I'm going to be good this year so you can help pay for these car repairs." That Santa Claus, naughty or nice list, concept where you do good to receive more is full of shit. You don't have to kiss some invisible ass to be rewarded with a promotion. It's already yours! You can't hustle a world that is built to give you what you want. Understand one concept and the rest will take care of itself... **You are Goddess Consciousness** playing a role in order to create this epic story full of twist and turns that ends with you being fulfilled. Life won't play out like a predictable script, but it will play out in a way where even spontaneity feels exciting, not scary. Your universe can either benefit you, or it can frustrate you; that's your choice, but it is always working to reflect your true self. Don't pump yourself up, go outside and experience something that upsets you, and run back to thinking life is out of your control. You have to remember to remember until you can detach yourself from the impatience, the stress, and the anxiety that will cause you to relapse into the lie that you are the character, not the creator.

That weak part of you is creeping in right now, you feel as if this is going to be hard, it won't really work, or you will screw it up. Believe what you will, either way, it will be made true. Fear and Confidence are the two words that will be repeated constantly throughout this book. You must have an abundance of one and zero of the other. Live in the now, and always remind yourself: *This Is My Theme Park*. Remember to remember that you're in on this secret no matter what you're in the middle of projecting.

Chapter 6:
How to Become a Game Changer

ebrand, embrace that brand, project that brand. Those are the first steps when changing the game. Who are you? Goddess Consciousness about to play the game of life. What do you do when you start a new simulation game? You pick a name and then create an image. Over the next few days rebrand yourself internally. Think of it like a superhero alter ego, your brand should represent your power. Avoid some random stripper name like "Mercedes" or "Sinnamon" or any nickname that doesn't resonate in your core as powerful. If you love your name, use it. If you have a name in your head that you always felt you should have been named, take it. Next, add Spartan in front of it. Spartan Kim, Spartan Simone, Spartan Amanda, Spartan Nicki, Spartan Jasmine, Ho Maria turned Spartan Maria, it doesn't matter so long as you know that from this day forward you're a fucking Warrior Queen, not a bystander bitch.

Now that you have your name, understand what your brand represents. Are you Tiffany, classic luxury? Are you Playboy, sexual yet elegant? Maybe you're Forever 21, young, carefree, down to earth. Your name should match the attitude you want to embrace. Yes, you're a Spartan, you don't take shit, you don't back down, you ooze charisma, but that's the foundation. Your brand is your external calling card, the image that the world gets every time you walk outside. That "S" on Superman's chest says "You can't fuck with me." You need to find your S! When you dress, no matter the outfit or the occasion, it represents your brand's attitude. When you do your hair, it's not whatever, it represents your brand's attitude. When you walk, that's your brand's switch. When you talk, that's your brand's swagger. Choose your brand's style and commit to it.

If you're Haute Couture, you don't walk with your head down, shuffling your feet, like some awkward cow. You float as if these motherfuckers can't afford you. Even in sweatpants on the way to the market, you're still rocking that get up and go outfit like it cost major coins. Even with your hair in a ponytail, you don't rock that shit like a soccer mom who is stressed and tired. You make sure it's on point like Ariana Grande on a red carpet. It's not the look, it's the feel. You are power, your brand is power, so don't only feel that, project that in your own unique way.

FIND YOUR SEXY

The next step is to fall in love with the mirror. Let's strip away all the clothes, the hairstyles, the makeup, and glossy material shit of your brand image. Now that you know the energy you want to project and the attitude, rebuild the actual woman who will be serving as your Spartan brand ambassador. This is about YOU and the MIRROR. All of this past bullshit about how you look good but you're not all that, or how you need work done before you can go snatch souls, it's all fiction. If you look in the mirror and see everything that's wrong, that means when you go out in public other people will also see everything that's wrong. No matter what you wear to mask yourself, if you give into the idea that a part of your body needs improvement, then it becomes a bulls-eye for others to hit.

You create your insecurity, not other people. If there weren't any thoughts in your head about, "my breasts are too small, my butt is too flat, my voice is ugly," then there would be nothing to be insecure about. Other people only notice what you first notice. Think back to a pimple you had, you were so sensitive to the size that when you were forced to go out in public, you felt as if everyone was staring at that bump. It's all in your head! You give life to your issues by thinking they are negatives to begin with. Get in the mirror and start changing that projection. I don't care how long this step takes you. It's better to get this right than to rush.

You have to want to fuck yourself. That's the only goal at this point. Wake up, and before you put makeup on, before you style your hair, before you push your tits up, or try to suck your stomach in, love what you see in that mirror! I don't want you to lie about being pretty. Don't turn to

84

the side and hit your best angle to feel sexy. Don't squint and imagine that you are blemish or acne scar free. Don't practice smiling with no teeth to cover up that mouth that needs braces. Don't comb that bang over your big ass forehead to hide your shame. Don't shove your fat into a waist trainer, shove your face into the mirror and accept yourself. Stand as you are every morning and embrace you for you before you start the day. The only thing wrong with your body is that you think there's something wrong with your body. You may not see this the first day or the second day, but you must keep working at this until you remake your avatar into the beautiful shell it was meant to be. Keep looking until you start projecting something that makes you smile, and that same image will begin to reward you when you go out in public. Think back to a day when you got an insane amount of male attention. You wonder what you did, if it was your hair, your outfit, the fact that you just got a new boo. None of that! It's about how you feel inside. Emit that feeling of flawless and you will make any dick hard.

What you feel inside, you will project outside—fact. Too many of you are walking the streets with busted avatars and only attracting men who you think would want this, "7 in a face, 9 with makeup" creation you call self. You don't have to pretend as if you're perfect to feel sexy. This isn't about delusion, where you lie about what you see reflecting back. Those women who swear "I look good" but really don't, know they don't look good. They're merely trying to boost themselves up via empty words and false swagger. I don't want you to be that typical chick that goes out full of hot air gets exposed by a man who isn't afraid to tell her she's a 6 with a bad closure, then crumble. You have to believe in your beauty on a real level. Take the negative and only see the positive in it so that if someone were to point it out, you won't flinch, because you are okay with that feature. Don't fix your mind to think "There are too many things wrong for me to believe that." This is your world, your character, your projection, it's all within your power to change. I want you to fall in love with yourself as is, because even with things you once called flaws, you will see that it's all part of the entire sexy package known as your Spartan Avatar.

BE YOUR BIGGEST FAN

Attraction isn't about being the prettiest, it's about that intangible sex appeal of knowing you're the shit. You've dated men or had crushes on guys who didn't look like token pretty boys. They were funny looking or a bit rough, but still gave you that tingle because they projected sex despite not being Prince in *Purple Rain* pretty. Physical perfection is an opinion. Your universe likes flavor, not vanilla. There is a reason the top movie actresses have weird features, as opposed to perfect comic book drawn bodies and faces. Julia Roberts, with her snort laugh and big teeth, became the epitome of the girl next door sex appeal. Madonna with that huge gap and mole, became iconic. Zoe Zaldana, no matter if she's brown, blue, or green, doesn't look like Jessica Rabbit, she looks even better because she oozes confidence with those *fuck me **eyes*** regardless of how big her nose or ears are. Cleopatra was portrayed as this great traditional beauty of history, but she had a hook nose and her father's features—Still brought down a fucking Empire with her sex appeal. The point is, there is no mold for beauty, you're the one creating it in your own head. It's time to revisit how you think about your looks in an honest way.

If you have a big nose, love that big ass nose, it makes you stand out. No one's laughing at it, if you aren't. No one's making fun of it, if you aren't. The moment you stop noticing it as a blemish, the rest of the world will follow. If you're a bigger girl and want to drop some weight, gold star for you, but for now, you are the size you are and you can't hide out until that gym routine begins to yield results. Your confidence has to be built on who you are right now, not who you will become after a diet or surgery, or that insecurity will always be in the back of your mind. There is no such thing as a perfect weight, breast size, or ass size because that cancerous way of thinking will always find something new to pick at and change.

Think different and think higher! Look in the mirror and love every ounce of body fat you have. Understand that the men in your world have more than just a fetish, they have a hunger for your body the way it's currently built. This goes for all body types and all facial features, if you love it, others will also love it. If you aren't happy, then you will continue to meet those people that mirror your own thoughts about your looks. Again, do not skip this step and jump to dating. If you still feel insecure, your world will point it out. A toddler who rudely yells out your flaw, a group of people who laugh as you walk by, a nail tech who is speaking another language but still shading you. Your flaws will get pointed out if you cheat this step! Don't leave that damn mirror until you love yourself minus any, "but I would change..." statements. Know that a man will want to plant his face in your box like you know the sun will rise tomorrow! Your avatar is that of a Spartan Queen: Sexy, Fierce, and Unbelievably Tempting.

SELFISHNESS IS YOUR SAVIOR

Up until now, the word "selfish" has been negative. It has been used to guilt you and make you give up more of yourself than you wanted to under the guise of being a good person. You don't have to put other people in front of you to be a good person. You don't have to sacrifice your wants and desires in favor of someone else's hopes and dreams in order to get blessings. Even when you were playing this game while asleep, events were nudging you towards the truth of, *Do you*. This world is made for you, but you keep letting people take your spot in line, out of some misplaced concept of kindness. Selflessness and servitude are hustles and you know it; that's why you feel a certain way when you see people who look out for themselves achieving things that, according to this imagined rulebook, they shouldn't achieve. Your true self keeps pointing you in the direction of "Put yourself first," but you're afraid to do that, so history keeps repeating itself because you can't take your own hint!

You are a Spartan, this is your world, it revolves around you like the earth revolves around the sun because you are the one powering it! Be nice to people, be kind, and be considerate all you want, but at the end of the day, never put someone else before you. This is your creation, but guilt has made you play Alfred instead of Batman. You aren't a fucking supporting character, you aren't a sidekick, and you aren't meant to wait until you die to transport to some other reality where you get a cookie for being a doormat. You have to take center stage now or this experience you call life will have been a waste. A boring generic waste where you let everyone ride the best rides because you didn't want to be inconsiderate. You have the right to ride the rollercoaster, get off and ride it again without getting back in line, because this is your theme park. You must cultivate the Spartan mind which demands: *Me comes before He or She.*

The old subservient mind led to women being used unabashedly by friends, family, and lovers. Family members borrow money that they never pay back, but it's okay because the weak part of you says, "They must need it more than me." Friends drag you along to places you don't want to go, but you play along because "I have to be a good friend." Yet when you try that same trick, they give you their ass to kiss with excuse after excuse. And men, they know best of all how willing you are to go above and beyond and never think of yourself. These men will prey on your kindness, and use it to their benefit in dozens of ways, all under the cover of "You're the type of woman I need on my team (a dumb bitch that does for me without demanding that I do for you)." A man will call you different and shower you with compliments because you let him take advantage, but you're no different than most women who puts *He before She.*

He doesn't have money to go out, so you sacrifice what you know is an important show of value and let him give you a house date—Selfless. He needs to borrow your car, your money, or your credit, and though your true self is screaming not to do it, you hook him up because you feel a sense of loyalty—Selfless. In terms of communication, you're always available to talk because you don't want him to be upset, but he has the option of ignoring you whenever he sees fit with no real explanation—Selfless. Even the concept of a relationship is a compromise. You know what's healthy, you know what you want, but you give in the moment a man says, "let's take it slow... we don't need a stupid title... I'm not looking for anything serious... You know I want to be with you, but I need to take care of things first." Excuse after excuse that tells you he doesn't want you is greeted with understanding because you choose to put a man's want to be free above your need to be loved—Selfless. This world that you have created comes across as stressful because you keep walking away from your power!

Every time your instincts let you in on the secret, you fight it and make a typical move that ends with you being fucked over because you are afraid of this power. To be a Master is scary when you're used to being a slave. You want to put your fate in the hands of Karma's reward, of some new era Zeus in the clouds with a white beard who decides if you win or lose based on his mood. You want an outside power to tell you what to do. You look for signs, read horoscopes, get palms read. Playing the game as if you're helpless and at the mercy of the stars...in reality, the only reality is that you are the stars! You have all the power, and you will keep repeating the struggle until you realize that it starts and stops with your thoughts.

Remember who is in control even when things seem out of your control. The universe testing you is actually you testing yourself. Never run back to the comfort of your old way of thinking, stay in the moment and know that the most powerful woman in this reality is you. Enlightenment is destruction in the sense that all of your old beliefs must die. In the past, you compared yourself to other people in terms of looks, wealth, and status to see where you ranked. If you lived around lower income people, you felt proud to be earning more. On the flip side, if you happened to go to a party with the young and rich, you would feel dejected, as if you should be doing more in life at your age. Your mood was dependent on what other people had or didn't have over you. As you wake up, you realize that comparing yourself to other people is like William Shakespeare comparing his looks to Romeo's and his wealth to that of King Lear's. It's all a part of your story! A Spartan doesn't compete with girls because there is nothing to compete against. Don't point to some rich celebrity as if they're better than you or proof that you are a nobody. They exist to entertain you or to inspire your character. They aren't meant to be goals or people to emulate, they're just playing parts in the background of your movie as it moves forward. This means jealousy should be the first human emotion you shrug off, as it doesn't make much sense to envy your own creation. Someone having more money, more success at work, getting married before you, who cares? Focus on moving your story forward, don't get lost in the background scenery.

HEAD BITCH IN CHARGE

Let us transition to your role in relation to other people. This isn't a world you share, it's one that you rule over, so stop trying to be so democratic. There's a saying, "the world doesn't revolve around you." It's meant to humble children and teach teamwork, but it's a Trojan Horse that embeds a slave mentality. Giving someone more meaning in your life than yourself is a self-defeating concept that goes against your natural instincts. This idea that in order to be good you need to be at the service of others is a con. Queens rule from the top, not the bottom. You are a Spartan, this is your kingdom, and it does revolve around you. That isn't ego, it's truth. You are here to rule, so rule bitch!

Think of life as your own version of the film *Mean Girls*, you are Cady, the star of the movie who needs to go through a drastic transformation to find her strength. This is the turning point of that movie where you realize you're the leader, not the follower. Embrace it! Don't worry about the Regina George's of the world and where they fit into your story? Don't try to share the spotlight with Janis Ian because she's your day one A1. This isn't an ensemble; your life only has room for ONE star, and that's you. The rest are supporting cast and background extras sent here to get you to your happy ending. Which means if a person isn't benefiting you in a positive way, then you have to write them out of your story by no longer giving them your time, energy, or attention.

You may have a best friend that's your ride or die, or maybe a circle of girls who you really love and trust, doesn't matter—they are here to support you, not vice versa. Be kind, be there to help, be there to listen, do all the things a friend does but never sacrifice your own wellbeing for their approval or benefit. Remember, this is your story! If you feel as if the relationship between you and another girl isn't balanced or isn't benefiting your experience of life, let that bitch go. Don't feel bad, don't feel guilty, she's just a fucking supporting character. Like Aunt Viv on *Fresh Prince*, another one will pop up after you fire that one to take that role in your life. If a person were meant to stay your friend, they would have stayed your friend. Don't be loyal to a concept. The universe will bring in people to advance your story and also remove those that no longer grow you. You may not want that person to go; you may want them to evolve with you. That isn't how it works. Some friendships last a lifetime, most only last until the next chapter of your life. You will have to shed people like dead skin in order to grow. Don't mourn change.

What about enemies? You will meet girls that don't like you, either outwardly or under the surface. They aren't threats. Nothing can truly threaten a Spartan. Understand their purpose in your life. Those haters are there to fuel you and to make your ascension feel that much greater. Life without overcoming adversity or shutting up naysayers isn't as fun. The end of *Mean Girls* doesn't taste as sweet unless Cady had a Regina character to overcome. Rocky isn't moved to tears in the end unless he had an Apollo Creed to bring that performance out of him. You need people that support you, but you also need haters to push you at times. If you pick your friends carefully you will see that their love reflects the love you have for yourself. Those whom you see as enemies are harmless because their resentment is also based on love. Jealousy is merely love and hate at the same time. People in your story will only hate you once they envy you. They envy you because you are ascending. If you begin to feel negative feelings towards someone, let it go immediately, you're giving them power. To see someone as holding you back or stopping progress means that you are giving into old habits of fear. Who is she to envy, to resent, or to wish pain on, but your reflection?

As you go deeper into Spartanhood everything will change, friends will leave, enemies will appear, but it will always reflect your growth from a low vibrational being to a universal power. Don't run from your evolution, embrace it. If you find yourself distracted by rival women who are looking to bring you down, remove them from your life. If it's no longer a motivation you need, then actively change the scene. If a bitch at work is giving you mean stares, ignore it until it kills her. A person gossiping about something that you supposedly did, shrug it off without giving it any energy. If your own sister, mother or even grandmother is calling you up to complain or be negative, stop being available for those kinds of conversations. You don't owe anyone your time or attention. **Bitch is not a negative word in Sparta**. That slur is now a spear that you drive into the heart of the status quo that tried to limit you. Be a bitch, be blunt, be rude, it's your top priority to be happy and unbothered! You don't owe anyone your kindness until they earn it and even then they have to maintain it. The idea of ignoring texts or cutting a phone call short with someone who annoys you makes you uncomfortable because you have been a prisoner to opinion. If you say you can't come out for drinks, stop entertaining childish conversation topics, or no longer pick up your phone for them, people will think you're stuck up. "I don't want them to think I'm..." rings through a guilty mind that is obsessed with how others perceive them. You wanted everyone to like you to the extent where you were willing to suffer through the nonsense. Never again! Old you played to your audience because you didn't want them to call you names. You are no longer a slave to outside opinion. You are stuck up. You do act Hollywood. You are too fucking good for the low vibrational bullshit of basics. You are a Bitch, but they better have enough respect to capitalize your B! Other people are only as powerful as you allow them to be in your world. Shrink the thoughts you give them, and you will literally shrink their role in your life.

A QUEEN IS WORTH MORE THAN A KING

Men are not prizes to be won, they are toys from which you experience whatever love story your true self feels will be the most fulfilling in this game called life. Remember, this story is scripted to give you a happy ending, but If you're a non-Spartan that thinks life is out of your control, then you will block that ending. Negative thought after negative thought will be made real so long as you hold on to ideas like, "I will forever be alone or end up settling." From your mind to physical fruition. The men who come and go from your life will be directly related to your views on men which were created while you were on autopilot. *Men don't want you like your father didn't want you. Men only want you for sex. Men always cheat on you. Men love you for a short while then grow bored. Men are all dogs, liars, and con artist.* That's poison you're injecting into your reality. Your belief in men as heartbreakers and pain givers will always be true so long as you give that concept life through your current perception and projection. Find a boyfriend, stay together for a year, then watch as you break up due to one of those things listed above being in your mind. Failure doesn't happen because the universe is out to get you, it happens because your weak mind was expecting it to happen! Thoughts create reality. You will always attract someone who gives you what you fear if fear remains more dominant than confidence.

A man doesn't determine the love story that happens in your movie, you do. The problem is, like the bias of Hollywood, your love stories tend to be ones where the man is in the leading role and you're merely the love interest. Your entire life has been built to make a man the most important character when it should be the reverse. Jack isn't the star of *Titanic*, Rose is. Kyle Reece isn't the star of *The Terminator*, Sarah Connor is. Yet here you are, believing you are more Cinderella than The Bride from *Kill Bill*. You don't want to be a man-eater like Scarlett O'Hara, you choose to be Aerial *The Little Mermaid*, a hopelessly romantic dumbass that would sell her own voice for a dick. Spartan's don't chase, they take! The first step in rewriting your love story is to put you in the leading role and never compromise that position. This idea that you need to be extra to show him you're different, you need to work hard to get his attention, or you need to sacrifice yourself to make him happy is for peasants, not royalty. You're the Queen; you're the one that needs to be impressed, inspired, and shown that this is indeed a real love and not just a false lust.

This isn't about snapping your fingers and getting a husband tomorrow, this is about enjoying the movie the right way. Once you understand your true self. Once you become a Spartan. Victory is yours. That happy ending will come so long as you maintain your center in this universe. That doesn't mean it will be instant, but it won't take long either. This is a journey, not a giveaway. There are still things you need to experience to grow stronger and more powerful. There are men who you will need to hurdle over in order to understand what you truly want in that ultimate mate. Rose in *Titanic* doesn't achieve final happiness when she meets Jack, his ass dies and she goes on to live for nearly a hundred more years! Jack was only one part of her story, an experience that revealed her true power, he was never her end goal. The men you are about to attract to you aren't meant to take over your life, they're meant to enhance it for the better. You aren't made for a man; men are created for you. As we move deeper into the art of conquering this thing called love, remember to remember that no matter if you hit a homerun or strike out a few times, it's part of the larger film you're creating that always ends with you victorious.

93

THE SPARTAN MISSION

The Spartan mission, in terms of love, can best be described as a game of survival of the fittest. You are the prize that must be won over, but standing in front of you are dozens upon dozens of men who aren't worthy, with only a few that will be revealed as King material. Some will be the most handsome men you've ever seen; others will be richer than you could have ever imagined. A few will be so funny or nice that you forget that they aren't attractive or rich. Some will even connect with you on a spiritual level where you feel a kinship beyond your character's flesh. Guess what? They're all just players in the game! Their true intentions are hidden from you on the surface, their words masking their motives, and it is your job to filter through them. *Survival of the fittest*! That doesn't sound like fun, does it? You want to just pick one that's the compatible and live happily ever after... but that's not the world you've created. You've spent years saying what you wanted in a man, yet you still don't know. Honest, hardworking, loyal, none of that means shit, they're basic characteristics. Handsome, Tall, Big Dick, really? Now you're just trying to build a man like Dr. Frankenstein.

I've met several women who were into making lists and on these lists they wrote down the traits they wanted in a man based on what they imagined they needed. One friend described to me how she found the man that met all ten of her checkpoints. It had been nearly a year since she wrote that list, so she went back to make sure, and on her paper there he was— The perfect boyfriend. She took this as a sign from the universe and the two began dating hard and heavy. Before the year was up, he proposed. Then all hell broke loose because she found out while he had all of those qualities... there were tons of things she never thought to ask for in terms of a man's own insecurities. These traits quickly proved that while he had those 10 Perfect qualities, he had a few others that were deal breakers.

The universe, meaning her true self, sent this man to her because she wanted it so bad, and she was so clear in that want that she would have never let it go. Nevertheless, that man and those bundles of traits weren't what was needed in her story. That engagement proved she was still ignorant of her true desires. She wasn't yet ready to find her "perfect man" because she didn't know what perfect truly meant. She needed more time in the story to play the game, not a rush to marriage.

You may make the same mistakes in an attempt to ignorantly wish or visualize a desire. Write down a list of qualities, go out and date, and you will meet that guy who fills out your basic bitch list just like my friend did. Then watch as it falls apart because you can't cheat the climb. This game isn't meant to bring you a list, it's meant to reveal a partner worthy of God herself! The boys you were in love with in high school or in college, the guys at your last job you crushed on, they may have been perfect for that current version of you, but they would have never worked for the being that you are evolving into. The number one relationship killer is that people grow apart. Why do people grow apart? Because to stay the same forever is worse than death. You will be fundamentally changed after reading this book. At this moment, your mind has already expanded, therefore, the men that will challenge this Goddess made flesh can no longer be made of past wants. **You will get the partner you both want and need, one that fits you forever… but in order to reach that you have to break a few eggs**. Spartans do not fear this mission. Unlike these zombies walking the earth, face full of bad foundation, body full of ill-fitting clothes, and a mind full of fear, you know you will win! Those other women over think and worry about men because they are afraid of losing. A Spartan cannot lose!

Meeting people isn't fun because you're nervous about how they will see you. Dating new people isn't fun because you don't know how to separate the real from the fake. Relationships are a test because you don't know if you are being dumb for leaving him too fast or even dumber for staying too long. This book will delve into all three of these things. <u>Meeting A Man.</u> <u>Dating A Man.</u> <u>Relationship Troubles.</u> However, the foundation is built on fun, not stress. There is nothing to stress about. *He won't want another date. He won't ask me to be his girlfriend. He's going to cheat on me. He won't want to marry me.* Negative, typical fearful thoughts are making this entire game called love into something serious when it should be played with a detached sense of freedom to choose without fear of mistakes! Once you become a Spartan and understand everything written in this book, then your thoughts will never lead you astray again. You already know that you win in the end, so let go, and trust yourself.

95

On Monday's you snatch souls. On Tuesday's you snatch souls. On every fucking day of the week, you snatch souls, because these men are yours for the taking, every single one of them! When I say, "snatch his soul" it means just that. Enchant him, seduce him, shatter his guard, and open him up until you see what's at his core. *Eat, Sleep, Snatch Souls, Repeat*! This isn't a race; you don't need to literally pull a man a day or date a man a week, there is no more pressure. They will be there waiting. Some men will be candy who you want to fuck. Some guys may be companions who you want to keep for company. Some men will be obsessed with you and not leave you alone. You don't need love from any of these peasants. Remember, you're in search of a King that can pull Excalibur from the stone. Why settle for a great dick, when you can get a great man attached to it? Why settle for friendship, when you could get both love and companionship? Do not shortchange yourself!

The old you was weak. She was desperate. She was egotistical. She was fraudulent. She was typical. Your avatar was built on a slave character that had to be thankful for men, take care of men, and submit to men. Fuck that! This new avatar, this Spartan Warrior who you are about to unleash on this world, she only has time for men that reflect her own strength. You need someone who mirrors you, who highlights you, who excites you, and who you can fuck and love like you've never fucked and loved before! The world is your buffet, but you must be choosy! You arranged this game of survival of the fittest to net you what you most desire in the long run, not over the short term, so be patient and don't question the process. This is Sparta, and your reign has just begun.

Stop. Meditate. Continue.

You cannot rush through what you have just read. This isn't a novel to be finished in a day, this isn't disposable fiction to be scanned through, and it isn't a hodgepodge of ideas to be cherry picked. This is meant to be read in order and inhaled slowly. Take this time to walk away and reflect. Small minds, weak minds, distracted minds, they will not retain this knowledge for long because they don't have the discipline of a Spartan. This is your first test. Relax and unwind for at least one hour. Then continue...

Chapter 7: How to Attract Men Without Even Trying

Y ou are a Spartan. You don't look for men; men look for you. The basic bitch frustrations of "Where do I go to find a good man in my city," will never apply to you. Which e-dating site to sign up for or dating app to download, are decisions left for peasants not Queens, you don't have to go through those motions. Settling for any old date with a random guy because you're bored, giving an ex one more chance because you're lonely, those basic thoughts won't even cross your mind. All the stress, all the frustration, all the searching has come to an end. You're about to make it rain men like the fucking boss that you are! This chapter will serve as the blueprint for building your roster of not one man, not two men, but as many as you want to bring into the next section's *Screening Stage*. Now that you have total confidence that this world and everything in it is yours, the hard work is done. Spartans don't have to jump from nightclub to bar to happy hour to house party to blind date and back around to find a man worth dating. There is nothing extra that you have to do outside of a normal social routine because the confidence you are now projecting will bring them to you! The only thing you need in addition to this new found Spartan confidence is to admit what you want. Verbalize it right now:

I Want Something Serious.
I Want Something Fun.
I Want Something Beneficial.

Choose one. There should be no shrug of the shoulder and feeling of "I don't know what I want right now, I'm open to whatever." If you can't decide on what you want for your life, then stop reading and pick this book back up when you're ready to put on your big girl panties and make a choice. Indecision is a sign of fear, and if you're afraid to open up to yourself and clearly admit what you want in a relationship, then you are no Spartan. The ability to create begins with the Will to Power. Power is never, "I dunno..." it's a mental and verbal declaration of, "I want this..." The reason all these non-Spartans fail, why you were failing on autopilot, is that you were conflicted and dishonest. You didn't know who you were. You were coasting, attracting a mixed bag of men into your life that netted you mixed results. Be honest and declare what you want. Why is it so hard for typical women to admit that they want a man? Why would a grown woman pretend as if she's happy with being single when she's really miserable alone? Because if they hide behind the excuse of not being ready or the apathy of "if it happens it happens," it gives them an easy out when they fail. Losers love to act indifferent because they're already mentally preparing themselves not to come away with what they really want.

If you tell the universe that you don't care about meeting anyone, then go out this weekend, what will your results be? You will meet no one, meet a guy who never calls you, meet a guy who has a girlfriend and is trying to make you his appetizer, or meet a guy who turns out to be just another pussy hunter. You did that to yourself by being weak and indecisive! Nevertheless, even in failure, you can save face by reminding yourself, "I was going out to go out. I wasn't looking for anything." Stop lying to yourself! Women don't get their hair done, buy new clothes, and do their makeup so they can sit in the dark and play on their phones. Women want men. You want a man consciously and subconsciously, so do you think making some false declaration fools your true self? Honesty is crucial to this process because you must kill what's left of this typical bitch ego, let down your defenses, and allow your world to give you positive results. Women who pretend not to be looking, declare that they're happily single, or swear they're focusing on themselves are full of shit because they are still out at the clubs, lounges, and other social settings trying to catch an eye. Just because you're not physically looking for love, doesn't mean you aren't wishing for it. I don't care what's going on in your life, if you're able to have a social life, you're able to date. If you're able to date, you're able to have a relationship. If you're able to have a relationship, then what's the problem?

Let me simplify this process. To want a relationship means that you want something serious. The days of friends with benefits, just talking, hook ups, situationships, and agreeing to see where it goes, are dead! If you just want fun, meaning hanging out, getting consistent dick, maybe a few light conversations; that's college dorm shit. You don't need to tap into any power to get that. If you want a man with money, fame, or status to help you along in life, go get those benefits! You don't need to be a Spartan, go read *Ho Tactics*. This Spartan road is about revealing someone special. That means you want one thing, aim for one thing, and verbalize one thing:

I Want Something Serious.

Men who are just "fun" won't make it past the dating stage and men who are just money tossing tricks won't make it to the relationship stage. Every guy you invest time and energy in from this day forward must be Top Shelf, A1, Alpha Male, husband material, not a work in progress, not a struggle story, and never generic Dick! Still, Queens don't just attract Kings, your magnetic pull is enormous. For every one diamond, there will be three cubic zirconia trying to break through, which is why we have the *Date Like a Spartan* game plan. Maybe you're impatient, and you want all this to happen quickly, snap your finger and the man of your dreams appears tomorrow. You're powerful enough to attract that, but never forget that this journey is about a rise to power, not a race to get a ring! You won't find a King based on some features you paste onto a vision board. You're going to create him through the process of meeting, dating, and elimination.

Typicals chase men, hold on to men, and fear letting the right man go or letting the wrong one stay because they feel as if life is out of their control. It is out of their control because they are not Spartans. No man who is meant for you will get away. There is no such thing as the right man at the wrong time or any other basic bitch romantic belief that make men into limited editions. You will get the man who is perfect for you, but first you have to declare it. Every morning that you wake up after you look in the mirror at the sexiest woman in the world, tell your reflection:
I Want Something Serious!

THE ART OF FLIRTING

To know what you want is to open yourself up to getting what you want. A chain will hold you back at this point will be the links of self-consciousness based on a belief that you aren't desired by the type of men who you want something serious from. How can you get a properly vetted boyfriend if you can't get a date? How can you get a proper date if you can't talk to a man in a way that makes him want to take you on a date? Why attract a man to you, if you don't know what to do when he's face to face with you? Before we get into the power of attraction, I want to make sure that you aren't still a weak bitch that skipped the Spartan steps and read ahead into waters where you aren't prepared to swim. Giggling like a little girl, freezing up when a cute guy asks you a question, saying something stupid because your mind goes blank, those are not Spartan traits.

A woman can talk to a guy she doesn't like or a platonic friend about any and everything because there isn't a pressure to impress. Flirting isn't about saying sexual things, winking, or licking your lips, it's about being comfortable in your skin around a man whose dick you want to ride. Giving a man too much power in your mind makes him larger than life, a celebrity, and in response you stumble over words, forget your train of thought, and revert back to a little girl who uses her sass and attitude to show a boy she likes him. **The key to flirting is to not give a fuck about how you come across**. Erase the fear of rejection or judgment and embrace the confidence of how you look and how you talk. Sexiness is a shield, you can't be nervous and sexy at the same time; those thoughts can't coexist. To be supercharged with the idea of, "He would lick my plate clean if I let him," will stop your heart from racing. Try it out with any man. Watch how quickly the idea that the guy in front of you is a slave to your pussy appeal will relax you enough to lead with your true Spartan personality.

Embrace your brand, and the moment you open your mouth to speak to that boy push his buttons knowing that he's more afraid of you than you are of him. If you are a seductress, use your sexual innuendo, put a hand on his leg when sitting, grab his arm when talking, make his dick tingle by smiling with your eyes when he's in mid-conversation. You will see him react, he will grin, he will fluster, he will laugh. No man is above being seduced, he will bend and he may even break. If you are more of a tomboy or someone who doesn't lead with a sex-kitten brand, let body language and wit drive home the fact that he should still want to fuck you. You joke with a smile, you don't "get smart" with an attitude. You laugh at his joke, and remark, "Oh, I like you already," using your blunt words to make up for your lack of Marilyn Monroe charisma. If you see him squirm or stammer hit him with a "do I make you uncomfortable," challenge and he will chase back. Men are turned on by women who don't shy away! Never hide your smile or cover your mouth as if you're the shy lead singer of a K-pop group, be bold enough to smack his chest or bat your eyes like a baby-doll, to let him know that he can get it.

Looking down, looking away, mumbling, all that proves is that you are still a coward. Rolling your eyes, talking back, keeping the subject on something safe and non-romantic such as business, other people, or any subject meant to hide that you like him is juvenile. Basicas feel that if they play their attraction off, a man won't think she likes him too much, and work that much harder to win her over. That's not how the male brain works that's how romantic comedy screenplays are formatted. Furthermore, lay off the backhanded compliments that protect your ego from coming off as soft. I don't usually date guys your height, but... I don't usually talk to guys that look like players, but... I don't really like guys from your fraternity, but...but nothing! When you add on extras to remind a man that you're making an exception, you show a lack of confidence. Don't hide behind attitude if you're a fan, be a fan. You wouldn't tell Rihanna that you don't usually give island girls props, but she's cool—it's insulting. It should be the same way with men you like and compliment. <u>Flirt 100% or not at all</u>.

How do you tell a man you like him without saying words? How do you project "I'd fuck your brains out," with only a smile? How can you direct your eye contact in a way that says, "You're not ready for me?" If you don't know those answers than you haven't done the work. Stand in the mirror and want to fuck yourself. Reach that level, and charisma flows like water! Spartans don't have to follow a flirting blueprint; they are one big flirt. If a man doesn't pick up on your eye fuck, doesn't notice that you keep gripping his forearm, or can't read between the lines of your words, then he's not a King, he's a moron.

Attracting Various Men in Everyday Life

Let's follow a day in the life of Ashley, a seemingly normal woman in the prime of her life. She's single, dates sporadically, has a few girlfriends who she hangs out with, but her schedule is normally filled with work or family as she's a single mother. Ashley was done making excuses, so she decided to Spartan Up. Ashley is now Spartan Phoenix, and nothing is going to stop her from her mission to find a worthy King. So where does she start? Does she set a schedule to go out on the weekends? Get her girls on the same page she's on so they can hunt in a pack? Does she ask someone where the best spot in the city is for a mature crowd? Fuck no. The moment Ashley became Phoenix, her life changed internally. She made a choice to go for something serious, and the pieces are already in motion. There are men everywhere. She doesn't need to wait for a weekend, pay to get into a club, overdress and hang at a bar, or plan her schedule around friends. All she needs is the confidence of a goddess and the swagger of a warrior Queen.

Phoenix sets a goal. Two numbers in a week. She says this aloud to herself but also writes it into her Smartphone's calendar, to make it real. That phone will buzz with a notification come 11:59 pm on Saturday night to remind her of the goal: Reminder Two Numbers. Old Ashley's fear and anxiety would have never allowed her to go this hard. She would have become instantly nervous under the pressure of a deadline and formed a counter thought such as, "If it doesn't happen, it's all good." Ashely was a weak bitch, a fraud, a would be Queen with a peasant's heart. Phoenix is going to get those two numbers with ease, no chasing, no going out of her way. Phoenix is letting go, and allowing the universe to guide her to victory.

The first day of this *Two Number Challenge* is exciting, as every man who Phoenix lays eyes on is analyzed as if he could be a potential meal. A new neighbor she sees when going to her car...a father she sees eyeing her when she drops her daughter off at school...the maintenance worker she spots while walking toward the elevator at work. There are men everywhere who she normally doesn't notice because she wasn't thinking about men in those settings. Ashley was one of those women who thought that you looked for men under two circumstances, if they approached first or if she were in a "night out" environment. She realizes now that there are always new faces or faces that she never noticed; a buffet of men and two will end up with her number by the end of the week. It's empowering. An entire world for her taking, and for the first time, she isn't afraid of what these men think or hung up on possible rejection. *Who should she talk to? Should she wait for one of these men to make the first move or just start up random conversations on her own? What's the protocol?* Phoenix doesn't waste her brain cells with such basic thoughts. When the time comes she will know what to do. She told the universe what she wanted, now opportunity will be presented. There are no counter thoughts holding her back.

On her lunch break, Phoenix decides to bask in this new power, she wants to see all the random guys that will pop into her world, so she gets away from her normal lunch spots, her desk & the break room, and goes out. Phoenix doesn't choose where to go based on where she thinks men will be, no need to sniff out men; they are already moving towards her because she's radiating her will—manifestation on fleek! Furthermore, her eye candy image, even in casual work clothes, is fire! She sat in that mirror until Ashley's flaws gave way to Phoenix's sexy. She knows she makes heads turn and dicks hard, and when you know you're the shit, you walk like it. As Phoenix switches by various restaurants, she feels that eyes are on her, but no one is popping out, that means those men thirsting for her from a distance are only background extras, not leading men.

Phoenix enters a sandwich shop. It's the lunchtime rush, but she doesn't feel overwhelmed. Old Ashley would have quickly jumped in line, took out her phone, and checked social media. Why? Because Ashley didn't live in the now, she was on autopilot; nervous, bored, phone always in hand because she didn't know how to interact with her world in a dominant way. Phoenix doesn't plan to take her phone out unless it rings. She steps into the line, but not before she takes in the store to see if anyone pops out. One guy looks up, checking out her ass on the low, but quickly looks away. Phoenix knows she's sex on a platter, but that kind of timid look, then look away move won't win her over. She is looking for a real man that won't shy away from the shine of the sun.

Phoenix makes it to the counter to order, and the cashier flirts with her immediately. He hasn't seen her come in for lunch before, and he's all over the possibility of this new pussy. Phoenix isn't surprised, *duh Spartan.*

She flirts back and gets a free drink out of the exchange...she could go further; he is cute...actually he's really cute now that she thinks about it. But he's a cashier; she has no time to waste on passion projects, struggle dick, or a work in progress no matter his looks. Phoenix is shallow, physically and financially, she has to be. Old Ashley, being soft and understanding, is the reason her daughter has a deadbeat father in the first place. She plays with the cashier like a cat toys with a mouse, but it's just a warm up, she has bigger prey to hunt. Phoenix exits the line with her free drink. There aren't any men in the store that pop out, but she's having fun, she feels the high of her power, and that makes this lunch break a success.

It will take until Thursday for Phoenix to strike gold on her mission. She brought her lunch for the last two days in order to save money, but her direct deposit hit, so she may as well treat herself to something special. Phoenix ends up in a nice littler café, not as busy as the sandwich shop, but she still takes her time to soak it in. She gets a tap on her shoulder, another customer asking if she works at his company. The Line Dick, swears she looks familiar. Isn't that cute...he's trying to run game. Ashley would have been nervous, maybe say something corny like, "People say I have one of those faces," and giggle. Phoenix doesn't giggle. She expected a man to try to start a conversation, and here it is. Phoenix lets him keep playing his game, he only has a minute before she's in front of the cashier. The Line Dick, shoots his shot, saying they should grab lunch sometime. He's okay looking, nice suit; he probably has money to trick, but there's something about him that doesn't feel right. Phoenix lets him off easy, "Maybe if you catch me out next time, we'll sit together." Curved. Phoenix never loses her grin. She's a **Bitch**, but a sexy one and she takes pride in being able to brush a man off, despite still needing two numbers. Ashley would have jumped to get his number, bad gut feeling in all, just to prove she did it. Phoenix feels no pressure.

The food is up and Phoenix looks for a place to sit, and there he is. Handsome, dressed okay, but he has an energy about him...she likes this one. However, what to do when a man is already seated and halfway through his food? A Spartan sits down next to him, of course. Phoenix takes the seat at his table. She doesn't ask if she can, she does so, then says, "You don't mind, do you?" with a grin and the loveliest eye fuck she can muster.

106

Of course, Table Dick doesn't mind. He introduces himself, and the game begins. Ashely returns to work with one number down.

By Saturday, the game is nearly over, and taking her daughter to the park, netted several looks, a few instances of flirting, but no man that stood out in a real way. It is only a few hours left before her phone buzzes with that reminder... Ashley would look at the bright side. At least, she got one, and technically she turned down one, so it worked. Fuck that! Phoenix doesn't see bright sides, she gets what she wants, and feels excited about how the end of the game will play out when she goes out for dinner with her girlfriends later on. The excited nerves of what will happen don't make this scary, it makes it exhilarating.

On the way back home, Phoenix stops at a gas station. She usually pays at the pump, but her daughter wants candy, so they go inside. A few guys are in line, and one, in particular, looks her up in down before he pays, Phoenix gives him a baby eye fuck because she's not too impressed with the way he's dressed. As Phoenix goes back to her car to pump, Gas Station Dick is standing by his car...he's pretending to be checking his tire, but he was waiting. He walks over, but Phoenix, like the Hollywood diva that she is, keeps walking, forcing GSD to follow behind. He begins with the usual: how she's doing, gives his name, asks her name. "I don't give my name to strange men," she smirks in a flirty way that doesn't come off as bitchy or confrontational. Now that she sees him in the light, he's handsome, he has a nice car, and she can always forgive his fashion sense. If Gas Station Dick is an idiot he won't pick up on the vibe that Phoenix is just playing hard to get, and fall back. Seeing that he has to show her something GSD fires back, "If I pump your gas for you, would I still be a stranger?"

Phoenix likes that kind of pursuit and instantly warms up. In what was only a random stop, Phoenix will leave with her 2nd number of the week. One was created by being forward, by not settling for the easy man, and going after the man she wanted. The other was created by being attentive, knowing when to flirt and how to lay out bait, to see if a man would chase. Two vastly different techniques, two wins. Phoenix never doubted herself. She knew she was sexy enough to get looks, she knew she was charismatic enough to flirt, and she knew that if opportunity knocked she was confident enough to take it. There was no need to go out of her way to find men, she simply lived her normal life in a much more outgoing way.

In the real life "Phoenix Story," I was the one that made her set the two numbers in a week goal, but that's where my involvement stopped, and her Spartan lessons paid off. She took me up on my challenge and did things, not like a robot, but like a woman who understood that, she was an attracting force that could have anything she asked her universe to bring. When there were chances to go out and explore her world, she took them instead of staying in her comfort zone. When she was out, there wasn't a love affair with her phone, a resting bitch face, nor was she rushing to get in and get out of places, like so many awkward women do. This all happened in regular everyday settings. With Phoenix's confidence and skill, she could have unleashed herself on the bar scene, even without her friends, and had free drinks all night. She could have gone to a museum with her daughter or by herself, and caught eyes. She could have Yelped the best happy hour in town, and searched for someone there. Nevertheless, she didn't need to. Phoenix, let go of the pressure, let go of the chase, and allowed life to give her what she purposely asked for. <u>Two numbers</u>. She may never use those numbers, or one man may end up being her next husband, it doesn't matter. A Spartan sets her goal then achieves it because she has zero fear of failure.

ATTRACTING VARIOUS MEN ONLINE

What if Ashley lived a different lifestyle, one where she didn't have many friends to hang out with and her job schedule didn't allow to explore life outside of work or school. It doesn't matter. A Spartan will always find a way to Spartan Up! I need you to erase any doubt that you can't find love based on some social hold up. There is no hold up outside of your negative beliefs. Let's use a new example with a new kind of Phoenix. She's single, no children, only one friend, doesn't have a job that grants her much free time, and lives in a tiny city where there are only a handful of places to go.

This Phoenix is stepping into the excuse-filled shoes of a millennial girl who is social media active more than socially active. Meaning that most of her interactions with men come through a screen as opposed to face-to-face. You don't have to sign up for a dating site to feast online. Forget a dating profile where you list all of these asinine facts about your life, when in all honesty, men your age only care about your picture. As an able-bodied woman, you shouldn't be paying a website to shop for Dick for you. That points to a non-Spartan, last resort mindset, based on the previous failures. You gave up on finding love in the outside world. You want to Amazon Wishlist a delivery husband because it seems safer than going out into a physical world where men lie, reject, and mislead. Not in Sparta. There is no fear of failure and no past holding you back. There is no bullshit excuse about not having time to date, because to not have time to date means you don't have time for a boyfriend in the first place. Spartans don't make excuses, they just win.

The truth is, technology is more convenient, but it doesn't change the fact that even when a Spartan goes online to attract men, she doesn't do it like a typical bitch. App hookups like Tinder and the various knock-offs will get any girl with good picture lighting an initial date. Where's the challenge in that? Why waste the little time you do have, swiping on some Community Dick who's just shooting his shot with every girl that will respond back? You aren't like every other girl, so why play the game like those basics? Instagram, Twitter, Snapchat, Facebook, whatever you're most comfortable on can be used to bring all the boys to your yard, in a more subtle way than any traditional dating website.

Millennial Phoenix sets her goal verbally and she writes it down. She's going to add two men to her roster before the end of the month, a Twitter boo and an Instagram bae. This is extremely easy, so she reminds herself that she won't get caught up with guys who waste her time, Phoenix wants something serious, not a cross country pen pal as if she's a 20-year-old attention whore. This means that both men must meet one further qualification—be local. Long distance dating is an easy trap to fall into, she wants someone she can actually see and touch, not Skype. This is the same power as attracting phone numbers outside, and in the end, Phoenix will come away with two local men trying to make her date roster. If you reach the advanced levels where you can juggle long-distance and local guys, go for it. Have guys across state lines flying you in and out, but let's not even entertain that complication right now, you should aim for something serious and fulfilling, and the ideal man is someone you can actually see on a regular basis. At this stage—it's local men, and local men only!

So where does this keyboard Spartan start? Add a bunch of random guys with nice avatars, and see if they react to her following them? Start sending direct messages to the ones that are already on her radar? Upload her best thirst trap picture and watch the mentions light up? Not at all. Attraction works the same as in person. You decide your goal, and you let the universe react to your will. This isn't something to rush after, it's *The Hunger Games*. Social media is 24 hours a day; men discovering you for the first time and battling for your attention. Know that a worthy victor will appear before your one-month deadline, so long as you move without fear. The internet isn't a scary place, but some women retain their insecurities even behind a screen, only able to be bold and flirty when they hide behind some catfish photo or mysterious avatar. They don't want to put the real them out there, so they create an online alter ego that says all the wild shit they wouldn't say in a room full of those same strangers. As a Spartan, you understand that life is one big fucking chat room, there is no need to be afraid of what someone thinks, what someone judges as not funny or too nasty. It's your world, and you don't need to hide behind a false image or persona. Your Spartan persona is the old you on steroids; fear removed and truth amplified. When starting this mission be proactive. You can't ask the universe to bring you anything you aren't first willing to walk towards.

You want someone local, you know your city, so start there. What are the places people talk about, the hot spots, the events, the slang, something local that is topical? Search the hashtags or specific words that relate to your city, and follow a couple of people talking about these things. That girl on Instagram talking about the concert coming this weekend will be a magnet for men in that city, so to follow her will show open you up to more local men than simply following some dude 400 miles away that's cute and tells good jokes. When things pop up that you may go to, be active and ask who's going. Not because you want to hang with these people, it's simply letting them know where your sandbox is, because the more local people that interact with you, the larger your box expands because other local people who are following them will start following you. Don't think because you have your location in your bio, the work is done. The game of attraction uses word of mouth, so don't sit back, and wait for a cute guy to pop up, put yourself out there in those online streets the same way you would if you went outside instead of staying in that break room. People have to be able to discover you, and you don't get discovered that by sitting in that same old comfortable place.

The first step for Phoenix is to refresh Ashley's online persona. Up until now, she's been kind of generic, posting tweets about her favorite shows, a few joke retweets, nothing that makes her stand out in the sea of typical fish. Instagram is the same; Ashley was good for a few selfies, a couple of meme posts, and some trite inspirational quotes, again basic bitch 101. There are guys who jumped in her mentions flirting, but they're always the same *4th Quarter Dick*. These are the guys who go after women online like a basketball player goes for points when his team is down. He's not worried about quality; he's going for the quantity hoping one of his shots lands. The average man on social media is 4th Quarter Dick. He's not going after you based on what you're writing or posting, he's simply casting his net hoping that you bite like a starving fish.

When a Spartan is on a mission she doesn't do anything average. Phoenix takes over, uploads a new avatar reflecting her new attitude, and attacks these sites as if she owns them. Similar to going out and attracting men in public, Phoenix won't try at all; she will let her magnetic personality and confidence pull them into her orbit. The second step becomes to take off the filter of fear. Ashely was tweeting about redundant shit or making random observations when she was bored. Phoenix is going to use Twitter like it's her own Spartan diary. Her brand is sex appeal, not humor, she's not the funniest chick in the world so she's not going to try and be a standup comedian, she's just going to be blunt and say what she feels. If you want someone to pay attention to you, say something truthful, if you feel it people on your level will feel it. You don't have to chase attention, just be unapologetically you.

Phoenix is at work bored; she has time to post a bit what's on her mind, but it isn't about how her day is going, what she wants to eat for lunch, or complaints about her co-workers. Her goal is men, so her mind is on men. She blasts off tweets about how amazing work sex would be, and the rush of maybe getting caught. She wonders if any of her co-workers secretly masturbate on their lunch break because some come back a little too rejuvenated. She's not baiting for retweets, she doesn't care who responds, she's letting her mind take her wherever it wants without fear. Phoenix doesn't have to be overtly graphic, she's not writing a ratchet sex novel about pulsating cocks and thrusting into showery vaginas, it's safe for work but with nasty undertones. Phoenix isn't the most popular person in terms of a following, but it doesn't matter. The things she's saying are truth triggers. Phoenix isn't talking hoish to the point where only the thirst buckets are checking for her; she's being frank to the point where she gets a few responses and retweets, which turn into more responses and retweets. At this moment, Phoenix is projecting her energy out into the Twitterverse, and it's not to get instantaneous responses, it's to rebrand her persona.

This same new found freedom spills over into Instagram, where her captions are no longer "Bored work selfie," they're engaging. She's taking pictures asking people to, "Caption This." If she is looking for attention, she owns up to it with, "Can I get some love for the way my ass looks in this maxi dress?" If she's reposting stories or quotes, she actually has her own personal take that she writes below it. This is done for her own amusement, not to feed her ego. Phoenix isn't thirst trapping with her boobs pushed up, sucking on her finger, or taking videos that show the curve of her ass. She is a Spartan, not a thot[8]. Her energy is fun, wild, and inventive; therefore, she's attracting respectful comments or compliments. A few thirst buckets will post comments under her pictures talking about "I need that in my life...You should be over here with me...I'd give that mouth something to caption." This is what 4th Quarter Dick does, but Phoenix is waiting for someone to pop up on her radar that makes her take real notice... someone who stands out in the sea of likes and comments, that makes her want to click on a profile. Again, this is a month long goal, so she lets her online persona breathe and grow day by day, there is no pressure to talk to all the new eyes that are on her, the right one will glow in the dark.

After a week of Phoenix's newfound social media swag, she's become more popular than ever in terms of men and women responding to

---

[8] Slang for a type of Ho that goes above and beyond in an attempt to get attention.

her more often. One guy, in particular, someone she's been following since before she became a Spartan, has begun to @ her more and more. Witty Dick, he seems handsome in his photos, is in the same city, and he's always saying something provocative and entertaining. Ashley never really interacted with Witty Dick; he had double her followers and that intimidated her weak ass. Not Phoenix, she could care less if he was as popular online as Justin Bieber, he's just another dick. Phoenix decides to have fun with Witty Dick, she knows his personality at this point, the things he loves, hates, and vents about, so she decides to have random conversations about those things that they have in common. He talks shit about Rihanna, she stands up for her in a way that's fun and not bitchy. He loves a Netflix show that she also enjoys, she pops in his mentions not only agreeing but adding her own two cents about what she enjoyed. Phoenix isn't trying to make this man like her, she's simply vibing off their shared energy. In response Witty Dick can either ignore her, only respond when he responds to her, or if he's smart, he will pick up on the vibe and do the same things to her when she's on her soap box. Their interaction grows over the next week, and while there are a lot of cute guys who she @'s from time to time, he remains a standout. What's a Spartan to do? Drop hints that she's single? Go through his timeline to see if he ever mentions a girlfriend? Stalk his mentions to see if he responds to other girls in the same flirty manner that he responds to her? None of that basic shit.

Phoenix goes for what she wants like the Queen of the Universe should, with no fear. Even if Witty Dick has a girlfriend, she's no match for Phoenix. There is no way she's going to get a "No" once she sinks her hooks in. Phoenix DMs him after their latest back and forth, and gives Witty Dick some of her own wit, "If you keep @'ing me like this, people are going to suspect that we're fucking." It's brash, bold, and tantalizing. If Witty Dick were a simp, he would probably fumble and come back with a corny line, but he's smooth and he responds with, "Well, let's give them something to talk about." From there she knows Witty Dick is down, and while they could just keep it on the app, a pen pal isn't her aim, she wants a man. A lot is lost in translation when typing and why waste weeks flirting indirectly on Twitter when you can save yourself the time and see what's good? By the next day, Phoenix only response is, "Here's my number, use it."

With one down, Phoenix is still batting 0 on Instagram. All the men who comment and direct message don't wow her. She's been curving a few guys a week, but it doesn't bother her, it's all fun. Old Ashely would have been open off the emoji game of that fitness guy who slid in her DMs and would have given her number to that friend of a friend who said he remembered her from back in high school. Both guys had the look she goes for, but they didn't have the fire. Phoenix doesn't rush to give out her number to just any man; she is okay with saying "I'm good," because rejecting these men isn't something to feel guilty about. A Spartan doesn't owe a man an opportunity unless he earns it!

While reading over comments on her favorite Instagram Ho's page, Phoenix saw a funny comment from a guy that made her smirk. She clicked on his profile, private. She sends a request, which she actually prefers because he knows this will force him to scrutinize her before accepting, meaning that this Private Dick will see the glory that is Spartan Phoenix from the jump. A few hours later, she sees that she's been accepted and followed back. After going through his photos, getting a feel for his personality, Phoenix finds him to be interesting, but unlike Twitter, there's no way to really gauge his wit or intelligence via those posts. Once again, Phoenix puts herself in the driver's seat and messages him. Unlike Witty Dick, she won't volunteer her number; she doesn't have a relationship with this man or a feel for him. Instead, she baits him with small talk about the IG Ho they both follow, and that leads into other basic subjects like real names, jobs, and where they live. Private Dick lives in the same state, but not city, but he says he visits Phoenix's city at least once a month. Phoenix plays her cards, "We might have to make that several times a month going forward." Got him. He asks for her number, and Phoenix is now able to do her Spartan Screening once she takes it to the phone.

This last example ended in the real life girl who I told to do these things entering into a relationship with the guy she met on Instagram. Again, this had nothing to do with me giving her a pep talk or blueprint, it was her going for what she wanted with the knowledge that she would win. All the bullshit she used to give me about how she didn't have time, was a cover for her introverted behavior, but I knew from the way she talked to me that she had swagger inside her that she could easily show if she felt confident around a man. She became a Spartan, took to her social media, and got what she wanted, proof that the only thing holding her back was her own fear. Notice how effortlessly it was to engage with men online without spending one cent or suffering through a Tinder date? Phoenix had multiple suitors flirting with her, as all women will have when a man has nothing to go off but her best-looking avatar picture, yet she didn't settle for just any attention. The key to social media attraction is to put yourself out there to be seen not only as a face but as a personality. Men are always watching. The lurkers you never see or who act as if they don't know you exist even though they follow your account will become your biggest fans so long as you are putting your energy out there in a way that pulls them in.

Phoenix wasn't being a thot, she didn't need to be half naked, talk about how good she rides dick, or flood her timeline with random shock statements in an attempt to attention whore her way to male interest. She unleashed her personality, embraced her Spartan brand, and let whatever was on her mind flow out. By doing that, the world reacted. She was engaging, comfortable, and open enough so that men would see her as approachable. At the same time, she didn't have a problem denying her number to those she had no interest in. The beauty of online attraction is that you don't have to pressure yourself to find a man or to look for one; it's always going to be there. Even if you get out of the house often and aren't necessarily looking for love online, this becomes a secondary outlet to attract men. All you need to do is open yourself up to the idea that it can and will work without any stigma, and the universe will move in a positive direction in accordance with your outlook. Yes, most men will be from out of town, but remember, your world shines on you and will bring you one that's local, not as a sign that he's the perfect one, but as a reminder that your thoughts are power. "All the good ones are from out of state," that's a defeatist attitude that no longer lives within you. If you want it, you will bring it. Let go of the stress, and have fun online, it's nothing but another playground for your amusement.

ATTRACTING A SPECIFIC MAN OR CRUSH

Attracting strangers is an ongoing mission that's always at your beck and call, but what about those men who are already in your life? That guy at work who you talk to but haven't mustered up the courage to actually go after. The boy at school who you chit-chat with but don't go any further. That person you see at your coffee shop, gym, or on your commute who you speak to, but don't even know their name. Men are in your life who you think you want, but your fear of rejection keeps those relationships stagnant and safe. Even extroverts become introverts when confronted with someone who intimidates them. Introverts sink even further into a shell when faced with a person they want. Shyness is a remnant of your past life, your fear based mind that was so consumed with outcomes and opinions. This is Sparta, there is no negative outcome even when you don't walk away with what you thought you wanted.

There is no rejection that will crumble you because you will never be rejected in a real way. "What if he has a girlfriend... or boyfriend? What if I'm not his type physically? What if he's nothing like I imagined from afar and I don't like him? What if I have to face him after he rejects me?" *What If* is the disease of a weak mind. A Spartan is 100% strong; her thoughts do not travel beyond the now, she embraces the moment with confidence. Nervousness projects as strong as confidence, and you must never allow another person to bring your vibrations down to that low level where you shrink your power. You see someone you like, you set your goal that you will go for him, then allow your universe to bend to your will accordingly. It all starts with a declaration in your mind, speak it to make it feel real in your projection, but it is always the vibration of your mind, that voice that's always speaking to you within, which you must announce your intention.

The opening will be there and I Will go for It.

This is the will to power, that specific declaration made with no counter thoughts. Notice the words aren't about "marry him" or "get him" because your crush on this man is most likely one formed before you were a Spartan, back when your mind was drifting on autopilot. Therefore, this man may be simply Fool's Gold laid out by your past self just to tease you. No man is special until he proves it, and at this point, he's just a crush. You will go for him, see if he is authentic, and regardless if he turns out to be the real deal or just another pretender, you win because the victory isn't in attaining these little boys, it's in attaining power over your reality.

Start with your platonic/secret crush male friends. You don't know if climbing his dick like a tree will ruin your friendship, nor should you care. As a Spartan, you follow your truth. Is this man someone you want because you can't find anyone else? Are you projecting boyfriend qualities on a buddy because he's the only man you talk to intimately? You know this now, there is no more confusion. Most likely, your guy friend is looking cuter than normal because you haven't been fucked in awhile or you haven't had a man show you affection, and he's in your face. Don't settle for the closest man to you, know you can now attract any man. Why shit where you sleep? If your everything is telling you that he is the one, then take him. He's right there, a phone call away, bring him to you. Flirt with him, break the rules, and seduce him. There is no more fear of rejection, so sit on his lap like you own it, he won't push you off. Use your words and tell him you two should do an experiment. Go on an official date, where you act as if you aren't friends, and see where it goes. If he agrees, date him like you would any man, don't fast track him to the pussy because you know him, relearn him. If he declines, that doesn't mean your instincts were off, it means that he needed to go anyway. You shouldn't have been sitting on a man you really wanted to be with in the first place.

Let's return one final time to Spartan Phoenix. When she was Ashely, she was the victim of crush anxiety. This super fine Work Dick started at her company, and every time she saw him, she would get butterflies like she was a Freshman. Work Dick didn't exactly work with her, he worked at the same company in the same building but on a different floor. This meant that Ashley would only run into him randomly during lunch breaks, maybe in the morning, and sometimes in the parking lot. Being this removed from her crush put Ashley into a Disney Princess mindset. She was free to fantasize about what kind of person he was outside the office, his hobbies, aspirations, even his sex stroke.

Work Dick wasn't an obsession, but it was something in the back of her mind that Ashely gave life to because the fantasy that he would one day get into the elevator, stare into her eyes, and kiss the soul from her body, had been allowed to fester for over a month. This, of course, was never going to happen, but it was a welcome distraction from her pathetic realistic love life. Typical Ashley did get her wish, however, as most women who crush do when they hold the idea in their head for too long. Work Dick happened to be standing right next to Ashely in the lobby and made a comment about the elevators being horribly slow. By the time Ashley realized it was him and reacted, what came out of her mouth was awkward and corny, "I know right! They're so dumb." This flaccid response got a pity chuckle and in Ashley's mind solidified that he now thought she was some idiot who believed elevators had actual personalities and control of their speed. Ashley, as she would always do when she got in her own way, failed.

Phoenix would not. Embracing her place in the center of this universe, Phoenix set in motion her goal of going for this crush. Note that going for a man does not mean: ask about the department he works, find out his office number, and ambushing him at his desk like, "Hey, so this is where you work, huh?" Nor is it an excuse to start googling pointless facts about him so you can figure out how to start a proper conversation when you meet him like, "Hey, so you like the Lakers, huh? And you used to swim in high school?" Spartans never have to do extra, they let opportunity knock. Phoenix does not change her schedule to fake a "bump into" nor does she tell any of her co-workers about her plans so they can help, she simply lives life with the thought that the opportunity is coming and she will go for him. By the middle of the week, she spots Work Dick across the parking lot, but that isn't an opportunity. The next day, Work Dick jumps in the elevator at the last moment, but it's full, and all they manage is a whispered "hello" as they stand inches apart. Phoenix is laughing, she feels what's going on, and unlike some typical she knows these aren't opportunities missed, but her magnet drawing him closer and closer. Her mind is calm, and steady, not worried in the slightest. The next week Phoenix has all but forgot about her mission, that's how relaxed her mind and effortless her power works. At the end of her workday, in route to the parking lot, there he is—Work Dick walking through the lobby a few feet in front of her. He is within speaking range; no one else is around...this is what opportunity looks like even from a distance.

"They had you working late tonight, huh?" Phoenix doesn't even yell it, the command in her voice is steady and powerful enough to make him turn. He sees her, that smile, those heels, that messy yet sexy bun, and he can't help but smile hard. Work Dick stops and allows Phoenix to catch up. He then tells her he always leaves at this time, inquiring why he never sees her leaving at this time. Phoenix locks in the most vicious eye fuck she's given all year, never shying away from his glance and with no little girl giggle, she admits that she always tries to leave early. This rolls into what department he works in, then if he likes it, the back and forth continues as they walk outside. By the time Work Dick walks with her towards her car, they've established names, positions, and a vibe. If Work Dick was inarticulate, weird, and didn't spark Phoenix's interest, it would be a cut and dry, "Drive safe, see you around," brush off. However, Work Dick is very articulate, charming, and keeps Phoenix engaged. There are no nerves or any "should I ask him for his number or just let it go," thoughts of an indecisive typical bitch. This is an opportunity, so she does what she promised the universe she would do. Phoenix tells him they should have lunch one day this week...if they allow him a lunch. Work Dick, bats down that ego check, he gets lunches, he's no company slave who has to eat at his desk. They set the lunch date for the next day and wish each other safe travels. Work Dick opens the car door for Phoenix; he's already trying to earn brownie points. Got him!

This same scenario can play out if a guy works in the same department as you, at your bank, if you ride the train together, if you go to school together but barely see him, it doesn't matter the circumstance! Declare your intention, and be ready to conquer him when he is drawn to you! A typical girl will rush in after talking herself up, walk over, tap a guy on the shoulder, and come off like a cornball. You are a Spartan; you understand that patience allows for calmness. Let the world work for you and then snatch that opportunity with full confidence. That swagger, that looseness, it will project as strength, not come off as some soft bitch, "Hi, my name is..." lameness. Will Phoenix end up liking Work Dick once she gets to know him? Will they go on a real date? Will they not vibe, and it ends up being awkward when they run into each other going forward? It doesn't fucking matter. Life unfolds in the moment, stay in the moment, and let your story play out in the way that benefits you the most. No matter if it's a happy ending or just a chapter in an ongoing story, it's all positive! The goal isn't the man; it's to flex these power muscles, so that any time a crush pops up, you know from experience, he's attainable.

RISING FROM THE ASHES

This is not theory nor is it a remote possibility dependent on outside forces. It does not matter what age you are or what city you live in. These steps will work 100% of the time when you believe 100% of the time in your power. Men are not hard to attract once you embrace Spartanhood because your mind will be clear of counter thoughts that have held you back and lead to mixed results up until now. Confidence is no longer fueled by how good your hair looks, what outfit you're wearing that day, if your skin is blemish free that week, or if you're in the "right place at the right time," at a given moment. Strangers will pop into your world, offline and online. Old flames will come back with new interest. Men who never noticed you before will suddenly be all over you. It will scare you at first because these things will begin to happen rapidly not long after you finish this book. This isn't a miracle; this is your new reality.

The Will to Power was always inside of you, and it will always be inside of you. Nevertheless, it is your responsibility to maintain your Spartan mindset, to not shy away and give your power to the first man who wows you or turn back into just another sheep on autopilot the moment you experience a situation that makes you uncomfortable. Know what you want. Get what you want. It's that simple! Set your intentions that you want someone as great. Feel your attractiveness, project your sex appeal, and bathe in the confidence of the truth: Life always works out in your favor.

Part II
Date Like A Spartan:
功率

Chapter 8:
The 5 Reasons You Failed at Dating

You don't really want to date. You don't have the time, the energy, or the patience to meet new people, chitchat about the school you went to, the city you were born in, favorites, dislikes, and other trivial shit. Why put effort into learning a person's favorite color, current job title, and future ambitions when there's a chance that they are just pretending to be interested in you? Does he really like you or does he just want to fuck you? You don't know. Even when you try to be confident in your value or look for hints that he's a dog, you can never tell what men think—and that's scary. Dating sucks because you've been down this road before and all it did was lead you right back to the starting point of *What Am I Doing Wrong*? This is where the excuses begin to harden around you like armor, protecting your ego. It's not you, it's your city. The problem isn't with the way you date; the problem is that men today don't date. You are a good woman in a world where men value bad bitches, and men are too dumb to realize how valuable you are. You wish you were born in the era of "I'll pick you up at 7 with flowers" courting instead of "Let's watch Netflix and chill" disrespect. Men no longer care about the dating process, they expect pussy on the first date, and that's why you will no longer waste your time attempting to date in this climate. "I haven't found a good man because there are no good men to find," is your story and you're sticking to it.

Weak women make excuses for losing and then set out to rectify their losing ways by never trying again. Anytime a girl tells me, "I'm tired of dating," I hear the agony of defeat in her voice. Napoleon Hill wrote, "When defeat overtakes a person, the easiest and most logical thing to do is quit. That's exactly what the majority do." He's right. The majority of people in this world are quitters. Excuse making, finger pointing, tired

123

minds, who just want to skip ahead to the part where they hit the jackpot because they don't have the fucking guts to push through adversity. A Spartan does not point to her past with bitterness, nor does she point to the current dating scene and cry about fairness. This world isn't fair... for non-Spartans. This world is tailor made for the strong to feast on the weak. These men lie and manipulate typicals because they know that these women are placeholders. In the presence of a Spartan, his lies fall flat and his manipulation falls short because Spartans know how to fucking date! Now that you've risen to the challenge, it's time to put your power to use.

There is no cheat sheet for dating—*do this, do that, now do this, congratulations, get the man*. Love is a war that only a woman who isn't afraid to stand up and do battle with men can win. He didn't call you after you gave him your number, Spartans don't cry, they shrug. You went out to dinner and he was boring and corny, Spartans don't give second chances, they block numbers. You've been having great dates and now he's pushing hard for sex, Spartans don't give in to make him happy, fuck his happy; just for applying pressure he can wait even longer. Relationships fail because women forget that they should be at the center of the universe. As a Spartan, you don't get tired of dating because it's through dating that you prove your mastery over your solar system!

#1 YOU DON'T UNDERSTAND HOW MEN DATE

Men play too many games, and I don't have time for that! Okay, Tina Typical, what do you actually have time for? Work, gossip, and checking timelines? You better find time to date and more importantly, find the attitude that will allow you to embrace this process without reverting into some annoyed little peasant girl who just wants "boys to be real with me." Dating is not supposed to be transparent and simple, it's meant to test your intelligence, heighten your intuition, and force you out of your comfort zone in order to flex your power. Confidence builds with every man you are able to break down and figure out, and that confidence opens a new door to a better man. You may be two men away from finding the perfect match or twelve, the ease of your success will depend on how quickly you pick up these skills. You are not yet at the level where every man you meet will be a quality catch. This is a journey. You will need to take on this challenge without getting frustrated or quitting because the one guy you like doesn't pass the initial screening stage.

Understanding how to break a man down on these dates starts with the Spartan knowledge of the way men date. Men today will always play some sort of game, even the honest and trustworthy ones because a wise man isn't stupid enough to treat every girl like a Queen. There are so many peasants pretending to be royal, who talk a good talk, walk a good walk, but are easy to expose in a matter of days or weeks. A man fears choosing the wrong woman, in the same way you used to fear choosing the wrong man. Even if he's aware that most girls are placeholders, that guy does not want to overpay. Why would a male walk around offering filet mignon to a burrito bitch? All he has to do is swipe on an app, meet up that night for a Mojito, and a girl that claims to be "different" will drain his sack because he had good conversation. Therefore, men purposely choose dates based on the following things that expose a woman as typical: <u>Privacy. Drugs or Alcohol. Limited Price</u>. Imagine if you were a boy. No matter how pretty a girl is when you first meet her, you don't know if she's just another basic chick. No matter how long you talk on the phone leading up to your date, you still don't know. Only on a date will you, as a male, expose this female as either a freak, a ho, a basic, or a Unicorn worthy of respect.

<u>Privacy</u> is crucial when setting a date if you want to expose a typical. As a man, you want to make it easy to touch her, kiss her, etc. Therefore, you don't actually want to go out where there are tons of people. Even if you plan a romantic dinner, the intent is to get her alone back at your place or hers. <u>Drugs or Alcohol</u>, dull inhibitions. A buzzed girl will not be as uptight or guarded. As a man, you want to get a girl drinking or high on your date, because if she is easy sexually, that will reveal her true self. <u>Limited Price</u> refers to the cost of taking a girl out on the town. If a girl is a jump-off who is willing to make out just because she sees you as cute, then why spend a ton of money trying to impress her, when she's already impressed? With this now in your head, if you were a man, even one looking for true love, would you be stupid enough to take every girl out to an expensive dinner, drop her off, and then do the same thing a few more times before you try to have sex? Or would you test her? You would test

her! If she is truly as high class as she professes to be on the phone or when you talk in person, she will pass these tests. Therefore, the only way to know if a woman is legit royalty is to lower the bar initially and see how she reacts.

If you are a handsome man, you will ask if she wants to come over to your place to talk and watch a movie, maybe grab something to eat. That's a feeler that men put out. If that girl agrees to come over, he will set the mood, pick a good movie, order great food, have the alcohol flowing. Maybe he tries to have sex and that girl doesn't go for it. Nevertheless, they had a good time, so he will repeat that "date" a few days later. This time she's more comfortable and will most likely do something sexual. If he would have taken her out to a restaurant like Outback Steakhouse or Olive Garden, gave her a kiss, and sent her home, he would have wasted money. A typical woman, even if she says she needs more, will always settle for less. So understand as a woman, that non-date offer is not personal, a man simply doesn't know you enough to respect you, so he must test you.

Dating is about exposing. From the day a man gets your number, he's trying to expose you as typical because handcuffing thots with low standards isn't what quality men do. Spartans have the same mentality. From the day a man gets your number, or vice versa, you should be trying to expose him as a typical Dick because a Spartan will never give her heart to a man who doesn't pass tests and prove himself to be exceptional. People are rarely who they pretend to be. Men are often times exaggerating to get pussy. Women are often times yapping about what they don't do so they don't come off as pussy. Only through dating, can you prove what's in the heart of a man, and only through dating (or the lack of real dating) does a man prove a woman's character—**Queen or Peasant**. Most women are afraid to expose men by being tough because they feel they will scare him off and lose out on a potential boyfriend. Fuck his potential. You can't go ring shopping with potential! As a Spartan, you know the male game and understand what the mission is in terms of exposing you by offering lame dates. You don't cry, "men ain't shit," you laugh at their hustle, and you train them to respect you. Not by trying to change them, but by showing these men what you will and won't do in very clear ways. This section is all about dominating dates by being one-step ahead of the men. You will learn not only how to say "No" to Netflix & Chill, group dates, coffee meet-ups, and all of the depowering ideas a man comes up with to check a basic bitch. You will show him that you aren't typical, get real dates, and prove that you are unlike any other woman he's ever dated, so long as you follow each step laid out in the following chapters.

#2 You Don't Understand How Important Dates Are

There are more women who come to me looking to fix an already broken relationship than women who come asking how to date properly. It isn't hard to find a man to give you the title of girlfriend, and that's the problem. Typicals are overly concerned with the bullshit of "I haven't had a boyfriend in years... I want to experience real love." These basic women don't realize that titles don't mean anything if the person giving it to you is unworthy. Once again, it's that kitchen bitch mindset that makes women feel as if they aren't complete unless they find a man who will commit. Think about all the people you know that are currently in a relationship, and based on observation, how many seem truly happy? The cliché that everyone goes through problems, all relationships have their bad moments, is another poison that is fed to you by unhappy people who are trapped in mediocre relationships. A friend that calls you crying over a boy who she was so in love with the week prior. Family members who are gossiping about how an aunt is being cheated on or taken advantage of by the latest Casanova. Hurt seems normal in bad relationships. Typical women vent about men days after bragging about them because they don't know what they are doing in terms of choosing the proper partners. They don't vet men, they jump at the idea of finally being someone's girlfriend, and that is why they fail!

Most women are in messy relationships because they didn't set their value during the dating stage. As a result, they are trying to keep a sinking ship afloat so they won't have to go back to the supposed shame of being single. Spartans don't struggle with false-start relationships, because when they choose to start one, they make sure he's already passed the screening stage and dating tests. It infuriates me when I ask a woman who is in a new relationship, normally for 6 months to a year, deep questions about her boyfriend and she can't answer most of them. It's not that these women don't care and just want a boyfriend to say they have a boyfriend; they are too afraid to ask men questions. Even before the first date, you should know specific things and by the third date, you should be all in a man's business no matter if it makes him uncomfortable or not. You can't afford to waste your time with someone that's hiding an entire secret life under the surface. Throughout this dating section, you will learn conversation skills and become a master of asking real questions.

#3 YOU OVERTHINK THE PROCESS

What do you say to make him think highly of you? What do you wear so he finds you sexy? What topics do you talk about to make him see you as the wifey type? Should you spend your own money to show him that you bring something to the table besides looks? YAWN! It's time to grow the fuck up and stop dating like a child. You are a Queen. Queens don't audition to be someone's girlfriend; they are the ones holding the audition. Your past life was based on living up to the opinion of men, which then created a fear of rejection. Your pre-Spartan mind was full of nervous energy, because "What if he doesn't like me," was your dominant thought. Your pre-Spartan mouth opened and all you could say were basic words and make obvious observations. You tried to come off as witty, but all you could muster was sassy. It's cute when a 13-year-old girl is talking smart mouthed and giving off sass because it's all she knows how to do at that age. For a grown ass woman to sit across from a grown ass man, and be so shy and nervous that all she can do to show her wit is backtalk, roll eyes, and get smart is pathetic!

Awkward women aren't awkward around their best friends, which means they aren't really awkward by nature. The awkwardness stems from being in a situation where you are overwhelmed by your own nerves and self-consciousness. You act anxious, come off as goofy, uninteresting, and corny because you aren't as relaxed around attractive men. Being awkward isn't part of your DNA, it's part of your WBW—*Weak Bitch Ways*. A Spartan is never awkward because there isn't a man that can sit across from her and intimidate the most powerful force on earth. Wonder Woman doesn't lower her head around Superman, she stares him in the fucking eyes because HE is not greater than SHE.

Over thinking is the result of wanting someone to want you and trying to figure out ways to get that across before you blow your opportunity. Fuck that. A Spartan is the prize, therefore, the man becomes the one in the hot seat, trying to figure out how to make you laugh, make you listen, keep your attention, and earn another date. Why should he get access to your Friday night? Why should he get the pleasure of spending hours talking to you over dinner? What makes this man worthy of you putting your heels on and leaving your house? What makes this man so special that you would ever press your lips against his, let alone grant him access to the best pussy he's ever smelled? You are always in control when you date like a Spartan because you never fear if he likes you or not. Dating with no stress gives you an opportunity to sharpen your wit through banter, and an excuse to share your knowledge via conversation. Talking to the opposite sex isn't some scary concept where you should be nervous or feel the need to impress. You are a Spartan, and that makes you impressive by default. When you go on a date, you're not just putting on lipstick and eyeliner; you're placing that warrior helmet on. That helmet is an invisible piece of armor that gives you the confidence to settle any nerves, and attack that date like a woman in control.

#4 YOU ARE IN LOVE WITH BEING IN LOVE

Spartans do not look for love. To look for love points to a lack of love internally, a need to fulfill something that's missing by finding someone to fill that void. Love is not a goal because love is easily attained at the Spartan level. Every time you wake up and look in that mirror, you are falling in love. Every time you walk out into your world with your sun shining down, you will know love. Many men will love you, but none of their love will ever match the love you have for yourself. This is important because heartbreak still exists in a primitive form, even in Sparta. To break up with a man who loves you, to lose a man who loves you, to find out a man has stopped growing with you and no longer shares that same level of love for you, that is enough to break a weak woman. A Spartan may lose the love of another, but it never breaks her, for it is her own self-love that fuels and strengthens her regardless of what man comes or goes. A typical woman is dependent on

129

outside love, she is only as happy as the man that is currently loving her, which makes her a slave to relationships. These lowly women cannot break up or be broken up with without theatrics and drama because they are hooked on a drug known as male love. You are no longer addicted to this basic feeling. A man's love will never be so necessary that you give up your power and betray your Spartan teachings in order to keep him.

The primary goal when dating is to find a boyfriend with the same qualities you have, who exhibits the emotional potential to grow with you. Throughout the deep talks, the outside of the house bonding activities, and the between date communicating, your mission is to peel back the various layers of a man, ensuring that he is who he is pretending to be.

In addition to the exploration of a man emotionally and mentally, you must also field test him by placing him in calculated scenarios in order to observe how he reacts. I'm not talking about dumb shit like "does he open the door for you or hit the unlock button," but real things that defines his character. The mission is to bait these men into exposing the good, bad, and ugly, in less than two months. "Wait, you mean I can find love in less than two months?" Fuck love! This isn't about love because love is plentiful, this is about character. You must find a man whose character matches your own because it is that character which the foundation of a strong relationship must grow. Stop thirsting for this endgame called "love" and focus on exposing these men early and often to see if there is true compatibility there. Dating isn't about falling in love, that comes at the relationship level, dating is merely a test to see if that person is worthy of your exclusivity. Dating isn't about finding out every single secret a man is hiding, again, that's relationship work that comes later, it's about seeing how much of the truth you can pull from those initial lies that all men tell.

#5 YOU ARE BASIC

Basic bitches have a burning need to be wanted because they think it is through a man that they are made complete. Basica Alba goes on a date with these things in mind: *I hope he likes how I look. I hope he likes how I talk. I don't want to sound stupid. But I don't want to come off as a know-it-all. I can't come off as quiet. But I can't be loud and ratchet. How much flirting is too much without coming off like a cock tease? I need him to try to kiss me at the end of the night so he knows I'm interested. But how much interest do I show without coming off like a ho?* An endless stream of fearful thoughts swirls in those women who aren't in control. When you make yourself out to be the one auditioning as opposed to the one who is casting, you feel pressure. Pressure creates nerves, nerves spread fear, and fear makes you weak. It is time to turn the tables, and understand you are casting for the role of Prince Charming, not these men who are casting for the role of Cinderella. This idea that a woman has to put her foot in a glass slipper to be chosen by a man is Disney bullshit. You are a Queen, not because a man puts that crown on your head, but because you have mastered your own inner Kingdom!

No matter your previous relationship experiences or those things you mislabeled as flaws, a man will be able to see through that forest and want you that much more. No one is perfect, but everyone is perfect for someone. In your pre-Spartan life, you tried to hide certain things, become something else. This lead to constant pressure to perform for others, as opposed to the comfort of being accepted as you are. You must never fake who you are when dating. When trying to pass off a counterfeit version of yourself for the approval of a man, you fail to realize that if this actually works, he will fall in love with the watered down personality, not the actual you. You can't spend 48 hours before a date trying to say words correctly, learn about current events, or change that annoying laugh. Who you are is who you are. Not every man has to love your qualities, but if he wants to earn a second date he has to accept them.

When you have been dating Cinderella style your entire life, trying to fit into that slipper, you can't suddenly flip that switch and be a boss, which is why you must get your mind Spartan strong before you even start the dating process. What do you like to eat? "I don't know whatever you like." That's weak bitch talk. You like chicken, you know you like chicken, so why are you waiting to hear what he likes before you answer? I use that as a metaphor for women who just want to say all the right things. I was on a date where this girl would respond with, "What do you think about it," every time I asked her opinion. Confident women aren't afraid to express their views. If that man doesn't agree with your opinions, so what! Be an individual, because if you don't really mesh well with him the way you're pretending to, then the relationship you enter will be built on personality lies. Know who you are, and never waiver. Dating isn't about having everything in common; it's about opposing half's coming together to elevate one another. The best thing that can ever happen is that you find a man that can teach you and who you can teach, and together, both of you can share your opinions with interesting conversation as opposed to timid agreements for the sake of fitting into that glass slipper. **What do men want to talk about on dates?** A Spartan does not worry about this basic bitch burden. Typical women see men as scary and mysterious. They don't know shit about the opposite sex, which is why their relationships are always in turmoil. Never try to be what you think men want. If you don't match up, then you don't match up. Don't fear that, embrace it, because the lack of chemistry on either side is proof that he isn't worthy.

Not every woman has a great personality, not every woman has interesting things to talk about... sadly there are so many *Zombies with Pussies* walking around just trying to find a dick. All they will ever get is a dick because they don't have anything a man wants other than a vagina. These basic bitches trot around talking about sports teams they don't really follow, ask redundant questions about a man's work hoping he enjoys talking about that and then falls into the habit of sending nude pictures because they have zero personality to keep a man focused. *Zombies with Pussies*! A Spartan does not fall into this category because you are always improving your worldview. You don't sit in the house, you go out. You don't just watch TV; you absorb all culture. You don't just see things from your POV, you try to understand other perspectives, be it political parties, religions, or unfamiliar music genres. A Spartan grows herself in order to have a rich lifestyle to pull from when dating; she is never a One-Trick-Pussy there to giggle and bat her eyes at a man.

What makes a girl boring versus enticing to a man? No guy wants to sit in front of a woman whose most passionate topic on a Tuesday is a *Real Housewives* show that aired on Sunday. A man doesn't care about the workplace drama that a woman pretends to be fed up with, but secretly gets off on and can't stop bringing up. A guy doesn't want to ask where a grown woman's traveled and have the answer be "Atlantic City." No man wants to direct a late night conversation towards sex and hear an adult shy away with, "You nasty, boy." Can you seduce like a woman or are you going to shy away like a high school sophomore? As a woman what life have you lived on your own that makes you fascinating? What thoughts do you think that truly make you unique? If you set in front of Oprah, how long would it take before she checked her watch due to your dry ass character? Can you bring up culture in a real way to create an engrossing discussion? Can you reference book topics that you want his opinion on? Do you actually go out and create experiences beyond what happened during your shift at work? Can you flirt and mind-fuck in a way that would keep any male engaged? A Queen is a master of many trades, not just work gossip, timeline drama, or TV show talk. Ask yourself if you are indeed well rounded, before you even agree to go on a date. If the answer is "no" then mentally, you are a Zombie with a Pussy, not a Spartan Queen.

THE FINAL TEST

Are you Typical or are you a Spartan? That's not rhetorical, answer that honestly based on your last two relationships. How did you get a man, did you pull or get pulled? How did you get a date, did you wait for him to ask or did you let him know that you needed to be taken out? Did you sit around guessing if a man liked you for you or did you not give a fuck about what he wanted and went about dominating him as if he had no choice in the matter? Spartans seduce and conquer; Typicals beat around the bush and get led. A man will establish who you are by the end of the first date, and he will never revise those feelings. That means that even if he likes you enough to be with you in a monogamous relationship, he will never respect you more than that first date. If anything, his respect will lower to the point where you become like most women in relationships, a prisoner who cries about "Why won't he treat me like I deserve to be treated?" As a Spartan you don't circle back and gain respect, you start strong, and take your respect from Day 1 so there is never any room for confusion about what you're made of, Steel & Ice, never Sugar & Spice.

Remember to remember who you are. The moment you became a Spartan was the moment you left the past in the past. No more stories about what happened to you once upon a time, how men treated the old you, or the laundry list of doubts that held you back. The word "scared" isn't in a Spartan's vocabulary, as a matter of fact, you can't even pronounce words with "sca—" because you would feel basic. From now on, you won't just go on dates, you will destroy dates. These men aren't bigger than you, they aren't smarter than you, and they don't have more game than you do. Even if they have more money, more social status, or more education, none of these guys are better than you! You are a Spartan Queen, you don't need to impress, you must be impressed, or off with his fucking head.

Chapter 9:
The Pre-Date Battle Plan

Y ou only get one chance at a first impression, so let's start with the easiest way to tattoo a man's brain—The Screening Stage. Think of this as *Pre-Date Reconnaissance* where you're mindful that not every man that gets your attention deserves to date you. A Spartan scrutinizes a man from the moment he enters her world. Red flags are missed early on because you don't pay as much attention as you should during the pre-date. This chapter will help focus you. The steps that follow do not require you to meet a guy a certain way. I don't care if you met on an app, in a store, if he was introduced by a friend, or if you sat next to him on the train and asked the time. The moment a man comes into your orbit, the battle begins.

As in *Ho Tactics*, I will use a composite of various women that I have gathered dating stories from in order to show you how these steps can be done the right way, as well as the wrong way. Similar to Spartan Phoenix, you will see how a confident and powerful outlook will make previously scary situations easy and stress-free. While reading, picture yourself in these situations. Visualization is key because you're actually going to do these things. See yourself in her shoes, feel yourself wielding her power.

Let's call this Spartan Dater—Cali. Through Cali's eyes, we will conquer the most common scenarios you will face: **The introduction. The initial reach out. The setting of the date. The actual dates. The Sex. Transitioning from dating into a relationship.** Don't picture some super woman in your mind physically, what Cali is about to do isn't because her ass is a certain size, breasts are perfect, eyebrows are on fleek, none of that shit matters when pulling this off. Everything she does is due to two things: Spartan Confidence & the ability to open her mouth and use that Spartan power to get what she wants. That is all you need.

135

DAY 0: Setting the Bait

Nicole is ready for war. She's made up her mind that she wants something serious from a man. No more random hook ups, no more entertaining bums out of boredom, no more wasting time on men with potential but no follow through. If the vibe doesn't scream King, she will not be bothered. Nicole focused in on her goal, transformed her mind into that of a fearless warrior Queen, and has begun to reshape her visual brand into that of a sexy huntress. Nicole has embraced Spartanhood, and renamed herself Cali, to reflect her laid-back attitude and approach to her game. She has waited patiently for the right man to manifest, and now the time is upon her to earn her Spartan stripes by putting everything written thus far into action.

STEP 1: THE EXCHANGE

Spartan Cali was in Starbucks when a man walked in, drawing here attention without even trying. Handsome, but not overly pretty; business casual, but with his own style added on. This was her type visually. Unfortunately, this guy was too focused on his iPhone to scan the line, so Cali missed her opportunity to eye fuck him like a fat kid eye fucks a Krispy Kreme box. Not one to chase, Cali simply waited for life to provide her with an opportunity to take. As Cali stepped out of line to wait for her macchiato, she again glanced over to the line; this cute guy was still missing his opportunity by overly eyeballing his phone. Cali remained patient, her own phone still in her bag, because no one in her current inbox was as important as adding a new member to her shrinking roster. Cali's macchiato was ready just as iPhone Dick finished ordering, so she waited a moment to see if he would come closer as she picked up her cup. Once again, iPhone Dick shied away, choosing to stand a few feet away, and not once looking up. Cali stayed poised, walked over to the condiment table to add an extra sugar in the raw to her drink, and then there it was... her shot.

The barista called his name, "Latte for Stephen." Cali put the lid back on her drink and turned ready to conquer. In a page out of Maria the Ho's playbook, she invaded Stephen's personal space and went to work with her pull game. "Stephen," she said with full authority as if she had known this man for years, "Did they misspell the name on your cup too?" Cali was now in his face with a slight grin. Stephen didn't know if she was serious or joking, so like any man that's not used to women speaking first, he fumbled around for a second before regaining his cool. He checked his cup to see if his name was indeed fucked up. Stephen revealed that they did ruin his name by spelling it, "Steven." From there, Cali confessed that she would have spelled it "the normal way," as well, poking fun at the actual spelling of his name with her own brand of tease-flirting. The two shared a laugh, and at that moment, Cali used her Goddess given opportunity to eye fuck him. A woman who masters proper eye fucking doesn't have to say she's interested, a man knows. After that it became elementary, the "So are you on your way to work," chit. The "Do you live in the area," chat. In the end, Cali walked out of there with Stephen's business card, and a half-promise to give him a call sometime.

Cali could call Stephen that night and start a getting to know him conversation or she could send a cute, "it was nice running into you," text before bed. However, she isn't in a rush and realizes that giving him a day to wonder if she was actually interested will make her that much more desirable. Cali is a Spartan; she isn't worried about looking thirsty by calling or texting too soon. This is a man she actually wants; she's not going to let gender sanctions turn her into some shy mouse. She's a lioness and she's going to eat him alive, but it's always good to play with the prey before sinking your teeth in. Cali waits until the next afternoon to reach out. On her lunch break, she sends him a quick text, "Did I have you in Starbucks daring them to misspell your name again this morning?"

Questions are always the best forms of texts, they exist to be answered, unlike a basic, "Hey, this is Cali from yesterday. Hope everything is good with you." That shit is sandpaper dry! Cali has set the bait by asking a question and making a joke at the same time. Any man who reads that will grin. Within five minutes, Cali has a response back, "I started to go hard, but I looked around and didn't have you as back up." Cali grins; he's both witty and handsome. At this moment, Cali has all the power. Before he fires off a, "How's your day going..." text that leads to chitchat that doesn't move this forward, she hits him with a *to be continued* reply. Cali texts "LOL" and tells Stephen that she will give him a call tonight after she's off the clock… unless his girlfriend objects. This bitch is bad. Not only did she lay the seeds of "Call me, don't text me," she has also girlfriend checked him. Stephen responds with, "I don't have one of those (smiley sunglasses emoji). Cool. I'm usually home after 7." Mission complete.

Cali only has to write, "K" and keep it moving. Stephen meanwhile is at work thinking about this new aggressive female, and assuming that it's going to be easy pussy…he has no idea he just crossed paths with a Spartan who is in complete control.

STEP 2: THE CONTACT

Cali is not a robot. She feels the excitement of nerves that any woman would feel when about to call a new man for the first time. This isn't fear, this is the anticipation of possibilities. Stephen could be fool's gold, a guy she talks to this one time and gets turned off of. He could become a guy on the roster she tests out for a month and then cuts when he starts to disappoint. There is a strong chance, based on the initial chemistry, that Stephen could be the one, not only her next boyfriend but her last boyfriend. There is no way to tell at this point, so why even give those "What if" thoughts energy? Nicole would be over thinking everything, but not Cali, Spartans don't sweat. Cali is about to bring the fire and do her part in presenting this man with someone who acts like a Queen, it will be on him to respond like a King. If Stephen comes off as corny, overly sexual, dry, or starts to preach about conspiracy theories, then he fails, not her.

Even when you are in pursuit, you are still the prize. "I went after him, so he's not going to work for it now," is bullshit. You took the opportunity to put your greatness on his radar. A gift fell into his lap, but he needs to appreciate you and understand that dating you is a privilege, not a right. Any indifference or behavior that points to him acting too cool gets him immediately cut. Men still have to be men, even when you are the one that initiates. This Spartan rule brings Cali back into focus. The nerves have been calmed, and now she can begin to visualize where she will take the conversation when she calls him tonight. Know where you want to end the conversation. **You are not calling a man for the first time just to talk him to death.** You need a date, not a four-hour convo. After your first date, then you can begin the deep conversation stage. There is no reason to spill your life story a day after meeting a man while on the phone. Becoming fast friends is one of the tricks men use to bypass dates. Not here. Cali has visualized and laid out three points she will hit when they are on the phone.

A. Put Him at Ease with Conversation
B. Recon His Life
C. Date Bait

Cali calls Stephen and he picks up in his best smooth voice, which lets Cali know he was already doing pre-game himself. Cali doesn't care about Stephen's game or how he thinks he's going to lay it down. She's a fucking Spartan, and she's going to control the pace of the conversation and lead him where she needs him to be by the time this call ends. Cali isn't a comedian; she doesn't have the insane wit of some geek girl that hooks men from behind her keyboard like some millennial Tina Fey. Cali knows her strength is in her seduction and goes about teasing Stephen in order to break the ice. She asks if he let the phone ring an extra time to show that he wasn't thirsty. Stephen responds that he didn't have his phone by him, assuring her he wasn't playing it cool. Cali doesn't let up. She playfully moans with disappointment that scheduling a call didn't get him so excited that he glued that phone to his hand. Voice emphasis on "Excited." The voice is sensual, the tone is playful, Cali may be a Spartan, but she's mastered the *Ho Tactics* that get a dick hard via inflection.

From that playful banter, she transitions into the nuances of how his day was, what he actually does at work, and if he enjoys it or is this just a stepping-stone in his career. These aren't big questions, just reconnaissance to see who this man is in general. Cali finds out that Stephen is an account rep for a heating company, just as his card said. It's boring work but gets him the experience and connections to branch out in a year or two. There is no need to talk about ambition or life's ultimate goal at this point. Stephen responds with his own brand of recon, "So what about you, what do you do?" Cali doesn't have the world's most fascinating job, so after she tells him her company and position, she follows up with more seductive personality. Cali laments that she doesn't have her own business card yet but she's definitely stealing his design when she makes it big. Notice the technique. A Spartan sidesteps questions about herself and redirects the conversation back to the man by keeping it light and flirty.

Next, Cali does what few women do; she admits her attraction in a real way. She openly tells him how sexy he looked walking into that Starbucks, and then brings it to, "I figured that you were texting your baby mama, the way your eyes were on that phone." Bam! She's telling this man that she finds him attractive on the highest level "sexy" which translate in male language to: <u>She will fuck me</u>. Once a man thinks he has a sexual green light, he's like a puppy on a leash, excited and trying to lead you, but still under your control. The sneak comment about a baby mama also opens it up to another recon; does he have children?

Stephen is passing the test. He has a decent job and ambition to get an even better one. Now he reveals that he doesn't have any children, but slides in that he would love to start a big family when the time is right. If Cali were a basic bitch, she would say something like, "Haven't found the right woman yet, huh?" However, she doesn't have to relationship bait by making asinine observations or beating around the bush like an idiot. Cali is not trying to put the pressure of her being the right woman, having his kids, or any long term thoughts in the mind of this man. All she wanted to know is if he had little crumb snatchers walking around. Mission complete.

Finished with the recon, and having shown off her flirty persona, Cali goes in for the kill. She asks, "So what's taking you so long to ask me out, sir?" Again, this is said in the right tone, with the sexual and submissive word of "sir" added to show him she's not being bitchy or matter-of-fact. Stephen, like most men, responds obediently and asks when she's free. Cali works a nontraditional schedule and her midweek is her weekend. She doesn't date for Stephen's Friday/Saturday convenience, so she tells her new man crush that she is only free on Thursday. Stephen is nervous, he's not sure if he should take control or let her pick a place. He steps lightly, asking her where she wants to go. Cali doesn't like that, he's the man, thus, he should pick. She pretends to think about, then sinks her fangs in with, "Let's have dinner this Thursday, but I'm going to let you pick the place so I can see how good your taste is, babe." Stephen begins to think of a place, but Cali's job is done, so it's time to exit. "How about you call me back this time tomorrow and let me know what you decide on?" Stephen says he can manage that and Cali tells him that she looks forward to his choice. After one last exchange of flirty banter, she laments that she has to go attend to something, but she will be waiting for his dinner choice. End of call.

STEP 3: THE BAIT

Although it was Cali who went for Stephen in the store, texted him first, and even called first, it is now Stephen who is put in the position to show if he's truly interested. A Spartan does not assume that a man is interested, he is either smart enough to realize the treasure that stands before him or dumb enough to let it slip away. There is never a worry about coming on too strong, or not giving a man a chance to show real interest. That phone call was the bait. All men are hunters, they pretend not to like to work, but they get off on it. Cali baited him with seduction and expressed her requirement to be taken out in a way that wasn't demanding or overly aggressive. Now it is up to Stephen to confirm if he is interested or not.

If Stephen doesn't call the next day, then his number is deleted, no second chance. That's how a Spartan rolls. If Stephen calls with some excuse as to why he can't go out but suggests a house date alternative, Cali will tell him that she will get back to him. Not really. Number deleted! There will be no *Come Over & Chill* here, you fuck boy! This is Sparta. Anything other than, "I picked such and such... is that cool... what time will you be ready..." and Stephen gets deleted from her phone without mercy. It doesn't matter how cool he comes off, how attractive he is, or how witty his conversation. A man's seriousness must be proved via his actions before the dating even starts. That's how a Spartan fucking rolls!

Day 0: Recap

You may have gotten that, or you may be nervous and unsure if your verbal skills are on par to do any of the things Cali did. Let's rewind and walk you through this as slowly as Floyd Mayweather reading *Hamlet*.

STEP 1: THE EXCHANGE - RECAP

It doesn't matter where you meet a man or who that man happens to be. Chapter 7 showed Phoenix in three specific scenarios and this example had Cali meeting her guy at an ordinary place, randomly. It's never as hard as the average woman tries to make it out to be. Why? Because when you don't fear rejection, confidence comes easy! The only thing that has held you back from getting what you wanted was the thought of, "what if he doesn't like me." That negativity has been erased, so what else is there to fear? There is no embarrassment to be had when you talk to men, so the real you, the confident you, will always shine. The circumstances may not be ideal, but you must not buckle. There will most likely be other people around, strangers or friends. You may be several feet away from one another and forced to step out of your comfort zone and get closer. Be ready but don't force it. Know that a path will open up if you are meant to talk to each other. Cali's path was blocked by a phone distraction as well as him being several feet away. She didn't walk away, she let the universe bend to her will. Cali eventually found an opening to get his attention, and that's all you will need, a clear path to work your magic.

You cannot be overly reliant on eye-fucks and traditional introductions, know what opportunity looks like, and take it. If there is an opening where you can walk over to him, or call attention to yourself in order to get him to come to you, follow your instincts and trust in your power. You will attract men, but that doesn't mean everyone that you want will notice you, walk up to you, and exchange numbers. Do not get caught up in the typical world of waiting for a man to move first. Ask your universe to deliver and it will deliver, but you cannot be so shy that you stand back and let opportunity slip away because it wasn't delivered two inches from your face. Spartans snatch opportunity, they don't wait for further signs!

The exchange of numbers sets the tone for the follow up conversation. Be confident in your initial conversation, as it will be the first impression you project and give you something to callback to later on. In Cali's situation, she was able to call back that he was looking good in his suit and had his face buried in his phone. She noticed the details and used them to get her prey open. Be in the moment! Also, avoid lingering around. No matter where you meet a man, at a party where you won't be leaving, a bar where they are buying you rounds, online typing back and forth in an app; get in your flirting, ask the small questions, and either lead him to take your number or you take his number. Don't hang out! I've seen too many women end up going home with guys from the bar. Kissing a guy in the car after a party. Don't get too close too soon because your guard may drop, you will become comfortable, and real dating never happens. No matter where you are, escape. Excuse yourself after your drink and go to the restroom. Excuse yourself after a conversation and pretend to spot a friend you need to go mingle with. Excuse yourself from the message chat, and tell him you need to log out and finish up whatever. It doesn't matter the excuse, just find an exit. The goal is to get in and get out and save yourself as a mystery to be unwrapped on a date.

STEP 2: THE CALL - RECAP

Most of you will have your number taken, and be in the position where you have to wait for the man to call or text you first. This step still applies. If a guy texts you a few hours later telling you that he was glad to have met you, text back and tell him the same, but understand the goal is to transition him to a phone call. <u>Follow up and ask if he's free to talk later on</u>. This is where so many women make a crucial mistake. They continue texting back and forth all day because it's not as nerve wrecking as being on the phone. You must talk to him verbally, not electronically, before you actually agree to go on a date. There is no, "Text Text Text, let's meet here, Emoji Emoji Emoji" bullshit. You aren't some Basica on a blind date happy to show up somewhere with a stranger. You aren't desperate to where you say "yes" and go out with any guy that's cute and offers. You are a Spartan. Your time must be earned, and these men can only earn that right by going through this Day 0 Screening Stage. Texting is a horrible way to leave an impression with a new person because you can't read the tone most of the time. The two of you are assuming based on your own ideas of how those words look on screen. Unlike your friends, you don't know personality enough to read sarcasm or jokes. Therefore, he can turn you off quickly due to you misreading flirting as insulting or misreading a question as an assumption. Get off that texting ship as soon as you can.

Men are just as nervous as you are when first reaching out. To tell him to hit you later can translate to you being too busy for him because you're not really interested. He doesn't know if you are brushing him off or being serious about talking later. Therefore, you have to take control of the situation and be specific. If you want him to call you, give him a time, and follow up that you will be waiting, not in a commanding way, but in a happy excited way by adding a meme or emoji at the end so he knows you're not gaming him. If you have a schedule where you would prefer to call him, tell him that! Again, the fear is gone. Use your mouth and be direct.

Always remember to have a time set and agreed upon. Too many people leave it open ended and miscommunication occurs because you didn't check to see if he was free when you were free. Two missed calls later and it all falls apart because you think he's playing games when, in reality, it's on you for not specifying the plan. That may sound like doing too much, but too much of what, winning? Get what you want, and take control while doing it so there is no room for error. If he doesn't pick up, leave a message. It's not that serious where you text after you call him like a psycho or flip out with an attitude because he wasn't around when he said he would be free. Remember, ego and pride are weak emotions. Let go of attitude and anxiety, shoot your shot, and allow it to play out patiently. Alternatively, if the man calls you without texting first—good! This means you don't have to train him. You may feel as if you need time to get your mind right and your goal visualized. Spartans don't run, they improvise. Realize that any man you meet could call in two hours or in two days. Know what you want to say in case of either situation. A superior warrior always expects the unexpected.

The same rules apply regardless of who does the calling:
Put him at ease. Recon. Date bait.

The initial date setting call shouldn't last more than thirty minutes at most. If you find yourself on the phone laughing and carrying on, snatch yourself away because you're doing too much. The point is to find out enough to know that he's not some creep, that he's employed, and that he's sane enough to meet in public. There is no need for a long conversation at this stage, but you won't be able to help it if you click. If the two of you are hitting it off neither will want to get off the phone, but you have to exit in 30 minutes or less. Men have their own game plan; they get in your ear, flirt, put you at ease, and then get real familiar.

Here's where that has benefited me. By the time I once got off a three-hour phone conversation with this girl I met the day before, we had bonded so much that all I had to say is, "I need to see you as soon as possible, this chemistry is crazy." It wasn't chemistry it was my dick. To her, it was a guy actually being blown away enough to want to skip work and see her, and that made her feel like hot shit. It wasn't so much my game; it was her ego that led her to meet up with me the next day. No date, no real recon on me, but real sex. Be smarter. Don't let a man lullaby you with phone boning before you go on an actual date.

In terms of the questions you ask and the answers you get, they won't all be picture perfect like Stephen's responses. You may meet a man who may not have a great job or doesn't want to tell you what he does. It's very important to know these things before you go on a date, so don't be afraid to press. No woman should agree to meet out in public with "Tavon who does a bit of everything." If your friend were to try to file a missing person's report, it's better that she knows that you were going out with Tavon who worked at General Motors. "I get money" or "I work for my Uncle," isn't a respectable response. Position—does he have one? Not all men will be truthful, but at least, do your part.

You may get a man who has children. You have to decide if that is a deal breaker for you right then and there. My friend told me how she dated a guy who met all her qualifications and then some, but he had one drawback, a young child. He looked so good that she revamped her views on men with kids like, "I'll play step mom, he's that fine!" After weeks of dating, she realized that it was always going to be a deal breaker. Her lust for him didn't change the fact that she was not about the, "My man has kids by other women," life. She wasted weeks, when she should have kept it real the moment he said he had a son. It's okay to have selfish standards, and it's even better to own up to them starting out on Day 0. If you front for a man and lie to yourself to make him work, it will eventually catch up to you, causing you to back out after you put in this work. Be honest with yourself!

What if you are the one with children and he does his own recon? In *Solving Single,* I talked about dating with children, and I stand by the notion that you don't have to volunteer that information until he earns a first date. However, it's never good to start out with a lie if directly asked. If he brings it up during this first call, keep it real, and give him the same opportunity to back out that you would want at this stage. No need to get defensive and say, "Yes I do, is that going to be a problem," because if he agrees and follows through with this date, it's not. Some men will lie to your face and say they don't mind, then fallback using other excuses. Leave room for that. If he chooses not to call you back to officially set the date, good! It means he didn't want to waste your time. Men won't always speak up, so allow their actions to communicate what's real.

The final part is the *Date Bait*. Men don't always ask to take you out by default because we live in a world where guys realize they don't have to court for pussy the same way men of the past did. It is not that modern men won't date; it's that they would be foolish to spend money when you may be a *Come Over & Chill* type of girl. How does a man know that you aren't Fast Food Pussy? The only way is to test you by seeing what you allow in terms of treatment. As noted earlier, typical women allow these good looking, gainfully employed, men to get away with half-ass dates. Other women have lowered the bar, in response, you must raise yours that much higher. This doesn't mean you offer to take him out and go Dutch, it means you establish your standards as a woman that only goes on traditional dates.

Cali used her sensuality to tease her prey into jumping at a chance to take her out. Depending on the type of woman you are, there are literally dozens of ways you can date bait. <u>Assertive</u>: *Check your texts, I'm about to send you the place you're taking me this weekend.* <u>Witty</u>: *Describe your perfect date with me, so I can tell you the day and time this will happen.* <u>Cookie from Empire</u>: *I hope you're not one of these niggas that think you going to get my nookie with Hulu and a home cooked meal*! Whoever you are, let it come out naturally. Never shy away from establishing your standards.

In the end if he doesn't want to take you to that place you suggest, doesn't give you his own suggestion, or acts as if he's going to be too busy to go out for anything other than a quick drink or a house pop up, then he is not the man for you. I repeat, if he doesn't respond to the date bait by actually setting up a date, then his contact information leaves your phone that night!

STEP 3: THE BAIT - RECAP

There will be women who find a man they really like and get over eager while waiting to test this out. "But he hasn't called for me to do any of this! How long do I wait for him?" If you meet a man and give him your number, but he never hits you up. He doesn't want you. If you text him and he never responds back. He doesn't want you. If he waits a week to hit you up and does so at 2 am. He wants your pussy, but he doesn't want you. If you go to call him and he doesn't answer or return that call. Say it with me—he doesn't want your ass. This isn't about making every man take an interest in you; it's about exploiting the interest that a man has from the start. You can't win over a man that doesn't see you as his type.

Some males will flirt with you, talk that talk, even ask for your number, but never follow up. Spartans don't sit around and sulk about what went wrong. The proof is in the effort. If all the signs pointed to him being "different," then this is the biggest sign of them all: He's not the one. Do not dwell. There are too many men out here, you can't let the ones who don't respond be a speed bump. Day 0 ends with you setting that first date. If he doesn't make it to that part, then he doesn't count. Now that you know the steps to getting to the first date, let's get into the Day 1 activity.

Chapter 10:
Date Night Domination

*W*here should we go? What should we do? What should I wear? I'm not going to be specific in terms of the place or activity. I want this book to be used no matter your personality, no matter your city, and no matter the time of year. You will be asked out on various dates that cover a wide net of creativity. Be it a dinner, a play, drinks, fight party, bowling, movie, lunch picnic, etc... I want you to understand that it doesn't matter the backdrop, the actual conversation is what defines the success of a first date. In a perfect world, your first date should be a dinner date, some place quiet where you can use that corner booth or table as if it is a police interrogation room. You won't get the full truth from a man on the first date, but you will get glimpses of the real him if you are smart enough to push beyond the jokes, the work talk, and those bias stories that make him out to be Batman, cool & mysterious.

The mission of a first date is to hear this man out in order to see where he's coming from with his sales pitch. Is he trying hard to impress you, or is he half-assing because he thinks he has already won? Is he trying too hard to seem perfect, or is he being a real dude who can poke fun at himself? The best way to complete this mission is to look him in the eye with your bullshit filter set to high. You can't do that in a crowded room, while a movie is playing in front of you, or on a group date. Keep in mind that while a date is social and you will have fun, the primary focus as a Spartan is sport. The Arena has to benefit your mission or you risk spending a night with a man whom you learn absolutely nothing about, just reacting to the external events of the date.

<u>Where should you go?</u> Out where at least half of the date allows for private conversation. You can agree to Go Karting if you want to, but make sure that before or after that race there is someplace, not at his home or your home, where you can talk. The same rules apply to a movie date. Find time to get in conversation; don't be cool with sitting in the dark and holding hands. <u>What should you do?</u> I understand that women love to plan and prepare, but push the pressure of coming up with a good date night out of your head. Your presence makes it a good date. All the romance and elegance should be left up to him. If you are dealing with a man that wants you to make all the choices, Yelp search a romantic restaurant in the area, decide on the one with the best ambiance, and wash your hands with any big decisions. This isn't your friend from out of town who you need to show a good time. The first date is *his* interview, not *your* interview. A Spartan doesn't need to perform like a monkey in order to get a man to take her out again. You aren't even worried about going out again at this point; he still has to prove that he's compatible by passing this first test.

This Basica once told me, "I don't want to go out and sit in front of him, won't he find that boring?" The reason she said that was because she was boring and scared of being exposed as such. This is a battle of the mind, a dance of wits, one long conversation that will reveal nearly everything you need to know about this man. Insecure women prefer the distraction of a movie, the cover of a double date, or the filler of a physical activity because she can get by with laughs and chitchat. **This is Sparta**; you want to strip away the diversions so you can get to know this man.

<u>What should you wear?</u> If you look good you feel good, correction, you already look good; now you feel even better because you get to express your personality through your style. Dressing for your date is extremely important, not because you want that man to like you, or you want other people to turn their heads when you walk by. Your outfit is your armor. Christians wear crosses to feel that holy protection. Ratchets wear fake septum rings to feel Cleopatra bomb. Spartans too need something external to provide that extra confidence reminder. The right outfit creates a force field that no hater can burst, and even if nerves start to build, all you have to do is look in the mirror and be instantly reminded, "I'm bad as fuck!"

It's not enough to know that you're invincible, it also helps to physically see it every time you sneak a look at your reflection. The outfit you choose will also set the tone for the date. What color makes you feel good? What kind of shoe makes you feel tall? What message does your entire outfit send to that man in terms of your confidence, sexuality, and style? You project how you feel. If you feel unsure about what you're wearing, you will stumble, so don't wait until the last minute to throw something together, embrace dressing up like you're Vivian on Rodeo with Edward's credit card.

Visualize the morning you wake up for that date; picture him and then picture yourself. He can have the fashion sense of Kanye West, but next to you, he won't get any attention. How do you go about doing this? How can you steal the show, while making it seem effortless as opposed to extra? Additionally, what can you wear that says who you are as an individual? I always laugh at this idea of women shopping at these super-secret boutiques so they won't wear something another woman has on. It's not the dress; it's the woman in that dress that makes it special. Having style and being dressed, aren't the same damn thing. Even in a Forever 21 off the rack pantsuit, how are you going to impose your style? Some of you get it; others are going to feel bad you're not stylish or fancy. You're missing the point. You don't need to be Anna Wintour you need to be yourself.

No matter your budget, you can create a look that makes you feel like a goddess. If your brand is 80's rocker girl, even when rocking a little black dress, throw some accessory on that says, Joan Jett. If your brand is goofy girl, don't try to hide that. Take that same black dress, and wear some Looney Tune Chucks. Yeah, people will look, but that's who you are and when you look down at those shoes they will put you at ease! I have a friend who is a huge Tomboy, but when she steps out she always has heels that look like they were created by Zeus. Even in denim pants, she makes sure her ass is cuffed in a way that lets guys knows that she can play wrestle and still make you eat the booty like groceries. Know your brand and perfect your date look the morning of your date or even a day before. You're Supergirl without the cape, but that doesn't mean you forget to show up with the "S" on your chest.

Let me address the male mindset and how over thinking about what a man likes or doesn't like leads to unnecessary stress about what to wear. Tight, says sex. Cleavage, says sex. Shoulders revealed, says sex. Even heels say sex. You have a vagina underneath your clothes; as a man, all he sees is sex. You can't bend to this idea of, "I don't want to look like a thot," and sabotage your own sense of style in an attempt to come off virgin pure. You will always be objectified! "Men don't want a woman that dresses like a slut." Don't believe the hype. Even if you're wearing a Christmas sweater with pleather pants, a man will find something filthy to think about you when looking you up and down. The idea that you have to curtail your sex appeal to be taken serious, is more inflated than the lips on Kylie Jenner. You are going to be looked at like sex regardless, so instead of trying to fight objectification, embrace it, own it, and weaponized your femininity.

    <u>What look turns you on?</u> That's what you go with. Some men will try to slut shame you and some women will try to set a standard of what's classy for you to wear. You don't dress for the men who wish they could fuck you, nor do you dress for the women who are afraid that you will take attention away from them. You dress for your own sense of style. All jokes aside, if you want to wear some low cut skirt that keeps rising and pair it with spiked heels because that makes you feel good, do you! I'm not here to tell you to be safe; I'm here to tell you to be the ultimate version of yourself. The one warning I will give is that if you don't know how to properly do your own makeup, have someone do it for you, or go minimal. Your outfit will inspire lust even if it is skanky, but there is nothing sexy about a woman who walks in looking like Puddles the Clown. Now that's out of the way let's check in with Cali.

The Date

Stephen has made reservations at an Italian restaurant downtown, nothing too fancy, but a level above the 2 for $20 chain restaurants like Applebee's. Cali begins her mental checklist by giving Stephen a gold star for being creative enough not to suggest some generic place that everyone has been to before. Picking a place off the beaten path tells her he's actually trying to impress her rather than reaching for an easy place twenty minutes away from his home. Cali has deferred being picked up, she's not ready for

Stephen to know her address, nor does she want to feel dependent on him dropping her back off when he's ready. Although her car is in the shop and it would be easier for him to scoop her, she is still going to meet him there on her own dime to maintain her privacy.

In terms of wardrobe, Cali's outfit has been picked out for a few days. She doesn't have money to waste buying something new, so she went into her closet to make something old look Easter fresh. A fitted pair of red leather pants, a drape neck black blouse, and a pair of six-inch open toe heels that she's been holding off wearing for months now. She is casual chic, and her makeup adds just enough, "Yes, I'm grown" sex appeal by highlighting her thick lips and seducing eyes.

Cali is not overdressed for this type of restaurant, so there is no fear of coming off like a girl who doesn't go anywhere trying to do too much just because she's been let out of the house. Cali isn't giving off a "he's just a friend," vibe by dressing down. She understands that men like candy, so she is happy to show her wrapper as if he has a shot at first night sex. Cali knows she looks like sex because she feels like sex, but her attitude is always that of a lady on the surface. The date is set at 7 pm, so Cali figures she will get there at 7:10 pm. She's not trying to be immature and make Stephen sweat it out, she wants to see what he's made of. There are men who will wait in front of the establishment unsure if they should go in. There are men who will go to the bar and order two drinks, one for him, and one for his arriving date. Then there are men who take this time to make sure the table available is the perfect one for his lady. Cali isn't expecting anything other than the truth. Stephen will have revealed one of many personality traits based on how he deals with her tardiness, and given Cali easy intel on his character.

Cali exits her Uber at 7:10 on the dot and walks up to the restaurant. Before she even gets to the hostess, Stephen is there to greet her. She apologizes for being late but doesn't mean it of course. Stephen compliments her outfit, and Cali responds with her own admiration of the shirt that he's picked out for this evening. Cali slyly pokes Stephen's chest, seeing how hard body he is, then shoots a seductive smile. She's already under Stephen's skin: Touch him, eye fuck him, and draw attention to her epic lips currently painted devil red. The date hasn't even started and Stephen's blood pressure is already on the rise. Stephen tells Cali that it may be another minute as he requested a booth instead of the table they tried to sit them at. Another Gold Star. Stephen arrived early and made sure to set the mood as he saw fit. He took control like a man and ensured they had a good seat, not a table tightly fitted next to another couple. Cali appreciates that take-charge attitude, and while she won't say this, Stephen is already winning in her book. The two are seated in the booth across from each other and like a referee starting a championship fight; the waiter excuses himself to allow time for the couple to look over the menu. Ding Ding! This is the official start of the first date and Cali came prepared to fight.

BREAK THE ICE

Stephen is anxious, nervous, and a bit excited. Cali can see it all over his face as his eyes dart all around her, not sure if he should give another compliment or let the first one stand as good enough. He will reach for conversation about the restaurant first, asking if he picked something up to her standards. Next, he'll scan over the menu, looking for something funny to bring up, maybe a strange name of a drink or entrée that will make Cali laugh. This is how most men come off on dates; they try hard in an attempt to seem as if they aren't trying at all. Stephen's grin hides his lack of control. He's unsure if he should be funny, serious, or a combination of both. In short, Stephen is trying to find the mask he should wear that will most impress Cali. A typical woman will sit and wait for a man to move his pawn first, and then go into a reactive mode trying to be a "Cool Girl."

Cool Girls laugh at any joke; answer all questions, and generally, only focus on following the man's lead so he likes her that much more. By the time, they have to order, the male who started off nervous, will grow with confidence and dominate the Cool Girl. He will control the pace, control the date, and if he's smooth enough, control her mind. Cool Girls don't understand male psychology; their only objective is to not fuck it up by being rude, opinionated, or goofy. Cali is far from typical. She doesn't need to be a Cool Girl because she's not trying to earn brownie points. She sees through the forced coolness Stephen is trying to exude, and like a true Spartan, she's going to use that hidden nervousness to control him. There will be no winning her over with slick talk, making her uncomfortable with questions, or causing her to submit with flirting. Cali is about to go on the offensive and take this date in a direction few women dare.

Men are little boys. Little boys like to play games. After the waiter leaves, Cali puts out her pinky finger, "Let's make a bet that you can't guess what I'll order." Stephen is a bit intrigued, "You want me to guess now?" Cali shakes her head and fills him in, "I'm going to text you right now what I want. But don't look. When the waiter comes, order for me. After you do, look at your text to see if you chose right." Now Stephen is charmed. He sits up in his chair, dropping all the fake cool shit that he was thinking to do in his head, and gets ready to have fun. This girl has already proven interesting, and he has to match her intrigue. Stephen, now super open, asks what he gets when he wins the bet. Cali is now prepared to fully break the ice that exists between all people that are physically attracted to each other. She leans in and says, "You get a kiss. Full tongue." Stephen jokes that he was already going to get one of those, and Cali says that she only hugs on the first date, never kisses. Cali hasn't gone full blown *Ho Tactics* with her flirting, but she still wants to plant the seed in this man's head that he may get something that no other man gets. Stephen, of course, wants to play cat and mouse, "So why don't you kiss on the first date?" Stephen doesn't know that he's the mouse, not the cat. Cali ignores his question and goes about texting him her order to start the game. After she's done, she rubs her foot against his foot and tells him not to cheat and look. Stephen has gone from confused date trying to throw on his playboy mask to giddy little kid. His cool is off, and the ice has been broken. Remember, men are little boys!

Cali's game is not really a game at all, but a recon. She gave this man the right to order her food for her under the guise of a joke. Will he order the cheap ass chicken dish, go for the sexy salmon, or cash out with the Lobster-Steak combo? This game gives insight into how much money Stephen is prepared to spend and what kind of class level he sees Cali at in terms of food. In terms of drinking, Cali will not push for a cocktail. If Stephen wants to ball out and order a bottle of wine, she will be forced to partake, but even then, she'll display her skill in terms of the fake sip. It's important to stay mentally sharp on a first date. Cali can drink with the best of them, but she knows that sexual chemistry and alcohol can cloud the mind. Stephen orders a Manhattan and asks Cali what she's going to have.

155

Cali gives the excuse that she just took her allergy medicine and has to pass. Throughout the night, Cali will make sure Stephen stays with a full glass because liquor can be a truth serum. He may think that she's being a prude, but no man's opinion matters. In actuality, she's laying the groundwork that will ensure that Stephen plays into her hand by getting turned on, slightly inebriated, and by the middle of the date, he will be open to her mind control. Now that the ice is melting, it's time to break this man down.

Let Him Talk

Random questions that come with long stories are a woman's bread and butter when on a first date. Cali is ready to settle Stephen down with some seriousness now that she's shown her playful side. Asking questions with personality as opposed to reading off generic inquiries as if you're going off a teleprompter is key. A basic bitch would begin with, "So how long have you been on your job." Who gives a fuck really? "Where did you grow up?" That's a one-sentence answer that will tell you zilch. "What's the longest relationship you've been in?" No man wants to talk about his old bitch, but all men are prepared to talk about it in a way that makes him seem innocent or a victim of a she-beast. Men are always trying to sound perfect and this plays perfectly into the heart of a typical female's ego. Most women want to hear that the man they are crushing on has been the right man for the wrong woman for all of these years, and finally, destiny has brought them to each other. Blah! These women don't want to hear the truth about this Blue Chipper being just as flawed as the girl he chose, just as prone to mistakes as other men, or anything that raises red flags.

Avoid ultra-basic questions like, "So what are you looking for?" Really, bitch? Do you honestly expect any man to tell you that he's looking for no strings attached pussy from a woman that won't call him too much, over-text, or stalk his timeline? Typical women ask typical questions that men are prepared to answer with preplanned responses that make them sound great. "He said he was looking for something serious on our first date... but a month later that's not what he seems to want because he hasn't asked me to be official." Do you want to be the moronic woman that says that or do you want to expose the wants of this man in a real way? It's all about the line of questions you ask, the more creative the more revealing!

Cali is not a simpleton. She won't lose the momentum she has and say something that will make her date retreat into his "representative" who says the right things. She wants to see the real him. Cali pumps the break on the current subject and asks, "What's the closest you ever came to smacking a bitch?" Stephen laughs. Cali is serious and expands, "I'm talking high school and above, not some little cunt that teased you in elementary school. Who pushed your buttons to the point that you nearly stepped out of character and laid hands?" Stephen tries to be politically correct and says he would never do that. Cali pushes forward, "Bored now! C'mon give me some fire, baby." Cali has just called this man out on several levels. She's the Queen waiting to be entertained, and Stephen feels pressured to answer.

Unlike, "tell me about your Ex," this isn't a question a man will have rehearsed nor one he has experience answering. Stephen has to actually think and tell the truth because there is no time to make up something. He submits and tells of a girl his first year of college who was the girlfriend of his roommate. She hung in their room all the time, eating their food, and acting as if she owned the place. As Stephen remembers this girl, he starts to get into a rage, that's how Cali knows this is real. No one recalls emotional moments dryly, they relive that moment. If a man's eyes don't widen or his hands don't move while telling a story, he's making it up. Stephen is actually recalling that moment and Cali feels the realness. Stephen and this girl got into it over her freeloading and she reacted like a bitch. He wanted to smack the hell out of her, but it wasn't worth it in terms of jail or ending his friendship with his roommate. Cali has him open; it's not about this college story from years ago. She's being a therapist, getting this man comfortable enough to start telling things that are more personal.

BE OPRAH, NOT ELLEN

Cali's random question now leads into internal feelings and motivation. Did Stephen really want to fuck that girl? Was his anger really a result of sexual tension? Stephen denies it, saying the girl wasn't his type. This opens him up to what his type is without being too forward. Cali doesn't have to ask, "So what's your type?" and have Stephen be PC. By framing it within a past story, she can say, "Why wasn't this girl your type," with the focus on that girl, yet it still tells her how Stephen really feels about all women. Cali teases, "in college I thought pussy is the default type for men, don't tell me you were one of those, I'm looking for wifey types in undergrad?" Again, Cali is challenging Stephen to be different, not some sweetheart. Men want to be men, but on dates, they are forced to protect how savage they come off, for fear of turning a girl off. Cali is unleashing this man's realness by daring him to be a bad boy. Stephen admits he hooked up with a few girls he would never take home to his mother, and that while his roommate's girlfriend wasn't ugly, she didn't have an attitude that turned him on. Stephen has been lead to talk, and like any man, he will explain his wants without any further questions because Cali triggered a topic that this man actually wants to expand upon. Stephen will go into how he doesn't like ghetto girls, his problem with women around his age, and even get on a soapbox about how women today don't know how to be women.

This isn't offensive to Cali because she too knows how annoying most women can be. She simply sits and nods, allowing Stephen to vent. As he winds down, Cali hits him again, "What's the nastiest thing you did in college sexually, and if you say something corny like doggy style, I'm walking out." Stephen again is faced with a random question. He was prepared to talk more about his "type" or "attitude" but Cali threw him a curve ball and made it about sex. Stephen has no idea who this woman is, and he's sweating. The waiter comes back for the order; Stephen is saved by the bell.

Stephen loses the bet by choosing fish. Cali reveals that she's a lamb girl. Stephen checks the text she sent for the right answer, and it confirms that she wanted the lamb. No kiss. His spirits drop, but Cali rubs her foot against his, teasing him, but also giving him some physical touch that makes it seem as if the door is still open for that kiss. Back to the conversation, Cali doesn't care about how nasty Stephen was in college, and the break in conversation gave him time to think about a lie, so she once again goes random. This time, it's about something she needs to know about his character, as opposed to another warm up question. Stephen is now drinking, and it's time to get deep. Cali doesn't want to make the same mistakes she made in her last relationship so the next few questions will be about personal deal breakers, and direct back to her last heartbreak.

Cali's relationship history includes two serious boyfriends. The one with the biggest red flag was her boyfriend of two years who felt held back by being in a relationship. This Ex wasn't ready to commit, but he knew that was the only way Cali would fuck him, so he gave her an empty title. This resulted in a hollow relationship that had more downs than ups. Cali blamed herself for forcing a man to enter into a relationship when the signs pointed to him not being ready and imagined after their breakup that if she would have lowered her bar and allowed him to play the role of "friend" with a little sex it could have developed into something stronger.

That was Nicole's theory. Nicole was a weak bitch. Spartan Cali knows that nothing she did would have changed that man's inability to be in a loyal monogamous relationship. **She was title hunting, instead of partner inspecting.** Her mistake was picking a boyfriend whose character she didn't research. She was too busy being Ellen DeGeneres, fun loving, sweet, and only asking softball questions that kept things upbeat and chill. As a result, she got in a relationship with a man that never really wanted her on a deep level. This could have been prevented if Cali went for the character instead of focusing on the title. Cali, back in those Nicole days, was concerned with being a cool, stress-free, zero pressure girl that did not scare men off. She allowed a non-serious man to give her a non-serious relationship because in her mind any relationship meant that she was wanted and that he would act accordingly once in a relationship. Cali is no longer Ellen she's Oprah. She's going to challenge these men to open up, and reveal their story before she even thinks about a relationship.

Cali plays Devil's Advocate in order to make Stephen comfortable. "What do you think about these title chasers?" Stephen has no clue what she's referring to, so Cali continues, "Those girls that live to get a boyfriend, just so they can say they have a boyfriend. If you were dating a girl who you wanted to take it slow with but she was giving you lame ass ultimatums, would you cave in order to shut her up? ...I mean it's not like the title really means anything." Stephen shakes his head, claiming that he would never be with someone he didn't really want to be with and that no woman can force anything on him. Cali retorts, "I mean if it was me with the dick and Jhené Aiko was bae chasing, I'd tell her I would be her white knight, fuck her, and then bounce." Cali seems serious, she is selling that her way is the smart way. At the same time, she's being totally understanding of a man's right to put sex first. Now it's on Stephen to answer honestly knowing that he has an out to be a dog. He could continue to say that he wouldn't compromise the title for sex, or he can be peer pressured into saying, he'd fuck and run because it is just a title. There is no right or wrong answer, only the truth that will tell Cali about Stephen's true character.

Stephen remains true to himself. He says the sex isn't worth giving someone the title. He takes the title seriously; he's not the type to call just any female his girlfriend. This is the answer Cali was hoping for, and now that Stephen is vulnerable, it's time to go in for the kill. "**Where did you go wrong in your last relationship**?" Cali needs to be giving out cars to the audience, that's how fucking Oprah she is right now. It's not about his ex-girl, how they met, how long it lasted, or any generic question. It's about the ultimate job interview question most people struggle with: *What are your weaknesses*. Stephen is exposed, and there is no way to retreat with this line of questioning. She is not asking where his ex-girlfriend went wrong, the circumstances of the relationship ending, or any outside forces involved. The only question is: Where did he go wrong. At this moment, Cali has full control over this date. Not once has she talked about her exes, her job, her family, none of that bullshit chitchat, it's all been about Stephen's life. She slowly built up from small random questions that told a little and patiently built it up to a big question that tells a lot.

INTERMISSION

The arrival of the main course is the best time to call a truce and let the man breathe. Therefore, Cali prepares to dig into the Mahi-mahi dish that she would have never ordered, and calls a mental timeout. At this point in the date, it's not about Cali eating, telling Stephen how good his dish looks, or complaining to the waiter about something being wrong. That's all surface level bullshit interaction. The real goal of this timeout is to ask, "Do I still like him." That question is something that many women are afraid to ask, but Cali can't afford to waste her time trying to make a man fit because he looks good. The first half of the date, from the restaurant selection to the way he answered those random questions, left an initial impression. Answering the "Where did you go wrong," inquiry solidified her views.

Let's go back and see how it played out: **Where did you go wrong in your last relationship?** Stephen opened up about his past, admitting that he didn't always make as much time as he should have with his ex-girlfriend because the transition from junior to lead account manager was stressful. It wasn't so much his job, but his own obsession to do good that caused him to shut her out. Stephen didn't blame his ex for being too needy, he took the bullet and confessed that he has to work on letting people in even when he's stressed and stop trying to carry it all inside. That was Stephen's "weakness" answer, which was an honest response that wasn't rehearsed because he was not expecting a question about his own flaws.

When women talk about dating requiring too much "energy" it's because most of them pour themselves into every man 100%. Cali hasn't given Stephen anything but flirty texts, a cute phone call, playful icebreaking, and a series of questions. Unlike typical women, Cali hasn't over shared. There has been very little emotional energy spent in terms of conversation and digging into her own life and views. Stephen, on the other hand, has been forced to open up and exert real energy. Men aren't used to dating like this, they are used to nodding and joking. Cali isn't in the habit of allowing a man to be emotionally unavailable; thus, she cracked him open thirty minutes into the date.

At this intermission, Cali will choose to put her own energy into Stephen by sharing a little bit more of who she is, a reward for being honest. Alternatively, she could choose to just keep things light, finish her food, and decide that the things Stephen has shared aren't in line with what she's looking for in a mate. Ultimately, Cali is in control of going south, meaning blowing her date off, or going north meaning that she continues to invest in her date as if he could be something real. Let's look at both paths.

GOING SOUTH

Let's imagine that Stephen answered all the inquiries in a way that turned Cali off. He had long pauses before speaking, seemed annoyed with her questions, and was dodgy with his answers. When she hits the intermission, what does she do? She can't get up and leave, it's not as if he disrespected or offended her to the point where she can't enjoy the meal gracefully. The dislike level on a date is rarely going to be extremely negative like in the movies where a man puts his feet on the table, calls the waiter something racist, and demands the woman order a salad appetizer as her entrée. Hell Dates aside, you have to be prepared to judge this man hard on how honest and forthcoming he is being with the small things. Most likely, the dislike will be subtle, not blatant in a petty, "I don't like men that chew with their mouths open," or "He didn't pull my seat out for me," way.

A real life deal breaker could be something like Stephen saying something offensive about the girl he wanted to smack, maybe about her race, skin complexion, or weight. It could be about Stephen confessing that if a girl is ready to give herself away just for a title, he would take it, she's the dumbass that's prostituting herself for the label of girlfriend. Finally, it could be one of the most common reasons I've seen women give in terms of turn offs, cockiness. That final question about weakness could have been answered not with honesty and humility, but with, "I didn't do anything wrong, the problem isn't with me. These broads expect you to lay up under them and not live your life!" If Stephen had let his ego and elite attitude throw himself a pity party, that would have shown Cali that their personalities were going to clash down the line.

Yes, they could finish the date with no problem, go on another, and even have sex, but in the end, she can't stand a man that thinks his shit doesn't stink, so it's best to stop at one date with a man like this rather than risk him hanging around and growing on her. Therefore, at the intermission Cali asks, "Do I still like him," and she answers "not really." She wants to like him because he's handsome, funny, and has his life going in the right direction, but a legit red flag has come out, so fuck him. The rest of the date plays out with less random questions that dig and moves into general chitchat. Cali no longer needs to interview this potential employee;

no way is he getting the job, so why keep up the third degree? Nevertheless, she's taken this break in her schedule so she's going to enjoy the entertainment of general conversation and a free meal.

Going South, Cali talks about basic shit like TV shows or celebrity gossip. The date died at the intermission, this is just the funeral. By the time she gets in her Uber, she won't be thinking of Stephen, he's literally dead. Alternatively, if Cali was feeling frisky she could use this dead date as practice. It's always smart to test out new tricks and new ways to flirt with men who don't mean anything. When you have reached a point in the date when you know you will not go out with the man again, it becomes like a comedian at an open mic, just trying out new material to prepare for the real gig down the line. Cali and Stephen share laughs, talk dirty, and in Stephen's mind, he thinks that this is going to end back his place or, at least, he'll set something up for the weekend... little does he know that all he will get is a hug and, "I'll call you." Stephen will be blocked the next morning. Cali does not date for potential; she has to feel that fire throughout.

GOING NORTH

Let's go the other route, where our guy Stephen has answered the same way as earlier in this chapter. He has been honest, funny, and showed vulnerability. Cali asks herself at the intermission, "Do I still like him," and the answer is, "I like him even more." This is what we call a "Good Date," in Sparta. So many people say the date was good based on basic shit or the fact that he didn't do something ignorant or come off as cheap. It is not about a man holding serve by being entertaining while you eat food; it's about him being impressive and candid. Has this man shown signs of being different from the rest? Yes. Stephen has answered every question with flying colors and now it's up to Cali to keep that positive energy flowing.

The entire date cannot be a series of random questions. You are always vetting character, but there is also a need to see if you connect. Cali isn't a serious person, she's serious about her heart and whom she lets in, but she loves to have fun in general. It's time to give Stephen glimpses of the things she's passionate about, to see if there is something in common besides sexual chemistry. The next part of the date will lay the foundation for future dates as it tests the things they have in common. Which of Cali's passions interest Stephen? Which of Stephen's passions interests Cali? What can Cali teach Stephen? What can Cali learn from Stephen? This is the next hurdle to see how far Stephen makes it after this date.

As Cali waits for the waiter to bring her fresh pepper for her bland ass fish, she poses the question, "There can only be three songs on repeat for an entire five-hour flight. Which ones would you pick?" Cali's a music nerd, so she can't be with someone who would put Young Thug on their playlist above Tupac or The Beatles, so Cali waits for Stephen to finish chewing and answer. He begins to smile because he's afraid to be judged, but he goes for it. Two rap songs that Cali's never heard of and Marvin Gaye and Tammi Terrell's "You're All I Need to Get By," this is the track that leads to further discussion. Once again, Stephen opens up. That song reminds him of his mother, as opposed to a romantic relationship, because she would always listen to it when he was younger. They then get into the old versus new debate, what era had the best music... Finally ending on Stephen reversing it back on Cali about her favorite songs. Music talk doesn't fizzle out, it goes from learning to debating, to each suggesting albums the other should listen to immediately. By the time dessert comes, they can take a break from that and start to venture into other topics. Cali just finished reading *The Tipping Point*, she throws that out as a feeler, and Stephen suggests that she reads *The New Jim Crow*. Stephen gives a rundown of the theme, and she can tell he has a lot to teach her about this area of sociology. Things are going great, but Cali isn't about to sit on a four-hour dinner date, so it is time to exit.

There is a lot more to be talked about that hasn't even been touched, and even though Cali finds Stephen easy to talk to and fun, she knows that those discussions need to be saved for later. Always leave a man wanting more, not struggling to think of more to say once you've exhausted the conversation. Cali doesn't have work the next day, but she's created a busy morning scenario. She has to be up at the crack of dawn, so she needs to get to bed soon. Stephen, like any man, will try to squeeze more time in. Cali hasn't said anything sexual or shared anything deeper than her love of music, but here this man is wanting to cage her all night. Why? Cali is in control and Stephen is smitten. He hasn't gotten her open yet, and he knows it. If men fail to enchant on a level, which they are used to enchanting, then they will always want to keep going until they win.

Every man wants to feel as if a girl is on his dick, and when that doesn't happen he will try to extend the date. The male ego is fueled by the sense of winning every time out, but no matter how "perfect" Stephen is, this game was rigged. Cali had no intention of letting him win no matter how smooth, honest, and open he came off. Cali has to go. She sees the sadness in his eyes, rubs his hands, and says, "Next week I'll pick the place, and I'll make sure I don't have a curfew." Kill shot. She's like a Marvel Comics movie, just when you think it's over; seeds are laid for the upcoming sequel. Stephen warms up to that, the no curfew line makes him think "pussy next time," so in addition to enjoying her company he has the motivation of possibly enjoying her body if he repeats this performance. This dog isn't quite on the leash, but he has just been collared.

WRAP IT UP

A man is water, your personality is Kool-Aid, and sexual chemistry is the sugar. At the end of the date, if things have gone great, there has to be a moment when you solidify the idea that you would fuck him by mixing in the sugar. The bill comes. Stephen grabs it to see the damage. Spartan Cali doesn't reach to pay half or offer a tip. This is the first date, it's on Stephen to roll out the red carpet, therefore, any generosity on Cali's end has to be held back until at least the third date. Cali does what any woman should, she says "Thank you, baby," and smiles. That thank you goes a long way. Men love appreciation, it's really the best reward you can give the male ego. Remember this, as your old pre-programmed mind likely felt that offering money was a proper form of reciprocation. Nope, "Thank you" is king!

Cali exits to the restroom while Stephen pays the bill and figures out the tip. Cali hasn't decided if she's going to kiss Stephen or not, but she's going to make sure her breath is fresh just in case. She exits the restroom and asks Stephen if he's ready. The two exit. Stephen doesn't know how Cali got to the restaurant and offers to walk her to the car. Cali tells him that her Uber ride will be there soon. The truth is she hasn't even ordered it yet. Cali wants, at least, ten minutes to pour her sugar on him.

Outside, Cali declines Stephen offer to drive her, again she doesn't know this man enough to be allowing him to pop up at her crib. Not to be mean, Cali moves in closer to him, "I'm fine, but you can keep me warm while we wait." When two mutually attractive men and women allow their bodies to break that personal space line, fireworks happen. Stephen wraps an arm around Cali; again, he's trying to be a gentleman. Cali moves even closer, her arms folded at her stomach, she pushes against his chest and lays her head on his shoulder. To wrap her arms around Stephen and stare into his face while talking would be too much for a first date, and at this point, Cali isn't sure that she truly is that dick disciplined to walk away if things get heavy. This position puts them close, the bodies are jumping, but it's not overly sexual. From here, Cali begins to reward Stephen for the date.

Men have paranoid egos, if they spend any amount of money without getting anything physical, a part of them will question if this was a hustle. Cali isn't running *Ho Game*, but Stephen doesn't know this. With her head nuzzled on his shoulder, Cali begins to tell Stephen how fun it was. She really feels as if they connected and that he's interesting. Cali is sure to use the keywords, "Connect," "Fun," "Interesting," because that's what men clamor for. They want to be a good time, they want to be unique in their presentation, and they want to feel as if a woman felt a deeper connection. Cali didn't find out the meaning of fucking life from this dude, but that's not the point. This is an ego stroke done with her body close to his dick. Cali is taming the snake by going through the earlobes instead of the zipper, and that's what makes her so good at what she does. The car arrives and Cali gives Stephen a deep hug. Cali isn't above a kiss, but she can't have him trying to steal control at the end. Cali quickly pecks Stephen on the lips. Stephen wants to keep going. Cali smiles, gives one quicker peck, and pulls away as if it's breaking her heart to do so. "Next time..." Cali smiles as she backs away and enters the car. Stephen knows that Cali likes him, he feels as if he's one more night away from having her, and any thoughts of her "bluffing" are long gone. This is all a mind-fuck, Cali does like him but he's nowhere close to sex. He is on her string and over the next few weeks; she will keep pulling until he reveals who he truly is.

NIGHTCAP

Any decent man is going to hit a girl up to make sure she arrived safely, but this is never to be used to have an After-Date. Text conversations about, "Did you make it home," shouldn't last more than two texts. Cali made it home, this date was better than she thought it would be, and honestly she's still excited... and a bit moist. However, this is just the first lap. There have been guys in the past who have failed after this point, so she can't get ahead of herself with fantasy thoughts. Stephen texts her that he's home and asks if she's in bed? Cali responds that she is, thanks him again, kiss emoji. Stephen can respond, but that is Cali's final contact for the night. Cali isn't going to be able to go to sleep, she's revved up with excitement like any girl who had a great date, but she'll chill out and stay away from social media. There no need to e-brag about basic shit, good dates are normal. Cali is going to lay back, chill, and get ready mentally for the next part of the game.

Chapter II:
Mastering the First Date

C an you do what Cali just did? I'm not talking about the specifics of where she went, what she wore, or the repeating the exact questions she asked. Can you stay in control, set the tempo, remain offensive, peel a man's layers back to reveal him as a turn-off or even more of a turn on, seduce him, and then walk away without compromising that control? Sounds like a lot, but it's easy. None of these things requires being overly intelligent or even quick witted. It's as simple as a job interview. As the employer you know what kind of employee you need, you go in with a list of qualities, and you hit each point throughout the evening by using indirect questions. I'm going to recap the big points you need to hit once again, but this time, I will use your own self-doubt to show you how easy it is to dominate any man on your first date.

Date Goal: Be Sexy
Rebuttal: But I'm Not Sexy

If you don't see yourself as anything special, then why the fuck would anyone else? I'm not promoting unrealistic thoughts like "all women are equally pretty," I'm promoting realistic thoughts that you aren't competing with other women of the world, only the woman looking back at you in the mirror. Your feelings on your reflection are the only thing you need to win over. The goal isn't to hold yourself up against Scarlett Johansson and take a poll of who men think looks the best. The goal is to appreciate your brand of sexy. Not every woman has a Spartan mindset when it comes to their physical appearance, it may be one of the hardest things to develop, but it must be done. If you haven't mastered Chapter V, then what are you doing this far into the book? Just reading? Seeing what bits you can take to use in your non-Spartan typical life? Stop it! Being unhappy with your looks will sabotage this entire mission because you will feel awkward instead of sexy. When you feel awkward, you hold back. When you hold back, you come off as basic. We do not date with that weak outlook on physical appearance, so no matter how long it takes for you to fall in love with that person staring back at you in the mirror, hold off on dating, and put in that time!

The first thing Cali hit on day one was her look. In terms of the actual outfit, Cali dressed in a way that made her sexiness obvious, tight clothes, tall heels, boobies sitting in a way that says, "I'll breastfeed you, daddy." That was on purpose. Cali knows how her body looks, she accentuated the positives and hid those parts she is still trying to chisel, but if she were to check a mirror, all she would see was a bad bitch. You project what you feel, which is why you must pre-plan the outfit so you aren't 15 minutes before the date hating what's looking back at you in the mirror.

Some women dress for a date the same way they dress for a hangout session with a book club, and then proclaim, "This is me, love it, or leave it." That's a cop out. Dressing in a way that makes you feel like a Queen is just as important as acting like a Queen. Key word being "you." I don't want you rushing out and buying some Instagram boutique thot dress because you think men want that, forget the men, it's about you expressing your own version of sexy. When you look in that mirror with the clothes you think are cute enough to hang with Karen, that isn't the same feeling you get when you look in the mirror wearing an outfit you would rock to Diddy's party. For those of you who aren't Fashionistas don't skip this step because you don't want to invest time and money into dressing up. It's just a date, but you need your armor to say, Slayer not Sister.

Makeup products are at an all-time high, not because women need it more than any other time in history, it's because just like cell phones, the innovations being done are incredible. Do not think of makeup as hiding. If you have bags under your eyes that you hate or scars that take your own opinion down a notch, cover it! If that gets you mentally where you need to be on this date, use it because your own mind is where the battle takes place.

170

However, don't use makeup as a crutch. If you're only covering things for fear of a man's opinion knowing that your blemishes don't bother you or that your nose being contoured doesn't make you feel any different, then you're placating. If you are comfortable in your skin then show up without the concealer because if you love it, fuck what he thinks. This is you 24-7, so it is better that he sees it now, than be surprised later. The point is to be armed for that first date with a look that makes you as confident as possible, but that real confidence should already be in place.

Date Goal: Protect Your Privacy
Rebuttal: I Want Him to Pick Me Up

A big rule my female friend has is, "No man is seeing my crib, I don't know if he's crazy yet." That's a great rule because access to someone's home can lead to problems if the date doesn't go well and your suitor isn't mentally stable. I'm not talking just in terms of violence but in terms of stalking, which happens often when a man won't get the hint. If you have a car, it's better to meet up at the location. Spending money on gas is a small price to pay for privacy. Someone popping up on you because you block them after the first or second date is not a situation that I want any woman to experience. Some of you live in cities where you don't need cars to get to work; others don't have vehicles in the budget. Don't feel ashamed if you do not have a car. Cali's example shows you how easy it is to date minus wheels.

A lot of dating anxiety comes from women not feeling as if they are on a level where a man would want them in terms of money and possession. A man won't care if you don't have a car unless he's a bum without his own vehicle looking to get rides or a cheapskate who doesn't want to spend his gas money. Don't let insecurities force you to refuse a date because you don't have transportation. Taxis are in every city. Uber is even cheaper. Having a friend drop you off doesn't make you look young. These are alternatives that protect your home life, so don't feel ashamed.

Let's say you do have a car, but you prefer the man to come pick you up like in an episode of *Family Matters*. Cool! You don't have to be protective of your address if that's not your personality. I don't want to make it seem as if all men are going to be waiting to Sharon Tate you the night after your date. There are more sane people than lunatics, so if you are comfortable and prefer the traditional, "Meet me at my address, bring flowers" method you are allowed to do that. In this case, the only thing that changes is that you don't arrive late and see how he responds to waiting. When he arrives at your house, be ready. This isn't prom; he doesn't have to park, come in, and talk to your parents. This man may not make it to a second date, so avoid any family or roommate introductions that don't have to be made. He can meet you at the door, walk you to his car, open the door, and drive off. Treat actual entry to your house, apartment, dorm room, trailer, or wherever you live, as special. A man only enters if he earns it later on, not the first night because he has to use the bathroom.

Date Goal: Break the Ice
Rebuttal: But How Do I Break the Ice If...

There are dozens of different date scenarios that don't have a clear start like the beginning of a meal. Even at a dinner date, it may not be in your character to create a fun game like, "guess my order for a treat." Before we get into variations of how to break the ice, understand why you must break the ice. As a man that's been on various levels of dates, from girls that I wanted more than oxygen to girls that were only pussy, there is always nerves on a man's end, no matter how cool he seems. A man that thinks you may be "The One" is just as masked as a man trying to fuck and fallback. Removing that mask by taking things from formal to casual early on will help make it easier for him to open up.

Even if you talked when you first exchanged numbers and talked when setting the date, you are still strangers. One woman spent an hour at a barbecue talking to a guy, and then their actual date was horribly dry. For some reason, the conversation wasn't as flowing as when they first met. Don't get cocky and think that the date is just a continuation of what you talked about when you first exchanged numbers. The stakes have changed, He doesn't know what you really think of him, therefore, he has to come off the best way possible to either get sex or get you on his team.

Who is this woman, and how do I act around her to impress her? That's the anxiety that men don't talk about because they have to seem as if they are cooler than a cucumber in Calgary. Just like Cali put Stephen at ease before digging into his psyche, you have to literally make that man feel as if he has nothing to worry about while still using that nervous energy as fuel for you to tease him. A great dentist develops a gift for chitchat because a comfortable patient allows a dentist to stick that needle in their mouth without even realizing they were being suckered into opening wide. You are about to molest a man's brain, so put him at ease.

Improvising will be a big part of any date, so be prepared to break the ice no matter the setting. Let's go back to the scenario where your date picks you up from home. If it's about twenty minutes to get to the restaurant, then that's twenty minutes you use to break the ice. Don't sit there listening to music talking about how your day went, that's nothing more than pleasantries. "Do you let women drive your car and by women I mean me later tonight?" That gets him talking and smiling. You don't want to drive his car, and you're not going to drive it, it's just something fun to say to get him loose about a subject most men enjoy—cars. If you two are at a bowling alley just drinking, then break the ice by giving the game stakes like, "Loser has to give a lap dance to the winner right in front of all these people." You two could meet at a park to walk and grab a snack, use your environment to spark an initial silly conversation that shows him this isn't some serious meeting. There is no such thing as being too goofy because as the conversation continues you will show your serious side. Walking through the park and asking to hear his best Squirrel Call doesn't make you seem crazy, it lets him know that it's okay to drop his cool and relax.

Environment observations may not work; if this is the case then observe each other's outfits, hair, accessories, and break the ice that way. If you're wearing something revealing, don't let it be an elephant in the room. If the girls are being displayed with insane cleavage, own up to it, "If one pops out, will you tell me or just throw it back in the shirt?" If you have a wagon behind you, don't make it awkward, you already know he sees all that ass, so make it fun. "If my dress gets stuck in my booty, you have permission to pull it out." It's all about making the mood light, so he doesn't feel like a stranger.

These same tactics work when going from a guy that's too lighthearted and you're trying to get him to take you seriously. Most men are jokers by nature, so if you have a guy that's being overly clownish to try and win you over, let him know it's okay to drop the Kevin Hart shtick. Let's say that you are grabbing cocktails with a guy that is hitting you with joke after joke, trying way too hard to tickle your funny bone. Counter that humor with something real. "I bet you're the type that only calls his mother once a week," he'll joke that he calls her so much that she threatened to block him. Follow up and ask about that relationship, how they get along. Things like family are serious, and even a clown will take off his red nose to tell you that his mother has been his rock or to regret that he and his mother don't get along. The Icebreaking doesn't always need to be silly it can also be heartfelt. If this man says he and his mother don't talk, don't bring up the trauma, show him that it's all good, "Her loss, more of your time for me, right?" If you see an opportunity to connect and be a friend, go for it in a warm way. Show him through your attitude that he doesn't need to try so hard to be hilarious, that he can be free to be a bit more real.

There will always be an opportunity within the first ten minutes to break a man from his cool. I could list example after example to use, but you shouldn't be on a script. This is the one part where you will have to improvise because you never know what type of date you will be on or his personality type. Trust in your confidence, be comfortable, and that will create a relaxed atmosphere. There is no right or wrong. A man not responding to your icebreaker in the way you imagined is not failing at this task, because either way you reveal his personality. You try to joke, and he doesn't laugh. You try to be serious and he still brings it back to jokes. That reveals who he is! Go for it, commit to your icebreaking idea, and then make a mental note of his reaction because it can and will be used later on.

Date Goal: Stay Sharp
Rebuttal: I Love to Drink

Drinking calms nerves, unwinds, and drops inhibitions in a short period. It also slows thoughts and disrupts your focus. What's more important, feeling "nice" or being on your A game? This isn't a social visit with an old friend, a celebration with girlfriends, or any other excuse to get buzzed. This man is a stranger who you're trying to unravel by using your wits, why the hell would you want to dull them. I get it, drinking is fun and you can hold your liquor no matter if you're taking shots of Tequila or sipping glasses of Prosecco. Don't get cocky. Although you may not be the type of chick that would ever get thot sloppy in front of new company, the real damage comes when you start feeling warm, he starts smiling hard, and the pleasure side of the brain gets you open. Instead of being on offense, you're now on defense as he distracts you from your mission in order to bring you back to the world of a typical date, where he sets the questions and controls the sexual innuendo. Next thing you know you're talking too much about your last date and hinting about the last guy that broke your heart.

Guys love getting women to drink because most become flirtier and behave more sexual. Additionally, it clouds your logic, which includes the part you need to figure out if he's full of shit or not. The representative mask he's wearing doesn't get tested. All he has to do is keep you drinking and keep you talking, and by the end of the date you'll be happy with the time you had. In reality, it wasn't a great date, you were just tipsy and everything is a good time when you're loaded. No matter how much you study this section, understand that you may be one and a half drinks from transforming back to that girl who talks too much about shit that doesn't matter. Talking about guys that did horrible things to you in the past. Going on and on about how you hate dating and just want a relationship but can't find a good man. You may even end up letting him feel you up, kiss all over you, or worse. Don't become some pathetic half-drunk that exposes her flaws because she can't say "no" to alcohol. The risk is not worth the high.

Date Goal: Don't Pay for Shit
Rebuttal: I Feel Guilty Spending a Man's Money

Cali's date didn't show any internal dialogue about what to order or if she should have been prepared to offer money if the check came and he asked her to put in. Spartans don't think about money, they expect what they want to be paid for, to have free range to order whatever is on the menu, and knows that any man who objects to any of those things is automatically disqualified from a second date. Let me delve into it regardless because who pays has become a touchy subject. You are the woman, even if you pushed for the date and set up the date, you don't take a man out, that man takes you out. You were the one who said, "Hey, let's meet at Cheesecake Factory, when you get off work," so fucking what—he still pays.

This is a big issue today as men look to use the idea of equality to be cheap or downplay the tradition of being a gentleman. Woman and men are equal, and a woman doesn't need a man to do anything for her that she can do on her own. However, we're not talking about workplace politics or social dynamics. We are focused on courting, and in terms of romance, traditions like a man opening a door, treating a woman on that date, and getting down on one knee to propose, stand the test of time no matter how independent the woman. When he becomes your boyfriend, that makes him a partner, and then the idea of taking turns or even treating can be discussed, but at this stage the first date, your purse doesn't open!

When a man wants a woman, the effort will always come off as effortless! There is no debate about price. If he takes you to a movie, he pays for both tickets. If he takes you to a dinner, he pays for that meal and he had better leave a good tip. If he takes you Go Kart racing, he buys those laps. Not because he's trying to buy pussy or a kiss at the end of the night, but because he sees you as a beautiful woman and wants to express his appreciation. It may appeal to your nurturing side to help in some way to show him you aren't a Ho or some broke chick that wants to eat on a man's dime. Stop feeling as if you need to contribute!

There's a sense of guilt that some women have, even when they aren't using a man for food or company because they feel as if he will eventually expect something in return. You like him, but you may not even reward him with a kiss at the end of the night, which will make him upset and feel lead on. That onus makes you feel as if you're doing something trifling. He's taking you on a date, not giving you a kidney! Men are motivated by sex, but that doesn't mean you go Dutch to avoid owing him sex. Even if you pay on the date he's still going to try for it, and you may still sleep with him. In the end, you just paid for half your date and gave up all your pussy. Who wins? A man who only wants to trick in order to get a treat, won't last more than a few dates. The objective is to weed men like these out, not help them low ball you. All you will ever owe a man is your company. Be comfortable in the role as a prize, not apologetic.

To date a guy whom you don't find attractive, or feel sparks with, would be using a man just for company or a free meal. In this case, there is an attraction; he has a shot at winning you over, so erase that weak bitch thought that you're a "bad girl" for ordering a $40 entrée and not putting twenty up. You deserve to be treated. If you act low maintenance, you become low maintenance, and you will never raise above that in his mind. Don't believe me? Go test it out. Offer to buy the popcorn because he got the tickets. Pay the tip because he treated you to a meal. The first round of drinks was on him, the next is on you. Watch how that becomes the standard for the rest of the relationship. A man doesn't think, "oh she's helping out," he thinks, "Oh she's got me." Eventually, he stops offering to pay, not to take advantage, but because that's what you seem to want.

You don't have to prove that you're an independent woman with her own money, he needs to prove that he sees a Queen worth spoiling. Stop trying to show that you have it to spend, and allow him to show that he believes in you enough to spend! You don't train an employee on the cash register, then say, "Do the first five customers, I'll do the next five," You show them what is to be expected by letting them do their job. Train that man to date you as if you are special, not some Go Dutch Diane, and watch how that treatment translates to other areas of the relationship. You can't promote yourself as a prize then give a man a discount. Set your price on the first date and keep it high.

Date Goal: Let Him Talk
Rebuttal: But the Conversation Stalls

Shut up and listen. That's the best advice anyone could ever give you about life in general, but how many of you actually do this? I was at my grandmother's house and both of my aunts came into the living room to talk to me. They asked me a question about Los Angeles, and by the time I was halfway through my answer, one aunt was talking about something she heard about LA on TV. Before she could complete that mini-story, my other Aunt interrupted her and brought up her co-worker's husband's opinion on LA. What followed was two grown women talking above each other about something they wanted me to talk about. My Granny looked over to me and gave a slight eye roll. That is the habit of many women, young and old. They want to be heard, more than they want to listen. When you're on a date, you don't want to be boring or seem too shy. However, the alternative isn't to just keep talking.

Most women who over-talk do so because they have all this stuff bottled up that they never get to talk about. *I did this... I'm the type that... I once went... That wouldn't have been me because I... Let me tell you what I would have done if... I know a person who...* Folks love to turn other people's stories and anecdotes back on themselves based on pure ego. Don't be the woman that stops a man mid-story when he's talking about Cancun, to say, "Oh, I went there too, I loved it. We stayed at..." He doesn't give a fuck. A man is trying to share his experience with you. That experience could reveal character traits about him if you listen. If you hijack his story, then he shuts up and lets you go on about your experience. Now, instead of letting him open up and share, it becomes a trip comparison as opposed to a character study. There will be a time to interject your own life story later, but never do it at the expense of your mission.

The following chapter goes into the ends and outs of asking random or indirect questions in the same way that Cali used to open Stephen up. For now, let's focus on the silence that may set in on your date if you ask a question that doesn't warrant a long response. Remember that men like to talk too! If you haven't experienced this in your life, then you probably talk too damn much and don't promote an environment where guys feel comfortable talking to you. I have a friend who is very quiet and laid back, but ask him about 90's hip-hop and he will not only talk about that subject, he will engage others about their opinions, sometimes to debate, sometimes to listen. His introverted side fades away the moment you give him a bone he likes to chew on. Every man has a trigger that will cause him to open up, and it's your job to find it.

The steps that I'm telling you to do on a date, men do these things naturally, which is why they end up getting easy pussy without ever opening up their own lives. **The best Dick Tactic is, "Let her talk."** Once a man sets a woman off about her ex-boyfriend, her job, her family, even her opinion on Kim Kardashian, she will go on and on and on...and it takes the pressure off of him to impress. 9 out of 10 of you reading this could date yourself, that's how much you talk. Meaning that you go out, a guy asks some trivial questions, tells a joke or two, and then triggers a big issue that has you reading your biography. A girl will go back home after the date and be on cloud nine, "Oh he understood me," he didn't understand shit; all he did was nod his head in a positive direction while you talked and talked and talked. When you came up for air with a, "So what do you think," all he had to do was check you with a, "You were right, I don't know why they treated you like that...you still talk to them?" That sends you back into more of the same story that no one gives a fuck about. A woman won't realize this, she will only remember that a man was receptive to her tales, and attribute that to her being so interesting...there was nothing interesting said, he's playing the same role I'm attempting to get you to now play.

Here's a real life example. I have a friend who was nervous about a date where he and this extremely pretty girl had agreed to get drinks. This girl lives in LA and is what people call "internet famous" because of her looks. I told my buddy the same thing I'm telling you: Let them do the talking and see how much they love you by the end of the night for letting them talk. My friend asked two questions that night, one regarding the girl's son and the other about the last guy she was dating. The son question only lasted for a few minutes, most likely because she didn't want to bring her little boy up and begin to miss him, or make herself seem un-sexy because here she is a mom on a date talking about mom things. The conversation hit a hiccup, the son inquiry went nowhere, and it left my friend staring at his drink struggling to come up with something witty to say. He later told me that I popped up in his head like Obi-Wan Kenobi, and he actually thought, "NC would say something crazy."

He did just that, I can't remember the specific question he asked but it revolved around her last relationship. The mood changed instantly. This girl poured out her feelings on that last breakup, transitioned into modern men wanting to be your boyfriend physically but not in title, and then by the time the drinks kicked in she was even talking about how the sex was weak but the head made her cum. They literally went from uncomfortable silence to her sharing stories about what it takes to make her orgasm. By the end of the night, my friend had his hands on her ass, telling her how he would treat her better than her ex. His game was not built on anything he said, it was built on him listening to see what this woman needed out of life, nodding his head in agreement, and then once her guard was down, he invaded her personal space and made her feel special.

This is what most men do. They shut up and listen! As a result of listening, they figure out the best way to endear themselves to that woman. By the time a woman goes home, she's under the impression that she found a man that gets her, is sweet, and also inspiring. All based on him listening and feeding her what she wanted to hear in terms of, *"That's fucked up...I can't believe he did that...then what happened...that dude's crazy; I would never have reacted like that."* Two hours of feeling as if a man understands you equates to a strong emotional bond. He looked good, he took you out, and he was easy to talk to... Check. Check. Check! This is perfect! You found Mr. Right, drop the balloons, and unfreeze your eggs! In reality, you just went on a date with yourself, and this man didn't prove a damn thing. All you wanted was a therapy session that ended with someone kissing your neck and telling you how sexy you are. This is basic game that these peasants let men get away with every day. That is not how a Spartan dates! A Spartan uses that same technique and flips it back on the man, because while men know how it looks to pull it off, they have no clue how it looks when it's being pulled on them.

When you attempt to spark conversations with a new person, you may hit a roadblock where your first question misses and reveals nothing. Don't choke and go on the defensive. If there is an awkward silence, a man will pick up the ball and begin to ask you questions because he's already experienced at getting females to talk about things typical females love to talk about. Don't let a drop in conversation serve as a change in who controls the dialogue. Let's say that you two have a good laugh about something fun, then after that laughter, it's quiet. He asks you about the last time you went on a date. How do you respond? Tina Typical will go into detail breaking down the guy, the date, how she felt, and forty minutes later when she finishes her dissertation; he has enough knowledge to push more triggers that keep her yapping. This is Sparta, therefore, you respond with, "It wasn't that interesting actually. Oh! Tell me the worst date you've ever been on." That's how you redirect a question and get him talking again about something that could be fun for him but also revealing. The same thing goes for general conversation. Let's say your topic of Lil Wayne doesn't go anywhere. Grab his hand. "Let me see your thumbs...too soft. You must not have grown up a gamer. I was the Queen of *Goldeneye*." If he's a video game geek, he will go HAM trying to dismiss your diss. If he was never into games, he'll tell you what he spent his free time doing instead. Be ready to flow from topic to topic, like a professional. That's how you control these men even when faced with a drop off in conversation.

Date Goal: End the Date on a High
Rebuttal: He Asks Me to Pay Half

By the time the check comes, you should be on a high. You did all the steps right and he responded like a man you can grow to really like. Unlike Stephen, however, he doesn't grab the bill to pay. He looks at you. Maybe you were the one to ask him on a date, and he thought you were going to pay based on that assumption. Maybe he's used to going Dutch. Maybe you're dealing with, "Damn, my wallet is at home," guy. No matter the reason, the result is that when the check comes and you tell him thank you, he asks for some kind of money from you...**What to do?**

181

Pay it. There is no need to argue your stance on how men should do things. I don't care if he sticks you with the entire bill or just the tip. Keep your cool and smile as you slide your card or cash in the fold. Internally, he has now committed suicide. RIP, because this dude is officially dead to you once you leave that restaurant. In the end, he revealed how much he values a woman like you. You may think that it's better to explain that you don't pay on dates, to give him a chance to redeem himself. Ignorance does not factor into the equation. Every man knows how to treat a woman, every single one. He's not asking for money because he's untrained, he's asking for money because you're the same as the rest. He chose to try you the first date as if you are one of these basic women—he has the wrong one!

Couples go Dutch when they are in a relationship. Platonic friends go Dutch. When a friend treats you, it's always proper to offer the tip. If this was a man that had treated you spectacularly over the course of three dates, you pick up the bill on the fourth to show him your appreciation. This is not one of those scenarios, this is a man that wants to be your man, and should have stepped up as such. *I bought you a drink now buy my drink?* Is he crazy? *I paid for these movie tickets now buy me some snowcaps.* The fuck? This is the first date, even if he doesn't normally pay the entire bill, this is that exception. It's not about his budget, it's about him checking you in order to put you in place. Even if he looks up surprised at the bill, or says he will pay you back, understand that a man always knows what he's doing.

I once went to a business dinner with a company that wanted to work with me. When the bill came I reached into my pocket, the President looked at me and said, "Don't disrespect us." There is proper etiquette in business, and there is proper etiquette in dating—**the one seeking the services pays**. In romance that is always the man, thus, the man always pays. Never allow a man to guilt you into thinking any different or let some faux-feminist convince you that you should pay half to endear yourself. This isn't *Ho Tactics* hustle where you have to sucker a man by treating him to things to set him up for the hit, this is romance. Refusing to treat you 100% is not how a man gets a second date, it's how he gets the Ax. Pay what he asks you to pay, no fuss. Then block him on the way home. No exceptions.

Date Goal: Seduce
Rebuttal: I Will End Up Sleeping with Him

If a man doesn't see you as sex, then there is no hope for anything serious. The way in which you seduce lets a man know if he has a shot at you or if he should leave now before he ends up in the friendzone. Men are a mass of insecurities because even the most attractive or wealthy man has either misread a female's signs or been played by a woman. If you don't have sexual chemistry, don't go on the date. If you do feel him on that level, project it on that first date. A little flirting will inspire a lot of lust.

The simplest part of a man to exploit is his dick, and no great romance ever began with a man feeling a lot of respect but very little lust for a woman he's courting. The idea that it's somehow counterproductive to come off as a sexual object is 4+4=9—false! I have seen the internet try to brainwash women into being less sexual as if being in touch with your sexuality automatically gets you labeled a whore. Understand the varying degrees of slut shaming. Another woman doesn't want you to be too sexy because you are competition, so they judge and throw shade in order to keep you acting conservatively. A man that can't have you doesn't want you to act too sexy because it's a tease that reminds him that he's not good enough. When society makes showing too much skin, making a sexual joke, or even rubbing a man's foot under the table into an act of Old Testament debauchery, women develop a complex and hold back. When you hold back from your true nature you come off as cold, prudish, and boring. Fuck that.

No man has ever sat across from a woman that's dressed sexy and said, "This is too much for me, I wish she wore a sweater." No man has ever thought of a girl as sweet and then was turned off because she played footsies under the table. No man has ever heard a sexual innuendo and thought, "What a disgusting freak!" Men love a woman that's comfortable in her skin and willing to be a little dirty in her conversation. The only instance where I have ever been personally turned off by a woman has been sex bragging. When a female lists her sex skills in a way that tells you that she gives even the non-exclusive lovers all her dirty deeds, it makes a man feel like just another John. Men like to chase, to earn, to feel exclusive.

The mystery of your sex life, is much more enticing than promoting your skills. You have a vagina; men don't need any more reason than that to lust after you. Pussy propaganda is ratchet in every sense of the word and reeks of insecurity. You orgasm while giving head, your ex said you had the best oral technique ever, you're flexible enough to do tricks on the dick... none of that should be shared during the first date. If you volunteer that information to him, you volunteer it to all men because sex talk is your crutch. You're the dating equivalent of a girl tweeting, "I just got out of the shower, and I don't feel like getting dressed." You are thirst trapping and he knows it! A Spartan doesn't need to put sex skills on her resume because she's not selling pussy, she's selling personality.

There does need to be some dirty talk or sensual flirting, but there is an art to seduction. Let a man think of you as sex by wearing an outfit that makes you feel sexy. On a date, sit next to him or get close enough, so he can smell your perfume and brush against your skin. When talking, emphasize certain words like you're Marilyn Monroe, but also touch an arm, hand, or knee, to get him worked up. None of this compromises your virtue, it's just flirting. In terms of being a cock tease, who cares. Men love to be teased when the woman teasing them is accessible. He has to believe that he will one day fuck you, or why date you. Don't worry about how he will perceive your seduction. Are you easy? Clearly you aren't because your panties will remain up at the end of the night and your hands nor mouth will touch his dick. You can be provocative all night, but leave him without doing anything sexual; that earns his respect. Unleash your inner Gypsy Rose Lee[9], and seduce with the knowledge that less is more.

Seduction is a double-edged sword. It's not just the man you are turning on, you also risk getting yourself worked up, and those hormones can lead to a mistake being made. Dick Discipline for women is harder than men understand. You may fall on the side of the coin where you won't have sex because you require an emotional connection, not physical chemistry. That other side of the coin is one where discipline depends on the man in front of you. Let's be honest, you are a sexual being with needs that a vibrator can't satisfy. You see a handsome man, and your mind can't help

---

[9] burlesque entertainer famous for her striptease act.

but go to a filthy place. What does his dick look like? Does he fuck gently or is he rough and aggressive? You visualize his face between your legs, you gripping his skull, guiding him to your spot. You picture your mouth wrapped around his dick, the sounds you can force him to make before he erupts. Your vagina is wet more times throughout the day than anyone will ever know, and the secret that you're holding onto is that you have the power to fuck whoever you want whenever you want to. All pussy may be created equal but you throw yours like Hera! An emotional connection is preferred, but having a good date is enough proof that he's worthy enough to get all the freakiness you've been holding in. Seduction is verbal foreplay, a little physical touch, maybe even a kiss...you know men have zero discipline but will you buckle sexually while playing your own game?

You can fake seduction like when a Hooters waitress flirts with her customer to get a better tip or like a stripper pushes up on a fat guy in order to get him into the champagne room. The *Ho Tactics* role-playing job doesn't apply to real dates because you won't be acting to get a mark open, as I wrote earlier, this is honest sexual chemistry that you're playing upon. To flirt for real will take your mind and body to the point where you are imagining all the things you can do with your date. Your mind may be patient, but your hormones have ADD. "Should I fuck him...? I mean he's doing everything right, and I would like some dick." Or maybe you run from your thoughts like a teenage girl, trying to disown them, push them to the back of your mind, only to end up with him making a move and you giving in because every part of you wants to fuck. You have to check yourself and show dick discipline! One good date is not enough to break your dick diet. Sex does not ruin the dating process if you are mentally strong enough to play the post-sex game and continue to vet him. However, I'm going to insist that you hold off on complicating things with sex at this stage. Sex on the first date is another monster with other steps that need to be laid out and hit, so, for now, act as if that isn't an option at all. I repeat, do not have sex at this point! You have to go home alone.

How do you walk away? Let's say you two are in the parking lot, he's walked you to your car. Like Cali waiting for the Uber, you take this time to get closer to him and mind-fuck him with a tight hug while you continue to talk. That man isn't going to walk away when you say, "okay, let me get in the car." He's going to say all kinds of shit to keep you in his arms. He's going to offer all kinds of incentives for you to follow him back to his crib or to let him drop you back at your car later on. Don't give in! The date has to end right there. You don't need to go get coffee with him, you don't need to see the artwork at his apartment, and you don't need him to sit in the car with you while it warms up. The sexual edge is slippery when dealing with new dick, if you play around you will fall. I don't care if your hand accidentally brushes up against his hard dick by "accident" or if he's the best kisser on earth, keep your focus on the bigger picture, not the easy nut.

A thought may cross your mind that to deny him on the date will make him feel as if you don't really like him. Women tend to worry about how to balance showing interest, without seeming too hoish, and when they over-think this it comes off as mixed signals. Give a little, show a lot! This is why you allow him to hug you like a lover not a friend at the end of the date. This is why you give him a nice kiss that proves that he's more than a buddy. Those small things are proof that you're not putting him in the friendzone. If you think giving a man head, fucking him, or even letting him sit in your car and feel you up, is how you keep him interested, then you've already lost this battle. Have some respect for yourself and set boundaries. A man won't like it, but he will respect it in the long run.

Date Goal: Go to Sleep
Rebuttal: I Still Want to Talk to Him

After you say your goodnights there may be one last communication before you go to sleep, and that's the, "Made it home" text. The adrenaline of a date doesn't end there. If this was one of the best dates you've been on and the chemistry was crazy, going to sleep becomes harder than trying to eat just one French fry. Remain strong. No phone sex. No nudes. No sexting. No Video Calls. Nothing! You went on a date; it was good, now put it to rest by putting your hormones to bed. I don't care if you stay up thinking about him for the next hour, it's better to crave than to cave.

Chapter 12:
How to Ask the Right Questions

i hope he doesn't say anything to ruin it! Allow me to break this saying down in a way that shows how men have been getting by for years without really opening up to women. A typical woman will develop a crush on a man based on surface qualities, and in order for him to win her over in terms of a second date or even fast sex; all this man has to do is avoid saying things that turn her off. Think about that... a man isn't judged on the way he opens up about his life or impresses her with conversation. He's judged on how well he remains inoffensive. If this is a dude who has radical political thoughts, anger management issues, or is still broken up over a past relationship, all he needs to do is turn his personality down and keep things light. 90% of the women I had sex with didn't know I had a brother, what my exact age was, or what part of town I lived in. All the conversation stayed on their past and their opinions, and I did that on purpose. We're back to the Dick Tactic of "Let her talk, more than I talk." A typical woman has already decided if a man is fuckable before the date. He's won based on looking a certain way, having something going for himself financially, or his sense of humor. This isn't a secret, it's known, and gives a guy confidence. If he tries to hit that, she will let him, maybe not on the first date, but it's going to happen the next date because she's already sold. All a man has to do is make it around the final lap without crashing.

Put yourself in a man's shoes. All you have to do is hold serve with basic conversations, come off as mysterious as opposed to annoying or abrasive, and a woman will sleep with you the first time you get her alone. Would you gamble on that date by being yourself...or would you come in with jokes and levity as you sit there and let the woman do all the talking?

187

You would put on a mask too, because why work for something that someone is going to give you based on doing absolutely nothing?

Have you ever asked, "Why do men lie so much over nothing?" This is a part of that larger mentality. *White lies don't hurt anyone and they get me what I want.* He didn't tell you about his girlfriend, he didn't tell you he was unemployed, he didn't tell you he still lived with his ex-girl; he didn't tell you he doesn't actually want a relationship, etc. Although these men are grown and shouldn't be afraid of scaring you off, they are controlled by habit. Logic tells a man, "This woman doesn't know me from Paul, but she likes me a lot anyway. Let me keep my mouth closed and collect what she wants to give me, because if I am forthcoming with the truth, my 'complications' will come off as deal breakers." You, or someone you know, have been in relationships that would have never been entered into if the whole truth was known from the first date. And that's the point, no matter how many women say, "Tell me the truth, it won't change anything," men know that's a lie. You would gather your shit and run if you knew what was in the mind of the average man that's sitting across from you.

Let's pretend that you fell in love with the looks of a man that had a girl pregnant at the time you were first dating. He didn't tell you this and you didn't think to ask anything that hinted at his past. After a few weeks, sex entered the picture, he knew how to lay pipe, and now you like him even more. Next thing you know, he's calling you his girl, and although you didn't agree to this, you love being called his girl, so you roll with it. A month later, you and Mr. Sexy still haven't talked about anything real in terms of his past. Now you see him tagged on a Facebook picture congratulating him on the birth of his first child. You don't want to be with a man who has a baby. You don't want to go down to the courthouse and stand with him as he demands a paternity test. You don't want to help him cover child support. You don't want to compete for attention with a woman that you don't know. But you will, because that secret baby doesn't change the fact that you've fallen in love. This is how a smart woman ends up that dumb woman who is in a ratchet situation called: *My boyfriend has a newborn but we're going to make it through this rough patch.*

You must ask questions! Men are never going to be totally honest but they will give you intel that you can continuously use to uncover him until he either opens up or gets caught in a lie. Do not buy into men only opening up to women they trust. That would mean you having to fly blindly into a relationship and then learn that he's not the man you thought he was. Fuck that. You don't need to know his deepest fears or secrets, but you do need to know the basics of his personality and where he's coming from emotionally. The truth is, most men will disappoint you with their back-story, their "representative" will be far more appealing, but you have to risk that disappointment. Too many women want the image to match up to the personality so bad that they avoid intrusive questions.

I asked a girl what her boyfriend did for a living, and she responded, "I don't really know, he works with his Uncle." What the fuck does that mean? This is proof that certain women don't even want to know if he's a piece of shit or not. The reason why so many bad liars get deep in your life is that you fear finding out the truth, you push it off to the side, keep things light, and refuse to uncover a man's character during the dating stage because you don't want your questions to ruin him. If you ruin him, then that means you have to do the process all over again. You don't want to start over with a man that's not as cute or paid, so you allow this applicant to get through without being vetted.

Who is that man across the table from you? He's not the smile that makes you want to kiss him. He's not the arms that you imagine wrapped around your body. He's not the watch on his wrist or car keys in his pocket. <u>A man is defined by his conversation</u>. For your date to sit there and not say anything real, merely promotes the image that you like. That image is what you want, thus, you will reward him with pussy, time, and a relationship. Six months later you're in love with a man who was never who you thought he was and you're silently unhappy... This problem could have easily been avoided in one fucking date if you did your job! A Spartan doesn't want a man to shut up and be perfect. A Spartan wants a man who shows her how imperfect he has been throughout his life so she can now determine if he's perfect for her now. This is what Spartan dating is all about.

189

The questions that Cali asked are the most important part of the date, and going forward they become the foundation of the things you test him against over the following weeks to see if his story remains or changes. After a few weeks of not only asking questions but also observing a man's actions, you should take all of his responses, and lay them out in your mind like this:

"James is a mama's boy that comes off as a bit of a control freak but he is genuinely sweet without being a trick. He takes pride in his relationship with his nephew and the way he looked at that baby in the stroller tells me he wants fatherhood. I assume that his father not being around has given him a complex where he wants to be the man of a house and right those wrongs. Looking at how his last relationship ended I can tell that he's done playing games and has matured to the point where he wants what I want.

However, I can also tell that James is afraid that I may be out to use him, based on the way he always initiates questions about how strongly I feel about him. He hasn't talked about being heartbroken yet, but something definitely happened that hurt him, I will bring this up on our next date."

Any woman who has been on two dates should be able to read a man in this way. The scary part is that there are women in actual relationships that can't even break down their boyfriends this good. I was emailing with one woman and she couldn't even answer simple questions about her man's personality other than what makes him mad, what makes him laugh, and the music he loves. The reason why the mind of her man was a mystery, the reason why most of you reading this don't understand how men think beyond, "they all want pussy," is that you don't interview these guys properly! You go on a date with this mentality that if a man wants to share he will share, if he doesn't share then that's his business. No! If you aren't trying to know that man's business enough to understand his current intentions, his past story, and his future plans then why date him?

EXPOSE HIM BY MAKING HIM EXPOSE HIMSELF

You get it now, you understand why questions are important and you're ready to get to the root of these men, no matter how much you like them... but you don't know what to ask. You fear going on a date and freezing up. Non-Spartan thoughts will start small then grow louder: *What if that's too personal... What if that offends him... What if he thinks I'm weird for asking that... What if I don't like his answer?* Nothing is off limits to a Spartan, no judgment is worth keeping your mouth closed, and no question is too personal. **It is more important to prove him incompatible now with answers you don't like than let him slide with lies you do.** When a woman says she can't think of anything to ask, it means that she can't think of anything safe and neat to ask. Safe and neat are how typical women walk through life. You know exactly what you want to find out.

The exact questions you need to ask are similar to the ice-breaking example. It's specific to your life and your personality. "What do I need to know about a man to trust him," is what you should ask yourself before the date, during the date, and after the date. I'm talking specifics. Women tell me generic shit like, "I want him to be loyal, honest, goal orientated, and God fearing." None of that crap means anything. It's literally like saying I like my pizza hot. No shit, really? How do you know if he has been loyal? It's not as if you can't test it right now on a date. How do you get the sense that he's mostly honest? Asking a liar to tell the truth about himself is like asking a 5th grader to grade his own test. How do you know that he's goal orientated? Because dude went to school and has a job? His religious side, what's really there, besides the denomination he tells you? Only you know what matters to you in terms of a partner's must-have qualities. Once again, truth will guide you, but I will frame it.

THE LIST

Let's say you want a man that you can trust around your girlfriends. A man who is stable in his employment. A man who appreciates money but doesn't obsess over it. You don't mind a working class man who doesn't earn a lot, but you want someone who won't hold you making more money than he does over your head. Finally, you want a man who is looking to start a family sooner than later. You don't just go on a date knowing you want A, B, C, and D, and ask if he can be that. Humans don't respond to directness. "Are you looking for something serious or nah?" Of course he is going to say "yes" dumbass, you have a vagina that he wants to bust open. Using this example, let's break down question asking in a practical way. What will prove trust? What will prove that he wants a relationship? What proves that he wants children? What proves that he isn't misogynistic? What proves that he isn't a criminal? What proves that he won't be offended by a woman with a good job and dreams? What proves that he isn't overly jealous? There is no magic question that will tell you that after a year, a man will fall out of love with you and choose another girl. Growing with a person in a relationship can lead to the development of all kinds of behavior that wasn't there prior. We will talk about relationship problems in the last part of the book. This list isn't about predicting the future; it's about seeing the present clearly in order to make the smart choice for a relationship that has a fighting chance.

A Loyal Man = Old Him vs. New Him: If you want to learn about loyalty, you don't lead with, "Do you ever think it's right for a man to cheat, even if he's not being satisfied at home?" How do you think any man who wants to fuck you will respond? "Yeah, cheating doesn't mean anything it's just my dick in some random girl who I'll never see again. Who cares, right?" Men aren't that dumb or that honest when they are attempting to get something from a woman. If you want to know about loyalty a better line of questioning revolves around him "back in the day" or him as a friend. For example, ask him if he would ever cover for one of his boys who was cheating if he were also cool with the girlfriend. A man will answer that question quickly and with emotion because he has a friend in mind who he

192

would ride for. Most men will ride for their brothers even if the girl he's cheating on is his own cousin because males truly do belong to a fraternity of loyalty. That's just the set-up. From there you can use the example of his friend cheating to ask indirect questions about his own thoughts on the subject that won't make him seem like a villain.

In Cali's story, we saw her play Devil's Advocate, and now you can do the same thing. "If my brother wanted me to cover for him, I would, fuck those hos." This gives him bait either to go with the typical male response or to show you something deeper. A man may never go along with covering for someone because his dad cheated on his mother. He may have been cheated on, and while he may not confess this, his mentality may be "fuck anyone that cheats," because he knows personally how it hurts. Those responses start to establish a morality based on something deeper than just sex being sex or a random opinion. If he uses words that point to him thinking about home and family being ruined or the personal pain, then he is a man who sees the bigger picture. That shows his loyalty. In the end, you won't know if he will or won't down the line, but in terms of this pre-relationship, you do prove that two-timing isn't a part of his current nature.

A Secure Man = Bitter Test: This may be the easiest thing to expose because men don't hide resentment. When you are dating, you need a partner who isn't going to be intimidated by your Spartan nature. You make your own money, can pay your own bills, men love that part. However, when you are making more, have more, or come off as smarter than he is, that can cause drama. It's the 21st century but certain men still love to keep women down to make themselves feel bigger. Don't wait until he starts putting you down after you're together; poke him to see if he has that Ike Turner inside of him now. I watched a documentary on the Ku Klux Klan, and one historian noted that the poor whites were more driven by their own lowly status than racism. They were failures and needed someone to be an outlet for their self-hate. Men who are working dead-end jobs, who are constantly trying to make it but face setbacks, or any man in a struggle that he can't own up to will look to others to take his frustrations out on. On a date, bring up the subject of athletes making so much money, the 1%, even the Kardashians, then observe.

A normal person may joke about the success of others or have some anti-capitalist sentiments, but a bitter person will be venomous. If your date goes on and on about how life is bullshit, that the system is rigged, that unrelated things are holding him back, then that exposes his "I deserve what everyone else has," pessimism not an "I'm still going to do me," optimism. A man that feels like life is keeping him down will never progress in a real way. Therefore, if you were to become a couple and he sees that you are progressing in this "rigged system," you expose him as a fraud. He will now be forced to find other reasons for your success. You're a woman so you get breaks, you probably flirt, etc...or he may work to bring you down to his level, saying that you work too much and can't spend time with him, that if you want a family you're going to need to switch careers, etc... Misery loves company, so on the first date check to see how miserable this man is.

A Man that is Ambitious = Resting or Climbing: Another easy feeler question is about ambition. A driven man isn't one that says, "I work two jobs and I go to school." I know guys that have been working on Associates for years and work two jobs because they drag their feet. There are people who aren't doing anything real with their lives but love the protection of saying, "I'm working on a degree." What degree are they working towards, and how long have they been in school? A problem that pops up later in the relationship is you bankrolling his lifestyle while this fool is still working on a degree. Unlike X-Box live bums, these men are actually doing something constructive, but they're not able to be a true partner. He's working on passing the bar, fails, has to take it again, meanwhile, you look at your account and realize that you've sponsored a guy who may never even become an attorney. It may not be his intention to make you a Sugar Mamma, but that doesn't make it right. In the old world, this is honorable, he's going to pay it back, and love you forever. Ha! I actually see the fallout from those relationships. Women resent taking care of men. Men resent being taken care of. The moment he does finish up school and land a job, the damage to his ego is so irreversible that there is no way the couple stays together. Your Spartan name isn't Sallie Mae. Before you take on a project under the assumption that you're building him up for your joined future, understand that appreciation, reciprocation, nor marriage is promised.

Another area to touch on is his actual career. Asking positions, not just assuming, is easy yet it gets skipped over. "He has a Benz so he's doing something right." Wrong! I know three guys with Mercedes who don't work... but they do get pussy. Don't let the smokescreen of what he's driving or where he works stand as proof of hustle. What does he actually do, how long has he been doing it, and where is it going? You can ask those easy questions on the phone. The date is where you delve deeper into true ambition beyond just a work position.

"Where do you see yourself in five years?" What kind of 17-year-old, smoking a blunt in the basement, question is that to ask a grown man? The reason women ask that dense question is because it's safe and sounds deep. That shit is about as deep as a Nun's vagina. If you want to measure a man's ambition, ask him something outside the box about life-goals and see if he inspires you. The most important part of finding a partner, and not just finding a dick, is how they grow you in return. No matter if you're a college student reading this or a woman in her 40's that's established in her career, the man you date should give you the feeling that he can upgrade your ambition. Is this man about his money? About his success? About his legacy? You don't get that with just one answer; you feel that passion and drive throughout his conversation as if it's a 2008 Obama speech.

"Do you believe in the idea of having seven streams of income? I have this friend that swears by it, he's even selling weave out of his car." You don't want someone who just agrees with a concept, you want to see his own fire and take on that subject. "That's cool, but I believe that success is a result of being passionate about something and waking up and doing that each day. How many passions to have is up to that person, but life isn't a Flea Market money grab, I'm here to leave a mark and that's why I'm going back to get my masters right now." That answer versus, "Fuck yeah, I'll go back to selling white tees to get this bread," shows the difference in life philosophy. It's not about right versus wrong, it's about which man matches up with your worldview. Some men are Steve Jobs visionaries, who take action and don't just dream, others are Dame Dash, finger in every pie types while others could be *Better Call Sal*, get paid by any means necessary hustlers. Know what you want, because if you go in there like, "I just want a man who works," you're selling yourself short.

<u>An Honest Man = Open Book</u>: You don't have to think about the truth, so why would any man hesitate for more than a few "how do I frame this" moments? Random questions, in general, catch a man off guard. Would you have sex on the first date? What complexion would you want your child to be? Have you ever seen a ghost? Would you let a girl eat your ass? What do you think we should do with homeless people? What's the craziest thing a girl ever did for you? What's the most you ever spent on an ex? How many girls you think still owe you sex? What do you think of Ray Rice's side of the story? How would you react if a black dude in a hoody were walking towards you? You can literally come up with all kinds of random things that get a man's mind working, but doesn't really tell you much about him. The key is to follow up with questions that actually matter to you. The bait questions open it up to deep conversations.

What was this man's life like growing up? You can't ask him to give you a *David Copperfield* novel, and expect to learn about his life in a real way. You need to see his thoughts, and then find out what shaped his thoughts. When's the last time you heard something in church that resonated with you? That's deeper than, "So when's the last time you went to church." From a real question, you get a real answer. From a real answer, you can then follow up on the specifics and put a person on a path of continued honesty. People have stories that they are willing to share, but they won't volunteer them. Be the one that gets them to turn the page.

<u>A Man Who Is a Narcissist = Rants on His Own</u>: You don't even have to ask questions to tell if a man is a narcissist because he won't shut up about himself, the things he's done, and the people he knows, all in a pompous way. General conversation about music, TV, the waiters serving you, or the guy passing you the popcorn can expose a man's nasty and obnoxious attitude. If you are dealing with some elitist asshole that thinks he's better than people his lack of, "thank you," to people serving him or his rants on the low paying jobs people do to pay their bills, easily expose his jerk nature. One of the biggest myths is that men with money are going to be assholes, so deal with it. Money has nothing to do with manners and humility, being abrasive comes from a dark place, and isn't the simple result of wealth or power. Stories about how many girls are after him, or how he has his choice of females, are also signs of insecure men trying to puff themselves up. Remember, true greatness doesn't need to pat itself on the back. You don't have to spend much time trying to expose this mentality because any question will reveal how much a man is in love with himself.

A Man Who Is Looking for a Relationship = Time: A man that's looking for a relationship is like Big Foot, I've never seen it. Men don't openly hunt for girlfriends, and if they do, they have esteem issues. Think about those guys who offered to be your man, to marry you, or who chased you after only knowing you for a short time; they didn't get you because they came off as thirsty. These men have holes they are looking for you to fill, and it won't take long to realize that they want you for all the wrong reasons. Typicals miss these signs, they see a man's affection as his truth, and never check to see what's under the hood. This is why we have so many false-start relationships, long engagements that end without marriage, and even marriages that end in separation or divorce within the first year. Be very afraid of any man that wants to settle down too fast.

You won't see a well-adjusted man out at the bar with the mission to find that perfect woman with whom he can settle down and put his last name on. This is what basic bitches hope for because they don't know how men think. "Don't you want to leave these hos alone and find a good woman that will hold you down and have your back?" Fuck no! That Game Changer is welcomed, but she is not someone a man is chasing at night. Men and women aren't wired the same in this regard. Males aren't on a shot clock. Males don't put pressure on themselves to get married before they start to wrinkle. It's not a part of the majority mind frame. Men expect love to happen because they know in their heart that the right woman will make herself known by being different from the birds he's currently chasing. A man's want for a real partner, a strong woman, is there below the surface, and that's where you need to dig.

So what do you ask exactly, because you can't be wasting your time with a person who is five years away from wanting to be married? This is the Catch-22; you don't have to ask a man if he's ready for love, he will show you by falling in love with you. In the coming days, he will clearly react to the things, you've done so far and you will either see a change in him or he

197

will remain unimpressed. By dating like a Spartan, you fulfill his prophecy of, "I'll know that she's special because she will be special." Each one of these steps works at revealing a man. Everything that Cali did on her first date works at seducing a man. While you are worried about interviewing, that man won't be sitting there, he will be internalizing your moves. He's not used to this, and genuine men, the one's you want, will be impressed.

By dating in a proactive way that forces a man to be honest, open, and treat you with value, you will separate yourself from the pack. Other women are not doing these things on dates, they aren't doing what you're about to do on the phone between dates, they aren't setting rules while also seducing dicks, they aren't being disciplined in a way that comes off as respect not teasing, and they aren't being a true shoulder a man can lean on. You are in the process of Spartan-Whipping this man. The question of if he is looking for a relationship will be clear in about 12 days, maybe less if you do these steps properly. A man may not be looking to settle down, but he will have no choice when presented with a Unicorn.

Chapter 13:
Post-Date Do's

the day after the first date is when most women give control back to the man. It's easy to feel powerful when you don't know a man and you can objectify him as just another guy trying to make your team. To actually go out and have not just a good time, but an excellent time will leave you thirsting for more "him." The day after the date, for typical women, is filled with nerves fueled by the unknown. *Will he text or call? Will he ask me out again immediately or will he wait? How long should I wait to reach out if he doesn't call first? Is reaching out to thank him for the date again doing too much if I did it last night? Should I add him on social media? Should I accept his request on social media?* The list goes on and on until your mind is a conflicting mess of weak bitch thoughts. Now is not the time to unravel. You are still in control, and you have to continue to flex those muscles and not revert to the regular habits of regular women.

Did he enjoy your date? Who gives a fuck, you enjoyed it, and now you have to be sure if this is something real or just a good first interview. Once again, remind yourself that this process isn't about hopping on a man's dick and praying that he likes you. He has no choice but to like you. You are a walking masterpiece who he just shared the same air with, who he just exposed his soul to, and who sent him home with a hard dick and a smile. You controlled the first date by being smart, and now I'm going to show you how to continue this winning streak. Know that the other women he's dating don't have the confidence or the playbook you have, therefore, between dates, there is nothing to fear and nothing holding you back from this Spartan takeover.

199

THE REACH OUT

Cali is off the next day, so she doesn't have the distraction of work to keep her mind off Stephen. She's talking to a few other men, but Stephen is already showing her things that they aren't. Cali isn't sure if this is the new dick effect or because Stephen was really that interesting, but she's not about to rest on her laurels. One date doesn't make her feelings authentic. She knows a little about Stephen, but now it's time to see how he does when he's off the clock. Post-date attention, how he fits her into his schedule, and further conversation are needed before the next date. **How can any man hope to become your boyfriend if he doesn't have time to talk, has to split his attention or majority of time with work or hobbies, or isn't able to recreate that same good conversation from the first date?** Cali has been with men who make a good showing, and then begin to act inconsistently. She needs to know Stephen isn't cut from that same cloth as the fuck boys. Stephen had to go to work, but he knows Cali is off, that means the ball is in Stephen's court to reach out.

Cali figures that she should hear something by his lunch break, but isn't being rigid in her mind. If Stephen texts while he's at Starbucks at 8 am, cool, but she won't respond back until she's genuinely up. If he calls when he first gets to his office, again that's sweet, but she probably won't answer until she's done her morning routine. Cali isn't hard up to talk to Stephen, she likes him, but this isn't the first new dick she's been around. Cali knows how to curtail her interests and show Stephen that she's still the prize to be chased, not a girl that's open off his attention or a bored Basica that waits by her phone hoping it vibrates. If Stephen doesn't text or call throughout the day Cali isn't going to react like some pride filled girl, "If he was interested he should have hit me up, fuck him, he wasn't even all that anyway." That's petty bitterness, and that behavior has no place in the mind of a Spartan. If Stephen goes the entire day without once checking in on her, she will take matters into her own hand and reach out around 8 pm.

Being offended by a lack of communication is jumping the gun. Stephen could be busy at work, have other life issues pop up, or maybe he's the type of person that always waits until after he's off to be social. Cali doesn't know the heart of this man, all she knows is that he showed that he had a good character during their time together last night. Based on that date alone, Cali is willing to give Stephen the benefit of the doubt, even if he doesn't reach out first. If he isn't interested, she's smart enough to pick up on the vibe during a real conversation. She's not going to let something as small as not calling or texting first, influence her mind and create a feeling of rejection that isn't there.

Stephen contacts Cali around noon with a text asking her if she's still alive. Cali isn't going to be dismissive of his texts the same way she was on Day 0; he's earned text convo because she knows she can get phone calls from him whenever she wants. The two text back and forth about last night's date, dropping inside jokes, flirting, and teasing each other about generic things. Stephen asks if Cali is busy tonight. He would love to see her after he gets off...smh, men are so predictable. Cali isn't surprised or flattered like a typical bird who isn't used to male thirst. Stephen wants to see her again within 24 hours because she's a bad bitch with a new vagina. Most women would jump at a chance to spend time with a man she likes, but Cali is smarter than that. She declines Stephen's offer, claiming she has some stuff she's going to be doing around her house. Stephen wants to come over and help her...again a man that got a whiff of Spartan magic won't let go. Cali thanks him, but says she has it covered. However, she does say that she expects a call once he's home or she's going to assume he just moved on to the next girl with his date invite. Checkmate!

Stephen has no power in this situation. As a man, he wants to see her because he wants to take it to the next level, now that he can't see her physically he has to take what she's giving, conversation. His hormones are on fire, but Cali controls how fast they move. If Stephen is only after pussy, then he doesn't want to be stuck on the phone. He could use that time to go out with another female friend. Cali is testing Stephen, is he the type of man that only wants to see her in person because he thinks that after the first date he may get some, or is he really interested in continuing to talk and learn more about her life? Stephen says he will call and that he's not asking any other girl out on a date. Cali responds back with one of her prettiest selfies and a kiss emoji. All women should have a default, "I'm pretty as hell," picture (not a nude) on their phones to break out for a new man. Send him something that wasn't posted to Instagram or any other social media, because if a man happens to follow your page and sees it, he'll just think, "This ho is for everybody." Cali sends an exclusive picture she's been sitting on, a small reward for Stephen reaching out first.

The aim for the pre-date was specific: Let him know you are a *Dater*, not a *Come Over & Chill* or *Phone Bone* type of girl. The aim for the date was specific: Who is this man beyond the bullshit mask men wear and do I like him? You set your goal and achieved your goal. It would make zero sense to slip into this "it's whatever" attitude now that he made it past the first date stage. What I've noticed in the advice I've given over the years is that I will find a woman who is a great student in terms of the pre-date game. She will pull men as if it's nothing, get dates, and have a great first date, only to say, "I've won, now let me do everything wrong!"

Those relationships where you start to text all day or talk all night are not the prize. You will fall into being lazy and stop researching his character. By next weekend, he's over at your crib with a bottle of Ciroc, and your legs are open because you feel as if you did all the work that was required to be smart. Negative! The work has just started. A second date isn't guaranteed yet; Stephen still has to keep climbing. Cali has to be sure that Stephen actually has time to be something more than casual; that the personality displayed on the date is actually who he is even when they are not face to face, and finally that she isn't made to compete for his time. Things like, "Does he think I'm Wifey or Pussy," doesn't concern Cali, she's a fucking Spartan she knows she's not Pussy and hasn't been so for a very long time. If Stephen is playing a good game to fuck, it will be obvious over this next week. Pussy hunters aren't good liars and are always impatient. There will be points on the phone where Stephen tries her, but men are supposed to try for sex, it's how you gauge their attraction level. Cali won't deduct points for Stephen trying to lure her over to his crib or get her out again because he's merely a dog sniffing, she has the leash and controls where this walk is headed.

THE LONG PHONE CONVERSATION

The day after a first date shouldn't be used to take a break and go without contact. Unless you are going out of town or he is indisposed of for a good reason, you have to keep the momentum going while he's in his feelings. Let me explain something about men to those of you that think males are hard or unemotional. The way you like a boy and it makes your heart race, a man feels that, double. Emotionally and sexually, a man is just as open after a first date as a woman is, if not more. He wants to talk to you and he wants to fuck you. So not only is his heart making him feel soft, his dick is driving him crazy to see you. That's why men tend to be aggressive in the 48 hours following a date, he's trying to get you back in the web. This is your chance to exploit those feelings on the phone.

The following day or night, whenever is a good time for both of you to talk, you must get on the phone and let it all hangout. If a guy wants to steadily text, do what Cali did, redirect it after a bit too, "let's continue this later on the phone," don't get caught up in texting being good enough. Some of you are younger and you are more comfortable texting than actually talking. I told you from the start that these steps require two things: Confidence and the ability to open your damn mouth. Set a time for him to call you or for you to call him and follow this blueprint...

Cali gets a call while she's online shopping and talking to one of her friends on the phone. She clicks over and greets Stephen with a warm hello, then tells him to hold on. Cali could have left her bff on hold, then apologized later. She could have clicked back rapidly like an excited school girl, "Oh my god, girl, it's HIM, call you back," without leaving him waiting for more than five seconds. Cali sees being on another call as an opportunity to establish that she has a life outside of talking to Stephen. Knowing Stephen will be forced to wait, and think about this, Cali takes her time. "Damn, she's talking to other people?" Is what a man will think while on hold. He will assume it's another girl, but male paranoia will also think it's another man. Putting a man on hold, as normal as it seems, is a small act of power. A man can't think he's your only source of conversation. Feeling as if all you have is him would make a man too comfortable, and there will never be any pressure to win your exclusivity if his feet are up.

Cali clicks back over and apologizes, without saying whom she was talking to, be it man or woman. Mystery casts doubt. Instead, she fires off an apology for not being able to hang out. Stephen is cool with it and says that they should get together again soon. Cali agrees, then changes the subject to his day, "Did anything exciting happen today that made you want to stay in Accounts for life?" Cali, like on the date, brings it back to Stephen's life, and in this moment, she becomes his shoulder to lean on. If the day went bad, and he had an asshole client, he'll share that and Cali will dig to see what exactly the client did, which allows Stephen to vent. Venting is wonderful because it is a stream of consciousness where you allow someone to just let loose while you listen. If Stephen had a good day, he won't really want to talk in depth about work. Topics are like Yelp reviews; people rarely want to go in unless it's negative. Cali will take this time on the phone to open up a little more about herself as well. The first date interview is over, so like at the end of their date, she can see if her personality clicks with this man by sharing things that she did that day and get into other topics of personal passion.

The goal is for this to be a marathon session. The longer you stay on the phone with a person the more at ease you are and the deeper you get into what makes them tick. **Think of each hour as a layer.** The first hour is joking and laughing. The second hour usually breaks down into history and stories of things a person does. The third hour forward delves into opinions, ideas, dreams, and even frustrations about life in general. Your aim isn't to jump from small talk to big talk because you think that a Spartan only needs to hear about important or deep things. Calm the fuck down and relax. This is your game, no need to rush. Let the conversation flow naturally, and if you are doing your job well, you will notice layers beginning to peel back.

I was once on the phone with a girl and it started with chitchat subjects, transitioned to a vacation story, and then ended on the meaning of life, literally. You can't start a conversation with the meaning of life if you get my drift. The conversation has to mature as each one of you become more and more comfortable. When you feel that he's most comfortable, ask any question that you forgot to ask on the date or that you have been curious about since the date. By the third hour, he's hypnotized, and you have a free ticket to get him to be honest about any subject. Use it!

Cali and Stephen will stay on the phone for four hours. Cali will have to stop and eat something, but she's going to take Stephen with her. Stephen might have to answer an email for work, and he's going to take Cali with him. If Stephen has to take another call, Cali won't be like, "Alright call me later," if it's only been an hour. She will be like, "I'll wait for you, baby," to show that she's enjoying him. Again, pride can't get in the way of connection. This little girl attitude about being put on hold or someone saying they have to call you right back is ashy. You don't get your way with attitude; you get your way by showing a man that you're down to ride. Every man you meet will have had long phone conversations with various women. Your mission is to go left where other girls have gone right. Stephen has to go to the door and let his neighbor borrow his garage opener. The phone remains on his ear, but Stephen isn't talking. Suddenly Cali hears a female's voice. Loud, giggling, "I'm surprised you're home Mr. Popular," Cali assumes this is the neighbor Stephen mentioned. Stephen chitchats but does the garage opener exchange without needless talk. Stephen is nervous. When he comes back to the phone and says, "hello, sorry about that," Cali could be like "Who was that bitch?" or she could take a passive aggressive attitude and mumble something about him being "Mr. Popular" in his building. This is the moment of truth.

Cali doesn't get protective and angry; Stephen isn't her man. Cali doesn't get passive aggressive or become quiet, she isn't insecure. Cali simply laughs, saying the neighbor sounded annoying. This is true, and Stephen confirms it. All girls know what loud and obnoxious women sound like. All girls know what a sexy voice on another female sounds like. Cali is going to be honest about her observation because this is going to show Stephen a part of her personality. She doesn't compete. If the girl sounded sultry, Cali would have replied, "I bet she looks like sex." The point is, there is no fear in terms of other women. Stephen is used to girls overreacting, and for him and Cali to now joke about his annoying neighbor is night and day from the other women who would call him rude or catch an attitude. Cali went left!

Four and a half hours into their call, Stephen's voice is tiring. Cali isn't going to pout to keep him longer. Her goal has been reached. Other girls would be like, "ten more minutes," or fake as if they don't care, "Go ahead, bye." A man will notice tone and vibe. Cali isn't going to be a spoiled brat that doesn't understand that he has to go to sleep nor is she going to be a rejected bitch who is being pushed off the phone. She blows Stephen a kiss and tells him she will talk to him later, maybe says one last witty comment or joke, and leaves it on a high note just like the date.

In the end, Cali knows several things about Stephen from their marathon phone call. What they talked about isn't important. Being on the phone for that long as a man proves that you interested him. As stated before, men love to talk about subjects they feel they are masters of or subjects which they are emotionally connected. The reason basic women can't get a man to call or stay on the phone is because what they have to say is lame or repetitive. Cali mastered the art of, "tell me stuff," which will always have men running off at the mouth. At the same time, she knows the secret art form of "shut the fuck up," so even when the conversation comes to her, she doesn't run on about her life. She makes her point and throws the ball back to him. Although Cali is willing to open up more, that doesn't mean she's now telling him everything. Questions about exes, enemies, childhood trauma, that stuff still isn't touched. Emotional discipline is withholding personal parts of your past despite being on a long phone conversation, master it. The more you tell a man, the more you trust a man, and when you develop trust too fast you will get burnt!

Outside of the fact that she is easy to talk to from Stephen's POV, Cali also learned that Stephen has time for her. Time is extremely important. There will come a point if you continue to date where you have to ask yourself if a man has time for a girlfriend. No man is too busy for pussy, but some are too busy for a relationship. He can get away to spend the night, but he can't get away to actually be there to spend quality time with you. He can get away for a morning quickie before work, but he doesn't want to be bothered hearing you out for a few hours if you're going through a rough day. "Too busy," has become an easy excuse for men who don't want to deal with certain girls they don't really like. Other times you can look at a man's daily life, be it school or work, and say, "Wow he barely has time to date me, no way is he going to have time to be my man." Being a good man doesn't make him the right man. Compatibility is key, if you can't match schedules, then that's a man you have to walk away from.

As a Spartan, you need a partner who can split focus and give you what you deserve, not just weekends or every other Thursday. This early in a relationship, the week following the first date, you must observe if it is logical to keep dating a man who can't get on the phone for a few hours a night but has time to meet up for an attempt at sex. You need a man who proves that he can and will make time, that shows attention to the details of your life, and who will be there to talk for at least one hour out of his day consistently. If he can't pull himself away from his schedule because he feels too busy or overwhelmed, how is he going to pull himself away to build a real relationship with you going forward? Cali researched Stephen's life in terms of time with this conversation. Now she knows that they have chemistry even when not face-to-face. Check! Cali knows Stephen has time for a girlfriend because he's opening his nights up to her for both a date and now for a long conversation. Check! Now it's time for the next mission.

FIT INTO HIS DAY

It's a thin line between being annoying and being desired. Too much of anything has the potential to become a bad thing, so there is no need to text a man every morning telling him how you hope that he has a good day or keep in constant contact with him throughout that day. Cali likes Stephen more than she should after one date, and she realizes that, but she won't allow her feelings to turn her into some weak bitch, thirsty to shower attention on a man she just met. The next morning she's back at work and sends a picture of her Starbucks order with Stephen's name spelled wrong. It's a teasing joke that is actually interesting, not a dry ass, "Good morning, have a great one!" Men do appreciate the sentiment of being hit up, it's sweet, but after two days it becomes routine. In reality, it doesn't endear you to a man in the same way a guy sending a good morning text or a wake-up call would earn brownie points with a typical female.

The majority of women get off on feeling as if they are wanted or knowing that someone is out there thinking about them. Men prefer fun to sentiment. Cali knows this, thus a joke picture that proves she's thinking about him, but also teases him and allows for a witty comeback, wins. It's not the action it's the creativity. Men want fun, not sappy and boring.

Cali's next mission is to stay on Stephen's mind but not in an annoying way where he would feel as if he needs to talk to her all the time or respond back to all of her texts. This man is working, he's on ESPN looking up stories about his team, he's fucking around with his boys on social media, and maybe he's even trying to make time for his other chick that Cali will soon push out of the picture. If Cali were to bombard Stephen with conversation all day, he would feel required to play along, not only to be nice because he likes her, but because new pussy requires attention that some guys don't mind giving in order to get it. Just because Stephen would respond back to her texts all day, doesn't mean she does it. Cali knows how Stephen is thinking, she's a Spartan, and once again, she uses her inner knowledge of how men think to position herself as an even bigger object of affection. Every day until the next date, Cali will make sure to have some contact with Stephen that shows that she's not too busy for him, but also shows that she's not a smothering kind of girl. At night, she can always call, but during the day how does a Spartan stay on a man's mind?

The real life Cali (one of the girls that make up the examples I'm using) told me about how when her guy was at work she would do a *Two Minute Challenge*. She called this guy and he had one minute to say everything he was thinking and she had another minute to say what she was thinking, then they would hang up, and not talk until later on. It was a silly and entertaining thing to do that bonded them as if they were teenagers, not two adults because as she put it, "We lose our goofiness when we first start dating because everyone is so scared." I thought that was a great example of fitting into someone's day with creativity.

Another example was *The Email Chain*. Cali would see an online story that was interesting, for example, there was a story where an Asian woman got so much plastic surgery that she looked like a completely new person...until she had a child with her new husband who was confused as to why his child would come out, "ugly." This man successfully sued his wife for misleading him with her surgical looks. Cali sent this story to her Stephen and they emailed their comments on it back between each other. It was just a silly article but it allowed them both to express their views and to interact throughout the day, without the "what are you doing boo" pressure that comes with being overly romantic.

You can use a quick call, you can text Memes, you can do the email chain; it doesn't matter so long as you aren't sending emails that run longer than a paragraph, texts that won't stop, or constantly calling him with, "I'm bored, what are you up to?" Don't be an annoying bird. The goal is to embed yourself in a man's life so he gets used to you in a way that's addictive. Give him something to look forward to when you call him that night; don't burn him out by being in his face all day. Fitting into his day in a low-key yet fun way makes him comfortable fast. This isn't about "get in where you fit in" submission; this is about being a shot of heroin with your personality. If you do this step, then you master how to make a man like you way more than you like him in a relatively short time.

THE DECLINE

Cali is tripping with Stephen during her workday, and talking to him at night. It's been three days since their date and she does want to see him again, but she's not ready to pull the trigger. During the conversations, Stephen asks if she wants to meet for lunch since they don't work too far from one another. He just wants to look at her. This is another mistake women make, "the quick hello" where a man is either in the area or near the office and wants to come and give her a hug or even bring a gift. Cali is always in control, and she will only see Stephen under her rules, even if her growing feelings are telling her, "bitch let him drive you home, that's bae." Cali declines, saying that she will let him know when a good day opens up for him to come by the office. This upsets Stephen, but the thing about men is that it is okay to piss them off; they bark but rarely bite. A man has to learn early, before the actual relationship, that he can't have his way with you. Highlight that, because at this point in the process, you will be in lust, and you will want to cave and see him. There will be time for that when he's your man. For now, you have to show him who's on the throne. This serves as another test for Stephen. If he's upset that Cali refuses to hang out after only three or four days, will he react like a brat or will he keep trying? So many basic bitches swear by, "you have to work for this," but the guys they date don't do anything but order them around, and they end up giving in any way. Remember, it's okay to say "no" to a man.

209

Cali knows that this is a handsome man that earns good money, and he's charming, therefore, other women are going to be after him. Other women are also texting or calling him. Despite Stephen saying he doesn't have anyone serious, any smart woman can look at a man and see that his market value points to him having, at least, one girl on his roster. Cali understands Stephen's market value, yet she doesn't bow down and give into seeing him. His ass has to work for the Queen, regardless. If Stephen gets frustrated and decides he doesn't want to talk to Cali after that, good. He's been exposed as a control freak or pussy hunter, and it will save Cali the pain of finding this out a month in. If Stephen starts ignoring Cali during the day or being unavailable to talk at night because he's not getting his way, good. He's been exposed again. Furthermore, if Stephen brings up anything in an attempt to make Cali jealous, other women, his ex suddenly calling him, etc., she will wash her hands. This is not about playing games, this is about establishing dominance over a man that proves that you aren't built like the rest of these peasants.

Stephen, like most men, will keep trying to win Cali over because Cali has done her job correctly. This isn't a corny woman that's chasing him or a Cool Girl that lets him set the rules, she's a strong personality that isn't overly bitchy, who takes time out of her day to hit him up. All men respect that. Stephen knows he has something special so he will wait for his Queen to give him the green light to take her out again.

THE DAY OFF

Absence makes the heart grow fonder. In a weak mind, absence makes the heart panic due to the paranoia that a person is no longer interested in you. Women and men both go through this and that's where I'm going to focus. When I was dating the woman that would become my wife, I remember not being able to get in touch with her one evening. I figured she would return my message, but 11 pm rolled around and no callback. Midnight no callback. I was up, mad as hell but it wasn't jealous anger, it was fear. *Did I say something the day before to upset her? Did she get what she wanted and was done with me?* Those are weak thoughts controlled by the fear of losing something you want. Those emotions are often

210

credited to women because females are known to blow up a phone, send way too many texts, and then leave a voice message like, "If you didn't want to deal with me you should have just said that, pussy!" This isn't some feminine hormone stereotype. The insanity that takes over after not hearing from a person for a day points to a fear of rejection that everyone has. No one wants to like someone and then have them suddenly fallback without warning. As with my story, you understand that it works both ways, but most men suffer in silence as opposed to going overboard and calling repeatedly or making threats. Between the first and second date, after you build up a daily routine; take a break, so that he has time to miss you.

Cali had a nice hour-long conversation with Stephen the night before where they had fun as always, but she got off the phone earlier than usual with the excuse that she had to be into work earlier than normal. Not true, but Cali didn't want to fall into marathon conversations every night with a man that she knows she has to go on another date with. The next day Cali purposely blocks Stephen. She doesn't want to be tempted to see any text messages or to answer any of his calls. She's going to be thinking of him of course, but she needs to decompress, maybe show some love to another guy on her roster, and give Stephen time to miss what he has so he understands what the stakes are if he fucks this up. Cali doesn't unblock Stephen until night. She has a voicemail but doesn't even check it. She gets a text asking if everything is good, but she doesn't even respond back. Cali is playing a game, an unfair game, but this isn't about being "nice" and "fair" she has to protect the only thing that matters, her heart. Cali texts Stephen in the morning with an apology and a picture of her blowing him a kiss. Yesterday was hell, and she didn't want to call and burden him with her work stress. Stephen doesn't believe the story, he's still mad, but Stephen has to buy the story because he now knows that not having her to talk to and interact with would be horrible so he has to swallow it.

"But what if he thinks I'm seeing another man?" Let me remind you this is only dating, he is not your guy and it is good that he would think that, because it further proves that you are still a free agent that answers to no man. This sets the foundation that if he wants 24-7 access to you in the future it's on him to either earn the right to lock you down or deal with you disappearing at times. You control his emotions; you don't bend to his!

Stephen will not have beef because he still wants her, and men don't act passive aggressive when there is still a prize to be won. A man that truly wants you will forgive and forget your day of absence just like I forgave and forgot when I was finally contacted by my future wife after that day was over. Dropping off the face of the earth will not damage things; it will make him want you more. Now that Cali tested Stephen and trained him to understand what life would be like without her, it's time to give him another reward.

THE SECOND DATE SET UP

Similar to *Ho Tactics*, you have to set the second date yourself in terms of where you want to go and how you want him to entertain you. This means you choose the activity, the place, and the day. This isn't about exposing how much money he has, this is about exposing your lifestyle to see if he can keep up. The first date was merely an interview; the second date is a day on the job to see if he fits into your world. Before we get to the actual date, you have to complete the setup mission. So far, you've given him good conversation, learned even more about his character, and given him glimpses of yours. You made yourself a part of his daily life, without being annoying. You successfully trained this man to move at your pace by declining his offers of pop-up dates or spontaneous meet-ups. Finally, you showed him that you don't need to talk to him every day, but he does. You, my Queen, are firmly in the driver's seat by this point.

Now it's time to research where you want to drive this man romantically. Do you want to go on another dinner date, this time at a more expensive place to show him that this is the way you expect to roll? Do you hit up a bowling alley and see how he reacts to your competitive side? Maybe you want to go to a stage show and dress up to see if he can hit the elegant switch. Maybe you want to go to a movie, grab a quick bite, and fuck him to get it out of the way, so sex isn't the elephant in the room going forward...just testing. This is the second phase of your vetting process, the part where you put his words into action. This means the second date will serve as a test to see if this man can be a real part of your life socially.

Some women only live to hang with their boyfriends. They go where he wants to go, and becomes interested in what he's interested in because their own passions in life may seem foolish and she doesn't want to bore him. There are too many, "I don't care, what do you want to do, bae" girls and not enough grown women who step up and promote their interests in a real way. Being that Cool Girl that can watch the game, but doesn't understand it, or who trails behind him to tacky restaurants when she prefers to fine dine because at least it's going somewhere, is pathetic. Women like that will forever remain boring Zombies with Pussies that find a man to love them for what they do for him (not fall in love), pop out a few kids, but most likely she and her man will live a bland and unfulfilled existence. Never sell your soul for dick. You must find someone that shares your joys or who is at the very least is open-minded enough to see new things through your eyes.

When you're dating, it's not about finding your place in a man's life; it's about him lining up with the things you love so you can share that. **Being happy together isn't about having someone to come home to; it's about having someone to explore life with**. I often talk to women who tell me that they want a man they can travel with, yet when it comes to normal dating are super basic in their wants. What's the point of traveling with a man if he can't event stand to do those things you enjoy doing locally? You can't jump to the fantasy and avoid the reality; you have to grow with a person in order to achieve real unity. A man can't complete you if he isn't willing to engage in your passions! The second date is no longer about him, you understand who he is, now he has to understand who you are.

A friend of mine had trouble finding someone local because he was gay and not comfortable promoting that to strangers. He took to the internet, found a match, and thought his problem was solved because this man was great on the phone. He would tell me how different this person was and how they talked every day about wide-ranging topics. This was a long distance situation, so I warned him to wait until they spent real time before he got his hopes up. No matter the orientation, men are men, and you never know a man's true nature until you drag him into a real world environment. In their case, my friend was a movie buff, and going to the theater was something he always did. When he flew up to see this new boo,

213

that's where they went. In public, he found out that the person he had fallen for on the phone was not at all someone who meshed with him in the real world. He insulted the ticket taker, made fun of the movie while in the theater, called people fat, and made racially insensitive remarks all in the span of two hours. It blew my friend's mind because when they were closed up in the apartment, it was perfect. **Like being on the phone, hanging out in closed quarters will never uncover true character.** Now that they were out living like real people, this guy's personality was fully exposed. My friend returned home earlier than planned and the two never spoke again. The phone and the house are not what relationships are built on, the outside world is the baptism that all potential couples need to go through if it is to work longer than a few months.

Back to our girl, Cali, she has been impressed with Stephen, they mesh on the phone, but how does she know Stephen fits into her life socially? A Spartan's mind shifts from just another date, to "What date can I take him on to further test his compatibility?" Cali isn't a homebody, she loves to go out in the city, and being a music lover her favorite pastime is to check out performances by indie artists. If a man is going to truly connect with her, he will have to be willing to share in this experience. This is a perfect litmus test to see if a man can date outside of his comfort zone. Cali has to see if Stephen is perfect in private or perfect all the time.

Cali asks Stephen to take her to a music show and sends him the link to buy the tickets. Stephen isn't into alternative music, but he's into Cali, so he agrees to take her out. The Second date is now set. We are passed the getting to know you chitchat, the ice has been broken, and this date will now match the more open and relaxed Stephen with the more informed Cali. What happens on this date will determine if Stephen stays in Cali's phonebook as a potential boyfriend, or is dismissed as just another cute guy who exposed himself as just another dick. Before we break down the second date, let's revisit all the ways you could ruin the post-date process by reverting to pre-Spartan habit.

Chapter 14:
Post-Date Don'ts

You may feel as if most of the things listed in the last chapter are unnecessary or can be dwindled down to simply having a few long phone calls and setting up the second date. Final warning, if you attempt to freestyle these steps or be lazy with them because you are impatient, then you will fail. This is five years' worth of research in seeing how impatient, lovesick, and know-it-all women lose. Don't get sloppy and make the same mistakes every typical girl that has one good date makes the minute she feels wanted. He doesn't actually want you at this point! If your goal is to win, not just date at a normal basic level, then take everything on these pages very seriously. You will want to go out on a date with him the next day or maybe a few days later, but you must take it slow between the first and second date. "I don't have time, and he's asking me out," I don't care! In order for a man to see you as a Game Changer going forward, he has to get hooked on your personality. Not your phone voice, not your nudes, not the anticipation of seeing you that weekend; he has to experience you as a part of his daily life, get accustomed, and then when he is fully open, and only then, do you give him another dose in person.

Some of you go on three dates in one week with the same guy because you don't know how to work a man emotionally from afar. Some of you spend all day on the phone with these men or text all day because you don't know how to create want through separation. Realize that these steps aren't made up out of thin air; these are real examples of how women dominate. As for the women who fail to follow the post-date steps, I have two inboxes full of "Don't be mad, but I fucked up," that clearly show that the old ways will always be the wrong way.

DON'T WAIT ON HIM TO REACH OUT

You wake up, check your phone... nothing. You try to brush it off, but an hour later your phone is back in your hand, this time, you're growing angry. That's pride fucking with you. "If a man wants you he'll rush after you," that's the bullshit women pile up and lean on so they can justify their fear. You want a man to talk to you first, call first, and then call after a date so you can be sure that he likes you. For you to move first comes with the risk of being rejected. You must not hide from rejection, you must run towards it because the fear of the unknown is why your thoughts keep you worked up, nervous, and doubtful. It's better to reach out and get curved, then to sit around for days hoping that he actually calls. Take things into your own hands, because when you do reach out first you exercise total control.

This is the 21st century and men think the same way as women in terms of coming off as thirsty. He took you out, fed your ass, and shared his life story with you. For him to pop up with a morning text, an afternoon call, or even an email makes him consider, "Damn she's going to think I'm some kind of loser that has nothing better to do but hound her." When a woman is too prideful to call and a man is playing it cool waiting at least 24 hours to reach out because he read to do so in some *Pick Up Artist*[10] book, then you ruin the momentum. In a perfect world, a man will hit you up after a date just to check in because you're on his mind and he wants to keep it going. However, you have to prepare for the new age man who may be unsure if reaching out is something you will respect or see as simp activity. Don't over think this. He passed your test, the date was great, so let him know that it's okay to hit you up by hitting him up first. The goal is to get on the phone and keep the conversation going so you can learn even more about his personality when he's not face to face with you. Your goal is not to be some, "If he wants me he knows my number," young ass pride demon.

---

[10] These are popular male advice books about how to be confident and pick up "hot babes".

DON'T BE ANNOYING

A friend was on the phone with me one night, and what was supposed to be a ten-minute conversation turned into 90 minutes of clowning around. Finally, his "girl" chimed in and said, "For someone who doesn't like talking on the phone you've been on that call forever." She caught him. Contrary to what they tell women, men do not have a problem talking on the phone. It's not the phone, it's the person on the other end that makes him lie and say, "I don't do phones." In terms of my friend, he doesn't talk to that particular girl for longer than ten minutes unless she's in the same room. Why? Because she's only good for pussy and light conversation. I hope you are on your way to being a full-blown Spartan, but the truth is, none of what you're reading may stick, and may always remain a Zombie who is only good for pussy and light conversation. The type of desperate girl that over-calls, over-texts, and annoys a man with a lack of real conversation.

What did you do today? When is the next time I can see you? How's your day going? Did you see that one video on vine? The weather was crazy today, right?

Most men play along because they know that after twenty minutes of this BS or "did you miss me...no I asked you first," chitchat they can lure you into sex talk and then set up when to come see you next. The days following your first date you need to establish that you aren't typical. When a man calls or texts he should get the sense that you're the type of woman that will always say something interesting, not ask what he's doing or asinine questions about his boring day. In Cali's examples, she found ways to keep her man talking about things that he couldn't shut up about. This isn't hard if you paid attention on your first date and listened to the things your date talked about and showed the most excitement over. Not every man is into the NBA, *Grand Theft Auto* games, or *Avengers* movies, you need to listen to the way his voice shifts when he gets on a subject he enjoys, and keep hitting those topics. The more he says, the more compatibility you can determine. Remember you're not looking to be his girl; he's looking to be your guy. Therefore, his interests have to line up or why date him?

217

Another problem, besides being so nervous that you can't create real conversation, is not knowing when to chill out and give each other a break. Let's say that you are fun to talk to and he loved your marathon phone conversation. Don't follow up by thinking that you're supposed to talk throughout the day or text throughout the day going forward. Have a life outside of talking to this one man. You like him and he likes you, but when you won't give him a breather to go live your life, you smother him. The ironic thing is that men don't mind this when you're first getting to know each other, they will happily let you over communicate. What man is going to tell you, "Baby, you're texting me too much, chill," and still get a second date or a first nut? Just because a man isn't objecting doesn't mean he's enjoying that kind of attention.

Clingy is never cute. A man will get sick of you without even knowing it. Once a guy loses his taste for you, he will figure out ways to avoid you, until he can see you in person aka try for sex. While you were a steak with lobster, days upon days of eating that has made you as special as meatloaf. Allow him to miss you, to want you, to chase you! You should be dating other men. You should be talking to your friends. You should have hobbies outside of work. "...but all I think about is him," no shit, because all you have is him, but he's not yours yet! The reason typical women struggle with over communicating is that their own lives are boring. Go to work or school, come home, play on the internet, watch a show, repeat. Your Amazon wishlist is overflowing, but your social life is empty as fuck. Right now, even with all the stuff you distract yourself with, how many times do you say, "I'm bored!" per week? If you are bored, that means you are boring! Men pick up on this vibe, they know it's not simply you having a crush based on how good things are going, he knows you don't have a life outside of him. The moment you show a man that you want him more than he wants you, It's game over. If you can't pace yourself during the first week or two, how will you pace yourself during a real relationship? Make this man a part of your day, not the primary focus of your day.

DON'T FALL BACK INTO YOUR STORY

A big part of preventing burnout is to keep up with the main thing laid out on the first date. Let him do the talking. When you get him on the phone and you get all the jokes out, you'll most likely be cuddled up in your bed, hair in your bonnet, and feeling all warm and fuzzy. This usually results in a woman telling too much to a man she barely knows. There will be plenty of time for your story. This is *Forrest Gump*, he's Forrest, and you're that woman on the bench that's asking, "What the fuck was up with Jenny?"

Do not get so comfortable in your environment that you feel as if you need to tell him about childhood trauma. Do not let his smooth phone voice drop your guard and make you talk about how worried you are about money or health. Do not revert to stories about your ex's mother, your father's drinking problem, your sister's loser husband, or anything that triggers your own personal therapy session. There is nothing wrong with talking about things that you plan on doing, or your views on life, politics, religion, family, etc...However, stay away from going into your own personal life stories to prove a point. The first week of calls is about him pouring himself out, so you can filter the bullshit. The same way you are relaxed, he's relaxed at his place, and he will start to snitch on himself the later it gets on that phone call. Your job is to listen to Forrest spin his tales, only interjecting to make a joke, comment, or to ask for clarity on something. I will say it again; people love to hear themselves talk more than they like to listen to others talk. Expose that on your first post-date phone call, and continue to hit that each night you two cupcake on the phone.

DON'T SOCIAL MEDIA STALK

Are you on Instagram? Should never come out of your mouth. Asking his @ name is off limits. Popping up on Facebook trying to add him the next morning is not only creepy; it's a recipe for disaster as you move forward in this blossoming relationship. Even if the man asks you for your social media info, have a response ready, "That's for fun, boo, you get the real me," or "I'm only on Facebook for my family, I don't really bring personal stuff online." Don't lie, Spartan Up and say "no" to him. He can stalk if he wants to; a Spartan doesn't put her business online anyway. But if he does bring something you said on the internet up, when you never told him any of your username information, you reveal the sneaky bitch in him. If he doesn't trust you and is willing to judge based on what you write or post, then let him bring that bullshit to your next date or a phone call, and cut him off like you just hit that 141st character.

If you two were already friends online, then don't suddenly censor yourself because you know he's looking. "What if he thinks that's a subtweet? What if he thinks that guy who I blew kiss emoji's is my other bae? What if I'm on another date and he sees me posting pictures of my dress and asks where I was?" You're slipping back into typical behavior. Fuck what he thinks. If you're dating other men, be smart enough not to blast that as a Snapchat story or Instagram post. You know you're out, you know you look good, and you know you're going to be able to take other pictures at other times, so don't let your vanity get you caught up. A Spartan has to keep her court private, not everything is for the public.

The other side of the equation is your own jealousy and insecurity working overtime. You may want to stalk him and find out info that you can't get on the phone, but again this leads to the path of being typical. Basicas over think everything, and they live to do deep Google searches on men because they're afraid to be hurt. Fear drives those peasants to stalk, but it should never drive you to stoop to that level. Is that his friend or is he trying to fuck that girl whose pictures he always likes? Is he @ing that girl because he agrees with the things she's tweeting or is he trying to soften her up so he can slide in those DMs...is he already in her DMs!? *See, this is why you shouldn't trust men they are always trying to double dip and blah blah blah*! Why are you driving yourself crazy by speculating about a man that isn't even your friend, let alone, boyfriend?

Here's the truth, men on social media are never going to behave themselves. It's a buffet where all of these women with avatar's that highlight their best features are accessible 24-7. Is he flirting with women on the timeline? He had better be if he's single or he's an idiot. Is he posting some Draya Michele looking chick, as his Woman Crush Wednesday and you don't look a thing like Draya? Yup, because he's trying to fuck her too.

Is he on Facebook dropping subliminal messages about how he enjoyed your date last night because he's feeling you or is it so his ex knows he's moved on? Who cares!? No matter if you find good or bad information, none of what a man does from the privacy of his social media account matters. Once you're in an official relationship then you can police that nonsense, but for now, stay away! All stalking does is put ideas in your head that make you jump to conclusions or turn you off.

The counter may be, "What if he's psycho, shouldn't me or my bff do recon on his pages to be sure he's not two-timing me or saying weird shit?" No! You and your bff need to go join a book club or something because you're doing too much with your free time. The truth needs to come to light via conversation, that's how you prove that you are doing these steps correctly. You aren't with him yet; therefore, the other women he's fucking or trying to fuck aren't your business. I once heard of a girl making her friend go on Tinder and match with the guy she was dating to see if he was really into her...he's single! He's not going to delete his Get Pussy App based on one, or even two, good dates with you. Why would any man get rid of his hos this soon? Stop letting your ego gas you! In reality, you should be doing the same thing with other men because one date does not mean you are no longer single. You are very single, which is why you should have a roster until you agree to give him the title.

Jealousy dictates that the man you like should barricade himself away from the rest of the women in the world and focus on you. That's not realistic. He doesn't know if you're going to turn out as cool as you were on the first date, if your compatibility is legit, or if you're just wearing a mask yourself. What fool cuts off his other options or potential options for something that has yet to be disproved as a mirage? Women have a bad habit of putting all their eggs in one basket the moment they meet a high-grade prospect; men have always known better. If you look hard enough you will find him online flirting with a girl, but that's normal. Using social media to see if he's psychotic is also pointless. His mental stability isn't going to be revealed in a selfie or twitter rant. Any excuse as to why you want to stalk him is just that, an excuse. Don't complicate your mission by bringing unrelated things into the picture; focus on how he's treating you, that's all.

DON'T BRING UP OTHER WOMEN OR MEN

Staying on the subject of minding your own damn business, do not bring up other women who may currently be in his life. In the advice I give daily, I'm often talking to women who are dating guys who already have girlfriends, who are in situationships, or men who are on break but not really free of their ex. People rarely clean break from relationships before getting into new ones, it's clearly the world we live in, or I wouldn't get so many emails on the subject. All you can go off is what he tells you on Day 0. If you do the baby mama check or the "your girlfriend" check, as I laid out earlier, you can only base the opportunity you're giving him off his answer. If a man lies and says, "I don't have one of those," then take his word... don't believe it, but give him the benefit of the doubt for now. If it comes up on the date or in a conversation post-date that he was lying, then you cut him the fuck off! Some men will tell you, "I didn't want to scare you off. It's complicated. We're breaking up." Do not buy it! If he lies, he has to go. No exceptions.

If he responded honestly and said, "I actually am seeing someone," or "I'm trying to end it with my ex, but she keeps holding on." Then use your discretion. I don't advise getting into a messy situation where the last chapter isn't closed. In a perfect world, a man will be single or at the most, only dating, the same as you are. However, your reality may push you towards someone who has some baggage but still seems worth the chance. I'm not going to tell you to close the door if he's being honest about that current relationship, but don't be naïve either. For anyone that read *Solving Single* you already know my stance on taking a man from a weak bitch being easier than buying food stamps from a junkie. A girlfriend isn't the same as a wife, she can easily be removed. A situationship dummy is just another placeholder, she too can be pushed out.

If a man is entertaining you, yet admits to having something else he's trying to get out of, it may be a lie so he can double dip, or it may be the truth and he is trying to find a reason to clear his roster. Nevertheless, you have to consciously understand and accept the boat you're climbing into or you could end up in the same situation a few months down the line. Dating a man with a previous situation is a choice you make when he first confesses to that, not one you decide on after your first date. If you are thinking, "He has a girl and I'm not trying to get mixed up with that, but let me see how our date goes before I decide for sure," then you already fucked up. Don't compromise yourself by being indecisive! The same way that you have to ask yourself if you can deal with a man with a child, you have to be honest about a man with a girl or a lingering ex. The more time you give him to win you over, the harder it will be to walk away.

During your post-date week don't say petty shit like, "You must have been busy with your other chicks," or "Let me know when you're free, I know you're popular." Those are signs of passive aggressiveness and unwarranted jealousy. His life is his life; he hasn't earned or accepted the position to come to work for you, so of course he's putting in other applications. In *Ho Tactics,* one of the biggest mind-fucks is to be okay with him having other women, in route to becoming that perfect unbothered fantasy woman. These steps are much different because you're not softening him up to buy you things; you want to earn his respect and, later on, his love. **To be cool with him having hos is to show him that you aren't serious, that you're a down for whatever type girl, no man wants to marry that.** While he will enjoy that easy going disposition, and tell you how cool you are, he won't see you as anything long term. Assume that you aren't the only girl, but carry yourself as if you are the only girl.

The same rules apply to a jealous man asking about the other people you are dating. "This is A and B, let's not talk about Z," or "I'm not talking to anyone seriously right now." That's all you need to get across when a man asks you about your life outside of him. For some reason, women are way too open about their "we talk" relationships. Stop being an open book with these strange men! You don't have a boyfriend, so why bring up some other guy who you are just dating or some random FWB who you call when the vibrator isn't enough? Keep your business your business, until that man becomes more to you. You aren't lying if you don't give him an answer, and you aren't being a mean if you tell him to worry about himself. You don't owe shit to this man just because he took you out. Therefore, at the first hint of jealousy, shut him down by either ignoring the inquisition, telling him to worry about himself, or downplaying the seriousness of the other men you entertain.

This isn't to spare his feelings; it shows him that you aren't one of these girls who becomes a girlfriend before she is actually a girlfriend. Some of you are guilty of letting your own want for a man stop you from talking to other men before that guy has even proved himself. Even if you aren't dating other men, carry yourself as if you are. This shows a man that you are desired outside of his courting. The thought of a woman having other men drives any truly interested man crazy. Use his male insecurity as a weapon! When you get to the step where you take a day off from him, he knows that he should be worried. At that moment, you are firmly in control because he knows that it's on him to take you off the market, you aren't a basic chick that takes herself off the market out of a thirst to be chosen.

DON'T SEE HIM

I was talking to a woman who told me about a good Tinder date she went on. This guy took her out to eat and then surprised her with an archery activity. That's a creative date. First you dine like a princess and then you get to play Katniss Everdeen for the rest of the night. How did she reward this? She called him the next day and asked for a ride as if the man was an Uber driver. When he didn't respond accordingly, she then offered to pay for the ride. This is how you turn fireworks to firecrackers. Dating is supposed to exude this feeling of magic. When you try to bring that man into your life to do favors like drop offs, furniture moving, house painting, or even have him stop by your job to say "hello" the magic vanishes. Don't take Prince Charming and turn him into Ray Regular. Some men will happily do these things just to get extra time with you, and you may salvage a relationship out of it, but it's too much too soon, and you are skipping over the necessary steps. You're forcing him to be a part of your life before you get to know him, and once that seal is broken you can't go back.

Even distribution of time is very important to getting to know someone properly. Pop up visits, or multiple dates in the same week, can bond you too fast in all the wrong ways. To lock yourself in the house and just get to know him will never be as effective as pacing yourself over weeks. The goal is to be a special attraction, that a man looks forward to, not an everyday appearance he takes for granted. Most of you know The Rock, former Pro Wrestler turned movie star. Well when The Rock came back to wrestle people were confused, it's like why leave 10 million a movie for 5 million a year? The genius was that The Rock only had to show up every three months. That ended up being 5 appearances that year—which broke down to a million dollars a show. Why the hell would WWE owner Vince McMahon pay that much for one man? Because every time he showed up it meant something! It was special. That's how you need to be with your time. Either you're going to be John Cena, the great vanilla champion that's out there every night, or you're going to be the fucking Rock, electric, magical, and has someone dying in anticipation of your next appearance.

Attached at the hip syndrome is the reason most college, workplace, and local neighborhood romances fail. When you spend time getting to know a person at an accelerated rate, it's like going forward in your biology textbook. You're supposed to be learning about DNA, truly understanding it, not glossing over it so you can rush to the chapter on the human body. Some of you probably rushed over earlier chapters to get to this part of the book, because you think you get it, but when you don't utilize patience to learn, you never get it. You could be in a college dorm or on a military base with nowhere to go, that doesn't mean you hang out each day because you can't date properly under the conditions. Patience must remain. You could walk over to sit with him and talk, but where's the build up? Wait a week and go off base for a drink. Wait until you are done with finals, and then go over to the local off-campus karaoke bar to trip with him. No matter where you live, take your time and be a special attraction!

I knew a girl; we'll call her Trina, who dated her co-worker. They went out once and then fell into the habit of eating lunch together every day. I gave advice to one girl, call her Eve to stick with the female rapper theme, who dated a guy in her apartment complex. This neighbor invited Eve out once, and then they fell into the habit of chilling in their apartments each day. "What's wrong with that, bonding on or outside of a date is still bonding," let me correct your flawed logic. Both of these real life people ran into the exact same problem. Trina's work buddy ended up talking to another girl on the job. The apartment guy ended up official with a girl that moved into Eve's building. Both stories had this burst of never wanting to be separated attraction followed by a crash and burn boredom.

These men didn't have to work for anything outside of that first date. They learned basic things about each other, had deep talks about life, but their relationship never grew outside of ordering in takeout or rubbing hands in the break room. By the time Trina and Eve both had sex with those guys, it came at a very cheap price. Just like that idiot who wins the lottery and blows the money, no one appreciates things that come easy.

If Trina would have gone to work every day, declined lunch sessions, and established dating and communicating as an outside of the building specialty, then Trina's guy would have seen Trina as something special. As it went down, he conquered Trina without breaking a sweat and didn't truly appreciate her as a person, just an object of lust during his eager honeymoon stage. Eve's guy had stairwell pussy, he got off work, ran up the stairwell, and there it was waiting for him. The girl he left Eve for wouldn't even let him in her apartment. Think about that! Eve was confused as to how a man could get everything he wanted, yet still pick the woman that tells him, "no." It boils down to the respect the special attraction woman is able to create, whereas the attached at the hip woman becomes stale, allowing apathy to set in. Similar to women in college who want to lay up under guys all evening, it won't work unless he sees you as a victory due to his efforts, not something handed over quickly. Dates make you a special attraction, utilize them to build your legend. A man will always remember what it took for him to get you and cherish that effort.

DON'T BE THIRSTY FOR ATTENTION

A question that comes up in actual relationships is, "How do I know how much space to give my boyfriend?" This is usually asked when the relationship is having troubles and about to end. Men wait until it's too late to carve out their space, and women, generally, never even think that their men want space to begin with. There are two types of women, the ones that love being free from their lovers and the ones that love being up under their lovers. The latter has a one-track mind, "he doesn't object to being around me so much, or talking to me so much, then he feels the way I feel." Wrong! A man is scared to death to tell his woman that he needs space, so he creates it naturally by using excuses such as work, friends, prior engagements, sporting events, etc. As a woman, you have to understand that even those men that want to be up under you need to be let loose. Most of the strong relationships I've seen revolve around the woman getting away from her man frequently to do her own thing. One of my best friends in Los Angeles has a super cool girlfriend that is into a lot of the things he is, but every other time I hang with him she's missing. She takes herself out of the equation because she understands that if it were up to him he would have her be his shadow. That's a woman knowing how to naturally balance the attention she gets and gives, in order to push her man to go be a free man.

After your first date and following your routine of talking on the phone or texting each other each day, you may get hooked. In your mind, you expect to get a quick text back all the time because you are used to it. You may expect him to call every night or be free to talk every night at 8, because you are used to it. For a man to have other things come up may cause weak bitch thoughts to pop up for no reasons. "Consistency" is one of the biggest desires women have, but in real life, consistency is not about a man reacting the same way to you five days out of the week. Don't get addicted to the habit of communication when you are first getting to know a man because he does have a life outside of talking to you. One of the goals is to become a part of his life by fitting into his day, not taking over his day.

You need to set that routine to talk, but if you see that the schedule is not working, adjust. If he wants to call you at 10 pm, understand the reason don't think that he's losing interest. If he doesn't respond to a text for two hours, understand that he may have been caught up with something, and instead of reacting with, "fine, I won't text this fool ever again," inquire about that when you talk to him and see what was going on in his day. Communication is the other C that needs to be used in heavy doses. When you actually become a couple, you need to be able to understand his behavior, not just expect things to go the same way every day. Know when to reach out, know when to fall back, and know when to set your own rules for consistency. This step will help you control any neurotic behavior during dating and teach you how to balance your wants versus his freedom as you move into a real relationship.

DON'T HAVE PHONE SEX

I think phone sex is the greatest thing in the world, and one of the ways women can easily hook a man during the "getting to know you" phase. However, the week after the first date is too soon to whip it out if you're trying to establish a legitimate relationship. You can flirt and be seductive, but to actually get into a position where you are on the phone making a man cum, before you even get a second date, sends the wrong message. The second date is where a man thinks he will fuck you, and if you start talking about all the ways you're going to suck his dick and how you want him to bend you over and pull your hair, then sex becomes expected. He'll take you out on that date, tell you what you want to hear, and play his position to get that fantasy in real life. Do not taint the mission by leading a man to believe that he's already in there, because then he stops being honest, and all the work you did on the first date is null and void. When you're about to get into a man's pockets using *Ho Tactics* phone sex is a tool for control, when you want to be respected, phone sex proves you're out of control.

Days after the first date, you're having a marathon phone session, and it creeps into how you have a sexy phone voice. You play around by saying something teasing like, "Do I really, daddy?" That's cool, but when you take it to the level of what you would do, what you're wearing, or allow him to guide you into saying something that will get him off, the game is over. Men are persuasive, and when a woman is afraid to scare a man off, she allows herself to be manipulated into making him happy. There are women who love to say what they won't do, but when a man is begging, they bend to his will, worried he will go find another girl to satisfy his needs.

You have to be willing to say, "No" and say it often. You won't be Jerk off Encouragement for a man you barely know, that's not who you are. If he wants to pout and get off the phone early with you, let him. He can go call up his other bitch and let her talk about all the ways she likes to deep throat. When you smack a man's hand down and prove through actions what kind of women you are, he may get turned off and never come back. Good! Each step of this section is meant to run a man off because only the men that aren't scared off by you coming off as a woman of respect deserve to stay around.

DON'T LET HIM PLAN THE SECOND DATE

Let's review the first date once more. You wanted him to give you his best shot in terms of creativity and romance. It didn't matter if he took you to a Yelp rated $$ restaurant or a $$$$ one, this was not about money it was about effort, seeing how this potential boo treats his women. He did a good job; maybe he already nailed your personality with his dating choice. Now it's time to introduce him to your normal style. Think of the second date as how you expect to be treated by a man going forward. Some of you are tomboys who don't want to sit and eat, you prefer to go hiking and have a picnic at the top. Some of you are hood at heart and the comfort of places like Red Lobster are preferred to some place that serves you one scallop and charges you $50 for it and an extra $12 for two pieces of asparagus. Others are more into the culture of the city, and love trying new places or visiting old stomping grounds. This isn't your ideal date in terms of Valentine's Day romance, it's your ideal date in terms of sharing your world. You need to show a man who you are beneath the sexy exterior and see if he can keep up with you because this is the final date before you make your first cut.

How do you become best friends and remain best friends? How can you create that once in a lifetime bond that leads to a strong marriage? You must find common loves or introduce each other to new loves. Sitting in the house watching TV shows is cool, but that's not a true reflection of life, so expose him to something deeper. There are so many 19 and 20-year-olds that swear their boyfriends are their best friends but they don't share anything in common, they sit in the house, watch YouTube, eat, and fuck. Those relationships always crumble because real romance doesn't confine itself to the house or revolve around doing what only one of the two feels like doing. You like museums, why hasn't he taken you to any? You prefer drama films; why does he only take you to see the comedy flicks he enjoys? You're a family-centric person, why does he always find a way to avoid dinner with your relatives? In response to a woman trying to be a "whatever you want to do, babe," Cool Girl, relationships form with the man at the center. Months or years later women realize the hustle: *I do everything he wants to do but as soon as I want to do something, it's a debate*. You created that life for yourself by not dating properly!

229

"I don't need to go anywhere. I just want to be with him." Women are not supposed to be dogs that serve to do as their masters say. Putting a man at the center of the relationship is outdated and overly submissive, and I refuse to see you date this way. The second date is your date, your activity, your type of food, or your type of romance. The words, "I don't feel like doing that," coming from his mouth already sets the stage for a man who will never truly be in a two-way relationship. I'm not promoting dating your way or the highway, I'm talking about establishing a compromise. A man will have you sit there and watch the basketball team he likes and you have to find a way to make it fun. A man will be quick to tell you he doesn't feel like going to a birthday party with your friends, but he will expect you to be by his side when he has to show up to his work party. That's what I mean by a man being the center. I know so many women who get led date after date and never have any say because they are afraid to speak up. "I don't know what to do, you decide babe," is a front used by cowardly girls who don't want to choose wrong. You fear that a man won't enjoy the things women enjoy, so you do what he likes to pacify him. When it comes to those things you enjoy, you push them to the side and do them with your girlfriends or by yourself. You don't become partners to do the things you love apart. Yes, there will always be disinterest and you will have activities that don't mesh, but there needs to be more you enjoy together than apart.

When you reach this second date point, before any of the "Let's do things I want to do," male-centric bullshit sets in, you have to create that foundation of compromise. You need a man that is willing to step into your world so he can get closer to the real you. What defines you? What are the intangibles that make you unique? These are questions that can't be answered verbally, you have to show these men who you are at the core. The second date is an entry level trip into your world. Don't over-think what you want to do as if you need to blow him away or seem cool, it's not about the wow factor. Plan a date based on the thing you would want to do the most on any given day. It's the personification of what *you* define as a good time. Before we get to that second date, let's dive into how to stay strong sexually when a man who you now like on a deeper level tries to test your Dick Discipline before that date, and after.

Chapter 15:
Is His Dick Spartan Proof

traditionally the third date is when a man's hustle is supposed to come together and he gets some sort of action—oral, foreplay, sex...if not all three. These days, I've seen the second date evolve into the new sex date because modern dating puts so much focus on texting and talking between dates, to an extent where women become comfortable around new men fast. I warn against consecutive dates back to back, because this is how men lure you into false comfortability. Date you on Tuesday, pop up to see you on Wednesday, get you over on Thursday, and a few hours into that session it doesn't feel like a date, it feels as if you've known each other for years. Courting isn't about cramming in three dates in five days and becoming fast friends, it's about seeing how his effort either grows or dissipates over the course of weeks. Literally weeks, not days. When you let men ADD date you, it sweeps you up in that honeymoon excitement of a new guy liking you so much that he has to keep seeing you or talking to you.

While he's blowing up your ego by giving you constant attention in a way you've always wanted, he's also disarming your safeguards. Everything written previously will go out the window if you allow a man to speed date you at his pace. Dating like a Spartan is not about how many dates you can get, or how big the bill is at the end of the night, it's about proving character via time and consistency. Before you go on the next date, you must be prepared to pump the breaks of any man looking to hustle you.

DICK ON A PEDESTAL

A longtime friend, let's call him Billy because that's not his name, once made a bold statement to a group of us who were busting his balls about why he chose to talk to a girl that was not his type. It wasn't that the girl was ugly, but Billy is one of those braggers that loves to talk about what he will and won't hit. Given that this girl he just pulled was not the "exotic with D-cups" type he always talked about, we called him out on his hypocrisy in the way that we men do, by clowning him. His response was, "Look at my height and my eyes, that bitch is going to give me head by this weekend." We all laughed at the time, then we got texted pictures, not of the act, but of enough evidence to show it was going down. Over the next three months, it stopped being funny to me when this same girl began to hang around like his personal slave. She wasn't his girlfriend, but she acted like it and he let her eat it up. Now, I see that she was a placeholder, but it was another story, however, that gave me further insight years later about *Pedestal Dicks*.

There was a young woman, I'll call Brandi, who was asking for advice. She had been dating this guy who started off nice, but then started to be a jerk after the second date. No more morning texts and no more date offers. It had only been about three weeks, and she was asking me how to get her "man" back to the way things were. By the time I was able to respond, she had seemingly solved her own problem. Brandi fucked this guy to change his attitude and said that "Oh, it's all good now, turns out he just needed sex." Not even a week later she came running back because the sex didn't fix it! I told her silly ass that she fell for the push and pull. Her response put it all in perspective. "You don't understand, he's super famous in my town, everyone knows him and every girl tries to date him, but he chose me." And there it was.

The same way my friend Billy knew that his height and light eyes made him appealing to certain women, Brandi's guy knew that his local fame made him a trophy for local basic bitches. The through line is that men will play the date to fuck game because they know that certain women will allow them to accelerate the process and lead to sex relatively easy. Billy's girl with on the chubby size, Brandi was skinny, but they both were physically attractive. It isn't that men treat certain women like shit and chase after other types, it's that men pick up on insecurities based on how a woman acts on a date or when he first meets her. Then he passes judgment based on their date thirst, "girls like that fuck guys like me because I'm better than what they normally get." For all the shit talk average women do about how men aren't all that, most are guilty when it comes to placing certain men on pedestals based on Market Value.

MARKET VALUE

A man knows what level he's on socially, economically, and physically. An unattractive drug dealer knows that he can still win because he can buy love. A handsome fast food worker knows that he can still be treated as if he's a perfect boyfriend candidate because he has default good looks that women don't pull every day. Unlike women, men can lack true confidence and still end up with the girl of their dreams. Why? As we discussed a bit in Chapter 2, Men understand market value. Males take self-inventory and then lead with something that they know a woman will respond to in terms of seeing him as desirable. In the case of your date, he will most likely see himself as a winner on two levels: He is attractive enough and employed enough to get most women in your city.

Mind you that we may not be talking super attractive or even a man that makes over 100k a year. He's looking at his competition to figure out how valuable he himself is to women. Men can guess by the area you live in and the places you go, what other men are in the race for your heart, and from there he can create a ranking system. He may not be Cam Newton, but he's better than Cam the Barber. The average woman may only meet one wealthy man in her city. This upper echelon man is usually a musician or executive who doesn't have time for love or a ball player who already has a main girl and is only looking to get a nut or expand his Ho harem. This leaves Mr. I'm a 7.5 out of 10 physically and make 55K a year, as the default standard for a lot of women who don't want to branch out from their normal lifestyle. The standards in the 21st century for women are low more times than not, therefore, a man at the level just mentioned or above will understand his own shortcomings, but still know that he has enough to make Tina Typical thirst for a commitment. Everyone wants to drive a luxury car, not because of the brand, but because it tells you and the rest of the world that you deserve the best and get the best. However, not everyone can afford the best even when they believe they deserve it. Men are the same. You deserve a man that makes just as much money as you, no prior kids, looks good, and treats you like the royalty you are...but during your Pre-Spartan life, self-doubt made you believe you needed to settle for what's good enough, and you ended up with a Camry instead of an S-Class.

This analogy is not meant to place blame on women, it's to understand why those who are educated and have money themselves, lower their bar. There aren't as many men on their level so girls downgrade, for fear that they will die trying to find luxury. It takes time to find a quality man in terms of looks and career, and non-Spartans are lazy. If a man thinks that you are a woman who will settle because you have zero dating options, and he has high market value, it will show in his attitude. They know they are being graded on a curve due to the rest of the men you meet being bums, narcissists, or undesirables. Therefore, they act cocky or don't feel a need to put in work. Why? Because like the Billy's of the world, they have determined that a woman like you won't do better—ever! Abusive husbands tell their wives, "Go ahead and leave, look at you, who would want you?" That cuts deep because there is truth to it in her own mind. The same thing with the guys you're dating. If you project this fear that you need to lock this guy with high market value in, before he moves on to the next girl, he will take advantage of your desperation.

Leverage is a man knowing that a woman doesn't have an offer on the table that's as good as or better than he is. She could find a more handsome man, but he will be broke or sharing his dick with the entire city. She could find a more paid man, but he is most likely unattractive physically or internally. She could find some guy that's even with him in looks and wealth, but she doesn't want to make a lateral move and risk being single another year. These circumstances are what gives many men the balls to walk into a date as if you owe him pussy. The first date he may try, but won't pressure. The second date he expects it, but will only try for foreplay. Third date he expects it all or he's prepared to use that leverage to drop hints that he won't be around for a fourth date. To say "no" to sex with him, or, at least, a foreplay session in private is to lose him...or so you think.

THE RUSH TO SETTLE

Your date knows that even though it's only been a week or a week and a half, you like him a lot, your body is attracted to him, and with the pressure of dating on the curve of "Only a few good men in this city," he will attempt to break you down using this secret: **Girls Hate Dating**.

"We like each other. Let's just be together so I can stop worrying about if you like me for me, stop stressing about if you have other girls ahead of me, and allow me to stop entertaining these other guys I only talk to just so I can say I'm talking to someone else."

No girl really wants to date for weeks or even months. She wants two or three dates and then to transition into a relationship where she's free to do things without fear. Fuck raw, nurture him, update her relationship status, bae brag, and most importantly drop her guard so she can truly fall in love. She doesn't want to do the legwork of three dates, 90 days, or any tests that could prove that she wasted her time. Men understand that traditionally, women are in a race to be chosen, not in a marathon to figure out what's real and what's fake. This is why the handsome, wealthy, or successful men are in the habit of making seemingly strong women move too fast or take chances too soon. Words like "exclusive" or statements like "I'm only talking to you," are music to a girl's ears because she doesn't actually want to do any of these Date Like a Spartan steps.

A typical just wants to land a man, using the lease amount of energy and brain power. Which is why I want you to take your time between the first and second date. Men think you're in a race like the rest of these birds, they aren't in on the secret that you're a patient Spartan. The longer you wait for the second date, the less power he has sexually, because fast sex happens when you spend a lot of time in a short period of time. A six-hour conversation, two back to back dates, a weekend together on a spontaneous trip, those things fast track a man to lower a woman's guard and get easy sex...not you. A Spartan does fear dating, waiting, and dating some more. A Spartan thrives in this strategic game, because she understands that it neutralizes a man's sex tactics.

BREAKING INTO FORT KNOX

When I was in London, I was asked in that accent that sets my heart on fire, "If a girl followed everything you told her to do, could you yourself still go after her and have sex with her in a short time?" I've never thought about anything I've written in the terms of the person who built the safe knowing how to break into that safe. However, it is a good point. I shouldn't be able to break you nor should any man thinking with my wisdom. There should be no such thing as Spartan Proof game no matter who the man is, myself included. The only way anything I'm writing fails is because you allow a man to expose your armor, and then chip away. I've seen three distinct weaknesses over the years in terms of a woman's vulnerability. Find the one you are hiding and reinforce it before you go on your next date.

<u>The Girl Who Wants to Be Loved</u>: This is the easiest type of woman to exploit while dating because her want to be loved is worn on her sleeve. These women have had a rough upbringing that included one of these things: Lack of attention from a father or having siblings that received more attention. Sexual assault of some kind that was never spoken about in a real way. Their looks put down by kids in school or by family members. Being chosen second or not at all by a childhood or teenage crush. A boyfriend that was perfect but was taken away because of death, prison, or moving away, and now she is haunted by the thought that her one true soul mate is already gone and she is forced to be alone. There are more examples, but you get the gist, these women have huge holes in their hearts and psyche's that have festered in a negative way for years. If a woman like this tries to follow the Spartan Code without doing the steps laid out earlier in terms of reframing that past and becoming reborn into a warrior that controls this world, her universe will continue to produce toxic results. Without true Spartan rebirth, her past trauma will remain a magnet for negativity and her weakness will be exposed by a man who knows where her hurt rests.

If I were to go on a date with a girl like this, even if she asked me all the fist date questions and made me do most of the talking, I would find areas to turn it back on her life. The same way I wrote about how bitter men are easy to expose, sad women are even easier. A woman who has real pain wants to talk about that because she never had a person that cared to hear her side of the story. Asking in a way that makes her feel as if I really want to know her story will get her talking a little, then a lot. There is no "Game" or lies a man has to tell, and that's what confuses women. Smart men are always honest because by being honest it proves that he is already different from the other men who try to kiss ass for pussy. A woman like that, who wants someone to want her, will project that onto that man who is being sincere. By the second date knowing that she wants to be loved, a man will do things like wrap an arm around her, give a layered compliment, or share something he can relate to her about to put her at ease. A man who eases into your broken mind by giving you the compassion you feared you would never experience becomes love. Even if it's for one night, that love will take over, and you will fuck him. Again, not because of game or false actions, but because you want instant love more than you want to wait for real love to develop. He doesn't beat you; you beat yourself.

The Girl Who Wants to Be Safe: These women are extremely common because their goal is to be overly careful and not engage a man because they know their guard is built out of glass. The goal is to use time to weed men out, but they aren't prepared for a man who can make time fly by. Girls in this category include relationship advice lovers, those girls who have read every celebrity advice book, Christian healing guide, Law of Attraction exercise, and even Google things like, "How long should it take a man to call after sex?" These women are afraid that they won't get it right, so they try to merge all the various advice together as if everything combined will finally be their saving grace. When you take something that works and add something else that you only think works on top of it, you don't get two things that work, you get chaos! Embrace Spartanhood fully, or not at all! **You commit, you believe, you achieve. Spartan life is that simple.** If you can't dedicate yourself to those three simple steps, then you will continue to live a life of repeated mistakes. Confidence doesn't get confused, so if you're trying to date in a way where you are overprotective and guarded, that tells me that you aren't confident in your ability to see through bullshit nor are you strong enough to deal with the pain of once again being rejected in life.

I would go on a date with a girl like this and use the same power *Ho Tactics* women use to win, the quick bond. I would sniff out her rules and shed doubt on them, not by saying, "The 90-day rule is for fools, here's why," because that does nothing. The proper way would require me to accelerate the dating process in a way where she herself feels that waiting 90 days would be stupid. Going back to the idea that women don't want to really date, I would be the man that is already talking about "this feels too strong too fast," or "I can't believe I want you this much and it's only been a week." These women who are playing it safe are only doing it to prevent themselves from being hurt again, they have sworn to do things right, and want to see that a man truly is into her by using time rules. However, as I've seen with women who crashed and burned when trying to Spartan up. These ladies aren't actually vetting; they are just trying to slow down their own over-eager heart.

I will be nice to her, show her not only the same affection as the girl who just wanted to be loved, but also add on my own panic about being afraid of too much too soon. Some women eat up the fact that a man is crazy about them and stop asking questions. These type of women want to see that a man is open because that proves that she's safe. Show me yours, and I'll show you mine, in terms of faking emotions is an easy hustle to pull off if a woman doesn't actually question the "why" of a sudden infatuation. This is how some of you will fail because you're looking for a man to get sprung, and tell you you're different as if that proves that your Spartan magic worked. That's ego, not the actual process of vetting a man! Let him cry about how different you are, let him offer a meeting with his mother, let him drop the "L" word too fast. But don't buy into that shit until time and effort match the words he's using to gas you up. Don't remove the locks on your heart because a man is looking through the window smiling, hands up like, "I don't have any weapons, and I really need to come in." Be smart and patient, not safe and fearful.

The Girl Who Wants to Be Hard: Most of my female friends fall into a category where they understand the male game, they truly get it, but the thought of playing mental chess with the opposite sex scares them. No matter how tough they pretend to be they are running from a fear of failure they pass off as "I don't have the energy." These women were in deep love previously, sometimes twice, and had their heart shattered by men they thought they understood. There will be no more trust, no more battle of wits, none of the mental wars that they could easily win, because like a shell-shocked soldier sent back for another tour—they've lost their nerve. These women date without emotion, they don't believe anything a man says, and their end game isn't love, it's finding a dick that doesn't annoy her so she can just get the physical and not have to spend the energy worrying about what's love versus what's game.

I would go on a date with a girl like this and once I see the telltale signs of her being emotionally hardened, I would drop the romance. These kind of women don't want to play the game so why play. If she wants to treat men like men treat girls, then I have to earn her respect as something beyond the normal man, and that happens by forming a partnership. If you want to be Harley, I'll be your Joker, no corny shit just fun. You don't want love; me neither, what the fuck are we even putting on fronts for, let's go party and bullshit. Men, especially athletes and entertainers, love the fantasy of the "good time girl" who isn't serious and who isn't looking to be something long term. The same is true here with those hard women that think they're Spartans but are really just filled with fear. By being okay with her "fuck love" lifestyle, and not trying to prove to her that I'm different or she should open up, I become harmless. Like a Smart Ho that gets calls at 3am from someone like Drake, just to talk, because she doesn't judge or try to make it into a love affair, I would be there for this fake-tough woman. Always down to listen, laugh, hear her vent no matter the time or day. It's not about being fake, because she can tell if a man's fake, being real wins her over. But this doesn't slip into the friendzone because I would still keep doing the hangout sessions that she doesn't call dates, but are. I'm not saying anything mushy, it's just chill, but I continue to grip her ass and kiss her on the mouth when it's time to say goodbye. This gangster courting will only take a matter of weeks to wear her down. Then she's sprung.

239

Now the guard is down and she has sex because that's what she thought she needed; rough punishing sex with no strings attached. Only then, after the sex, will she remember what was behind that heavy armor, a big heart. **The coldest women are really the warmest if you hit the right spots.** Sadly, the way she let this man into her heart was done with him going through the backdoor, no real vetting. He was a cool guy, he didn't lie or bullshit, but was he the right guy for her? She never finds out because now he's moved on to the next emotionally frustrated woman who pretends to be hard. When her once frigid heart warms up, how will she deal with this man not wanting her on that level? She will go even deeper into her shell, only to repeat this same mistake later on in life. To those of you that cling on to this, "I don't care, I'm going to act like a boy," attitude, it won't save you from heartbreak, it makes you a target. Being too hard to date or too exhausted to date, doesn't mean you get to skip the steps, it means you stop throwing yourself a pity party and do the work that must be done to erase fear, reset your avatar, and become a Spartan. Women who are weighed down with heavy hearts are even easier targets because their apathy blinds them to being attacked in other ways not used by the normal players.

In *Think like a Man*, the movie's twist came when the men found Steve Harvey's book and used the women's rules against them. Even if a man knows that you're a Spartan, he can't beat you. There is no "say the right things, and get pussy," game any male can use on any date because being a Spartan changes your entire mentality to be war ready no matter what curve a man throw's at you.

Chapter 16:
Slaying the Second Date

t he first date was a job interview, but the second date is an on the job tryout for a man. No longer do you ask him who he is, you push him to show you via his actions. Remember he is still on his best behavior, no matter how honest you feel he's been in the week leading up to this date, you can't put anything past this man. Does he want the job for real or is he just trying to get a quick paycheck *aka* your pussy? Is he not tripping on the benefits, and sees this as a career aka wants to be your man for as long as you will have him? Don't assume anything at this point good or bad. Observe.

Cali has chosen an intimate concert being headlined by a new up and coming singer she likes which takes place at a coffee shop/bookstore. This is Cali willing to show her bohemian side. On the first date, she came off as elegant and sexy, but could still make sexual jokes or sassy comments, but that's just attitude. Now Cali is going to show another side, her soul. She loves music and loves chilling at cool places filled with artist types as opposed to the hood crowd or even the buttoned-up luxury folks. Cali knew this was important, which is why she laid the foundation by asking Stephen about his taste in music on the first date. Although they aren't really into the same artists, Stephen claimed he was open to new things. She will now see how true that really is. In terms of the outfit, she will dress to the crowd, casual, but as before retain that, "I would fuck me," image that will make her a head turner even in a room full of other women. She's going to allow Stephen to pick her up this time. At this point, she's not worried about privacy, he's earned enough trust. The show starts at 9, but they will have a quick bite at 8, which will give Cali a chance to re-break the ice.

Stephen pulls up to Cali's apartment, but by the time he steps out to go to the door, Cali is already walking towards him. She doesn't want to go through the fuss of inviting him in or being hit with the "can I use your bathroom" excuse men use to be nosey. Stephen gives Cali a hug, and opens the door for her. He's all smiles because in about four hours he thinks he will be back in front of this apartment, this time being offered to come in and chill (Ha!). The ride over is filled with compliments and small talk about how it's been too long since they've seen each other. It's only been six days, but Stephen is openly annoyed about not having more access. This isn't a red flag, however, men are big babies who will always bitch and moan when they can't have what they want when they want it. This isn't Cali's first rodeo, she plays to this man's ego, promising that she badly wanted to see him too, but needed it to be the right time where she could focus on him without work or family stuff distracting her. Although this isn't an honest answer, it's mandatory. There is always a bit of a game to be played between men and women when first getting to know each other, and right now Cali is following these dating rules in order to vet Stephen. There is no guilt about lying in order to test this man because the ends will justify the means.

The two decide to go to P.F. Chang's to grab small plates at the bar and maybe a drink. Cali could have chosen something as simple as a Buffalo Wild Wings or a TGIF's, but when given a choice, she will always pick a place more befitting her classy side over somewhere loud and catering to a rowdier group of people. She is a special occasion. This is still a special occasion. To go to some basic place in a basic setting would make Cali seem like just another girl. Even in a hurry, a Spartan never does anything generic. At the bar is where Cali takes the time to listen and observe. Whenever a man is seeing you for the first time since you've communicated so much, it's like a brand new person. No longer is Cali "some bitch" who he took out to see what was good. Cali has become a real person, so a new set of nerves rush over Stephen. It's time to re-break the ice using what I call, *The Girlfriend Experience*. Before they can even ask for a menu, Cali wraps her arm around Stephen's arm, gripping his hand in the process. She then leans into his body, nuzzling up to his shoulder with a sensual, "I'm so excited to see you again." This turns that phone "like" back into physical "like" which avoids any awkwardness or long build up to get back to a place of comfort.

Cali used the oldest trick in the book, she not only touched him; she pressed her body against his. That's Animal Kingdom 101. The closer you are to a man, the more excited he becomes. Feeding him an appetizer with your hands or fork... Continuing strong eye contact that either has him engrossed or makes him laugh out of nervousness... Placing a hand on his knee... These are all tricks Cali uses to regain the physical control. Stephen can't help but be open because in his world all of these things point to sex, he has no idea that he's being hypnotized.

Cali and Stephen arrive at the show on time, and the mood is romantic and fun. Cali has been here before and like most niche activities in a city, she knew she would run into people who know her from that scene. This is the first test, and why it's always important to go places that you are familiar with on the second date. **How will your date react to other people you know?** A male employee greets Cali with a hug as if Stephen wasn't even there. Cali is warm and makes small talk, but is sure to bring Stephen into the picture and introduce him as her "friend." Men do not like being referred to as "friend" it sounds unimportant and doesn't hint at what is actually going on. To Stephen, this guy may see him as some chump who's tricking on Cali. Stephen's mind will race to, "Did she call me a friend because she's dating him too? Has she fucked this dude? Why is he smiling at her like that?" Cali could have said, "This is Stephen we're on a date," or "This is my boo, he offered to take me out." Something more ego stroking that would have made Stephen more comfortable. However, Cali knows that this is important to the future of the relationship.

If Stephen can't handle male associates coming up to chat in public, or to give a hug, then this won't work. Cali goes out regularly and she's a social woman that has various associates. Men that used to date her will be out, men who she friendzoned will be out, men who she fucked, and who still want to fuck her, they will all be out on any given night. Stephen will have to deal with that and not flip out, judge her, or make snide comments. Cali isn't a ho, but for an insecure man, popularity with the opposite sex can be hard to deal with. Stephen is about to show how secure he really is.

Cali asks her male employee friend if he can hook them up with seats closer to the stage. The friend tells them to hold on while he checks. Stephen hasn't said anything at this point, so Cali takes this moment to ask him what he thinks of the decor. Stephen is still distracted by the other man hugging "his bitch," but says that it's nice. Cali could tell Stephen who that guy is and how she knows him, but it's always, *don't ask don't tell*. If Stephen is truly a big boy and is curious then he has to ask himself, not sulk and act passively. Cali and Stephen are taken to a seat closer. Cali once again hugs the employee as thanks for the hookup. The friend tells them both to have a good time and shakes Stephen's hand with a smile.

Let's pause. This is why you MUST take a man out to familiar places when you're dating because men will tell you how they aren't jealous all day when it's only you, him, and maybe a waiter. To go out with another man puts thoughts in his head that he may not be able to hide. Right here we have Stephen and Cali's friend exchanging pleasantries, but what's under the surface? A dap and a smile to a rival man who knows your girl could mean, "Good luck, brother, she's a tough one," or "Damn, you tricking on a ho that I slept with on a Chipotle budget." Stephen has no way to know if he's a fool unless he asks Cali.

Once they're seated and comfortable, Stephen man's up and asks Cali who that rival male was. Cali smiles internally, she is ecstatic that Stephen asked directly, opposed to internalizing and fuming for the rest of the date. Cali explains that he works at the coffee shop, and she would come in every morning before she began working closer to the Starbucks where they first met. Stephen states the obvious, "He looked like he was in love with you." Cali smiles, "Aren't they all?" Then follows up with, "He gave me so much free coffee trying to get me to go on a date, but I need more than caffeine to give out my number." This makes Stephen happy. Without being too direct Cali is letting him know that he should feel honored to be sitting next to her because plenty of men have tried and failed to take her out. Cali didn't need to pander to Stephen; she let her personality tell him that he has nothing to feel threatened about in regards to that other man.

The show is about to start when another friend of Cali's, a woman, comes to say hello (be nosey). Cali introduces Stephen in the same way, as a friend, to prove to him that she isn't the type of woman that acts one way in front of men and then tries to stunt in front of rival females like, "Oh this is my baby, girl." Cali always keeps it low key and real, she doesn't need to impress anyone. The woman is here with some friends and asks if Cali and Stephen would like to sit with them. Cali defers to Stephen for another test. Right now Stephen could play ball and let Cali enjoy the company of her girlfriend, to prove that he's cool. However, by doing that he sacrifices alone time for a group of strangers who he doesn't know. Stephen answers, "We had to kill the people sitting here before us in order to get these nice seats, and plus I kind of want this young lady all to myself." The girlfriend raises an eyebrow excited by the romantic answer and leaves the two lovebirds to it. Cali promises to come over to talk at intermission. Cali turns back to Stephen, "Somebody likes me." Stephen doesn't front, he has waited all week to see her and wasn't going to share. This turns Cali on, and further makes Stephen stand out in her eyes. This man is taking control in a good way, and not being an overly submissive little bitch who only wants to make her happy, even at the expense of his own enjoyment.

During the show, there is not much for Stephen to do except listen and attempt to stroke Cali's leg every now and then. Cali is caught up in the vibe and doesn't flirt like she did at P.F. Chang's, and Stephen is a bit bored. Between songs, Cali asks him his opinion, if he's having fun, etc. Stephen plays along and is responsive. Cali knows that this isn't his scene, but that's not a deal breaker. Even uninspired Stephen has yet to pull out his phone to check a sports score or his timeline. He's conscious that he needs to show support for her interests. After the final set, Cali meets up with her girlfriend and her associates to discuss. Cali makes sure to bring Stephen into the circle, to see if he's going to chime in, or just sit there like a bump on a log. It's no surprise to Cali that Stephen retains his wit and humor even in the presence of these strangers. He also keeps his eyes from gawking at some of the pretty women in the group, another gold star effort.

One of the best things about meeting friends while out on a date is that they ask the direct questions that you shouldn't. Cali's girlfriend asks how long they've been dating and if it's serious. These are the invasive questions that a Father, Mother, or Aunt would ask, but on a smaller scale. Stephen says this is only their second date, but he hopes it won't be his last. Cali's girlfriend doesn't care about embarrassing him so she follows up with, "Do you see her as someone you can be serious with?" This isn't a question that a Spartan asks because it's not going to garner a real response, but as a wing woman or friend, it's a perfect question because you allow your friend to see if a man has to over think his answer in front of others. Stephen doesn't hesitate and says that although it's still early he hopes it can be something serious. PC answers but Cali can sense the honesty in his voice. Stephen may have earned himself a spot on the team.

THE SEX PUSH

Stephen attempts to get Cali to grab one more drink before heading back home, and though she is drinking more than on the first date, she still knows her limit and declines. Stephen drives Cali back to her apartment and pulls up as if he will be invited inside. Cali tells him how much fun she had, and apologizes for forcing him to sit through non-rap lyrics for 90 minutes. Stephen counters that most of it was good and that he was there to be with her, and that's all that matters. Cali goes in for a kiss, a reward for Stephen doing everything right. She could have waited for him to do it, but her taking the initiative is more important. To kiss a man as opposed to allowing yourself to be kissed means that you are into him, and defuses any worry that she's only letting you kiss her out of politeness.

While this may sound stupid to some, numerous women tend to go with the flow in terms of things like kissing and even letting a man feel them up, because they feel they owe it to him. Cali isn't going to fuck Stephen, she isn't going to even let him inside, so she has to prove that she's not playing him, and the easiest and most efficient way is to kiss him first. Stephen responds like any man would, as if this is an invitation for more, and that one kiss turns into a make out session. Cali's body is on fire, and maybe if she was drunk she would slip up, but she's a professional. After five minutes of kissing, neck sucking, and thigh rubbing, Cali backs away. "I have to go before I get you in trouble," again, Cali is exercising control.

One of the biggest annoyances men have are women who are still scared of sex. There are grown women who don't have sex, not because of moral reasons, but because they fear judgment. Men don't understand why a woman would deny herself the sex she wants, but they come prepared to put her fears at ease with Dick Tactics.

Guys drop the L-word, swear they won't tell anyone, and even promise that nothing will change. It's a sales pitch that all women hear when a man is trying to get inside. Guys smell your indecision and they use that moment of confusion to their benefit. No matter how dick disciplined you are, know what you need to see from a man before you have sex. We'll examine "when to have sex," later on, but at this point have a solid reason that's not based on the fear that it will hurt, the fear that he will judge you, or any phobias at all. Any fear-based reasons you can think of, a man can destroy with logic, and he will have a point because fear is never a good reason not to do anything in life.

Stephen isn't the type to guilt trip Cali into doing more than she's ready to do, nor is Cali the type of woman to respond to, "C'mon don't be punk!" Cali isn't afraid of dick and doesn't care if she fucks tonight or next month, but she won't because Stephen hasn't earned her pussy yet. Sexual chemistry and a good date are normal in her dating life because she doesn't entertain losers, she's been in this position before and she knows to stay strong. There is no pressure on Cali to have sex just to keep him around or to have sex because she wants to cum. Her reason is simple: Only have sex after a man's put his heart in my hands. **Spartan's snatch souls, they don't wait 90 days or 3 dates, they wait to until a man is putty in her hands and then the panties come off**. Nevertheless, she can't tell him, "You got a long way to go to even eat this box," because that will be a blow to his ego, so Cali turns the tables and uses reverse psychology.

Cali's pussy will whip Stephen. She's a Spartan who has mastered the art of retracting muscles, sucking her own breasts, and asking to see the dick go in and out. The things she can do in that bedroom are legendary. Cali doesn't have to go into detail; she merely states that Stephen will fall in love if he were to fall into her. She's not acting as if sex is an elephant in the room, she goes directly at the subject. "I'll have you sprung, baby, and it's way too early to get that serious." This could lead to more back and forth, where Stephen tries to play his own game of reverse psychology, calling Cali out as all talk, offering to pull his dick out, or any other little boy tricks men use when desperate for sex. Cali shuts down all the fast talk before Stephen can get started, she doesn't want him wasting his wit trying to fuck when she is 100% sure it's not going down.

Cali gets serious, "You know it's going to happen, baby, just keep being you." That's a buzzer beater response as she took it from being nasty to being heartfelt. Hos promise pussy, to get treats, Spartans predict pussy, to calm a male's ego. Cali owns up to her sexuality, she is good at sex, loves sex, and will most likely fuck Stephen if he keeps doing what he's doing.

That's the only reward Stephen is going to get at the end of the second date, and he can either accept that as truth or dismiss it as bullshit and never take her out again. That's on him, for now, Cali has done her job. She says goodnight, gives him one last kiss and exits. Stephen is pissed, here he is a guy with a lot of other women trying to get at him, and he can't even get into the home of the girl he just spent the last week and a half tricking on. Cali turns back to the car and trots over to the driver's seat. Kisses him again and tells him that he's the best. Then she hurries back to her door. Cali knows how men think, and any man that leaves a woman without fucking is going to feel some sort of bitterness, this last kiss turns that negative back positive and gives Stephen the one thing that all men love, the hope of new pussy coming soon.

Chapter 17:
Second Date Check List

the second date is not more of the same as the first date, with random questions and basic dick teasing seduction. It's about role-playing. You take him out as if he's your boyfriend and see if he sinks or swims. I stress that the reason bad relationships get a chance to graduate to actual relationships is because women and men don't let the outside world in fast enough. Men act funny and reveal other parts of their attitudes when forced to do things like wait, be waited on, have to interact with someone annoying, see other men showing you attention, etc. You as a woman may reveal the dark sides of your attitude if someone messes up your order, bumps into you without saying "excuse me," or if you run into someone you or he knows. Both of you need this type of real life experience or the relationship you're building will be based on a fantasy. House dating isn't real dating! Outside dating can be a baptism by fire that can let both parties in on the stuff human beings keep buried. In Cali's scenario, she was more reactionary than in her first date. She observed Stephen instead of prodding him with questions. This is your job now, to observe as opposed to lead. Don't worry about what situations will or won't arise that will allow you to test these things. Trust that unless you go to an abandoned warehouse for a picnic, obstacles will pop up naturally. Be prepared to use them to benefit further vetting of your date.

Mission: Girlfriend Experience

You can't be afraid to disarm a man with physical acts of affection. There are women who stay in their personal space and wait for a man to do things like hold hands, place a hand on a shoulder, or even hug. These traditional women don't want to send the wrong message and be a tease, but the moment you agree to date a man you already pass the teasing stage. He is assuming that by accepting a date or asking for one, it means that you want to fuck or at the very least are attracted to him enough to consider it in the near future. Forget sending the wrong message, who cares about the message? You aren't going to be having sex so you must show him that you are interested in a different way because to stand around acting reserved tells him that you may only be using him to finance these dates.

Another thing I see is the fear of physical rejection, as if this man that's courting you will somehow reject those advances because you're not pretty enough or because he doesn't want you touching him in public. I'll never forget the girl who asked me, "Is it okay to put my hand on his leg, I don't want him to push it off." Think about that bullshit. Those fears are deep rooted because non-Spartans are so consumed with being curved that they curtail their actions to the point where they are like prisoners on their own dates. Stop carrying your insecurities on your sleeve, and understand that no man who is out with you will push you off in any way.

The Girlfriend Experience exploits sexual chemistry in order to re-break the ice. I once met a friend of a friend for the first time, and this girl was so smart in her flirt game that it surprised even me. The moment she met me, before exchanging names or any of that, she hugged me tightly, and then led me by the hand to sit next to her on the couch. Internally, she already won me over in five seconds. Why? Because men, even smart ones, are simple creatures! Show us physical affection instead of dry basic interaction where you sit there and keep your hands to yourself and you have our attention for as long as you want it. Even if you're in the line at the movies, to lean your head on his shoulder while you wait, takes you from that sterile date vibe to feeling like you're already his girlfriend. Take control of these men as if they already belong to you! If he were your boyfriend, you wouldn't be shy physically, right? You wouldn't keep your hands away from your boyfriend's hands or wait for him to initiate a hug. This person isn't your boyfriend, but make him feel as if he is, so he falls in love with that potential future. It doesn't matter if you're at a bowling alley and sit on his lap, or come up as he's about to roll, and wrap your arms around his waist. **The more physically free you are around a man you're dating, the faster you hypnotize him**. You aren't his girl, but it feels right, it feels like something he could get used to, and once you imprint that in his brain, you become a prize beyond your pussy.

Mission: Show You're Wanted

Cali went to a spot where she was known, but many of you aren't known socially or won't choose events where you may run into an ex or even your female friends. That's okay because there are other ways to show a man that you're not some unwanted dandelion, but a rose that everyone wants to smell. One of the biggest reasons not to enter a relationship is jealousy. Nearly every woman reading this has dealt with a jealous man who started off so nice, then showed his true colors. Jealousy or potential to show signs of abuse are always present. We talked about being mysterious and insinuating that you are dating other men. A lot of men will run away as soon as they think you're dating other guys. It's a double standard: <u>As a man he talks to four other women, probably sleeps with one of them, but expects you to date one at a time</u>. You've already tested him in this area by letting him know that you have friends and you showed via your actions that you aren't breaking your neck to see him or talk to him all day every day. If he didn't like you being a free agent but hid it, then this date will expose him. Let's say your date choice is something low key like a cooking class where there is nothing but other couples. Men aren't going to be looking at you and other women aren't going to be trying to chat you up, so the room to show jealousy isn't there, right? Wrong.

You two are in a cooking class; you glance over to one of the guys to his left, and remark, "Oh shit." Your date asks what's wrong. You look again, this time, relieved. "I thought that was this guy that won't stop blowing up my phone." It's a total lie, but what it does is put it in your date's head that you are wanted out here in these streets. The same way Stephen started to get upset with Cali's coffee buddy, your date won't be able to hide his curiosity or worry. "What if it was him, would you introduce us," should be countered with, "I don't mix the guys I date from the guys who I merely talk to," bam! You show him that you're a treasure not by pretending you only talk to him, but by insinuating that he is the one guy currently standing out. Don't be afraid of these little boys! It's in your best interest to get guys to look at you, to mention off-handedly that

251

you may see someone you know, and to make him realize that he needs to do all he can to take you off the market because you are in high demand.

Mission: Test His Engagement

It's rude for you to play on your phone when on a date, but it's downright disrespectful for a man to split his attention between the spectacle of you and his phone. If Facebook is more important than you are on date #2, imagine how more important it will be in the weeks to come when he's really comfortable around you. Some people may need to check emails or other important things, but you should know by this time what kind of lifestyle this guy leads. A dude who works in construction doesn't need to be checking his email multiple times at night. A man without children shouldn't be worried about his phone vibrating. Another observation to make revolves around other women. If you're going to a place where you're dressed sexy, then other women will be there looking almost as good— almost. All men look, you can't turn that off, but it's how a man look that determines his respect level. Full head turns, gazing too long, or even the old school, "look at what she's wearing, do you like that color," disguised stare, all point to a man who isn't giving you your proper attention. The main event is in front of his eyes, he shouldn't be looking at people in the crowd.

Mission: How Does He Talk Around Others

When you're on the phone late at night sweet talking each other, a man isn't going to offend you or talk down to you. Maybe there will be a debate on a topic that you two disagree on that may show his elitist or narcissistic side, but usually during the first week, a man will refrain from getting on a soapbox about a touchy subject. In terms of jokes, a man who is courting you will also keep those above the belt. Girls can be sensitive, calling a woman teasing names like, "genius" after she says something stupid. Making fun of an accent or how she pronounced a word. Throwing innocent shade at something physical like her big ears, hairstyle, or nose shape, even as a joke can ruin a man's shot. Guys stay away from things that can be taken the wrong way, but it only lasts until they become comfortable. This is why deep conversations followed by the second date works so well because you put him at ease sooner and lessen his filter so the real him comes through in terms of how he talks to you in public.

One woman told me how a guy she was seeing for months got comfortable and called her "Thunders" a name that referred to the size of her thighs. I saw it as a cute joke, but she took it to heart due to her history with men verbally bashing her weight. It wasn't until they were at one of her family gatherings that he called her Thunders in front of her mom who started to laugh. What could have been a quick, "Don't say that to me, please, I'm sensitive about that," became a huge blowup. They should have crossed that bridge during the first few weeks. If they were on a date, he would have called her Thunders, but they didn't date properly nor bond in a way that uncovered his jokey persona. All they did was house date and phone bone. Even after knowing him for two months, he was still a stranger. When you're out and around more people than the waiter or the bartender you hear a man's thoughts on society, but you also experience his reactions to you in terms of his temper, jealousy, or humor.

Let's say that you want to go to a Paint and Sip, one of those events where you drink wine and paint pictures. The conversation will be between the two of you, but it's also about something specific. Unlike on the phone where it revolves around "I want to see you," "what are you wearing, bae," bullshit. A guy you're dating may be super competitive and will begin to talk down on your painting. Saying things like he can tell your parents didn't send you to camp or that your school must not have had funding for the arts. He may be a jokester and start to clown you in a malicious way that you don't like. Calling you "big dummy," or "retard," because you make a mistake. These real life responses come up all the time after you're with someone, but rarely before you commit because people don't spend enough time outside of the home observing true personality.

Different women thrive with different personalities. A man doesn't have to be a saint, but he has to line up with your disposition because after the lust wears off that's all a man is, his opinions and behavior that reflects those opinions. It's not a deal breaker if a man tells offensive jokes or is strong willed, but how does he respond to you checking him? Is he the type that listens or the type that doesn't respect your objections? If you don't like him calling Asian people derogatory names, be blunt and tell him that's not cool. If he tries to undermine you by continuing to say similar things, then he's a man that only listens to himself. You can't flourish in a relationship with a man who doesn't respect you enough to watch his mouth or see things from your perspective.

The final point is observing the shade a man throws at you. Snide comments that appear to be jokes but are really judgments often come out when you're around other people. I've spoken to women in abusive relationships who didn't see these *Bitch Checks* as anything out of the ordinary because a man will sneak disrespect you in a way where it seems harmless at first. You come out the house for a date, and he's saying, "I thought only whores wear red." You're laughing at a joke the waiter makes and he feels a need to say, "Maybe I should give him my seat." You correct him on a word and he says, "Oh damn, a person would swear you had more than an Associate's degree." When a man you like is saying those things, it can work in terms of eating away at your self-esteem or making you feel guilty. Men use words like whips, and while it sounds like jokes at first, you will start to curtail your behavior based on his reactions. "Let me wear this dress because I don't want to hear his mouth. Let me not say anything to this bartender because he may think I'm flirting." You can wear what you want, laugh with whom you want, and if a man chastises, even under the cover of a joke, that tells you who he is, a controlling asshole.

This test will not only expose how he talks to you in a public setting but how he compromises when called out. "Could I be with him? Yes, because even when we bump heads he's willing to explain himself to help me see what he actually meant or he's willing to apologize when he sees that it wasn't appropriate." Don't wait until it's a month in and you bring him to a family cookout or a double date to see he has a disrespectful mouth around other people, competes for attention, or judges you openly.

Mission: Let Him Down Easy Without Being Easy

You want to have sex... You're horny, frustrated, and he's said all the right things to get you to do more than just kiss him when he drops you off. You want to invite him in, fuck the soul from his body, and let the chips fall where they may. Don't do it. This isn't about you cuming tonight and again the next day when he wakes up next to you, this is about finding a man that can give you that for the rest of your life. Your mission is all about defining a man's true character in a fast and efficient way. There is no better way to define who a man truly is then by withholding pussy he thinks he is going to get. To be all over him on the second date like you can't keep your hands to yourself, to kiss him first, those things all signal you want the dick, and you do, but it's not going to be that easy. Trust in the process and don't over-think what his reaction will be. No matter if he thinks you're a cock tease, a Ho that just wanted concert tickets or a woman that's on the fence—let him judge. Typicals worry about the minds of men; Spartans determine what's in the minds of men by exercising control over those brain waves.

Most likely, you will be tried physically with him kissing on you, but you can't break because he kisses that spot on your neck that gets you leaking. Next, you will be called out as a bluff verbally. He will tease that you are playing games in order to goad you into doing a little bit more to prove that you aren't scared or bluffing. Play this off without an attitude and keep it sexy. "You going to have to keep working, daddy." Men like to chase, so never feel guilty about pushing him away. Alternately, the men who get denied like a kid that has been told he can't stay up late, rage silently. They may fall back the next day and distance you from their lives out of spite or they may keep dating you in a more nonchalant way until you are forced cut them off due to signs of "acting funny." You must not fall for this *Push & Pull* Dick Tactics. If you shoot him down and he starts to distance himself passive aggressively, it's not your fault. You having sex shouldn't be the sole reason a man wants to see you! If he proves to be only in it for sex and develops an attitude after the date, he's finished!

There's a thin line between leading a man on and being overly guarded. At the end of the date, be empathetic to what a man is feeling. Let this guy down slowly by showing him via your actions that you like him.

255

Example, you are sitting in his car or standing outside of your car about to end the night. He really wants you to go back to his place. "Don't worry we'll get there soon enough." Kiss and exit. This shows him you are attracted to him, not using him. Let's say he drops you off and wants to come in your apartment, just to talk. "I don't want to talk; I want to ride you like I was down by a lap in the Kentucky Derby. But that wouldn't be smart right now." Kiss and exit. Again, your words are a turn on, and help extinguish the idea that you're playing him for free dates. Let's say you two are in the car and he pulls his dick out and tells you to stop bluffing. "Don't disrespect my womanhood like I'm a thot." Roll eyes and exit. Be as polite and interested in him as you can possibly be, but never entertain disrespect. Let him know that you are attracted to him, prove it with kissing, but don't compromise your mission by giving more than that.

Be smart and safe. No man should be allowed inside and you shouldn't go inside. I've heard all the war stories of girls who let guys in for fifteen minutes thinking nothing would happen and ended up sleeping with a man just because. Don't become that girl who felt bad and jerked him off or went down on him so he wouldn't go home hard. Never confuse being sympathetic with giving in. The moment you show a man that your word means nothing in the face of his sexual pressure, then you lose all control. No man will ever take you serious if one minute you're talking about how you don't get down, then the next minute you're letting him eat you out in your living room. That's like a mother who says, "Eat your broccoli or no dessert," yet still gives her son dessert. Once it's been established that mom will always go back on her threats, he will manipulate her for the rest of his life. Be stern! No means no, even when you want to say "yes." You are who your actions prove you to be. Your mouth says you're classy, your mind says you're a Queen, but your actions just proved you to be a jump-off. If you give a man what he wants just because he wanted it, you're weak. You can't argue against your own actions or excuse them, you are how you live, not how you imagine. So don't go on dates saying who you are, leave these dates proving who you are—Not Easy.

Chapter 18:
Add Him to The Roster
or Release Him

two successful dates out on the town and two weeks filled with candid and consistent communication. What's next? A third date where you have sex? Do you have "the talk" about how you see him as someone you could be with? Do you wait for him to bring the "R" word up? None of that shit. You aren't hunting this man; this man is now hunting you. By dating in this way, you made him expose himself internally. If you were dating like a typical bitch, this man would try the Push & Pull technique[11] on you, where he takes away his attention and forces you to run after him. Dating like a Spartan eliminates that because he has invested real energy into you to the point where he won't risk reverse psychology.

The reason these steps are so specific in terms of questions, letting him talk, and keeping your mouth closed, is that men who tell women their history, their secrets, their truth, are reluctant to walk away. If you followed each step like Cali, your man will now be emotionally vulnerable. This doesn't mean he is defanged and is no longer playing games, it only means that he is invested. No matter how cool he comes off, know that his feelings have spilled into his hunt for sex. Unlike most women, you require true effort. You didn't say this, you showed him this during the first two dates. You are now the type of female he will respect enough to genuinely pursue.

---

[11] For more detail on this dick tactic read *Solving Single*.

A Spartan will never have to chase after the title of "girlfriend." A man will throw that title on you because you are now a must-have whom he can't allow to remain on the market. Be selective. A man wanting you doesn't mean he gets you. What you've done is vet this man enough to know if he deserves a spot on your team, not vet him enough to be your boyfriend. Being your boyfriend means something special, correct? You don't allow just anyone to come in and lay claim because they fed you and told you about their past. Even if this man calls you the day after the second date asking you to be his girl, the answer would be a resounding, "No"! Why? Because that makes you a passenger moving fast inside of a car that a man is driving. You've impressed him, you've seduced him, therefore, he wants what he wants. Regardless, he's not in control of when you take a boyfriend, you are, and this is just the beginning because after the second date the rubber hits the road.

MAKING THE CUT

Time is your best friend, yet women treat it as if it is their worst enemy. Going forward, you must check your "in like" emotions and take things slow. Being in like with a man feels like love because he consumes your thoughts, pushes out other men, and when you're around him you light up. It's just a honeymoon high! You are supposed to like this man a lot, don't see it as "a sign" from the universe. He's told you his life story, but what have you told him thus far about your life story? Nothing. These steps were meant to protect your heart, not share it. The average woman, even those that claim to be emotionally unavailable, falter by putting too much into a non-relationship at this point. You have avoided over sharing your life story and avoided making him the center of your daily life, and now that's going to pay off. He's not your friend, he's not your bae, he's not your man; he's a new recruit who just made it through basic training. A man doesn't go straight from basic training to leading the platoon, he earns his stripes.

"But I want to give him his stripes, he does something to me that I never felt and he's been a perfect gentleman. Why can't he just be my boyfriend or just a guy I date exclusively at this point?" If your brain waves are still set to those pathetic thoughts, then you can't read! Don't forget where we started, you were accepting applications not promoting a man to boyfriend status. There is no exclusivity until he's your man, so don't fuck up by becoming friends with benefits at this stage. To get a shot at you as his woman takes longer than two dates over the span of 10-14 days.

The mission was to expose this man, find out who he was by making him drop his mask, then see if you were compatible by pushing him to move at your pace on the second date. By the end of the second date, you are firmly in control of this man. He won't be happy with just dating; he now wants to take it deeper. This is as deep as he gets. No sex, no pre-relationship title, and absolutely no taking yourself off the market for him. He's in your company. Now, how is he going to climb that ladder to earn a promotion? The final step is to see how he handles his new position.

Cali and Stephen have been talking normally for the past two days since their date. They joke during the day, talk at night, and it's as if nothing has changed. It's now time to see if Stephen has been properly trained. Cali won't ask for another date; she will allow Stephen to offer on his own. If Stephen is pushing house dates, then he hasn't learned what kind of woman Cali is, and most likely, he'll be dropped by the end of the week if he doesn't come up with another suggestion that fits Cali's status. If Stephen wants to slip into the routine of Cali always making the plans, he'll be cut just as fast, she needs a *take charge king* not a *sit there simp*. The past two dates were training; a man has to pick up on how you like to be treated going forward or he wasn't paying attention. Right now Stephen is up in brownie points, but he's also one week away from being cut off if he doesn't continue to work for this. A Spartan only leads a man to water once, if he doesn't figure out how to drink after that, then he fails. Bye Bye.

Stephen finally asks Cali if she's free to meet up with his sister and her husband. They're in town for a day and he wants to introduce his sister to his girlfriend. **Pause.** Stephen just made the first mistake of this blooming relationship. He claimed Cali as if Cali had no say in the decision. Typical women would go with this phantom title and be excited, "OMG, he called me his girlfriend! I have a boyfriend!" Not in Sparta. Cali has plenty of men who want the title, she's not desperate to get rid of her singlehood just so she can say she's not single, that's basic. More than that, what does Stephen really want? Always ask yourself what a man's true motivation is for wanting a relationship so early. This man barely knows Cali, the real person. He knows her as the shoulder he's leant on, the fun time girl who says random things, and has a basic understanding of the hobbies she's into. Cali hasn't talked about her exes in detail, her mother, her siblings, or even her feelings on commitment and marriage. For all Stephen knows Cali could be a smart ho, seducing him with charisma, and one week away from hitting him up for a tennis bracelet.

Like a ho's mark, Stephen is open, and when men are open, they try to regain control. By making Cali his girlfriend, he protects his heart from being played because it's official. Those men who Cali may or may not be talking to, gone. The fear that Cali is going to hit him up for money, gone. By making it official, he also takes control of the pace and schedule of the relationship. Going out on dates, gone. Hello, house dates. Cali making excuses not to fuck, gone. You can't deny your boyfriend, so hello in-house coochie. Understand that the title isn't always about a man wanting you; it can also point to a man gaining control of a woman he's unsure of.

Cali doesn't need to be rude, so she responds, "Girlfriend? I didn't know you had one of those." Stephen counters that it happened so fast, but Cali is there to tell him, "Let's keep this where it is, daddy, I'd hate to have a false start to something that could really work." Cali is a grown woman; she uses her fucking words without fear of hurting a man's feelings. It is always better to tell a man what he can't have than to give in knowing that it can ruin everything you're building. A Spartan always speaks up, even if a man won't like her response. For those who don't understand what a "false start relationship" is let's break it down. That honeymoon lust, that initial excitement can lead to going with the flow a bit too much. A man will be obsessed with you, and you will be smitten with him. So why not be together and see if it works? The problem becomes it was just a new person high, and after that wears off, you two quickly burn out within the next 3 months. Basically, a false start relationship is so short that you barely want to call it a relationship because neither of you were prepared, you just ran full speed, and like a track runner, you paid the price for that false start.

Stephen is a bit hurt, but tries to keep his chin up, still asking if the dinner date with his sister is cool? Cali would have normally gone, but she can tell that Stephen is wounded and to sit in front of family and have to fake like his girlfriend will hurt him more. Men have insane egos, as I have pointed out repeatedly. A woman who can protect his ego in a real way is more valuable than some chick that can cook, clean, and swallow. If Cali were to make Stephen her man she would protect his feelings in regards to how other people see him, and right now, she's going to show him that is her character by declining the invite. There is no need to have his sister being blown away and asking, "So what up with that Cali girl, I liked her, don't ruin it." Men don't need the pressure of family or friends telling him to wife a chick that can only be wifed on her own terms.

Cali counters the date offer with her own reward. "How about the next night you come over, and we'll order dinner and watch that documentary I mentioned the other day?" Stephen was told he can't have Cali as a girlfriend, this is an ego blow. However, she was smart enough to reverse the momentum by giving him an olive branch. He can see her, no money spent, no getting dressed up, and he can finally come over. Stephen happily accepts and his ego is now healed, but he doesn't know that he's still under Cali's control. She's not going over to his house. He is forced to come over to her home field where Cali controls what they watch, where they sit, what they drink, and when he has to go home. While Stephen is thinking sex, Cali is thinking, "I hope he has a Pornhub subscription because his dick is going to be so hard when he leaves here..."

This isn't a third date test that Cali is about to embark on. Letting Stephen come over is the reward for making the team. He invited her out to a dinner, proving he now understands how to date her. For that effort he doesn't become her boyfriend, he becomes the third guy who she's officially "dating" regularly. Now in addition to going out to places he picks, taking her out to places she picks, she can throw in a house date for those nights where she doesn't have the energy to deal with the world. There is nothing wrong with chilling inside after a man has proven himself. Cali couldn't lead with that, she would never allow a man over her house until she vetted him over two or three dates and he passed those tests. Only now that her value is established and her rules followed, is coming over an option.

GETTING CUT

Let's step back and go an alternate route. After the second date, Stephen doesn't ask Cali out, he instead asks her to come over. Cali isn't afraid to come over because she's not worried about having sex before she's ready. The point is that the first two dates were training this man to pay attention, and here he is just trying to fuck or simply being lazy by not following the path that was laid out over the last two weeks. This isn't about money; this is about value. **I make a big deal out of dates because it is the only act that a man can do to prove effort.** Not the way he talks to you, not how often he calls you, but how he tries to court you! Consistently trying to see you in order to get access to sex, is lust. Consistently trying to see you just because he enjoys your company, is passion. Don't confuse the two! Stephen is only concerned with getting Cali alone, not to talk, but so he can get his dick wet. A Spartan knows a man will always want sex, but a man who doesn't get the hint that she is not typical and keeps going full speed with his dick leading him, has failed. As in the last example, if he would have made a date suggestion, she may have canceled and let him come over to her place. Why? Because his intentions showed he knew how to treat her. This isn't a trick to get men caught up, it's evidence of his true feelings on how you should be treated. If he doesn't offer a proper third date after going through two great dates, he's not the one. If he can't do this simple step to make the team, then he will never do enough to become a real boyfriend. Cut him.

In terms of cutting a man off who hasn't done anything horrible, how do you go about it in a nice way? Do you block his number and delete him from social media? Call him and say, "Sorry it's not working but you're great," or maybe act like a boy and simply stop responding to calls? Fuck being nice! I don't care how nervous or shy confrontation makes you feel. You have to Spartan Up and treat this guy like you would want to be treated. If a man didn't want to date any longer, would you want him to ignore you or tell you straight up so you're not left wondering what went wrong? You would want the brutal truth! So don't be some pussy that beats around the bush or becomes passive under the cover of "nice" because faking the reality of this situation is far from nice.

Call him up, don't text, and tell him that it's not going to work. Use those exact words. *It's not going to work*. He's going to ask why. Was it something he said? Yes, and be truthful here, "I thought we had an understanding, I'm not a come over to the apartment type of girl. I know you didn't mean any disrespect, but I showed you how I roll, and it seems like you threw that out the window." He will argue with you, saying he doesn't see anything wrong with a chill night for once. Your rebuttal, "It's not about being inside, it's the fact that we're just getting to know each other. If we were to become an item, we would be inside all the time. I love watching movies and laying up with my man, but you're not my man. That's earned with me." Voice inflection on "earned" and drop the mic.

No more debates. No allowing him to come pick you up and take you out that night to make up for it. No hearing him out, so he can try to butter you up. Get off the phone, even if you have to be rude and hang up in his ear mid-sentence. What this does is either piss him off and reveal his true attitude. Maybe he will call you all kinds of bitches on the phone, go online and rant, send you a text the next day about how you're a stuck up cunt, or whatever it is that men do when they lose. If he acts like that, self-hi-five, because you just dodged a bullet. On the other hand, and this is more likely given the energy he's put into you thus far, he will give chase in the proper way, and tuck his tail between his legs like, "please, let me make it up." You are allowed to give him another shot...

When you cut a man, he doesn't have to stay cut. This isn't the same as dropping a boyfriend or even a roster member. He got cut early enough where you can be understanding. He didn't comprehend the rules of dating a Spartan, maybe it wasn't due to him not paying attention, just a force of habit because he's used to Basicas. How do you know if he's worth giving a second chance? When he calls you a day later or maybe that next week, asking to take you out, you will feel it in his voice when he apologizes. Men don't like to admit when they are wrong. To call you, not to talk, but to offer what you wanted from the jump, means that he fucking listened! If you feel that his heart is sincere then agree to that next date, and let him kiss your ass. If that date goes well. That doesn't mean he's on the team. Repeat this step. If he truly learned, he will ask you out again, proving that he is now trained to your standards. Once that happen. He's made the team.

TEAM BENEFITS

There is no need to go specifically through each date at this point, date four, date five, do this on date six, now follow up with that on date seven. Forget the date numbers. Once a man proves himself during dates 1-3, he's on the roster, which means you can ease up with being overly guarded. Just to be clear, you don't tell a man, "You're on my team." This isn't public information. At no time, do you even mention the word "roster" this is your private game. There is one final test remaining, becoming real friends. When people say, "I married my best friend," it's not to be taken literal. Even if you attract someone old like a classmate or childhood pal and make them into something new, there still needs to be a re-learning period. Becoming friends on this level is about finding deeper things to have in common and sharing each other's world more regularly. That's why he's on the roster, it is a clear break from interview dating where you give him access to more of the real you in order to reveal more of the real him. You don't put a man on the roster just because he's been hanging around, he took you out, or you think he's cute. That's not what a Spartan Roster is, that's a basic bitch roster. Basicas consider any man they talk to as on the team. It makes them feel fake-powerful to brag, "I have four men on my roster," they aren't guys whom she vetted, they're just random dudes that text and try to fuck her—difference. When a man makes your roster it's an honor and it's serious, which is why your team should only include men who made it through every test before this point, every one, or he's cut.

House Dates: There should be absolutely no house dates until after the 3rd date test. Make him work for the right to sit next to you in private. You may think that the fourth date is too soon to be sitting on a couch next to him, but it isn't unless you lack dick discipline. Too many women avoid private dates because they know they can't keep their panties up around a guy they want. You can't run from a man, you have to test yourself, pass that test, and prove to him just how atypical you are in terms of how you get down. The average woman goes over to a guy's house or lets him over, and she will let him feel her up, engage in foreplay, maybe even spend the night with him. Why? Because these women lack real resolve. They can't control themselves around a dick and know it. The idea that women who are Hos will fuck any man that shows interest is overblown. The truth that I've seen repeatedly is that the Hos cost, but the normal "I don't usually do this," women are the ones who fuck quick and easy. Making it through a house date will separate you from the *Betty Bust It Opens* of the world, and solidify that no matter how horny you are, you have a Spartan discipline.

A house date should have an objective. You're not going over just to hang out, it should literally be a date. If he wants to cook for you, then you are going over to eat as if it's a restaurant. You will talk with him. Help him with his dishes if needed. Have a nightcap conversation and leave at a respectable time, same as a normal dinner date. Pretend his place is Olive Garden. It closes at 10pm on a weekday and 11pm on a weekend night. Set a curfew and stick to it. What happens is you will hang around until 1am unwind, and think that cuddling won't hurt. Tell yourself that sleeping over while he stays on his side won't lead to anything…and maybe it won't but you're sending the wrong message. You are doing exactly what all women do. Most women try to play tough but end up lying next to a man in the bed, his hands on her breasts, while she pretends to be sleep. He knows you want the dick at that point, and all the work you've done will go out the window because both of you will be so comfortable that house dates are all you will want to do because it feels amazing to cuddle with a man you like each night. The problem is he isn't your man!

If you two want to make it a movie night, the same theater rules apply. Go over, watch the flick, keep the hands above waist, and once it ends, maybe have a conversation. Nevertheless, you have to be out of there within an hour of the movie being over or you lull yourself into a comfortability that will lead to you doing something you shouldn't. I get emails from women who come off apple pie sweet, they're mild-mannered, talk about respect, rules, blah blah blah…and then they pop up, "I ended up jerking him off in the bed because I felt bad for not having sex with him." You should not put yourself in a position to be on his bed! You should not be giving out back massages that lead to blowjobs. You should not be getting foot massages that lead to his tongue exploring your body. I don't care if taking your bra off feels like heaven, keep that shit on around him. Prove to yourself that you don't break by setting standards even when in the house. Just because you can do something freaky, doesn't mean you do it. You're not a 17-year-old whose parents are gone for the weekend, you will have plenty of opportunities to turn him out sexually. It's much more important to tame him and make him respect your discipline so that when you do finally have sex, he appreciates it.

Meeting Friends: Dating reveals personality because you place males in uncontrolled environments where they have to react. The reason why house dates should only be sporadic treats is due to the continued need to see the real him before you can ever upgrade him from roster member to boyfriend. One of the biggest signs of true personality won't come from a one on one date, but from a group date where you meet his friends or he meets your friends. This should happen naturally during the first month of dating. The first two dates are too early to be hanging out in groups because you need to vet one on one, but once you go beyond the third date, start looking for opportunities to meet his friends or vice versa.

Let's say that you guys had a great fourth date where he came over and helped you put together furniture and you ordered food. He may feel that he's going to do the same house chill session the next week, but you throw him a curve. No matter if you have one good friend or a group of several, plan something where they can meet him. It doesn't matter if it's Six Flags, the beach, a friend's party, a cookout, or simply grabbing drinks. This gives you all time to interact for more than a quick "Hi. Bye." You want to create opportunities where you can walk away and let him carry on a conversation with your friend. When you go to the restroom, he shouldn't be stuck with nothing to say to your girls. This date, much like the second date, introduces him to deeper aspects of your life. Your friend or friends will show you how he is in mixed company. It's not about them liking him or approving, fuck their approval; you're a Spartan you decide on your own. What it does is give you a chance to observe his raw personality. Similar to exposing a man as a narcissist or the jealous type, the things he says in mix company may reveal more than he would ever reveal one on one.

In terms of his own friends, don't be the basic bitch that moans, "So when am I going to meet your friends?" That sounds insecure, as if you don't trust he has buds outside of other women or guys he chases ass with.

Allow him to offer. If he doesn't you can suggest things like, "The music festival is this weekend would any of your friends want to go?" or "If you guys want to watch the game over at my place, I don't mind, it'll save you money on drinks." Listen to who his friends are personality wise and offer something based around that. If they're into sports, that's an easy sports bar or in home meet up. If they're into music, mention a concert. If they're single, maybe a group club night so they don't feel as if they have to behave themselves around you. Even something like a Grammy or MTV Awards viewing party can be used to initiate this meeting. It's important to see a man around his boys because the character could be night and day.

Meeting Family: Unlike meeting friends, meeting the family isn't something that you need to push for this early. He isn't your boyfriend, you are dating, so a man will be on his best behavior when his family is around. Outside of nicknames and old stories of when he was a kid, you won't learn anything about your guy from a visit to the family. A mother's approval of you isn't needed when you don't even know if you approve of her son at this point. Too many women get sprung once they visit a guy's home, bond with the mom or sister, and feel as if it's a family she could thrive in. Mothers, Grandmothers, Sisters, aren't judges, they are women, filled with their own animosity and bias opinions. If your guy is used to bringing girls home, the women of his family will most likely be desensitized and just play along. I was the king of parading chicks in and out of my mother's house, and my mother put on a nice front for all of them. A few of them, she would later say, "I really liked her," others she would roll her eyes at. Didn't matter. You don't need pleasantries that gas you up as if you're different because you're not at this point. Even when a man says, "I never bring women home," don't flatter yourself... I've said that lie too.

Many relationship problems stem from the family not liking the girlfriend, so you may think this is a necessity to weed out if he's a mama's boy, a product of a dysfunctional family, or anything else that would pop up later on. Trust that the deep family dirt will not come out at this stage. When you become a man's legit girlfriend, his family will then be authentic. They will not waste time hating you at this "she's just another ho" stage. If he offers for you to meet his folks, decline. If it's a wedding or a gathering in his honor, go because it's not a direct introduction where you're made to be the guest of honor. If you can, hold off on meeting family until he wins that spot, as this is something you will need to vet as an official girlfriend.

Spending The Night: In a true roster, you will have 2-4 men, however, many you can fit into your week and for as long they remain consistent in trying to win the top spot. By the time you get into deep dating, you should have exposed most of these guys. Meaning that no man should be on your roster for more than two months. **If it's been 60 days, and you're not ready to upgrade a man to boyfriend status, cut him off**. Not by being nice because you have no real reason, but by being real, "it's not working!" You can never be afraid to hurt feelings and cut a man off, don't leave guys dangling on your team, it will come back to bite you. Keep your ship tight. Any woman with a roster of more than five men is "talking" not dating, and she's also wasting her time because you should always be in the process of dropping a man who isn't working out and picking up a new guy. These Spartan steps are set up to filter 90% of the men you meet that will waste your time. Look at your roster, and if it's too big, you aren't vetting properly. I bring this up because spending the night is a huge step that should be reserved for that ONE GUY who is on the cusp of being your man. You don't spend the night with a man on the third, fourth, or even fifth date. This is a deep dating, first place on the depth chart, benefit.

To have a roster of 3 guys whose houses you sleep over at any given week makes no sense. You may not be having sex, but you're allowing a man to be extremely intimate with you, and that's not something you hand out. There can be only one. In terms of timeframe, spending the night should be done when you feel confident that he is a week or two away from being promoted. *Why do it at all*? Because staying the night, without sex, is a great character study. I'm not talking about if he leaves the toilet seat up or farts in his sleep, but real insight into his normal routine and habits. His place will be clean, he will behave as if a girl is there because one is, but he can't control other people. What you do at this stage is reveal how active his phone is, and what his nights and mornings look like when you're around.

When you spend the entire night, his other girls will receive the same treatment they get when you two are on dates, their texts and calls ignored. However, come morning time his phone will be blowing up if he has a legit girlfriend or a high-ranking girl on his roster. Numerous women have shared stories of spending the night (having sex) and finding out during the night that a man has a serious girlfriend or a girl who is actually ahead of her on his "team." One girl said that she was made to hide in the bedroom for an hour because a maintenance man came over to fix a sink, and his landlord didn't allow company overnight. Come to find out, it was the neighbor he was fucking, and the two of them had sex while her dumbass was hiding in the bedroom. A man will lie to protect his roster at this stage. You can't ask him if he's been slowly letting go of his other women nor can you demand that he stop talking to other women because you're not exclusive at this point. It's only dating and dating should never be exclusive. However, you can observe how he acts and find out on your own. If he's rushing you out in the morning, nervous about you touching something, or displaying various other signs that someone is up to no good, you're still near the bottom. That's what spending the night does, you infiltrate his routine to find out where you rank in regards to his love life.

Start leaving things at his place. You're not his woman, but you should now lay claim to his spot as the girl in first place. Spartan's Manifest Destiny, it's what your world revolves around, taking what you want when you decide you want it. Therefore, feel comfortable leaving your hair care products, makeup kit, hygiene necessities, and be sure they are easy to get to, not hidden. Dare any man to tell you that you need to move your deodorant from the dresser to the bathroom cabinet. More importantly, follow up the next time you spend the night. If things are moved and put back in a different place, you know he's had his other bitches over. This isn't to get mad over, again, not your dick. It's for you to gauge how serious he is about you at this point. A man who is falling for you after weeks of dating may not have given up other girls, but he will start to limit them to make more room for you. Your products are merely a test to see if making you happy is worth pissing off other girls. Top priorities get to keep tampons in the bathroom, low priorities just get explanations of "oh that's my sister's stuff." Be the one he lies to cover up, not the one that he hides.

Retaining Space: A huge benefit of being on the team is that you can drop your guard to the point where you don't worry about being strict in terms of when he sees you. When he's trying to make the team, there are no late night booty calls, no meeting up at whore hours, or anything that disrespects your status as a classy lady. Once he makes the team, you can talk and hang out whenever you decide. Once you establish house date rules and train him to respect you, you're now allowing him to earn the spend the night (no sex) benefit. This can feel as if you're moving too fast on both ends, and this is where you have to give and take. You give him the comfort of lying next to the sexiest woman on earth, but you have to take your time away as well, to keep him from being comfortable.

There are seven days in a week. Never see a man that is only on your roster more than three times in one week. How can you date Jason when you spend 5 days a week with Stephen? How can you maintain discipline and observe Stephen outside the house when you're staying over every night? Understand that everything written is to protect your heart, and increase a man's desire! That means just like the post-first date step of disappearing on a man, the actual dating should be sprinkled in with enough space for him to miss you more than you miss him. Remember, men are big babies, they want you when they want you, and will pout and cry when they can't get their way. Yet, it doesn't push them away, it brings them in closer if they legitimately want you beyond the sex lust feeling. It's Friday, go on a date, spend the night, leave in the morning and don't talk to him until Sunday. *Where were you at? What were you doing?* It's none of his business. He can ask you, but you don't answer with specifics because he's not your man. What this does is drive him to what? Regain Control!

Pay attention, I told you that men need control. They want a woman off the market once they realize they can't control her by just dating and talking big. So many women give men "Exclusive but not official" relationship statuses after a month. Meaning these typicals take themselves off the market because they like a guy. Yet it's not a real relationship, so why would any self-respecting woman think of dating as exclusive? You don't become his until you officially become his, which means you can pop in and out of his week when you feel. This space creates an obsession where he will need you, and that need will lead to him asking you to be his, fast and in a hurry. Alternatively, you may meet a man who tries to outsmart you by playing the same game. He won't answer your calls as consistently or he may try to pull your same disappearing act in an attempt to put you in check. This isn't a "two can play that game," hustle, so you must reverse it on him.

No Selling is the art of not internalizing someone's fraudulent moves or attempts at reverse psychology. He disappears from Tuesday until Thursday, doesn't respond to your daily texts, or return your routine calls, and you know it's because he feels powerless. You made him feel weak, so he is trying to fight fire with fire. The problem is yours is Phoenix fire, his is a fucking Bic lighter. This man is trying to make you obedient, but you don't sell it by acting mad, getting an attitude, or making it an issue that needs to be corrected. You "No Sell" it by acting as if you don't mind him living his life. When he does call, you keep it real and tell him you miss him. Share all the stuff you wanted to talk about. And you two can go out on another date to catch up. There is no passive aggressive, "Look who decided to use his phone today," or attitude filled, "Oh that's how we do, okay, I got you." Control those weak bitch reactions and don't sell any typical emotions. What this does is show him that you can't be mind-fucked. You like him, but you aren't hanging on his dick and chasing him. While the other women he's fucking may have to call over and over, and rush over to fuck him because they fear him losing interest, you NO SELL. By being unflinching in your control, you become even more of a must-have.

To recap, once a man becomes a member of your team, he gets benefits like house dates and meeting your friends. The longer he stays around, he earns deeper benefits like spending the night and you offering to pick up a dinner bill once and awhile. Nevertheless, you retain your power by knowing that he can be cut at any time. If you agree to one house date, and he wants to keep it that way all the time, then he didn't learn. If you are over his house and he won't stop trying to overstep his boundaries sexually or "chill," doesn't make him take his hands off of you, then that's Cosby dangerous, and he has to go. If you take him around your friends and he's acting like an asshole or trying to flirt with one of your friends, then you expose the dog in him. If you go around his friends and he fronts as if you're invisible by ignoring you or if he pretends that you two are fucking or together when you aren't, then he's a fake. All of those things get him cut off no matter how much you have been enjoying him over the past month.

A month into dating is when the true him begins to pour out more and more. His true attitude, his jealousy, his selfishness, his loyalty and where you rank in comparison to other women he may be dating. Don't be understanding of a man after this point. Anything he's showing you is no longer a representative, this is the real him. That means you have to be no nonsense in what you will and will not stand for going forward. If you let him yell at you, he knows you're the type of woman who can be bitch-checked. If you allow him to pop up at your placed unannounced, you set him up as above the rules. If you ignore him talking to other women in front of you, he sees that you're a pushover. If you let him cancel dates and blow you off for his friends, then he knows you're okay with being on the back burner. If you give him the power to make you his girlfriend before you're ready or lure you into a situationship where you two are "seeing where it goes" then he knows you're a fool. Keep your eyes open! Being on the roster means that you are lifting the sanctions enough so that a man gives you a sneak preview of himself as a boyfriend…but it does not make him your boyfriend. In the end, you may be falling in love with this man, but you cannot fall head over heels and think of him as irreplaceable or even special. He remains on the chopping block.

Chapter 19:
When to Have Sex

*W*ish... think about that word. If you're blowing out birthday candles, it's said with hope and excitement, but when talking about adult relationships, it loses that magic and takes on a melancholy uncertainty. I searched my inbox for "wish" and there it was: I *wish* he would listen to me. I *wish* he would tell the truth. I *wish* he would let me go. I *wish* I could move on. I *wish* he would realize how good he's got it. I *wish* he knew how it feels when he treats me like this. Hundreds of women making despondent wishes, but the most common phrase that had been sent to me— **I wish I never had sex with him**.

The reality that keeps younger women clinging on to their virginity and older women running towards the protection of celibacy is that sex is rarely looked back upon as a good decision when you're a female. This isn't about sex horror story, embarrassments, or laughable dick strokes. The regret that women feel is that of wasting an intimate experience with a man who never deserved it. The paranoia this creates becomes which man wants her for her versus which man wants her for pussy. Men lie about their intentions as effortlessly as a dog shits on a lawn. There is no guilt; when men chase sex, the ends justify the means. Which means you can't expect males to be honest, you have to demand that you be smarter. *If the next man I sleep with doesn't end up being my husband, then I failed.* That insane pressure can make the strongest woman revert back into just another weak bitch. A Spartan doesn't devolve, she understands that sex pressure is easily conquered when you erase the fear of being played, and embrace the truth that no dick alive can outsmart a woman who sees through the smokescreen of male lust. Sex shouldn't be a prison, it should be an act that you are able to master and control.

CHESS NOT CHECKERS

You can't reset your body count back to zero. You can't pretend penetration never happened. You can't disqualify him as never having you the same way a 6-year-old yanks the power cord from a video game when he screws up. It's already been saved! No matter what repressive technique you use to keep your sleep number lower than the real number of men who have been inside of you, the truth remains. No matter how big or small, fast or long, if you had an orgasm or went to sleep unsatisfied, that man can still say that he had you, and at what emotional price? This isn't bad sex versus good sex, it's about what sex means to you. No matter how much of a free-spirit you are or how sexually liberated you think, this is where you have to decide if you want to throw pussy like a college girl simply looking to have fun or maintain pussy power like a Queen intending to reveal a King.

Virgin, prude, ho, reformed ho, church girl, Anastasia Steele, it all comes back to you understanding that your pussy can no longer be given away for kicks. No matter how cute a guy is, that orgasm won't feel any better when he's pulling up his pants, walking out, with no intention to call again. Fake-tough women proclaim they fuck like men, no emotions, just a nut, it's a lie. You know you deserve greater. The universe was created for you to reach the highest level of happiness, to become indescribably special, not to be a piece of pussy. You wanted him too, he was just a dick, it's not that deep, blah blah blah...those days are over. A Spartan doesn't sell herself for a thrill. That momentary feeling of a man inside of you, pushed up against your body, telling you things he doesn't mean just so he can cum harder, is a cheap high. Experiment, experience, excite yourself, that's healthy when you're in the cocoon, but you were never meant to live in cheapness! Evolution demands change, and it starts with sex value.

When you started this journey you were asked what you wanted. You continued to read, that means you chose something serious. Therefore, sex becomes the most serious aspect of dating. Typical bitches fuck to feel momentary love because they know a man will never truly love them. Basic bitches brag and boast about how good their vagina is because that's the only substance they have to give. In the end, sex is honey not glue, it may bait a man in, but it won't make him stick around.

You are a Spartan. Your pussy is gunpowder, the most game-changing invention in this world. Weaker women want to know how you developed it, and thirsty men will tell you anything to steal it. The days of regretting who you fucked, regretting a drunken hookup, or being talked into a relationship just because a man wants to lower your guards, are over. No woman reading this will ever WISH that she never had sex because the next man you have sex with will have earned it. I am not a proponent of celibacy pacts or women who keep their virginities into their late twenties. I've met numerous girls like this, and the majority are fear based individuals who do themselves more harm than good by making sex a burden. This isn't about "I can't afford to add another body to my list," bullshit. This isn't about "Sex complicates things," cowardice. This is about control.

So many women walk around as if having a vagina is a briefcase full of money, and they don't know who to trust and who to run from. Your pussy is priceless, that doesn't mean you covet it like some paranoid billionaire afraid to let people in. Sex feels good for a reason because you're supposed to have it! I want you to have sex, not because he will put a ring on it, but because the man you are dating unlocks the code romantically, physically, and spiritually. When a man hits all three sparks, on top of passing these dating steps, then he has climbed a hell of a mountain. That's who deserves to sip from your pussy, a fucking Jedi. Spartans can respect their bodies and scratch their itch, but they do so in route to the bigger conquest. Understand that sex at this level should be chess, not checkers. You can't think about the day after, you have to think about the year after. Is this a man who shows the signs that he could build a dynasty with you, or just someone who's cool for now? You don't need three dates, 90 days, or any arbitrary line in the sand that determines when to spread your legs, all you need is Spartan intuition and direct proof that a man has what it takes to not only make the team but become the only player.

YOU DON'T NEED A TITLE

The default safeguard is wait until he is your boyfriend to have sex. This proves that his intentions are legitimate and that he wants you for you...in theory. Let's put that theory to the test and look at sex from the male POV.

Why do men date? To charm a woman into having sex. Forget the crap about how he wants to take it slow because sex ruined his last relationship or how he is more concerned with building a friendship. If he has a dick, he wants sex, and he knows it. Sex does not ruin a relationship for a man, those annoying women who become too clingy afterward ruins it for him. **Over emotional or erratic behavior that comes after sex is introduced will make a man leery, but it will not make him abstinent**. Men aren't all raging hard-on's that are waiting for a green light. A man who can get sex on the regular, can afford to be patient. This patience isn't born out of wanting to be your friend first because he thinks you're special, it's about him seeing how you act over the course of these dates to determine if you remind him of those women that have proven to be easily dick whipped. When you date like a Spartan you extinguish a man's "she's crazy like that last girl," worry.

Let's detour for a minute and talk about dick whipping. The concept that a man has such a good penis stroke or foreplay game that a woman gets hooked is bullshit. The feeling of good sex makes you want to do it again, but it is not addictive in a way where it chemically forces a woman to step out of character the same way a crack addict transforms mentally. What's going on is a physical trigger built on an emotional response to a man making her feel good in a way that's rare. If a woman is lacking in the father area, and a man is dominating her sexually in a way that makes her feel loved, wanted, safe, then sex becomes tied to filling that emotional hole that Daddy left, it isn't just the physical release. If a woman doesn't feel beautiful or has a history of being made to feel subpar in terms of looks, sex with a man that goes above in beyond completes her. Sucking toes, rimming, a constant stiff dick that never gets soft, signifies that he truly finds her attractive. That dick turns her ugly duckling mentality into a swan swagger, and that makes this man seemingly irreplaceable. Again, we're dealing with what he does to her mental hole, not inside the physical.

I once talked to an older woman, around 40, who said she was dick whipped by a man who was sixteen years younger. As we broke down her obsession with this young man over the course of a few weeks, I finally led her to uncover what was going on. It wasn't the orgasm because she admittedly only reached climax twice, and only during oral. Her addiction was, that as a divorced woman who lived with a man who never saw her as

276

exciting or desirable, the energy that this boy was putting into her was new and fulfilling. He wanted to go multiple times a night, he let her be in control and lead him, he was spontaneous, aggressive, eager, all traits that she had never experienced before with a man. She didn't need to cum because emotionally his behavior was enough to elevate her to cloud nine. What was supposed to be a fling to knock the dust off, turned into her stalking this kid, chasing off other women, and eventually ended after she spent the money she was saving for her daughter's high school graduation party on getting her boy toy's car repaired. She hit rock bottom, but still craved him. This was not a dick being insanely good, this was a woman being insanely empty. There is no such thing as being dick whipped, it's all mental. Men, even with Dirk Diggler[12] sized egos, know that a woman in emotional need can lead to a headache, which is why they could be slow to engage in sex even when you want it. For guys who don't need a female to pay for car repairs, loan money, or offer a place to live, getting a woman sprung isn't worth the annoyance. It's not the sex that ruins things, it's the woman attached to the vagina's emotional stability that he's worried about.

Now that you understand this, you can see why a man could be waiting to see if you show signs of insecurity and instability. Even before he puts his penis in you, he wants to feel as if you aren't acting clingy or trying to smother him. If you do those things just off of dating and kissing, imagine what will happen after sex? He waits, says he isn't worried about sex or doesn't go for sex, cool. But don't jump for joy and feel as if he's different from the more aggressive types, his patience reveals nothing.

Let's go back to the idea of become official, then have sex because it proves true intentions. If a man asks to be your boyfriend and you agree, what does that really mean to him? It means that it's time to get serious. Seriousness means sex. You may not intend to have sex with him until six months after giving him the title, but he doesn't know that. A woman taking on a boyfriend is a sign that it's safe to move to the sex stage, in the mind of the average man. **It is not above a man to play along to see what being official gets him, fast**. If you are the type of girl that only has sex when in a relationship, then he's banking on hitting that within the week.

---

[12] The lead character in *Boogie Nights*, a well-endowed male porn star.

If you were a boy, and a girl said she wanted to take it to the next level, even if you didn't see her as girlfriend material, you would still see an opportunity to get what you came for, new pussy. Allow me to break down how we men turn this to our favor. Instead of agreeing to be your boyfriend, he will make up an understandable excuse, something that he needs to get done before he can agree to commit. <u>This is rejection without rejection.</u> To say that he needs a little more time to get over his ex or needs to wait for the stress of his job or school to die down makes it about the situation, not the woman. Your ego thinks, "he wants me too, it's just the wrong time." In reality, it *is* about you not being what he wants fully. This is a calculated risk. Although you aren't going to be together, he has manipulated you into believing that you're on the same page. Therefore, when he tries to go for sex, what's holding you back? You admitted to wanting to take it to the next level. He has admitted to feeling the same. You two will be together soon...or so you think. Most women have sex with a guy who is technically theirs because it feels safe, and the man wins. He no longer has to date you, nor will he have to enter into a real relationship. If you get dick whipped aka emotionally hooked, then you will keep busting it open for months maybe even years, as a FWB[13] while he keeps shopping for a Game Changer.

Alternatively, if he asks you to be with him first, you have to question the motive. Earlier, we went over how Cali shot Stephen down because she realized it was a power play. Men can move fast in terms of making you their girl, not because they are lying about how they feel, but because they are in lust and don't know how they truly feel. If you agree to a lust title without asking yourself why he wants you so bad, you give into your own egotistical need to be wanted. Once you give him that serious commitment, you will be pressured to perform girlfriend duties. You won't mind because you are his girl, but by moving this fast, how can you tell if this is like that leads to love or plain old lust that leads to a breakup?

---

[13] Friend With Benefits, sex buddy, situationship boo, you get the point.

Once your pussy expires, meaning that months later after he's had you in every way, the novelty is gone, and that lust dissipates. He will begin to get stir crazy because your personality was never what he wanted, he was just filled with desire. Now, he either sabotages the relationship or grows apart from you. You should have dodged the quick lasso of a title, and waited to see how he held up to dating. The vast majority of women are so hard up for a boyfriend, they rush in the moment he asks, not in Sparta!

If you think like a typical woman then your thoughts may center on, "why waste his time when he doesn't want me when I know he can go get sex elsewhere for no commitment?" When a man is given access to new pussy, it's never a waste of his time. Our time is never squandered if we cum in some girl we've never had before. A man will never spend several months having sex with a new girl, get broken up with, and feel as if he wasted his time unless he invested money he didn't have. His time was well spent because he got something new out of it! That's how men view sex, it's always a win if he achieves that nut. Those other girls he can have sex with, he either hit it already or got shot down. Newness is what men chase. The title of Girlfriend and Boyfriend is only as powerful as you make it, it's not legal or binding on a physical level. Nothing will stop him from deciding that he needs to go because it was just lust, or make him treat you better when you threaten to take away that title down the line. A man can and will let a relationship die and not feel robbed because his investment paid off.

From a non-Spartan viewpoint, a female will see the title as final proof that they are on the same page, and it's okay to have sex. I repeat, it's not about the title. Once you reach the upper levels of Spartanhood you could care less about "be mine" because you demand an actual effort that speaks louder than words. You must visually see and physically feel that he is already treating you like you are his before you are official. You must witness him investing so much of himself emotionally, financially, and time wise that it's safe to say that he's in too deep to leave after he gets sex. An investor doesn't pour money and time into a business then walk away, they stay involved because it's a part of them by that point. That's how Spartans determine if a man is sex ready, over-investment, so let's move onto that.

GIVE ME YOUR HEART MOTHERFUCKER!

"Come Harder, This Won't Be Easy..." -King Bey

Don't say you want me, show me. That's the burden of proof that all men have, and no exceptions can be made. Showing you is determined by three things, the first being <u>Time Spent Creatively</u>. Once you break into the post-third date world of him making your team, his efforts should increase, not level out. How much time is he putting in to talk to you about non "can I see you" topics? Any man can put in the effort to see you when he is trying to get his dick wet, but in terms of calling you during a normal boring weekday, how active is he in chiming in with a creative conversation that continues to keep you hooked? In terms of continuing to date at a high level now that you have introduced the possibility of house dates, what has he shown? Is he still interested in going outside with you to show you things that he loves and treat you to things that you love? Is he being as romantic or creative as week one, or is he content with indoor chilling and grabbing takeout? Why would a woman who's looking for something real agree to fuck a man who is merely doing the bare minimum? Yes, you will enjoy those basic talks about how much he wants you and how great you are as well as the nights on the couch with his arms wrapped around you, but that isn't exertion. If he were to have sex with you based on that effort, how invested would he be in actually building something real? Even if a man is technically your boyfriend and that's the routine, he's still on easy street. Flirting with you on the phone—free. Telling you how much he's starting to fall for you—free. Snuggling up on a lazy Sunday—free. Taking you to the movies to see a movie he was going to go see anyway—free, not in terms of money, but in terms of EFFORT.

The currency of true love is undeniable time and effort. If a man does not show that on his own, then it reveals how he feels. This isn't about the demands you use to make him take you out or the tricks you can use to lead him to put in more effort. You did your job by dating like a Spartan, you interviewed him, opened him up, showed him how you expect to be treated, and rewarded him with a deeper level of intimacy. For a man to settle into complacency a month or two into the process is the revelation that costs him his spot on the roster. Far too many women lead a man during the dating process. **Now is the time to take off the training wheels and see if he can *King Up* on his own.** Stop suggesting things to do, stop dropping hints, and allow him to take the ball and run with it. If you continue to plan romantic outings and come up with unique date ideas, then the actual relationship will be an extension of this lazy ass effort. Do you want to be just another typical that has to make her man take her places, only gets flowers on occasions, and has to remind him of date nights, or will you demand a man that reaches that level of independent effort before the title? Sex isn't given to men who put their feet up, it's given to those men who continue to work and show you value without reminders.

The second sign that you have genuinely won a man over is <u>Aggressive Pursuit</u>. You aren't going to fall for the "We go together," power play during the first few weeks when honeymoon butterflies and new dick lust is at an all-time high. However, even if you tell a man he's moving too fast, his effort should continue to be that of a full court press. This is what makes a Spartan a Game Changer, a man will not take "No" for an answer in terms of locking her down. That's the hustle you want! Michael Jordan didn't make his high school team, so what did he do? He worked harder! This man isn't dating you for his health, he's trying to win you over because he recognizes something special. Unlike those thots that chase dick, give into fast titles, and sell their pussy for the right to be called his, you challenge a man to fight for the right to be called yours.

You need to see that he feels a certain way that he can't have you. The fact that you are still living a life outside of him should piss him off. The fact that you do go a day without talking to him should frustrate him. The idea that you aren't exclusively dating him should make him jealous. None of these feelings should be thrown in your face with anger or pettiness, but they should come out naturally. You will always know when a man wants you seriously because he pouts and gets into moods when you pull rank. Your old instincts have been to be up under a man that wants you up under him or to make an agreement that you won't see anyone else as long as he doesn't. <u>That weak shit doesn't exist in Sparta.</u>

By continuing to reserve your dating rights and taking breaks from seeing your friend, you force him into an emotional corner where few men are used to being. Males love control, they don't like the idea of a woman having power over him, but you need to see this struggle. If he can't express himself, don't be brutal and cut him off, a Spartan opens her mouth. If you sense that he wants to be with you, ask him if that is the issue. Be forward, not passive. A real man will open up to you, especially given your communication history, and at that vulnerable moment, he will confess that he wants you. This doesn't mean you agree to be his, it means that you reward him with your own feelings. That you're falling for him too, but not ready. Emphasize that you aren't scared of being hurt or dealing with trust issues, you are merely enjoying the process until you feel 100%. It is important to communicate this. A man who feels as if a grown woman is afraid to commit will lose respect. How can he trust a girl who still believes that he will do her like some ex once did? You are a Spartan, trust issues, daddy issues, commitment phobia, are non-fucking-existent. The only reason you are taking your time is because you want to pull him apart mentally and get him to over-invest so that he can't live without you. That takes time. Don't hold back, express your feelings that you want him so he's not assuming you are playing a game, but internally you are on this secret mission...you must remain un-exclusive until after you finish vetting.

The final proof of worthiness is <u>Shared World Companionship</u>. Being friends is extremely important. A friend isn't someone you are getting to know, talking to, and laugh with occasionally. Friendship is created through mutual interest and sharing of views, ideas, and secrets. A true friend falls in love with your soul, not the surface of your personality. Why would a man see you as a friend, and not just some girl, only three to four weeks into dating? Because a Spartan brings a fire into his life that he can't duplicate with other people. You have a viewpoint his other friends don't have. You grow him in ways he can't grow himself. In response, he becomes invested in your life as well as you remaining in his. To lose you would be to lose the one person he can call and vent to about a certain subject. To lose you would mean he won't have anyone to go to that place that you two discovered and fell in love with. To lose you would mean that he no longer has someone who gets those particular jokes that only you get or understands those wild ideas that only you understand. Any woman can bring him pussy and jokes, but what you bring are intangible feelings, reactions, and opinions no one else can replicate. You are priceless!

Spartans aren't fake deep, their depth is natural because they communicate in a real way, and their personalities aren't hindered by fear of "I don't want to say something offensive or ignorant." Spartans speak their minds to those that earn the intimacy of their conversation. This isn't about sexual chemistry or some honeymoon false high, the proof of your friendship is in how you two can hang inside or outside without sex coming up. Can you go places and enjoy the silence of each other's company without the physical affection? Can you two debate passions without catching attitudes when the opinions defer? Companionship is needed for any relationship to flourish, and by dating like a Spartan, you bond on a level few people reach. In the end, ask yourself is this man treating you like a friend or just a chick he wants to fuck? Are you the first one he calls when something crazy or funny happens, or do you hear about it later on? Are you invited out only for dates or does he bring you into his hobbies and interests outside of romance? Does he bug you like a little boy bugs his older sister, because he wants her attention, or is he still trying to play it cool and mysterious? This man should want to make love to you but also want to be up under you like you're Ash and he's Pikachu.

Time Spent Creatively. Aggressive Pursuit. Shared World Companionship. If a man doesn't meet all three, then he doesn't get you. No matter how nice, fun, or sexy he is. Earning sex isn't about seeing if he lasts 90 days, remains sweet and affectionate, offers a title, or spends money every week to court you. Any Dick can wait three months and behave himself if pussy is coming. Any Dick can call you every day and tell you he loves you if pussy is coming. Any Dick can buy you a plane ticket, set a romantic weekend, and bust it open in a hotel. Any Dick can agree to be your boyfriend! None of those things that makes a typical bitch's heart flutter dents a Spartan. You need to see deep proof that this man not only wants you but needs you in his life. He must achieve all three of these prerequisites, and then you will know it in your essence that he has climbed that mountain and earned the best pussy he will ever experience.

Chapter 20:
How to Transition from Dating to a Relationship

O ne dollar confidence transforms "When will he make it official" into a million dollar question. Legions of women are currently in situationships where they are waiting for a man to lay claim and either ask for or confirm that they have a monogamous relationship. Others are stuck in a post-dating/pre-commitment purgatory where they treat a man like a boyfriend and take on girlfriend duties, but if someone were to ask what was going on it would be met with a shoulder shrug. *I don't know what we are*, is the common answer. *We're taking our time and seeing how it goes*, is the defensive answer. *I'm ready but I'm waiting on him*, is the truth. No matter how much he treats you like you are his girlfriend, you are not his girlfriend until you both are in agreement. This need to be direct and straightforward with one another about what each person wants from the other is scary and has created this gray area where fearful women sit on the bench waiting for confirmation.

The longer you sit on the bench waiting for a man to decide, the more likely it is that he's already decided—you aren't girlfriend material. The longer you sit on the bench, even if you pretend to still be "talking to other guys" the more comfortable you get. In the end, you will feel as if being his purgatory bae, is better than leaving him and starting back over dating a new guy you have to relearn and retest. That's the one-dollar confidence that typical women have. They act passively and drop hints about wanting to be with a man, they may even ask "so where do you see this going," but their lack of self-esteem will keep them clinging on to this idea that it's better to go with the flow of being unofficial but exclusive, than to rock the boat and get what she wants. Men don't lose in this game, if he wants to be with you, but doesn't ask, he still gets your girlfriend experience—win. If he doesn't want to be with you but doesn't say this, he still gets the girlfriend benefits until a Game Changer appears—win. Alpha males don't suffer in silence when they want a woman exclusively, they speak up, and so should Spartans. These men may get shot down, but it doesn't matter because it's always better to confront this want than to wait on the "what are we," bench hoping the relationship bus shows up.

Tina Typical would rather Google, "When will he make me his girlfriend," than directly ask a man who she talks to every day. Fear makes cowards of women in relationships and slaves to signs. The reason women Google for answers and ask for opinions on the male mind is because they don't want to put their heart on the line by asking for a relationship only to be rejected. Instead, they look for signs that friends, family, or the internet claims that men show when they are falling in love. "If he likes me, he's going to do XYZ, and then I can stop worrying because that mean he's serious." This cowardly way of thinking must be eradicated. **Spartans don't ask for commitment, they field offers**. This entire *Date Like a Spartan*, section has been about creating a brand that an intelligent man would have to be blind not to buy into. If you went step by step from the Pre-Date to the Roster Spot and finally to the point where you would have sex with him, that means he opened up and showed most of his true colors and you have revealed the true power of your personality and character. This should only have taken six to ten weeks max, depending on your schedule of dating and bonding. Which means that in less than 75 days, this man should be Spartan whipped! The final step for any free agent is deciding who to sign to, and that's what I mean by fielding an offer.

Why do college athletes make millions before they even step into the pros, while others from that same school go work at Foot Locker while struggling to make the practice squad? Value based on past results and projected potential. You are a Spartan, that makes you the top free agent in the land, not some average bitch that has to wait around while a man decides if you're good enough. In the past six weeks you proved your value, and more importantly, this man has proved to be someone you can win with for years to go. That's how you decide if you become official.

Commitment should never be about if you like him a lot and he likes you back, if you want to have sex and not feel guilty for doing so, or if he happens to ask and you don't have anyone better, so you agree. That's basic settling, not Spartan power. To get a relationship from you, the top free agent in the world, means that this man has proven without a doubt that he is exceptional. He is King Arthur pulling Excalibur out of the stone. And while this does not prove that he is worthy of marriage, it proves that he is worthy to share your power for now. You are a Goddess, that isn't a metaphor, you are a Goddess! Will this man fall short when he's actually with you or will he grow and solidify what he's shown during the dating stage? You will not know until you see him in action as your boyfriend. That means, that while the title and role of boyfriend may not be the same as that of a husband, you must treat it with the same reverence. You have reached the end of the dating stage, this man has passed all tests, and all your instincts are pointing to him being the one, so let's break down the Do's & Don'ts of transitioning into a relationship.

WE GO TOGETHER

When we last left Spartan Cali and her man friend Stephen, they had reached the roster level. Over the course of a month, Stephen proved to be a quick study in terms of how to treat a woman and proved that his charm was authentic, not forged in an attempt to lure Cali into sex. He showed a want to be with her officially within the first few weeks, proving he was decisive and attentive to the fact that Cali is not the kind of girl you leave out on the market. As important, Stephen flexed his King muscles by being a man that doesn't bow down just to earn points. He's not afraid to say "No" and he doesn't agree with everything Cali says for the sake of keeping things calm. This man is not a simp or pushover. What's taking Cali so long to agree to be his girlfriend? That's the same thing Stephen is wondering.

Cali has a two-week plan to seal the deal and take Stephen on as her boyfriend. Similar to the way she visualized her pre-date conversation, Cali is going to use the one vision board that actually works—her mind. With this final game plan, she will lock Stephen in as either her next man or her next blocked number.

Day 1 of 14: *The Commitment Talk*. Day 7: *The Penis Test*. Day 14: *We Go Together*. Life is never out of a Spartan's control, consciously Cali wants Stephen, but who knows what her subconscious true self wants. Instead of waiting for a sign, she decides to take the plunge, but not before those things are explored over the next two weeks. Does Stephen understand what being a boyfriend means on a deeper level? Is there true sexual chemistry beyond the flirting and lust? Will they both feel the same about each other after the post-sex cooling off period? Cali has to find these things out, and there is no tarot card, dream reading, daily horoscope, or any indirect sign that will tell her these things. Cali is willing to put herself out there to find out the truth, and she's confident that her universe will show her exactly what she needs to know: Is he truly boyfriend material?

****

Late night conversations reveal a person's soul. Add in the close proximity of two bodies, and a man who trusts you will spill his truth like Wonder Woman's lasso. Cali goes over to Stephen's house for a date, this is the second time she's been over, but it will be the first time she spends the night. The cover of the date is a cook-off. In the days prior they've been teasing each other about doing some Bobby Flay type cooking battle, and Cali has gathered a simple recipe they will both try their hands at making to see whose comes out better. Cali could do this at her place, but she knows that the line of conversation she plans will last into the early morning hours, so this is a good opportunity to sleep over and do the overnight test. Cali doesn't just pop up with a sleepover bag like some Basica that assumes coming over means staying over. She verbally tells Stephen when they set this cooking date, "I'm going to bring my stuff to stay over unless you have to be up early." Stephen did have to be up early, but he is so excited at the prospect of Cali finally staying the night that he doesn't mind leaving her unsupervised in his crib. Like the Spartan she is, Cali uses her mouth to establish the rules of the night, there is no guessing or assuming.

While cooking, Cali doesn't drop hints about how cooking is what he should expect when they're together or ask dumb shit about if his ex-girlfriends have ever done this with him. She's not insecure, thus, insecure questions don't slip from her lips. After dinner, they position themselves on the couch to watch TV, but the TV will be watching them. Cali puts her feet in Stephen's lap and begins the first wave of contract negotiations...

"Do you think we would make a great couple? Wait," she holds a finger up for emphasis, "I said great, not good, keep that in mind." Stephen smiles, he knows Cali at this point, she doesn't do one-word answers, so "Yeah," or "I think so," won't fly. "I know we will, there's nothing that I can see that will point to us growing apart," he says, and before Cali can respond in her typical forward manner, Stephen keeps going, "What do you think? Would we be great?" Cali loved that Stephen said, "I know we will," that sureness makes her kitty tingle, but she can't let him off the hook. Spartans don't answer questions that they asked first, ever, so she keeps him in the hot seat. "It's only been a month," Cali reminds him, "how do you know that this honeymoon period won't wear off the moment we have sex or the day after our first dumb argument?" Stephen takes a second to think. Finally, he speaks, "I know that I love you, and that doesn't happen this quick with a person like me. That's enough for me to try my best to make it work no matter what we go through." Good answer.

At this point, Cali won't keep grilling him, no one wants to be made out to be full of shit, so to keep asking "why this why that" will sound as if Cali has trust issues. Instead, Cali opens up to communicate her inner struggle so Stephen knows she's not a typical scared girl unsure who to love. "I'm not afraid to love you, baby, and I know this could be something special, but I want to see that we keep growing in this direction. I know how you date, I love how you date me, but I don't know how you are as a boyfriend," Stephen begins to talk because he needs to sell himself, but Cali uses her feet to dig into his chest and shut him down. Being playful yet stern she keeps going, "Hold on! What I expect in a boyfriend are dates like we've been doing, fun outside stuff as well as fun indoors stuff like tonight. I also expect a man that takes the relationship seriously. I'm not talking about don't ever look at another girl's ass or having to show me off to your friends, I don't need that. This is about the role of being my man being something that you take pride in and always want to make me happy." Stephen responds that it is the kind of boyfriend he will be and was, and goes into his own story about how even with his exes he took the title seriously.

Cali, as always, will listen, not to look for another chance to talk, but to learn more about his past. If Stephen brings up something generic like "I was the one that communicated first in my last relationship because communication is important," Cali won't just eat it up, she will ask, "Give me an example of where you were open and she wasn't." This conversation is about expectations. Cali wants to hear real relationship thoughts, not a theoretical, "If I was your man," dream selling.

The two will drink a little bit, but keep talking about this issue in terms of the things they hated in past relationship, but also the things they loved about their last relationships. People rarely say, "My ex was really good at this," because bitterness creates this tunnel vision of negativity when looking back. Cali will bring up that she enjoyed how an ex planned a "staycation" for their anniversary because he knew they couldn't leave the state due to Cali's schedule. Stephen will internalize that as "Remember to spoil regardless," without Cali having to spell it out. Stephen will talk about how he had a great relationship with his last girlfriend's dad and he missed him more than her. Cali doesn't have an active dad in her life, but she does have a great uncle who she knows Stephen would love. Again, this isn't something she says, "oh I can do this," it's internalized as something that she should remember to do because he likes those things.

This is what communication is all about in terms of making sure a man and woman can mesh well as opposed to reacting to needs that pop up. Too many people enter relationships where they assume they can make each other happy, but they never learn what makes their partner smile. They assume and adapt on the fly. **This isn't a one-sided conversation where you make sure a man knows how to keep you happy**. Can you do the same for him? This will be a partnership where you have to be sure that you can be a woman he feels understands and completes him, as opposed to one with incompatibilities. Learning about a man's needs gives you direct knowledge of what's to be expected as his girlfriend. A guy could be great, but needs too much attention or demands a woman be too much like a mother or therapist. Talking openly about what you both see as must-have traits, ensures that there are no personality surprises once you enter into a union. Relationships are about moving in sync with one another, you learn a person during dating so that you know their likes by the time it's official.

The more Cali and Stephen talk about a potential relationship in a real way, the more comfortable they get with the subject. Commitment talks are rarely had unless it's "So what are we!?!" By pointing out the elephant in the room, Cali takes "girlfriend" from a dirty word to one that seems like fun, but also carves out that it's not going to be just "dating with a title," this is real commitment that will require consistency and maturity on his end. A male's brain thinks that if she's bringing up titles and what to expect as her man, it means she wants that ASAP. Stephen doesn't want to offend Cali by switching topics to who really killed who on some Netflix series, so he goes for the score.

"We established we would make a good—no, a great couple, so what's the holdup?" Cali smiles, she scoots over to him and lays in his lap. "You tell me?" She's playing her hard to get games now. Stephen lights up, "You! I've been ready." Cali could take that and run with it, there is no reason not to as he's passed all the tests. However, she's still on her schedule, she's going to spend the night, she's going to fuck him next week, and then she's going to see if it's still all good. "I like making you wait; it turns me on," Is Cali's dodgy answer and to stroke his ego, she follows this teasing statement up with a kiss. Stephen is on her string. He used the L-word in a natural way that wasn't forced and is continuing to show his vulnerability, not tell. His heart is in her hands, and it feels good.

By the next week, things have continued as normal, Stephen's joked about the boyfriend stuff, but he hasn't been pushy. The night they spent together was nice. Stephen, of course, tried to move his hands down below, but Cali checked him. There were no late night or early morning texts or calls from other women. Stephen even made breakfast before having to go and left Cali with a key to his place. This is the sign of a man who's focused on one woman. He didn't have to say it, Cali saw it. To be sure, Cali did another sleepover a few days later, this time leaving her toothbrush in his bathroom... a nice bright Nicki Minaj style pink one that tells his other bitches that the Queen has landed. As far as Cali's other men, she didn't go on any dates this week, she's had conversations, but even the guy who was once in front of Stephen on the roster doesn't seem as great these days. Stephen's about to win, so it's time for the *Penis Test*.

You may not need a penis test. Don't feel as if sex is a mandatory part of the boyfriend decision if sex isn't a part of your life. Cali has her own rules for love that other women may not share, but her needs must be met. Maybe testing out the equipment isn't important to you, but Cali went through a boyfriend who was a three pump Paulie, back when she was Nicole, and there is no way she's going to spend her prime years faking content while only being able to achieve orgasms on her own. She could wait until Stephen is her boyfriend to test it, but what sense does that make if good sex is important to her happiness? Fall in love with an untested penis, then have to learn the angles to make a semi-hard dick hit the right spots to get her off consistently? Not in Sparta. Cali doesn't need a certain size but she does need a certain effort because she fucks like a champ, not a contender. Unlike the sleepover date, Cali doesn't need to say, "Ay, we're fucking Friday, have condoms and whip cream." The spontaneity of sex is fun. Why spoil it with an announcement? However, she will drop hints by engaging in the one thing she has yet to do—phone sex.

****

To this point phone sex, Skype sex, Facetime sex, sexting, have all been off limits. Sure, there may have been a few nasty lines or jokes about sex, but it was contained. Understand what phone sex really is, it's the act of bringing you or the person at the other end of the device, to a climax by painting a vivid picture of what you would do to them. Sex itself is a mental experience, simply moaning the right way is enough to make a man's dick begin to leak pre-ejaculate. Men are easy to get off if you aren't afraid to put on a performance or too shy to say something utterly filthy. Nevertheless, phone sex isn't a one-way street when using it as a pre-sex warm up. Can this man make you dripping wet? Again, it's all mental, a woman's inability to cum is due to the physical and mental stimulation not matching up. A shy mind may hold back, but a man should know the combination to open you up. Cali will test Stephen's ability as a warm-up for their showdown. Breaking into phone sex is as simple as the ways I covered in *Solving Single*, no need for any big build up, there is never a wrong time so long as the both of you are alone in a private place. Late night, when you're both in bed, is ideal, so let's pick it up there.

Cali transitions from the day in the life talk they were having, and tells Stephen that he should be over there to feel how soft her new panties are. Men are simple, any talk about what you are wearing gets them perked up. Stephen wants her to Facetime him the underwear. Cali wants to keep this verbal control, so she responds, "I would, but I'm in the process of taking them off." Stephen will try to play it cool, but like most men his wit will leave him once his dick begins to grow. "Oh really..." He asks. "Yes really," Cali purrs, "are you jealous of my comforter?" Stephen is being lead to take the bait, but he's built up enough respect, that he won't blurt out, "Fuck, I want to put this dick so deep in you that it bruises your soul." Phone sex is a gradual build from nice to nasty over the course of about ten to twenty minutes. Cali leads him to drop his gentleman act and play along. "How hard is it? Take it out for me," will take the conversation to a new level. "Can I taste it, daddy..." will take the conversation to the point of no return. The goal isn't to cum. In reality, Cali doesn't have to actually touch herself or play it out on her end. She's merely seeing how freaky Stephen can get, so that when they do have sex for the first time it won't be any awkward nerves. No matter how long you date someone, if you don't cross that filth line before that first sex session, the odds are that without alcohol a man that's built up so much respect for you may not put in his best work. Phone sex takes away performance anxiety, and that's what Cali is doing. She's training him to be a freak with her, not a gentleman who handles her pussy with kid gloves.

Time Spent Creatively.
Aggressive Pursuit.
Shared World Companionship

Those are the three things we went over last chapter that you need to see before determining if a man is worthy of sex. Stephen has passed all those previous tests, and has just lost his phone sex virginity, so it's time to do the deed. Stephen wants to know if Cali wants to go out with a few friends for Karaoke, Cali only wants to rock one mic. She has a better idea, why don't they get a room at a hotel downtown and make a night of it, it'll be something different. Stephen isn't dumb, hotel = sex to any man.

Stephen is down, and Cali tells him to find one with a nice restaurant they can eat and drink at aka *don't Holiday Inn me, motherfucker.* The date is set, Stephen doesn't know it's a sex date, but he's praying it is. Once again, Spartan Cali is in control of this man's mind and she's about to blow it.

The day after sex shouldn't be awkward, it should be comfortable. What routinely happens is that people over think the situation and speculate about what's in their partner's head. For men it's about performance, was he weak or did he leave his mark? For women, it isn't about performance as much as what happens next. "Does he think I'm going to want a relationship? Does this mean we're in a relationship? Is he going to stop calling as much because he got what he wanted...is he going to start calling more because he thinks I'm now a fuck buddy?" When people get paranoid about what sex means, they stop communicating, and that awkwardness creates a divide. No one wants to call first or call too much, thus, a fun relationship falls apart due to miscommunication about the seriousness of sex. In Cali's case, she is going to be forward...*duh, Spartan.*

The sex was great, they did it twice that night and once again in the morning, with Cali reaching the mountain top two out of three times. She doesn't lay on Stephen's chest and say, "Was it good?" she knows her throw game was bomb. She doesn't change the subject to, "So what are you doing for the rest of the day," as if this man is a stranger she should be shy around. He was just inside of her, they're as close as you can get. Why be timid? Cali does what she's done since day one, asks a question, "Are you sad, that I test drove you before making you my boyfriend?" Stephen doesn't know if it's a joke or serious. What Cali did was objectify him as a piece of meat, while also bringing up the elephant in the room "the title" forcing him to react. The words "making you my boyfriend," keeps the power with Cali. Stephen asks if she test drives all of her potential boyfriends. Men love to ask about a woman's sex life, it's in the male DNA to compete. Cali lightens the mood by jumping on him and joking, "worry about yourself, boyfriend in training!" They play wrestle around, and with the post-sex ice, now broken, they gather their things and leave the hotel. Cali may not even call Stephen that night, he's not her man, and she likes taking breaks. But Stephen will call Cali because he is now hooked.

The final test is the week after sex. If Stephen has true desire, he isn't going to call her to come over to fuck, he's going to call to see her—difference. Cali needs to see that level of continued respect and effort after sex or Stephen reveals himself as non-boyfriend material. A man calling to get a rematch does not prove interest, a man calling to set up a real date, does. Stephen and Cali hang out without having sex and then have a movie date a day later. Cali invites Stephen back to her place after the movie because today is "the day" and she wants to be on her home field. The two-week schedule is complete and now it's time to take what she wants.

Over the course of the past six weeks, you witnessed a woman who played by her rules without fear that the man she wanted would fall back because he couldn't get what he wanted or go find another woman who moved at a faster pace. If you have the mind to comprehend what you are reading and lack fear, then you can pull this off in the same time frame! The open communication about "I want you, but on my terms, and it has nothing to do with me not trusting you," has created an environment of rewards. Every time Stephen acted like a man instead of an angry or temperamental little boy who didn't get his way, Cali has rewarded him. He dated her with respect and tried to commit early, so he got the benefits of being on the team and getting house dates. He still continued to date her and open up to her on a real level, without getting lazy, so he got the benefit of sleepovers. He didn't cry about not being together or pressure her for sex, so he got the benefit of phone sex. He proved that he knows how to hit her spot mentally, so he got real sex. Is Stephen perfect? No, he gets on his soapbox about issues that Cali doesn't care about. He isn't as ambitious as he first seemed, but he does have above average drive to move up in life. He sometimes jokes too much, but Cali is sometimes too serious, so they balance each other out. The thing that makes Stephen better than the other men on her roster is that he tries the hardest to win her over.

With those things in her head, she pulls Stephen down on her couch, and looks him in the eyes with the confidence of Cleopatra, but with a Mona Lisa smile, and tells him, **"I'm ready."** This isn't a question, this isn't a conversation, this is a statement that a Spartan makes when she's made her choice. She is ready to grant him exclusivity and uses her words to say it clearly. What if Stephen says, "I think we need to keep building," or

"I'm not sure if I'm ready now." It means that none of the steps that Cali did were followed. A man will not reject a Spartan that has reached this level, ever! There is no "What If's" to be worried about, there is only the truth that a Spartan who sinks her claws into a man this deep over this much time while dating in an exposing manner, always win. Men are not complex creatures, and women aren't stupid, most relationships begin the wrong way or never begin at all because despite how confused a girl pretends to be, she knows if a man wants her or not. The little tricks men do to act as if they are putting in work, or falling for you, those things are transparent. Dating like a Spartan strips away the lies you tell yourself. You will see clearly after the first date if he's on 10 or on 7 in terms of how he likes you. By the second date, it solidifies your first date intuition. A man does not make it to the *We Go Together* stage without you feeling, seeing, and experiencing this man's obsession with you. I repeat, you always win.

Chapter 21:
The Thing Every Woman Must Do
Before Agreeing to A Relationship

these steps don't require you to be a carbon copy of Cali, but they do require the same confidence, the same communication, and the courage to confront your own wants. A Spartan doesn't chase, she doesn't hold on, and she doesn't wait around. Dating like a Spartan takes out the guess work of "is he into me?" If he made it this far, moved at your pace, and opened up in a real way, then he is genuine. A Spartan does not give ultimatums or ask questions about where a man sees it going, she knows where they stand because it's already been established numerous times over the past several weeks. Any man dealing with his own trust issues, emotional scares, or immaturity, is not compatible. A man who isn't compatible will never make it to this transition stage, he gets cut at the roster stage. You will always sniff out his inconsistent, fake, or weak behavior. You will always be protected from choosing wrong, so long as you put in the work of vetting a man in this manner.

I don't know if I'm strong enough must always be greeted with *I Am*! Do you want to vacation on a beach with some settle Dick or do you want to vacation on an island with your name now hyphenated? The days of dating on a man's terms are over. You will never sit by your phone waiting for a man to call you. You will never sit on the phone wondering when he'll ask you out. You will never worry yourself with basic shit like where to go or what to say. Your thoughts won't be consumed with when to have sex, when to kiss, when to allow him over, when to spend the night, or any of the trivial things that do nothing but keep a man in control of your mind!

This is your entire universe, your Spartan Avatar is the Sun, and this all revolves around you. All the pressure is on these men to earn your attention, to respect your rules, and to endear themselves. The ones who think their market value is too high to do that, the ones who would rather chase easy ass, the ones who try to play mind games, you don't stress over them, you dismiss them. Your aim is compatibility, the manifestation of a man who reflects the new you. Don't cry over a CZ as if he were priceless. You will attract multiple men that want to give you the world, but you need to hit one final thing before you give your top choice the title...

THE FINAL CHECKLIST

<u>Has The Effort Been Established</u>: At the end of six weeks, can you say that he's been working as hard to win you over as he was during the first two weeks when he couldn't wait to see you and talk to you? The answer needs to be a resounding "yes," not "I guess," because you know damn well that you can sense effort. The first week a man will break plans to see you, stay up late to talk to you, and revolve his world around getting to know you. Over time, if he thinks sex isn't going to come anytime soon, or feels you aren't worth his effort, these things begin to fade. Plans can't be broken, he doesn't have much time to talk, and you have to basically get in where you fit into his schedule...if this is the case, do not confront him with, "I need you to step it up," or lay any threats at his feet. A man who wants you should never be reminded to treat you the way you deserve to be treated.

Once a man makes the roster, it's a probationary period. If you show a new employee their job, then they get lazy before they even secure the position, you don't confront them so they can give you an excuse, you fire their ass. If a man is getting lazy, you don't yell at him to do better, because all that gets you is an excuse, "You know I've been busy...My job has been stressful...My mother is sick..." When you corner a man who's in the wrong, he will always try to make it right by feeding you lies. The moment he feels his life is becoming complicated, he should communicate like a man. "Hey, sorry that I haven't talked to you in a few days because..." should be "Hey, I may not be around for the next few days because..." There is never an excuse for lack of effort. Check this off before making it official.

<u>Can He Communicate How He Feels About You</u>: "I think he likes me," is something that women tell me about their guy friends. Don't assume a man likes you, know! There are women who ignorantly believe that men don't show emotions because that's just how guys are wired. That stereotype is bogus. Unless a man is a sociopath, he can and will express his romantic feelings. Does he want to? Maybe not because guys, like girls, don't want to be left vulnerable and rejected. Regardless, it is in your best interest to get him to speak about these things openly. Stop relying on indirect signs like the way he holds you, the way he kisses you, the way he spends money, or the way he breaks his neck to see you. Communicate like a human being, not a fucking ape, and use your voice box. "How do you feel about me," is not a good question. "Do you miss me," will not get you an honest answer. The best way to get inside a man's head is by listening to him talk about you over the course of these six to ten weeks.

Men are romantic, they will hint about missing you or ask you about missing them because they're trying to open up. "What do you miss about me," is a real question. "What do you like about me," is a real question. Tease him about falling in love with you and see how he squirms. Listen to how a man points his words like fingers to tell you what he sees in you, don't let him blow smoke about how he likes you because you're different, cooler, or smarter than other girls. That's generic! Make him communicate the source of his feelings. A man who risks being emotionally vulnerable has invested in you. Six weeks in and he can't tell you what he likes about you means you haven't connected deep enough to be official.

<u>Is He More Than Attention</u>: Let's be honest, you are not a perfect creator. You are still tied down to immature needs that may cloud your own quest to manifest true love. Even after you have destroyed most petty insecurities, you may fall into the trap of attention thirst. Most women make the mistake of loving back those that love first. You are a Spartan; the way you carry yourself will intoxicate a wide range of men. The world will suddenly become a buffet, and it's easy to get caught up with guys who kiss your ass, and stop looking for men who challenge you. Butterflies. Excitement. Combustible energy. A feeling that he has something to teach you. Do you feel that with this man or do you simply love that he loves you more?

Without the magic of chemistry, a relationship can't sustain itself. Without the challenge of an equally powerful person, you will grow bored in a relationship. You want real love, so that's what you hold out for not a fan. Let's talk about "nice guys" for a moment. A man can be nice without being a pushover, and you know the difference. A man who gives you whatever, does whatever, and kisses your ass isn't who you want. You may pretend to like servitude but you want that *spark*. Sparks don't mean true love or any other superstitious bullshit. You will see your own qualities or your most desired qualities pop up in random people, and you will be attracted to them. If you haven't mastered your mind and learned to focus your thoughts on what you truly need at this point, and are still focused on creating some hollow dream guy based on lust, those sparks will be meaningless. You can have sparks with a man who's a total bum and would never take you out on a real date, that's not love, that's the presence of a vibe that turns you on. You can have zero electricity with a man that dates you like a Queen, pays for trips, and opens his soul to you, that doesn't mean you are a bad person, it means his vibe is off. The solution isn't to find the spark and deal with the asshole attached to it. Nor is it to ignore the need for a spark and be grateful for the nice guy. The Spartan way of life is about finding the perfect balance. You need a man that brings both excitement and treatment to the table. If you think that's impossible, then you aren't thinking with a will to power. You are still letting settle thoughts manifest into half-ass results. If you don't feel your potential boyfriend is the culmination of that balance by now, don't force it, leave him be.

<u>Do You Complete Him</u>: When a man talks do you listen? A guy's past paints a picture that points to the map of his future. It's not about who his exes were and their faults or the various incompatibilities of his prior relationships. What was he looking for from these women in terms of love? Not just with women he's slept with, but with the ones that raised him. A man who was trying to save a ho has a reason for that soft side. A man who spent years with a woman he didn't love has a reason for that sacrifice. A man who grew up without a mother or treats his mother like his wife does these things for emotional reasons. You can't guess, you need to uncover these things when dating. For a man to spend a month or more talking to

you virtually every day, there has to be something you take away in terms of what his burning desire is when looking for a partner. Earlier, I mentioned that a relationship isn't a one-way street where a man kneels before you, meets all of your qualifications, and you lay claim. You both need to get something out of this union. Knowing his story, can you complete this man? The men who I give relationship advice to, they are honest, noble, and loving. They prove that men do have hearts; but they have their own insecurities which causes them to lust after women that use them or to stick it out with women who don't know how to change. The reason these men fail at love is because they rush in. They would meet a Spartan like you, become infatuated with how you act, and then do anything to have you. They fail to see the bigger picture. Any relationship can last six months or a year, but it takes something special to grow year after year. A Queen does not reconfigure herself to fit a man, but she does pay attention to see if her power source is compatible with his power supply.

Are you the right woman for the man who you are falling for? Just because he meets *your* requirements doesn't mean you spit in the face of *his* requirements as if you can either bend to become what he needs or bend him to no longer need those things. This is a fatal mistake typical women make. They don't pay attention to the details and figure they will make it work once they are together. Why are you dating if not to test these personality traits out? Women tell me about petty arguments they have with their boyfriends ranging from, "He expects me to be like his mother," to "He tries to give me advice about my career when I don't ask him for it." When you date a person, these kinks should be worked out. You shouldn't transition into a serious relationship thinking the love you have, which is infantile at this point, will survive. Know his story, know yourself, know if it will work? A man may need a woman to give him space to make his own mistakes without saying anything. If you prefer full transparency, you will bump heads thinking that he's hiding things from you. In reality, it's just how he operates. A man may need a woman who accompanies him to places 90% of the time because he doesn't have friends. If you are a Lone Wolf, even in a relationship, then this will become an issue. A man may be very matter-of-fact about what he wants, and while that attitude is good for picking restaurants when you don't want to decide, it will lead to riffs when he tries to boss you around. How long before him being him, gets under your skin? Some traits, negative and positive, are so embedded in a man that you cannot change them, nor should you try. Understand each other, and then ask yourself if you two could co-exist after the lust wears off.

<u>Can You Say the Words</u>: Everything in this chapter boils down to one statement: **I'm ready to be with you**. Those are the only words you need. The million-dollar question isn't a question at all, it's a declaration of power that communicates what this relationship now has to be in order for you to continue. There is no waiting on a man to be ready, there is no waiting for you to be even more prepared. If you aren't prepared to finish this through then you don't need to date like a Spartan in the first place! If you wanted to play house, cuddle, and get consistent dick, then you could have kept down that Tina Typical path. I challenged you to change your life, and you accepted. At this moment of truth, you must Spartan Up. People are bundles of uncertainty that use indirect words and hints to say what they mean, not you. If you want this man, if he has survived cut after cut, and proved himself to be special, say the words that will catapult you: *I'm ready*.

     In less than 75 days, you can establish something that can last a lifetime. Fully grasp how powerful these steps make you, and own it! To put this book down, and pretend to understand it or to highlight a few things, and take them as suggestions, will get you nowhere. This book found you for a reason, do not turn away from salvation because you feel overwhelmed by the magnitude of this power. **Are you a little girl or are you a Goddess**? You are not meant to Spartan Up overnight, read and re-read the first two parts of this book until it becomes more familiar than the alphabet. This is your life now. This is how you date, how you flirt, how you seduce, how you open a man up, and how you test a man to see if he is worth you. Know the weapons you now have will always work, and use them! If at any time your thoughts betray you and that inner Basica attempts to overtake you, close your eyes, and remember how far you've come. Visualize that old weak girl you once called self...Picture her, with all of her flaws, insecurities, excuses, and doubts standing over a pit...then kick that bitch in the chest and watch her fall into the abyss. You are Sparta.

Part III
Risk The Dick:
Conquer The Relationship

Chapter 22: Do You Know How to Be a Girlfriend

In sports, the consensus is that winning a title is harder than defending that title. In relationships, making a commitment is much easier than maintaining that commitment. No matter how confident you are in your ability to love a person through thick and thin, there is no cure for growing apart. Let me define what growing apart means. It isn't being mad at each other for a few days or a week, and feeling that you should just end it. That's basic anger. You are emotional and annoyed, so your mind goes off to dark places, but it's nothing cooling off won't rectify. To grow apart means that a person stops caring, stops investing, and begins to distance themselves emotionally. A man can grow apart from you while sleeping in the same bed. It's not the physical space, it's the feeling that you no longer connect mentally. The vast majority of relationships that are brought to me, the man has grown apart, and the woman missed the red flags months ago that it was happening. They still had sex, they still had fun, but the signs were there. He didn't talk as much, he didn't share as much, he didn't have as much patience...these small character changes stand out, but they get ignored. Unlike a man cheating or going through a depression, there aren't Ah-ha moments. You slowly break apart, and by the time you realize that he's now playing by his own rules, you are too far away to reach him.

To be a "good girlfriend," means you pay attention to your partner, you stand up to mistreatment, you communicate without fear, and you curtail your own bad behavior no matter how agitated you become. There are women who become pushovers in a relationship because they fear losing this great once in a lifetime man, so they let him get away with murder. There are also women who are bullies. They see that a man lets them do whatever, so they push his buttons to bring that "real man" fire out of him. Both of these personalities lead to huge blowups. A pushover is always going to cry about neglect, stress that her man doesn't appreciate her, threaten to leave, then repeat the cycle after he apologizes. A bullish woman will make a man react like a victim, with his own ultimatums about how he's leaving because he can't take her controlling attitude or bi-polar behavior. A woman like this will apologize, cry for forgiveness, and pull the man back, only to do the same thing when she feels bored or unchallenged. You shouldn't be a pussy that lets a man run over you, nor should you be in the habit of committing to men who you can manipulate and push around. The dating stage was meant to empower you, as well as net you a partner with a backbone, not some simp you could settle for, kick around, and then cry, "come back, I really do love you." That's not what a Spartan does.

Beyond those extremes, there is a more common flaw, and we call her pride. The downfall of a woman in a relationship can be traced to an obsessive need to make it work, not for love, but to prove herself. Red flags aren't missed, they are picked up and thrown under the rug because you can't afford to have another failed relationship. Your parents, your friends, your co-workers, even the folks on the internet, can't see you go through yet another man who doesn't work out. After talking all that sugary shit about how great he is, how he treats you, and acting as if you knew everything about what makes a relationship work; **how will it look to be single again**?

You will spend so much energy investing in a man, trying to understand a man, and putting up with that man's shit. Is it really because you love him? Or is it because you hate to fail? To tell the world how loved you are, then have to explain why it's over—stings your pride. To get engaged to a man, then have to call it off—stings your pride. To get married, to throw your vows in the face of the world as if you figured out the secret to love, then have it end in divorce—stings your pride. You hold on to a sinking ship because you know that the rest of the world is waiting for you to fail, for you to prove that you aren't as good as advertised. Are you the type of girlfriend who has this chip on her shoulder, who is fueled by pride to the point of self-destruction, or are you in it for happiness?

Will you leave your boyfriend if you are no longer happy? Be honest. It's easy to say "yes" when you don't have a boyfriend, but the true answer only comes during the relationship stage. Women in relationships are rarely 100% happy, but they continue to stay. They may complain to a few close friends or family members, but they refuse to tell themselves the complete truth—it's not working. Shame, embarrassment, the myth that a "good girlfriend" can make any relationship work; these things keep the average woman trying to fix something that broke a long time ago. *This too shall pass, if you love each other you will make it work, hang in there...*no one gives solutions, they serve up positive clichés that do nothing! You don't know anyone with real answers, so you look for books on how to "rekindle the love" or seek advice in secret to figure out the mind of your man. Why? Breaking up is not a real option because your pride sees it as giving up, so you stay. For the Non-Spartan, the answer to the above question is "no" you won't leave your boyfriend. Happiness isn't as important as maintaining your relationship status. What a sad life to live.

SPARTAN GIRLFRIENDS DO IT BETTER

To date like a Spartan from the onset will make basic relationship problems a non-factor. The typical things women struggle with like, communication, constant lying, mommy or daddy issues, narcissism, being controlling, jealousy, abusive tendencies, all of these things a Spartan sniffs out during the dating stage. She doesn't speed towards a title or get swept up in lust to where a man can get away with being his false representative. Learning a man before he has the job of boyfriend, creates an entirely different relationship experience than learning him while he's on the job. Nevertheless, you may find this book while in a relationship that's been going south for some time. You aren't going to cut your boyfriend off and start over as a Spartan, you aren't that strong. You want to save what you have, upgrade what you have, or maintain what you have, because you are in love. Your dilemma isn't how to become a Spartan, date like a Spartan, and get into a relationship like a Spartan. You want one thing: To learn to Spartan Up in the midst of a relationship that you are losing.

How does a non-Spartan find her way back to power? You must <u>Risk the Dick</u>. That's how you win back control of a failing relationship. Regardless of the backstory, if he is the problem or if you caused the riff, you can rebuild and refocus your life together. This section will reshape how you approach the ups and downs of a relationship. It demands two things: Confidence and the total lack of fear. You have to take a gamble, prove that you trust in yourself, and literally risk losing the man you love, to get your relationship back to a healthy place. Before we get to the solutions, the first question which must be asked is if your relationship is even worth saving.

Forget being in love, all the good times you've shared so far, and the potential you see for a better future, and let's look at reality. Some people are comfortable sleeping on a mattress on the floor. It doesn't bother them, so why waste money getting a bed frame? Most relationships are that mattress, it works well enough, and it's comfortable, and so long as no one discovers that you're living like a fucking hobo, who cares? You should care! Relationships aren't about being comfortable; they're about being happy. Are you happy? *I guess. Sometimes. When he acts right. For the most part.* Are cute ways of saying, "No" and it tells me that you're the type of basic ass woman who holds on to mediocrity because it's easier to deal with the shit he puts you through than to make a lot of noise and lose him. No one is happy sleeping on the floor, they just get used to it. No woman is happy in a mediocre relationship, she gets used to it and calls it love. If you are ever going to reset your relationship like a Spartan, you must first diagnose it with the honesty of one.

GIRLFRIEND MENTALITY

Do you even know what it means to be a girlfriend? Pause the bullshit about "I'm the best kind of girlfriend a man can ask for," ego propaganda. Are you really that amazing? Yes, I know you are loyal and don't talk to other men. You make time for him, throw the box even when you have a headache, and deal with his attitude like a good woman should. Yawn! Being a girlfriend isn't about how great you are at putting up with a man's shit, not giving out your phone number to new dick, the time you spend laid up under him, or how much sex you give him in a week. Are you mature and honest enough to be the kind of woman who a man falls in love with or are you the average placeholder who men put up with for the benefits? A large percentage of women I advise have been engaged before. One even told me this as if I were supposed to give her a gold star like, "Oh, you got an engagement ring once, you must be different." Fuck your prior engagement! It didn't lead to anything, so welcome back to the boat.

Understand what makes a girl start to lose points in her man's mind—the headache factor. He can't talk to you because you nag. He can't own up to a mistake because you bring it back up after it's supposed to be forgiven. He can't help you with your own issues because you fear he will throw it back at you, so you play the role of this "everything's fine," strong woman. You are the type of girl who says "We need to talk," days later instead of talking about a situation when it first happens. You say basic shit like, "Let me cool off because if I talk to him, I may say something I can't take back." Really? Are you so primitive in your communication skills you can't address an issue without the fear of losing control? You are a grown woman. Yet here you are sucking your teeth, rolling your eyes, balling up your fist, and swelling with rage because you can't handle a conversation where you say what must be said. You are so afraid of being honest with a man, so afraid of unleashing your true feelings, that you wait until it boils to the point of arguing. Realize how annoying a personality like that is, and how difficult it is for a man to confront this because he feels you will see it as an attack, get defensive, and it's war. Men put up with this, but only to bide time for someone better. No man is in love with a ticking time bomb.

Communication is everything. If a man feels as if he can't talk to you and you can't talk to him, it creates an enormous separation. A girlfriend mentality shows a man that you have the seeds of a wife mentality; meaning he can grow with you without fear of feeling trapped, bored, annoyed, and emotionally unfulfilled. If you're being a headache within the first five months, imagine how big the communication gap will become by year five of a marriage? The typical attitude is that if you were special enough to get a man to commit, you will be special enough to get him to stay. What a fucking joke. Commitment means nothing, it's the longevity that matters! 99.9% of women have been in a committed relationship, getting there isn't hard, staying is.

Do you think you're the only chick with a stove that can ride a dick? You aren't. A man will always find a girlfriend capable of the basics. These girls are placeholders just like you, doing enough to stay in the game until a better woman appears. To be a true girlfriend means you have to put emphasis on the "friend" aspect in a way that tells him you know how to communicate and that it's okay for him to do the same in a transparent and mature manner. Do you speak your mind when he does something that upsets you or do you inhale your frustrations and go run and tell your friends how mad you are? Your friends can't fix your problems; all they can do is listen to you vent. *Tell me if I was wrong. I wasn't in the wrong, right? ...exactly! That's my point, but he acts like he did nothing. Men are so dumb!* What does that do? Is telling the person you aren't mad at about the person you are mad at, going to solve the issue that may break you up?

A girlfriend should be transparent and blunt. "You know what you did, don't play dumb," is not communication. A man shouldn't have to guess why you're mad, he shouldn't have to wait until an unrelated issue happens for you to finally talk about the first issue, nor should you walk around feeling as if you have no voice in your own relationship. The fear that you will get into an argument, that he will call you petty, that he may break up with you. I smell it. Your passive aggression, the forced silence, the explosions that happen because you keep things bottled up, it's all because you can't talk about what's on your mind in an adult way because you think that will scare him off. It doesn't matter if the problem seems small. If you can't speak on it, then those small problems become big arguments later.

Think about what an argument is, in terms of getting to where you're raising voices. It's an escalation of a problem caused by not dealing with it earlier. How does it make you feel when he doesn't do what he promised? Disappointed. *Say that shit.* How does it make you feel when he puts someone else before you? Unappreciated. *Say that shit.* How does it make you feel when you see him look at some other girl with a glimmer in his eye? Jealous. *Say that shit.* How does it make you feel when he does the same thing you told him not to do? Disrespected. *Say that shit and stop holding back*! A good girlfriend doesn't make a big deal out of small things, she makes a small deal out of those small things before they ever get too big!

Internalizing is a huge problem, and while a man's actions may create the friction, your own cowardly handling of your emotions causes a rift that widens with each new problem. Men stereotype women as these hand on their hips, overly emotional, overly sensitive banshees because the average woman holds her feelings in and only speaks to erupt. Speak your peace every single day. Before you worry about how to deal with all these other issues, start with yourself. Are you a good girlfriend? Are you honest? Are you truthful? Are you verbal? If your response is, "I have to work on some things but he needs to also…" then stop right there. **It's not about what he needs to do, this is about you being at your best.** Your man may not stay your man once you read the last chapter of this book, but you will have to continue to live with yourself, right? Strengthen yourself, fill your holes, and then worry about what a man does. Don't let ego point to him before you evaluate yourself. All of the men that didn't work out, who was the common denominator? You. Fix you first. There is no Spartanhood without the destruction of personal baggage and defensive excuses.

BOYFRIEND MENTALITY

Is he a good boyfriend? This may be harder to admit to than your own faults, because if you answer, "No, he's not really a good boyfriend," what does that say about you that you're trying to discover a way to keep him? When I first conceived of *Date Like a Spartan*, a close female friend responded with, "Does it come with a time machine, because how is that going to help me deal with this current asshole I'm already with?" The prison mentality that if you're already with him, you have to stay with him and make it work, is something that a Spartan would never entertain. All couples have bumps, times when things need to be smoothed out, but no matter how long you have known each other, even if you live together, have children together, or have a business together, a woman always has the power to walk away from the romance aspect of that relationship. You chose to chain yourself to the relationship. Now you can choose to unchain yourself. For every excuse of "I can't leave him yet because," there is an example of a woman who has walked away under similar circumstances. Are you not as capable? As smart, as strong, as independent as other women?

The only difference between a woman who frees herself and a woman who stays chained to misery is the Will To Power. Being in love has to stop being the ultimate scapegoat for weak bitch behavior.

Let's look at these flawed men who you fall in love with and refuse to let go of, and let's see if they are worth it or you're just another typical who thinks she can fix broken a man. During Spartan Cali's journey, she picked at Stephen's past, observed his behavior, and purposely did things that made him uncomfortable to see what kind of boyfriend he would be. In your relationship, you most likely found out the hard way that your man has anger issues, gets extremely jealous, expects to know where you are at all times, forgets things you tell him, and behaves differently around his friends than he behaves around you. That's spilled milk at this point, so let's go deeper into what boyfriend mentality means, and not dwell on those flaws as complete deal breakers. Why should you make a man your boyfriend? Are you trying him on like a new bra, with plans to discard him if you outgrow him, or are you trying him on like a pre-husband? To become your boyfriend once you are over the age of 24 should take on a bigger responsibility, that means the man you choose can't just be cool, sexy, or funny, with a couple of annoying habits. He has to show you things that tell you that he's mature enough, responsible enough, and driven enough to put your life in his hands. Your future, your time, your exclusivity; do you realize how important those things are? Do you realize the power you are going to share with a man that becomes your husband?

A grown woman isn't dating just to kill time, she is looking for her match, her Game Changer. This doesn't mean your relationship is a race to get married, but the man you choose to be exclusive with should have one quality: <u>I could see myself marrying him</u>. Typicals see themselves marrying any guy that's half cute and has a job. You shouldn't. Think about what you want in a husband. Now think about the guy you are with now or if you aren't with one, think about the last man you were stuck on. Did he have a boyfriend mentality that pointed to him being what you wanted in a husband or was he just a dude you were with that was good enough? "Some of the times," or "Most of the time," is not an answer.

Either a man has what you want forever, or he is lacking. If he is lacking, then why the fuck are you still holding on to him? You do realize that you have the power to attract better, right? Go inside of your man and examine for incompatibilities. A guy who spends time with you, but doesn't share his thoughts with you, is a boy, not a man. A guy who listens to your problems, but can't offer solutions, is a boy, not a man. A guy that opens his wallet, but won't open up about his life, is a boy, not a man. Who is this guy you have committed to? You know his name, but do you know his soul!? No matter what's on the surface, males can be incredibly insecure, mentally broken, and emotionally scarred. Your guy may still be healing from another woman, struggling with money, or in the midst of pressures unrelated to you, and barely keeping it together inside. Do you even know what goes on in the head of your man? Are you aware of his daily struggles or do you simply fuck him, laugh with him, and eat with him? "He doesn't tell me things," then ask him! What man leads with his pain? This is a macho world he's in. Men hide their insecurities in plain sight, and most women can't see this because they are more concerned about their own needs being met, rather than inspecting a guy for cracks in his foundation.

Is he financially secure, or is he putting on a front, living off credit cards, school loans, or hustle cash that can dry up at any moment? Know this! You will be asked to help out with his bills and lift him up financially if the bubble burst on his sketchy investment or if a risky idea he's trying to do fails. You didn't know that when you were dating, but you figured this out now, so ask yourself is this the type of man you could one day marry? This isn't about his finances, it's about his mentality. Fake like it's all good, bring you into his financial mess, and then let you bail him out? That's not a boyfriend mentality, that's a struggle dick that will drain you.

Does he love himself, or is he self-loathing to the point where he takes out his bitterness on other people? You will constantly have to stroke his ego, listen to him make excuses for his position in life while blaming external forces, and suck it up when he starts an argument with you based on his own insecurities. That's not a man you stay with. Some women put up with this, even buy into the excuse of a man having an unlucky hand, and because they know that he can be sweet when he's happy, they excuse his dark side. You should never marry a man who is battling demons nor should you be the Save-A-Dick that diagnoses a man as bi-polar and tries to be his therapist. A girlfriend's job is not to be a man's medicine; a man with that kind of sickness has to be the catalyst for his own change, his own growth, his own therapy. Does your man even like women? Comments about women as whores, about what girl's wear, or any condescending observations about females, points to more than an opinion, it points to a deep hate. Certain women gobble up misogyny because they feel he's shitting on other women, but sees her as one of the good ones. That's like being a house slave and hearing Master talk about the slaves in the field as being stupid, but smiling because he loves you. Use your brain! How long before he's calling you out your name? Accusing you of cheating? Banning you from hanging with certain friends? Basic chicks think it's cute when a man acts jealous about an outfit she wears. "Daddy told me I had to change," is said with pride because she wants the world to know that her man loves her and doesn't want any other man looking. That isn't love, that's control, you simpleton. To stay in a relationship with a man like that or to have a child by him will become life in a prison where the warden secretly hates everything you represent. That is not a boyfriend mentality, that is an abusive husband in the making.

Finally, let's look at a man's past because it creates the deepest insecurities. The same way women grow up with daddy issues or become a reflection of the men that rejected them, males can also stay stuck in the past. <u>Who is this man you committed to and what kind of hurt does he come from?</u> Do you not care so long as he hides it, treats you the way you like, and puts on a smile or do you understand that it's only a matter of time before his traumatic past creates a problematic future? Men are competitive, and the majority are at the end of the winner's spectrum in terms of self-esteem. His dad didn't think he measured up to the other boys, and he's still trying to prove he does. The girls he wanted never wanted him back, so he had to settle for what he could get. To feel better about not being good enough for those girls, he overcompensates in other areas of his life to validate his bruised ego. Maybe he was molested, abandoned, or watched his mother go through abuse. A man like this hasn't forgotten, it drives him. The average woman jumps at the opportunity to mend broken birds, they have the love to give, and think it will save him. They fail to understand that love is not enough. If you love him, a broken and undeserving man, then what does that make you? He sees his weakness in your affection. You love him like a puppy, not like a man. No matter what you do, how often you come with a shoulder to lean on or have inspirational words to make him see that he is good enough, he will reject you and resent your love.

A man who feels that he's not worthy needs more than the easy love of some woman that never even bothered to ask about his hurt until they were in a relationship. Allowing his insecurities to go unnoticed proves that you didn't care who he was, you were settling for the surface representative because any man is good enough. How can you sit in a man's face and tell him what you love about him, when you don't even know the hell he's been through or the depression he's holding on to in private? You can't love someone you don't fully know, but you do, because you are only worried about landing a boyfriend that loves you back. A man knows where a woman's love comes from, and if he hates himself, he will hate you for loving him for nothing. This depression doesn't necessitate that he verbalizes it, but you will see it in his actions. Sabotaging the relationship, acting indifferent to your feelings, being ready to walk away the moment a problem occurs, and being abusive. This is how these men handle their emotions, they rage, they run, they sulk, or create an environment of apathy because they feel as if your love is based on bullshit.

A male's past could create insecurity in the opposite way. Instead of being a repellant for love, he could become obsessed with being spoiled. Weak mothers, usually those who see that a boy's father isn't showing him proper attention or where a boy's father isn't present, can overcompensate by making a man feel as if he deserves the world, and doesn't have to reciprocate. A man that grows up like this will face instances where he's not treated special, where the world shows him that he's just as ordinary as the next man, so to feel better about his life that male seeks a new mother and calls her "girlfriend." Again, we have a woman who has so much love to give because she wants to receive that love back due to her own insecurities, so she accepts this challenge. You put a spoiled mama's boy in front of a damaged woman, it's heaven on earth for a while. The relationship is built on him getting his ego stroked, getting his way, and getting catered to, which means he will never be in love with that woman, but only what she does for him, because again he recognizes where her love comes from, desperation. In his professional life or his social life, he is most likely near the bottom compared to how other men view him and he knows it, but in your arms, he's a king. "Men are so selfish," is the disgusted frustration that pours from the lips of women who thought they could give unconditional love and have it boomerang back. When you think a man acting needy is cute, when you fall in love with playing house instead of vetting, you become guilty of feeding into his addiction. Do you really believe that a man who gets it all will without working for it knows how to return that love? Do you think you can train a man to be less spoiled by curtailing how much love you show him after you've already given him the world? A man like that will pout to get his way and you will go back to spoiling him because you don't want to lose him. You're being hustled by a boy not loved by a man, understand the difference. The name of the game is Boyfriend Mentality that shows a pathway to Husband mentality. These tortured souls, can't love themselves so how will they ever be able to love you?

Ask yourself if you have the mentality of a girlfriend then ask yourself if the guy you're with, trying to get with, or trying to get back with has a boyfriend mentality. You can't love your way out of incompatibility and you can't fix something that never worked. Before you go on to the next chapter, is your relationship worth fighting for or should you break up? Evaluate your relationship by asking one simple question: <u>Am I happy?</u> If the answer is no, then where is the difficulty in that decision? Fear of starting over, fear of being judged as a failure, fear of making a mistake and not finding another man, fear of never being good enough for any man...these things don't exist in a Spartan's mind. They exist in you because you put too much value in men. You want to fix that which can never be repaired. You cling to his comfortable in the face of his disrespect. You will never be happy until you see all men, even the one you call yours, as replaceable. Risk the dick! Mentally, bring yourself to the edge where there is no longer a fear of losing him. Know that you don't need any man, and the battle will be won. You will behave like a woman that has nothing to lose, and he will react like a man that doesn't want to get replaced the next day. This power ensures that you will never be taken advantage of.

Chapter 23:
First Cracks – Conquering Early Relationship Problems

ay to day relationship life is the goal you were aiming for, that place where you know him and he knows you. No one is trying to play games, and you can settle into doing all the happily-in-love things that couples do...or so you thought. Even when a man measures up to your screening standards, you do as much vetting as dating allows, and you have your own life in order, it doesn't guarantee a happy ending or even a smooth beginning. The honeymoon period in terms of a new relationship is usually the first three to six months after you two make it official. Things are good and there are no legitimate beefs other than the occasional, "I miss you," separation anxiety that comes from spending a lot of time with a person. He's great, you're great, and together you're happy, but then, the universe throws obstacles in your way that are outside of your individual control. Are these signs that it's not going to work or are these tests meant to strengthen your bond? If you are a Spartan, you understand there is always a method to your madness.

Never look at the bumps in the road as bad things, look at them as drills that train and prepare you. "Why is this happening, I just want to be happy," stop being so damn dramatic. Understand that your game of life will only challenge you in order to grow you, to solidify a truth or to rip apart a lie. You wanted something serious, right? This next level will prove or disprove how serious this new relationship is, by throwing one, if not all of the following hurdles at you...

FAMILY OR FRIEND INTERFERENCE

Friends and Family operate on two stages. When you're casually dating, you are seen as a non-threat by his family or group of friends, and depending on your circle, the man is usually seen as a non-threat as well. Just another guy trying to lock you down who may or may not be around next week. Few people are looking at the two of you like, "Oh, they're going to be together forever," you may have a fan in his mother, and he may have a fan in your best friend, but this isn't the first person they have seen you date or take an interest in, so why would they get emotionally invested? Once you switch over to being official, things get interesting. The family members that embraced you during dating may talk behind your back. Those friends of yours who liked your guy may admit they don't like him; they were just staying out of your business. For those that care about him and those that truly care about you, they need to see proof this is a legitimate person with real intentions. The *smile and get along* stage has ended, and you could be left stuck in the middle of personal bias that can rip you two apart.

I get an enormous amount of "mama's boy" emails where women are suddenly blindsided when a man's mother fights to keep him tied to her hip as if he were her husband as opposed to your boyfriend. One story that comes to mind is a good example that shows how a man who is not a typical mama's boy, can still be influenced by outside interference. There was a woman we'll call Miss Tanya, who had a son and a daughter. The daughter was married to a man who was a deadbeat, but she didn't seem to care; her investment wasn't in her idiot daughter but in her smart and handsome son. Miss Tanya's son Kenny had the potential to do great things and needed a woman to fit Mama's vision. Kenny began dating a woman Miss Tanya referred to as, "a 5 out of 10," so I'll call her Lady Five. Miss Tanya first met Lady Five early in the relationship when Kenny had to stop by his mother's house. Miss Tanya looked Lady Five up and down, and marveled at her pretty smile, and even invited Lady Five in. This proved to be fake, as when Kenny saw his mother a day later and asked what she thought, she replied, "She's a 5 out of 10, but better than the redbone with the kid you brought by." Kenny actually told Lady Five this joke...two months later once they were in a relationship.

It was at this two-month mark, that Miss Tanya realized her son's relationship may have legs. Suddenly Miss Tanya begins to call Kenny during his nights over Lady Five's house, telling him she needed him home to do things in the morning. One week it was the cable man, the next week it was a package that may get stolen, and one night she even made Kenny drive to her home because she thought someone was trying to get into the basement window. When Kenny brought Lady Five along to check for the potential burglar, that's when the game was fully understood. Lady Five told me that the look Miss Tanya gave her when she came walking in behind her son could have melted steel. The next plot revolved around Kenny's nephew. Miss Tanya had the little boy Facetime Kenny something like, "you don't come around anymore. You have a girlfriend now." Clearly, he was reciting what Miss Tanya told him to say in order to make Kenny guilty. In response, Lady Five set up a play date with her cousin's son. Now the sister, who liked Lady Five initially, jumped on board the hate train. She told Kenny he wasn't allowed to have her son around Lady Five because she took her son around project kids who taught him to curse. This was in response to Miss Tanya saying something along the lines of, "he didn't say that word until last weekend when he was with that girl." Once again, Miss Tanya was putting thoughts in her children's heads, and Lady Five was forced to sit back and hear all of this second-hand from Kenny.

We have Kenny's sister and nephew now in the mess, but it gets better. Lady Five felt as if she wasn't being heard, but she loved Kenny and decided to let it go. That was until Kenny's ex-girlfriend spotted them at some local restaurant and gave Lady Five the third degree about the part of the city she was from, who she knew, and who she dated before Kenny. Lady Five felt unprotected by, what was supposed to be her man, allowing a woman to talk to her recklessly. By the next week, Kenny's ex began texting him. Telling him to watch his back, and coming with stories about Lady Five being an opportunist. Kenny's ex even sent him an arrest record of Lady Five's father who had struggled with drug use years earlier. This was to somehow prove that Lady Five was some poor girl looking to hitch her family to Kenny's wagon because Kenny was young, had a great career, and no children, something apparently rare in their city. This should have never made it back to Lady Five, Kenny should have handled it, but instead

Kenny asked if it were true. Despite Lady Five defending her reputation, Kenny began to act differently. He didn't want to pay on their dates anymore or spend the night as often. After a few weeks of dodgy behavior, Lady Five confronted Kenny about his attitude and the lack of time being spent. Kenny responded, "You tell me, Mafia." This was referring to a stupid nickname Lady Five had when she was younger, based on her love of Junior Mafia member Lil Kim's rap lyrics. Only close friends in high school called her that. Somehow, in the hands of Kenny's ex-girlfriend, this became Lady Five's *Ho Name* that the local guys knew her by. "I think his mother set all of this up. She called his ex-girlfriend to dig up dirt, and when they found out I didn't have any, they made up a story," that was Lady Five's theory about why her relationship collapsed. Lady Five was emailing me about a new problem with a new guy. This was the story she told me in her introductory email to point out why she had trust issues, a full two years after Kenny broke up with her and got back with that ex-girlfriend.

Learn from Lady Five's passive reaction to being bullied and slandered; understand that you can't respect anyone to the extent where you let them play you. Most women sit with arms folded, and say they would never allow this, and maybe they wouldn't if it were just woman on woman, but add a man to the mix and things change. To take on his loved ones means that it's a slim chance that you will ever be welcomed into that family, but that's the risk you can't be afraid to take. Family interference must be confronted head on, not brushed under the carpet.

This isn't only on the man's side, it's on your side as well. If you feel as if someone is giving you a cold shoulder or fake smile, you don't kill them with kindness, suffer through the times when you see them and go about living your life. Haters become cancers in the ears of those getting to know you, and it will spread fast and kill your reputation if you don't take action. His mother, sister, or grandmother don't like you but they sit there and make conversation. You see the condescending looks or you hear something said in passing. Mention it to your boyfriend immediately, not so he can buck up and go back to his family and say, "You better stop it," he won't disrespect those that raised him, but he will need to inquire about the cause. If this man is to be someone you build a future with he has to be brave enough to defend you in a way that bridges the divide, not some chickenshit who says, "That's how they are, ignore them." A King can be both protective of his Queen and respectful of his family. A man who turns a blind eye shows you what he's made of.

Your engagement party, your wedding, the birth of your child, they are not situations where you want to feel uncomfortable because some weak bitches feel threatened by your power. To go with the flow, means you are guilty of allowing yourself to be victimized. If his friends, boy or girl, have ulterior motives and are looking to drudge up dirt, to cast doubt on your past, or say something slick to you in private, then stand up and put an end to it the moment it happens. Not by fighting, by cursing them out, or by going to him and making ultimatums. Defer the argument and tell him to handle his friends, in the same way you would want the opportunity to handle your friends if the roles were reversed. "If you don't handle it, I will," doesn't come out of a Spartan's mouth. Pride will make you want to act like an ape and flare up on anyone who you feel is trying to play you, but you can't give into that primate behavior. You are a woman with intelligence, not some middle school ratchet swinging fists for the Vine. The moment a man fails to come to your aid in dealing with his people, then there is nothing to be handled because he has proven to lack the true heart of a man you could one day marry. You didn't give up on him, he gave up on you.

In terms of your own friends or family having something to say; lead by example. Don't leave it in his hands to go confront them, and don't rush to take a side of someone new over someone old. Get to the bottom by communicating. The entire process of finding love was about being fearless, and in friendship, you must behave with the same courage. You don't know why your mother gives your boyfriend mean stares, why your brother makes smart comments, or why your best friend is telling people your man was flirting with her, but you need to go to those sources and inquire about what's actually going on. You know your family and you know your friends, you know who has an attitude, who exaggerates, who never lies, and who lies all the time. How you both react to outside sources, that you care about but who test you, will tell you how strong your bond has become. This isn't drama that will ruin your perfect world, it's a revelation that there are things which must be corrected if you are to stay together. If you can't stand up to a person's family now, you won't do it later, and you will end up miserable. If you can't stand up to your own family or are afraid that you will be seen as taking sides, then you will make the person that wants to be with you miserable. Not all family or friend issues can be patched up, but they can be carved out so you can identify the problem, and make sure that whoever it is, will never interfere with your happiness.

DIFFERENT LIFE GOALS

You want marriage, so does he. You want kids, so does he. You want to stay in this city, so does he. While dating, these things are talked about loosely and in a generalized way. However, when you are actually together those same topics become real and inconsistencies pop up. Big wedding or money saving wedding is a serious question not an "in a perfect world" wish. Who doesn't want to own a big house? The style, location, and color, fantasy talk becomes a conversation about credit scores and down payments, again a very serious conversation to have with someone who may not make it a year with you. How many kids? This is no longer a *Brady Bunch* dream scenario, it comes with the reality that you have to push those kids out, and he has to make enough money to afford you being sidelined with those kids. Those are heavy conversations to have with someone new, but they will come up, and that is where the divide begins.

One of you may not be on the same page, and the other will feel as if they are wasting time if this relationship won't end in their imagined married, nuclear family, still living in the hometown, dream. Actual relationships force you to think, "The fantasy sounds wonderful, but how do we actually afford that without it crippling us?" Most women assume their boyfriend wants what they want, only to hear him tell a friend or third party something counter. "Man, I don't even think I want kids...Weddings are stupid...I think I may want to move down south next year..." You can't wait to overhear that the man you are recently attached to really doesn't want your ideal life. No matter what he hinted at while dating, you have to revisit the topic of goals before you get in too deep.

A frequent new relationship problem I get is when a boyfriend wants to move to another city or even country for job opportunities, after previously ruling that as out of the question. A new job opportunity pops up and it's "Fuck this city. I'm moving, how about you?" A man has his own life agenda and he doesn't curtail that for other people, especially one he's just falling in love with. Males have no problem putting themselves first, they don't feel guilty, it's a survival instinct. He has to move to where he feels he will have the most success, and unlike average females, love is not what he includes in that success box. You've seen this before, a man is confident that he can find a new woman, it's career or financial opportunity which he fears he will never get another shot at. When a guy moves to the beat of his own drum instinctively but gets in a relationship with you, that doesn't mean he will settle down for you. Suddenly he says, "Hey, I got a job offer, if it goes through I'm leaving." It's not something you can put your foot down and stop. Arguing that if he truly loves you he would stay, will get you dumped. It will always be his career over you. Which brings up the heart of this problem, follow your dreams or follow your heart?

There are women who don't have any goals besides being married and having children; a girl relocating for love is as common as a blue sky. **A Spartan always puts her goals and interests ahead of a relationship**. There may be a need to compromise at times, but you must weigh the cost. Can you do what you love in the same place as him? Can you have as many children as he wants to have, and still follow your dreams? Instead of waiting to see what your boyfriend wakes up one morning and decides is your future, decide for yourself what this relationship, or any future relationship, is worth sacrificing. He's a boyfriend, not a husband, your loyalty to his life is misplaced if you think following behind him means he will appreciate it and reward you. I've met more women who moved and ended up getting left, than those that moved and it worked out. A man will try to sell you on moving with him. He's afraid, he wants companionship, but the moment he becomes comfortable in that city, will he need you?

What if his move can lead to you making an even bigger move? That's called an opportunity, so take it! If it's about your life, not playing the wife, then you're ahead of the curve because you are already mentally prepared to cut him off and still thrive in your new location. I worked with this producer whose girlfriend left him a month after coming to Los Angeles, she was every bitch in the world when telling me the story, but in my mind, she was smart. Clearly she came for the opportunity, not the man, and when she realized the relationship would not work, she quickly dumped him because her plans weren't dependent on him. I juxtapose that story with one where my wife's former classmate moved to Los Angeles to be with her boyfriend. He didn't think the city was to his liking and went back to New York. She couldn't leave, as her parents sacrificed their savings to send her across the country. The man wasn't loyal to her struggle, he put himself first and flew back to NYC. She remained miserable for over a year, sunk into depression, developed a drinking problem, and finally went back to the home she never wanted to leave. Men put their dreams first, and so should you; not out of ego, but out of your own want to conquer life.

All of those late night talks about ambition don't mean shit when put to the test. People imagine what life will be, but opportunities that spring up can't be imagined. The fun of your game is that it could take you anywhere, but remember, if these life choices don't benefit your true self, then every move you make based on a whim or for a man's love, will prove ill-fated. His goals must line up with your goals, not the other way around. There is no need to declare, "I follow my ambitions, so it's my way or the highway," to your boyfriend during the first month. Know it in your heart. Share your dreams as he shares his from the outset, but be prepared to have the courage of your convictions if they begin to differ.

MOVING TOO FAST

You become boyfriend and girlfriend after a few weeks, you move in after a few months, you get engaged in less than six months, you get married within a year, those types of relationships are like the Powerball; the odds don't point to you pulling it off. There are so many factors that determine if a relationship lasts at the marriage level which you must take your time with. Going in with hubris and expecting your greatness to outweigh learning a man is asking to be checked. Yes, you feel a deep love for this person, and it hasn't dropped off after the honeymoon stage, but that doesn't mean rush in. "My best friend's cousin met a guy and they got

engaged after only a few months, and now they're on their honeymoon."
This is said by typicals as if it's something to aspire to; the relationship
equivalent of getting rich quick, but it points to a dangerous ignorance.
Humans fall in love with others humans who they don't fully know, every
day. Love itself is not proof of long term compatibility, you must know a
person like the back of your hand before you even consider getting married
or even engaged. **You don't accept offers of forever just because he asked.**
Typicals chase a ring because it represents validation. A man not only
thinks she's good enough to marry, but it didn't take him long to decide, so
she accepts with a swollen ego. She's imagining her bridesmaids dress, the
color of the flower arrangement, the haters reacting when they see her
Facebook pictures. These thirsty women never think about the day after the
wedding and if the man she's yet to see the worst of, can handle the pressure
of being legally bound. This isn't about you being good enough, it's about
him being good enough. Understand that you don't move at a man's pace,
society's pace, or at a speed determined by how quickly you want to quench
that, "I need to be married by this age, or I'm a loser," fear.

Let's say your boyfriend is more in love with you than you are with
him, this isn't a bad thing, it's to be expected in Sparta. He wants to have
children with you because he's one of those men who's obsessed with
reproducing, and he feels that you would be the perfect mother. "Why not
just start a family?" Is the motto. He may say this or he may hint. The next
thing you know, he's not reaching for a condom, and in the moment of that
"you know I'm going to marry you and take care of you" passion, you give
in. Oops pregnant. He may be the type who talks about it with you openly
and convinces you to get off birth control. This is the comedy of, "let's see
what happens" as if you don't know what happens when sperm fertilizes an
egg. One girl told me that her boyfriend's sales pitch was, "Let's have sex
normally, and if nothing happens in two months, get back on it. But if you
get pregnant that's God's way of telling us it was meant to be." She got
pregnant, and they never got married or even stayed together! That's what
happens when you pressure yourself to do what other people want under
the cover of fate. You determine your destiny, and when you allow yourself
to be led, you give your power to that person. Your true self won't stop you
from transferring your power, but the universe will play out in a way that

tells you that you fucked up! Be a Queen Regnant not a Queen Consort. No matter if he has Lil Wayne level baby fever or if you saw a chubby kid in the store that lit your maternal fire, know your goals and put them first.

If you want to be married before you have a child, be married. If you want to be established before you have a child, be established. If you want to wait for any reason before becoming a mother, then there should be no pressure that makes you shortchange your ambitions. The pressure of men, the pressure of time, the pressure of other people reminding you that even if you get married, it's not guaranteed that you will stay together. What are those? They are doubting forces, causing you to go in a direction you aren't 100% sure about. As a Spartan, you know what you want, and you know that to compromise yourself for the benefit of others or to rush because you're on a time clock, points to fear! You may never be shit in life, so you may as well have this baby now with a guy that wants you. That is negativity which points to you needing to bend your rules because you fear failure. You will get what you want and you must not listen to this shit about, "you know you're getting older," or "Let's start a family, you know I love you." **Never settle for anything less than the vision you keep in your head!** You have the power to tell him, "no." You have the power to assure yourself that it will happen as it is supposed to happen, and not be time crunched. You have all the power when it comes to the when and who of reproducing. Take your time and be smart.

Moving on to cohabitating. I know a woman that let her boyfriend of all of two months move in with her. He spent most nights at her apartment, it was like he lived there, so why not make it legit. They split the bills, money wasn't an issue, they didn't find out anything crazy about each other's living habits, and it was good sex wise. I told her that she was moving too fast, but for nearly a year it worked, and she loved to remind me, "see, there's no such thing as too fast when the love is real." I was happy for her and glad to be proven wrong... then she texts me at 4 am in the morning, saying he moved all of his shit out and she doesn't know what to do. All of this right before their one-year anniversary. So why did it crumble? <u>Pressure</u>. When you move at an accelerated rate, you can say you need to slow down, but you can't emotionally hit a switch. You get in the habit of keeping the train going at that same speed.

People will always stick their nose in your relationship, most of the time they're trying to throw shade by suggesting you should already be further along than you are. To hear people ask you over and over again, "when are you going to get married," weighs on a person. When you are in a long relationship that question is to be expected, but when you've only been together for a matter of months, you shouldn't get that question. Moving in made the people around her apply that pressure sooner. *Are you living together just to live together? Does this man actually want to marry you? Why are you shacked up with a man who isn't your husband? You may as well get married, you're being his wife anyway.* Guilt is a motherfucker because it pulls at a part of you that feels the same way. There's no such thing as laying a guilt trip on someone who doesn't feel guilty, but this girl legitimately felt as if she moved too fast and that she was giving away too much just to cuddle up and split a cable bill. This man was laying up with her each night, beating up the kitty, no ring on her finger...she never wanted to be that girl. This made her feel as if she played herself. In response to this guilt, she dropped hints. Picked out wedding pictures from magazines, asked his opinions on wedding topics, etc. The pressure was on, but her live-in boyfriend told her he wasn't ready to think about those things. **Imagine yourself in her shoes, a man lives with you but doesn't want to talk about marriage in a real way.** Predictably she became defensive in a "you want me to play the role of wife, but you don't want me to actually be your wife," way and their relationship suffered. There were two options for this guy, propose or leave. He made the smart choice.

This situation could have been avoided if they took their time and let their relationship build to moving in. In your story, there may be a boyfriend who pushes you to move fast. So, how do you handle a man who wants to move in together? To tell him, "No, I'm not ready," sounds mean. It's telling him that all the stuff about being serious is a lie. Don't fall for your own guilt. <u>To live with a man is to be his wife in everything but name</u>. It's so tempting because it allows you to show a man how great of a wife you will make, how happy you two will be when it's for real, but while it saves you money, it also lowers your value. During the date like a Spartan phase, you were positioned in a way where you came off as unique, a special occasion, something that must be had. To turn around early into your relationship and give a man that has only earned the title of boyfriend the benefits of a husband tells him that he's won. His feet are up, his effort is complete, and just like that girl who stays in that "exclusive but unofficial" situationship, you will not be upgraded anytime soon if at all. Even in a relationship, you are worse off than women in situationships. The ultimatum you will have to make is, "So when are we going to do this for real?" It's too late, it is for real.

You are giving him everything you would give him as a wife, so why would he buy you a ring, pay for a wedding, just to do the same thing he's already doing? Living with someone before marriage is a smart step, it opens up that world of true home living, but it's something that you make a man earn, so he doesn't get complacent. As in the story of the girl whose boyfriend moved out in the middle of the night, waiting alleviates pressure, because before you move in, there should be a conversation about what moving in means. This isn't about being able to wake up with him, being able to consolidate bills or the convenience of being closer to your work commute. Those are basic bitch reasons for moving in with a man. Both of you must discuss moving in as a huge step that points towards marriage. This shouldn't be done passively, "oh my roommate is moving out, move in." Give yourself a year. Sit and talk about what's to be expected, and communicate your motives. This bullshit assuming and hinting has to be replaced by real conversations. Moving in should either happen after an engagement or be treated as a pre-curser to an engagement. Which means it shouldn't come within the first six months. The day you two decide to cohabitate should not only feel special, it should signify a move towards forever. Never assume that this is understood by a man, spell it out for him.

Becoming Too Routine

When you are not in a relationship, you long for the mundane activities that couple do. Relationship memes showing a boyfriend and girlfriend play wrestling, him combing her hair, goofing around in the bathroom, playing video games, etc...it projects as even more romantic or sweet than images of flowers or vacations, because it's the small things that are so attainable, yet so far away that makes the heart ache. Single women miss those minute expressions of companionship, but for those in a relationship—they're over it. I didn't write *Ho Tactics* to be a Sugar Baby manual, my intention was to help women in boring relationships get treated the same as women who are considered new pussy are treated in terms of excitement, creativity, and pampering. The concept came from my inbox being bombarded by women who reached the relationship stage, but who were now stuck in the house every night with the exception of the occasional trip to Strugglebees and a matinee movie. "I'm boring, and I like the house," may have been true, but any woman who wastes her prime years doing the same shit every single night will eventually feel unattractive, unloved, and uninteresting. Training a man to treat you like a Queen starts at the dating stage, and once a Spartan enters a relationship it becomes a partnership where you both find ways to spend time doing things that excite you as a couple. I want those women just becoming Spartans to do these things in a current relationship, so let's look at how to light a fire when things have already gone cold.

Dating is more important in a relationship than when you're single. If you two aren't going out, that's a problem. You can't sulk your way to change. The moment you feel disinterest brewing, address it. The common response is to catch an attitude, act passively, and then blow up on him with, "You never take me anywhere!" Do you understand how that comes off? We talked about communication being transparent, not letting things erupt because you lack courage, and this is a specific example of that. You shouldn't have to tell a man to buy you flowers, he should want to. You shouldn't have to tell a man to take you somewhere you can dress up for, he should want to. You shouldn't have to beg him to go to an event that interests you, he should want to. Before you can get on that soapbox about "he should," ask yourself what kind of man your boyfriend is in terms of romance? A young guy, still in undergrad, came to me after his girlfriend threatened to break up due to him not being romantic enough. He didn't understand what romance meant to her, but his romance meant being considerate and asking how her day went, offering her food whenever he was ordering for himself, and making sure if his dick didn't make her cum, he went to work with the mouth. He vented to me about all the things he did for his woman, but like most men, he didn't get women.

He wasn't stupid, he just thought his basic affection was romantic. He didn't know that she wanted more traditional and outgoing expressions because she never mentioned it until the breakup text. Some men are cavemen, and that's not a knock, it's truth. To assume that a man knows how to be a *Don Juan* and then become angry with him without saying a word is immature as hell. You probably didn't introduce this treatment at the roster stage because you didn't go through a roster stage like a Spartan. Doesn't matter, catch up by using the only thing that works: <u>Your Voice</u>. Don't assume your boyfriend knows what you're thinking, knows what you want to do, or knows you expect more than Cheesecake Factory to go and cuddling on the couch every weekend. Romance isn't having sex and him giving you a warm rag to clean off with or texting "I love you" every morning. A man doesn't necessarily know that his romance is lacking because you say, "thank you, I love you, you're the best," based off of him not doing anything special! The way he won you over wasn't by doing anything romantic, he took you to eat, complimented you, and made jokes—show me the romance in that. In relationships, it's expected that the other person either comes in with a definition of how to treat you or they learn to read your mind because you are afraid to say anything until it becomes an issue. This is not how you Spartan Up, it's how you grow apart.

If you are enjoying his normal romantic treatment, meaning not openly complaining, then he feels he's doing a good job. You shouldn't have to tell a man how to love you, but the way he's acting may be how he shows his love. Know who you entered a relationship with, is he a little slow on the take? If so, then you will have to lead him by taking action. If sitting on the couch, both of you distracted by your phones, is how you spend most nights, then you need to upgrade your social life. Instead of scrolling a timeline, search for something to do in your city, and do it. If laying on his chest while he plays *Call of Duty* is fun sometimes, but not five days a week, then be forward and tell him, "Babe, you know I like to dance, let's go do that on Friday." Basicas say stuff like, "Spoil me with your time and love, not your money," give me a break! You need to be spoiled on all sides, a real woman recognizes the importance of being pampered, taken out, and traditionally romanced. If he says he doesn't have the time or suggest that you go with your friends, then you fucked up. You chose the wrong man, and no matter how much you want to work it out, either you toss him now, or you grow depressed as his wife later. Let's say you were dealing with a man who used to treat you like a Queen when he was trying to lock you down, but has fallen off since he landed you. Spartan Up and take it to his face with your words. This isn't a case of ignorance, it's a case of laziness. Point out what you would like to do, and dare him not to do it. If your boyfriend greets you with bullshit excuses or acts as if he's too tired or too busy to show you a good time, then why are you with him? Love should not glue you to a man who treats you as if you're a burden! If he has time to do what he wants to do but is too busy to do anything with you that isn't generic and routine, then help him out. Lighten his schedule by removing yourself from his life. Now he's free to go find a bitch that's thirsty for a man who just wants to lay up, fuck, and eat.

PAST OR CURRENT SUITORS

Men don't care that you have a boyfriend. Your relationship is not a dick repellent; it actually works to attract more men to you. Your happiness, your glow, that new dick smile that upgrades the resting bitch face, it's so transparent. You may have had the driest phone in the world before your current bae, but in the weeks following your commitment, many men will pop up. This may seem harmless, but if it's not handled in a decisive way, you can and will allow outside forces to tear apart what you thought would be something special. Let's first look at your ex-boyfriends and the guys who you were only dating. Regardless of why you stopped talking, or who broke up with who, they will reach out under the front of "just checking in, hope all is well." **Once an old fling finds out that you have someone or that you aren't quick to respond with the speed of a lonely bitch, they will become aggressive.** They don't know who you are with nor do they care if they make you happy. Seeing a new man with his old girl lights a fire. This competitive nature isn't about him realizing he messed up and wants you back, it's ego. Most women believe that a man coming back is an admission that she was the right woman for him, and he simply wasn't ready. Bullshit! Men never come back to placeholders and upgrade them to Game Changers based on her having a new dick on the team, this is a hustle.

"You didn't want me then, so why are you coming back now?" is said in anger, but it makes a girl prideful. You are gassed off finally getting good treatment, the problem is, the treatment is due to another man possibly being better than him, not you being any better than when he left. Don't be Tina Typical, feelings as if she's no longer a placeholder because a man circles back. He didn't want you and he still doesn't want you. Exes can be petty or they can be strategic. A petty ex will do something along the lines of liking the Instagram post of you and your new man, he knows that it will signal your mind to respond with, "Why is he liking this...Why does he even still follow me...Maybe he wants me back." It's a petty mind-fuck he uses to stay on your brain. To remind you that he's watching and to possibly tempt you into communicating behind your current boyfriend's back is his aim. Men notice you, noticing them, noticing you. You're telling your friends he has started following you on social media, texting you, or calling. Why? Because you secretly love the attention.

A Spartan does not give a fuck about some ex showing up, liking a picture, sending a text, or any form of communication meant to snake his way into her mind. She is too strong to fall for manipulation, and if you aren't, then you still have a long way to go. The other side of the coin is an ex or an old "we used to talk," guy being aggressive and laying out a strategy to actively get a girl open. I've been that guy on the other end of the phone trying to squirm my way back into old pussy under false pretenses. Not because I was jealous or wanted a do-over, I wanted to prove to myself that I was better than her new man. Understand this, don't let your own ego lead you to believe a past man's interest admits anything more than competition. I've had sex with virtually all of my exes after they moved on to new guys, because I knew they were mentally vulnerable, they had egos that made them want to show me what I was missing, and in the end, meaningless sex was all they got, which is a waste of any woman's time.

I will assume that if you are in a new relationship your old wounds are healed, and unlike my exes, you won't be talked into reuniting for one last roll around. Regardless of your standards, you can't think because you aren't ever going to have sex or go back, that an old bae can't affect your relationship in other ways. The cool ex with a girlfriend but still flirts with you, blocked. The guy you were dating, but want to put in the friendzone because he's funny, blocked. There is nothing wrong with having male friends, but realize an opportunist when you see one. A person that wants you will always be after you. The smarter the man, the more stealth his moves. He knows you have a boyfriend. So? He can still send a text or call during a late night session with your current guy, and now you have to explain why that guy is hitting you up. He can still drop hints that you two "still talk" which can be taken back to a friend of your man, and made into a situation you have to defend. Being naïve isn't an excuse, a Spartan understands the chess board and knows how each piece moves in any situation. These men want pussy, not friendship, and they are looking to snake their way back in so they can then wait for an opportunity.

He may sabotage from a distance. He may wait for the week you and your new man are arguing and strike at that moment of weakness. You can't subscribe to this idea that, "I have it under control," because you're taking a risk that need not be taken. A friend serves a purpose, they shouldn't be someone you know and want to keep around just because. **Look at each man in your life, old and new, then ask their purpose.** If a guy is your true friend, he would always be there for you, not to keep flirting, simping, or giving you bad advice that leads to him getting the next shot. Maybe you didn't date like a Spartan and in terms of letting go of your multiple men, perhaps you let guys from the roster hang around. Well, now you know better, so mow your lawn and rid yourself of the snakes.

Let's discuss the role known as <u>The Backup Dick aka BUD</u>. These aren't men you sleep with, keep on the side to talk to when your boyfriend's not around, or have any affair related interactions with. He is simply a man you meet, whose vibe rubs you the right way, but since he met you in an offseason (already taken) he doesn't get a shot to be on the team. However, you can file his number away for a later time and contact him if your current relationship ends. Backup Dick are men you notice, but don't move on, they aren't exes or men who had a shot who come back around, know the difference. Let's say you meet a guy during a business conference, doing some service for you such as auto or home repair, or at a formal event, and it's all professional. He looks and talks like your type, and if you weren't taken you would snatch him, but you are taken. File him away. Take his business card or info, and store it. Focus on your current situation. Don't start a romantic-friendship during a relationship, it's too much to juggle.

What about those men who randomly come up to you asking for your number or who flirt with you? Do you become that girl who screams, "I have a boyfriend," when a man asks the time or starts a conversation in an elevator? No. You observe. Who is this man and why is he coming into your world right now? If he's trying to get your number, then you can tell him that you're seeing someone. That's easy. If he's someone that can benefit you socially or professionally, hear him out. In Los Angeles, I've seen actresses blow jobs because they mistook networking for flirting. You live in a world where there will be men trying to chase you sexually, and others trying to offer opportunities. You can't let a relationship cage you, but you can't be so naïve that you don't pick up on a vibe of what a man is selling. Not all men are trying to fuck and not all men are trying to help, this is where you use your Spartan mind to read between the lines. If you make a connection platonically, communicate that to your boyfriend, even if it will make him jealous. Seeing "Roy D" text you will lead to an argument where the consensus will be "Why didn't you tell me about him if it's nothing?" It's not about explaining yourself to a man, it's about treating your man as you would want him to treat you in terms of transparent communication.

Speaking of your boyfriend, his ex-girlfriends, former fuck buddies, or current social media crushes, they don't just disappear the moment you get the title. Men are notorious for keeping their relationships on the low. Not because they are trying to be sneaky, but because few men feel a need to broadcast their relationship status when first getting into one. Guys see how quick people break up, and who wants to be that person that declares they are in love and then has to eat crow? In terms of your guy being off limit, this is his test to pass or fail, not a mission where you shield him from other women. If women only stay away from your man because you are active in promoting that you are together, how do you establish trust outside of your control? The moment you aren't around what happens? A man has to be put through the fire early, not protected for fear your relationship will go up in flames. **If your boyfriend can't handle being seduced by another woman, then you need to know that, not guard against it.** Don't be the girl who demands he post you on Instagram, change his Facebook status, or that he gives you the security code of his phone. Fearful tactics and basic bitch announcements meant to scare off other women train him to be sneaky. You as a female know that the average woman gives zero fucks about if he has a girl. See what he's made of when put to the test. He knows he's yours; a picture of you two hugging doesn't do shit but bring the vultures out quicker. It's on your man to defend himself from other women, not on you. Observe this early in the relationship to understand what kind of man he is by his actions, don't correct it, simply observe at this stage. Letting him hang himself will save you from falling in love with someone who is going to be sharing his dick before you even reach the one-year point.

What about those women who were already in your man's life before you? Are they really his little sisters or are they just low hanging pussy, there for him to reach for when you annoy him? Don't get paranoid. Remember, men are too nice to women, especially attractive ones. I've mentioned before how males rarely burn bridges, so if you see that your boyfriend is being too generous with his time, bring it up. "Why are you still talking to that bitch?" Will not get you on the same page, it puts him on the defense and nothing will get solved. Communicate that you trust him, but you don't think it's proper to maintain a relationship with that girl. If he says they're real friends, don't counter with anger, "Okay, well watch me call my exes and be friends again too," that's immature.

Here are the magic words: <u>I don't want you talking to her</u>. This is where dating like a Spartan pays off. When dating a man in the ways laid out in that section, you learn his past. This includes all of his female friends and the roles they play because you asked him stories about his life. You know Emily was the jump-off that was too clingy, you know that Cynthia was his ex's little sister who became his little sister, Renee is the one that got away but evolved into his best friend, and Briana is his last official girlfriend who hurt him. If those names pop up, you understand what's a real friendship and who's just old pussy that's hanging around. If a new name pops up that wasn't mentioned during dating, then you know that something is up. Be forward! You date a man so you can know a man's life, don't allow someone from the past sneak in because you want to believe this man wouldn't slide off into new pussy while your pussy is still relatively new. Don't trust anyone fully, trust in your research.

TALKING NOT COMMUNICATING

Every early relationship problem has the same root cause, a failure to communicate. You spend every day with a person, you sleep with a person, you say you love a person but are you communicating or are you simply talking? Talking is the crust, communication is the filling. When you stick with the crust, you don't get to see what the pie is made of, you're falling in love with a basic ingredient that all people have, a buttery flaky top layer. You talk to people at work, you wouldn't say you're close, because you know there is a limit to how much you share with the majority of them. You talk to certain relatives but aren't close enough to give them the same access that your mother has. Talking is safe because you don't have to let anyone in. Communication requires you letting someone in on your problems and your doubts, which requires vulnerability and courage. Your internal feelings could be called petty, insecure, or silly, and be dismissed by the one person you want to understand you. You don't want your boyfriend to take your feelings for granted. You don't want to be made fun of or to be seen as another dramatic girl complaining about nothing. This is why most relationships stay at the talking level, the safe level, and only delve deeper when pushed to an argument.

Don't ask a man to do something that you aren't prepared to do yourself. To open up is to demand that he do the same. It's a give and take. If you don't give him real communication, he won't spill his feelings. If all you two do is talk, argue, apologize, and repeat, then you have a weak understanding of one another and an even weaker relationship. A boy hides behind "whatever," "Can we talk about this later," "I don't know what you want me to say…" a man opens up and discusses his point of view with respect for your point of view. That allows you both to come to a solution or compromise without the fussing. Push him to open up by not being afraid to ask questions even at this stage. The first six months of a relationship determines the foreseeable future. If he refuses to communicate now, it won't get better. By allowing your man to remain emotionally lazy, you tell him it's okay. Before losing yourself in this man's positives, push yourself to discover his negatives, and then be Spartan enough to communicate what needs to be improved. That's what teammates do.

Chapter 24: Emotional Support – Helping a Man Without Emasculating Him

"It was pride that turned Angels into Devils..." – Saint Augustine

Your boyfriend seems to have it all figured out, he has his life in order, his plans make sense, and he projects his strength on you in a way that's both sexy and reassuring. Similar to how a father becomes a giant to his daughter, your boyfriend's drive and command makes him the epitome of male power. What if I told you that most men, including your boyfriend, aren't as strong as they seem? You deal with a certain societal pressure as a woman which you can either let stress you or you can shrug off and maintain control. A man has that same pressure, but may not be as emotionally strong as you have become after you embraced Spartanhood. If you know that he's unsure, worried, or in need of motivation, you can take measures to help, but you must go about it in an empathetic way. You aren't a man, you may feel as if you have them figured out, but when trouble is brewing, males not only breakdown they lash out at those trying to help. You can prove how great of a woman you are by showing your man he doesn't have to do this alone. The problem is that most men will not admit to their anxieties.

You can't help someone that won't let you in, and your boyfriend's troubles won't come like in the movies, where he breaks down in your arms, his troubles will slowly leak out. You may think it's just a funky mood or a bad day, and while it will draw your attention, it is soon dismissed because these kind of men hide stress behind a smile. The truth will eventually come out that he's barely keeping his head above water emotionally. Not only is life taking a toll on him, he would rather handle it alone than ask for help.

337

The common response from a strong woman is to take the lead the moment she sees that her man is in trouble, which sounds like the proper response, but creates a hostile environment of resentment. Fear of being emasculated will drive a man to desperate measures. You see yourself as being a good mate, he sees it as stepping on his toes, and his frustration will cause him to turn on you. Arguments, avoidance, turning to other women, even breaking up—a man will do these in response to you trying to fix him. Why? Because trying to fix an independent man in a brash manner is the same as pulling down his pants and laughing at his dick. Male pride doesn't care about your intentions, it only cares about protecting the image of a strong, tough, man.

He can't get ahead in life. He can't afford the things he needs. He isn't at the same level as others his age or below. He can't do for you what he feels a man should do for his woman. He made promises he hasn't been able to live up to. Everything he portrays as going good is caving in on him, and he's not allowed to cry about it, he's expected to keep his head up and hold it together until things change. There are countless things that are tied to a man's pride, and he doesn't want any of them exposed by a woman. If you discover that he isn't as big as he pretends, you will still love him, but he doesn't want that pity. We talked earlier about daddy issues, and how you had to look back upon your own father as just another flawed man. **Now you must take this same knowledge and apply it to your boyfriend**. His bravado is a mask, his carefree attitude is paper thin, his cool demeanor is an eggshell, and what lies beneath could be a deep dark depression. "We got this, baby," will not make a man feel better. Saving him puts him at your mercy, and you are proven stronger than him. This leads him to question what kind of man he is.

These thoughts are negative assumptions and condemnations based on an overblown ego or the results of a culture that promotes macho men as Kings who rule alone. This fucked up male psychology is why you can't rush into your man's life with a cape on as if that will solve the underlying issues. A man has to be a man, but even a man needs emotional support. So how do you help the person you love rise above their own self-doubt without causing more insecurities? You develop an unconditional trust that lowers his guard and extends his boundaries in the following ways...

THE MAN WHO HASN'T MADE IT

Success means different things to different people, but the measuring stick that most men use are other men. Don't be of the mind that if your boyfriend has material things and talks about various moves he's making, that he feels successful, is successful, or is on his way to being successful. Use your brain to go beneath the surface. Look at your man's life. How old is he and how advanced into his career is he? If you dated like a Spartan, you know what age he is but you also know his position, and how long he's been doing his current job. A 27-year-old man working in tech support, looking to advance to a network administrator will most likely have a different outlook than a 37-year-old man whose rise in a company has reached the ceiling at tech support. He has a decent salary, he can afford things that someone who works a lower paying job may see as luxurious, but when he looks at other men his age he doesn't see that he's making a living, he sees that he's behind them. When he looks at his new co-workers, he doesn't see himself being a veteran, he sees himself doing the same job a guy ten years younger is doing at roughly the same pay rate. Consider being in his position for a moment. Do you go home and cry to your girlfriend about how life sucks and ask for suggestions? If you were raised to be unconditionally strong then you suck it up and smile. Have a drink to forget, have sex to feel like you're still a man, spend money on things to show that you're a winner, and then go back to that depression when no one is paying attention to your circus act. That's life for this kind of man.

Maybe you have a boyfriend who doesn't have a career that comes with the stress of moving up, he has a regular job. He clocks in and clocks out, is told when to take a lunch break, and he can be told he has to stay late or come in early, depending on his bosses wishes. To have a boss at a higher level in terms of an advancing career doesn't come with this slave like routine. If it does, it's balanced by having others under his supervision, which makes him feel less like a little submissive bitch, and more like a leader. At a low level, there is no bright side. Your boyfriend feels like shit because he does have a boss, he does have to ask another man permission, and he does feel emasculated by a time clock. While he can claim, "As long as my direct deposit hits, I'll do anything," that's not true. He wants to be a boss, but can't. Which makes him just another cog in the machine, and that hurts his pride. When going to school, a job is a means to provide until graduation, it doesn't bother a man on a deep level. When gathering experience or trying to gain entry into a larger company, a job is still a means to an end, it doesn't sting his pride. However, if your boyfriend is working where virtually anyone can get hired, and he's been there for years with no end in sight, will he feel like a winner?

Finally, let's look at guys with hustle jobs, musicians, businessmen, property investors, promoters, any job where it is on him to bring in money or close a deal. When dating a guy who is on the verge of greatness, or is living a fast life where money seems as if it's no issue, it will blind you to what's under the surface. It's common for a woman to think that just because a man isn't lying about his career, then it's all good; they rarely think deeper. To talk to a guy with these bright ideas about launching an app or opening up for a performer who can give them a big break, hypnotizes you. It signals that they have it all under control, that they are fearless, but again look at the success they have had so far. A barber trying to open his own shop for over a year knows how it looks to the outside world, they see him as a fraud. A rapper or singer with some local buzz, but hasn't reached real fame, knows that people are dismissing him as just another guy who will never be as big as Trey Songz. Even a man with money from something like real estate, construction, fashion, or a public relations firm, is in the same boat as the 37-year-old tech support guy, because while they aren't going to starve, they have pressure on them to do better based on those men who are doing it bigger and better every day. To keep telling people they're about to close that million-dollar deal from their million-dollar idea, that never materializes, makes them feel like failures. The cost of living mixed with the cost of maintaining their business or profession, drains them financially and emotionally.

Put yourself into the shoes of any of those men. Their dreams haven't quite worked out, and all you have to do is look at the effort they've put in to see if he's rising, at a stand-still, or on the verge of falling. If you are in a better position than he is, that hurts, but he keeps quiet. If he hears about guys you used to date who were successful, even when pointing out that he is a better boyfriend, he still feels like less of a man. All of these things he hides. Why? If you were to see his horrid financial statements, you would judge him as wasteful or stupid for letting his debt spin out of control. Maybe you would tell other people that he's struggling, and this exposes him as just another ordinary man who may never rise to the top. These men hide their emotions, flash money, spend extravagantly, and party like it's all good, but are slowly falling apart under your watch. So what do you do to help someone that fears being judged?

Do not go out looking to meet people who can help him, do not collect business cards of people in his industry, do not seek someone who knows someone that can hook your boyfriend up, and do not wait until you see the stress in his face after a bad day to chime in with, "Maybe you should do it this way." All of those things emasculate him. As a woman who has just come into his life, telling him he doesn't know shit about how to be a success, and then giving him a boost, will break him. The intentions are pure, but him needing help projects back as him not being capable. Instead, you need to open up the dialogue, not to stroke his ego, but to let him know he can let you in on his fears. The moment you suspect that he may not be happy, he's been worked to death, he's stressing over a deal that didn't happen, he's having beef with a supervisor or boss, or he's venting about life in terms of his position, don't be just a shoulder, **be a journal**.

This technique goes: Bring up how things are going in his professional life, don't push, simply ask him. Listen, and like a journal entry, you read it back. "So the one guy who was supposed to invest in the project, is saying that he has to wait for his money to free up?" He will confirm this, and keep going because hearing it back will make him add another two cents. "This is the second time he's done that, and I can't afford to wait around." It doesn't seem proactive at first, but it's the first step in gaining his trust, similar to what therapists do. You think you're paying all this money per hour for them to tell you solutions, but they're repeating what you said, so you can open up enough to work towards your own solution. Once you establish that a man will share these thoughts, don't force your opinion, make being his journal a normal thing. By chiming in, "You need to just find a new investor or maybe I can find someone." You're doing the exact same thing as mentioned earlier, undermining him. Instead of taking over, gain his trust, and build on it.

After he opens up, no matter if he gives a little or a lot, thank him. Literally, say "thank you for talking to me about this stuff, it means a lot." Mothers and other girlfriends, maybe even ex-wives, were probably in the habit of judging him. Scolding him for his mistakes. You aren't tied to this man's life so deep at this point where you're on the line, you're simply his girlfriend, which means you aren't supposed to save him, you're supposed to build trust so he feels comfortable letting you deeper into his world.

Establish this journal routine. It could take a week or it could take months, don't rush it. Remember, you aren't being a cheerleader, there is no "You got this baby, I believe in you." Fuck that noise. Talk to a man like a man, don't coddle him. Saying affirming things based on the fact that you love him, not based on him making a smart move, will only fuel him to keep doing the same shit. Play it straight and be affectionate in other ways for now. Once you establish that you can say, "how was it going with such and such," and he sits down and opens up in detail, his trust has been earned. From there, show that you have been paying attention by offering solutions that have been thought out. No one wants to hear common sense responses like, "Try harder. Find a new job. Go to HR." Show him you aren't like other women by thinking outside of the box in terms of offering help. He may take it, he may not take it, but the point is you tried to help him out in a progressive and non-condescending way.

In terms of your personal relationship, what does his response to your help tell you about his character? You are still playing this game of life, still revealing compatibility, don't shake it off as if things will get better. Observe how he opens up, but also, how he responds to solving his internal strife. You can't seriously continue on with a man who doesn't learn, who only wants to complain, and who dismisses anything you say because he's committed to doing things his way even when it's not working. A man like this is destructive and self-defeating. This isn't something you could have sniffed out during dating, again, this is one of those "wait until the relationship" situations you go through to further prove if he is or isn't husband material.

THE MAN WHO STRUGGLES WITH MONEY

Money ruins more relationships than cheating, bank on that. When you become husband and wife, even if you keep your finances separate, money or lack thereof, is most likely to become the issue that leads to the biggest resentment. He can't afford the house you want to move into, but he doesn't tell you, he tries to make it work because he's ashamed. He can't afford the baby you want, but says nothing; by the time that kid is starting school, he's still trying to figure out ways to bring in extra cash. He got you hooked on expensive gifts, and in order to keep up the appearance of a provider, he's staying at a job he hates so he can afford you. He can't take a financial risk and start a business because he has to be practical in order to maintain the lifestyle you two started. Instead of going to you to figure it out together, he secretly begins to hate you for holding him back. These are common issues in marriages that lead to divorce, but they should never have made it to the altar in the first place! A relationship is the time to discover money problems, bad spending habits, credit scores, and future financial goals. Let's keep it real, women don't want to talk about money with men. Most men don't have as much as they feel they need, and you don't want to insult his manhood. At the dating stage, you can hint at this, but in an actual relationship you need to ask these hard questions.

A funny *Ho Tactics* story was sent to me by a girl who hooked a mark, then tried to put a ring on him. Thinking she hit the sponsor lottery, she made her trick her man, only to find out that he was swimming in debt and needed her to help him out with a loan. "Why would a man buy me a Chanel bag when he couldn't even pay his rent? Is sex that important to y'all," she was disgusted, but by that point she was in love and the Ho became the trick. More men live on the bubble than women think. In your own life, being broke may mean you only have your savings, with your current paycheck going to bills, so you claim to be too broke to buy anything extra. In a man's life broke means, there are no savings and he's taking his credit card to borrow this, and borrowing from this 401K to pay for that. All so he can go take you out to a $200 dinner date to prove that he's not broke. See the difference? A man living paycheck to paycheck will go to Dubai quicker than a man with real equity because 21st century males live in a world of "fuck it, I need to live." Keeping up with the Thots isn't stressful to him when he's single. No one knows that he's splurging on shit he can't afford but him, so his secret is safe. Once he enters a relationship, these spending habits become harder and harder to hide.

It's easy to play the "I'm not broke game" when a man is dating you because the rug won't be pulled out financially during the courting stage unless something obvious happens like all his cards get declined or he has his home foreclosed on. Most likely, a man living on the edge financially will keep this under wraps, no matter how good you vet him. Unlike the guy who comes to the date and asks you to pay half, he is too prideful to admit that he's a broke dude trying to afford a luxury woman. He lets you order whatever and shows you his big tip. It's all about impressing you. Once you become his girlfriend, that's when you see what's really been going on. The way he tries to avoid doing certain things, the mail notices you may see at his home, or the stress level that goes up for no apparent reason. A man won't hide that he's upset about his job, he'll own up to that because work is work, but he will not volunteer that he's in debt, that he can't afford to repair his car, or that the random calls coming to his cell phone are for student loans he owes. Regardless, you will know that he's hiding something, and trust, it's not another woman.

Use your brain, not your heart. You know how much things cost, you know your boyfriend's job, and you know what that averages out to even if you're not sure of his ancillary bills. **Can he afford the lifestyle he's living when you do the math in your head?** At this point, are you going to be the girlfriend who goes out to an expensive dinner and assumes he has it, asks for red bottoms knowing he will buy it, and plans a fancy future with a man you think is balling? Or do you do the math and observe his behavior? Typical women don't think about a man's money; the same way a brat teenager spends Daddy's money as if their father has it to burn because he never breaks her heart by saying, "no, princess, Daddy's in the struggle," they help their boyfriends throw away money. You are smarter than that, you know that a man with an ego will never tell you "no" he will tell you "yes" and then figure out a way to make you happy. "Well that's dumb, he shouldn't do that, I don't really need those things." No shit, but it happens more than you think, so pay attention now because it will burn you later.

If your boyfriend works for the post office as a clerk making upwards of 50k a year and that's going to be his job for the rest of his life until he's old enough to retire, there's a limit to his finances. Even if he has some additional side hobby job that makes him an extra few hundred a month, understand that if he tries to spend like an NBA rookie whose minimum is 500k, then he will be destitute in a month. A good job with benefits should be looked at like an adult who understands the cost of living, not like a hoodrat who thinks that anyone with a government job is balling. Even at 100k, tax rates, housing, and debt can leave your boyfriend with less money than a man who works in the Macy's stock department and lives with his mother, because that Macy's Dick doesn't have a bill outside of Sprint. No rent because his mother pays it, a hand me down car with no car payment, and no education loan because he didn't go to college. Macy's Dick can afford every color of Air Jordan, endless video games, and even fly down to Miami to blow money fast, because he lives like a teenager; no bills, all disposable income. Your boyfriend may go broke trying to replicate that. As a logical woman, you may think only an idiot would live life in this manner, and given that your boyfriend is intelligent, you don't understand why he would try to stunt on someone he's better than.

Here are the reasons men getting into pissing competitions with each other, and why you must be observant. If a man who doesn't have a fancy job is driving around the city in a car better than him, how does that make your boyfriend feel? If a man whose only job is "dropping bars on Soundcloud," is on Instagram living a larger life, how does that make your boyfriend feel? If the guy who works below him on the job is taking trips to exotic locations and coming back with stories about how foreign chicks love his accent, an insecure man will want to compete. Hos love flash, and men love hos, you get the picture. By the time this man with a good career or well-paying job, meets up with you, he's probably in the habit of spending over his means. You didn't become his girlfriend for the money, it was a plus that he spent so generously, but it was his character that won you over. That man doesn't know that fully, he can assume, but he isn't sure if you are materialistic or not. It's not your fault for only dating men who know how to treat at a high level, it was his fault for fronting. He was trying to portray a dream life that left him broke, but it landed him his dream girl. Now he's stuck. How can he tell you that the interest rates, the back taxes, or the cost of maintaining what he has is piling up and he feels trapped? He can't.

This isn't your battle to fight, it's his. You may be able to afford to financially support a boyfriend or help here and there, but I have women in my inbox who thought the same thing, and those money troubles never stopped. If anything they increase when you add on things like bad business deals, medical emergencies, or a raise on child support from a previous relationship. If a man isn't willing to talk about this, then you have to bring it up, and there is no easy way in. Ask! If you see signs of overspending or careless purchases, inquire about it when you are together in private. Give him your credit score, and ask about his, not to judge him, but so you can build financial trust. You don't need to ask him exactly what he makes a year, you have an estimate from when you were dating; instead ask him if he has any big debts. Again, show him yours first. Meaning, if you owe Discover card and Sallie Mae, bring it up in terms of how you plan to progress from that debt. You aren't waiting to hit the *Sex and The City* casino game to pay off your bills, so share your plan, then ask what his plan is if he does have chunks of debt. The key is to make these things easy to talk about by letting him know that he will not be judged. A man who feels as if he can open up and be real as opposed to being a fake baller will do so because living with financial stress is lonely. You don't write him a check, you don't offer to pay a bill; you get him to confront what's going on, so he can change his habits. You can also help by not adding to the mess. You deserve to go out to nice places, but it doesn't have to be a five-star restaurant every month. You want a pair of shoes, but you know that man needs to pay off his bills not add to them, so decline those types of gifts.

If months go by and you're continuing to communicate about money in this open way, you should see a change. He should have created a budget or his credit score should have risen. If he doesn't want to talk about it, or you see that he's still splurging, then you have a huge fucking problem. Spending can be a drug, and like any narcotic, it won't just bring that person down it will bring you down with them. Don't be so loyal to a man that you feel it's better to brush it under the rug and prevent an argument. He will continue to be that sweet loving guy, and romantically nothing will change, but do you want to fall deeply in love and marry a man whose lifestyle will have you dipping into your savings, readjusting how many kids you can afford, and dragging down your credit? Do you want to be that superwoman that took on a man's finances, he ends up leaving for new pussy, and you're the one left broke? Observe. Ask. Observe again to see if anything changes. If they don't, walk away. Talking about money is only uncomfortable if you fear exposing the truth, but as a Spartan, your first priority is always getting to the truth of a man before things go too far.

THE MAN WHO WANTS TO COMPETE WITH YOU

A story from Ronda Rousey's autobiography recalled her relationship with a fellow UFC fighter, a mediocre talent in the midst of a career decline when they were together. This boyfriend, who I will call Bull (she can't name him in the book for the same reasons I can't name the women I mention here) would tell Ronda, who had just begun her historic rise to the top, that she had it easy because she was fighting girls. At the time, she brushed it off defensively, but it had an effect on her emotionally that she didn't realize until they broke up. Think about that bitch check. Bull telling Ronda that her accomplishments were tainted would be like you rising to become C.E.O in a Nebraska-based company, and someone telling you it means nothing because you didn't pull it off in New York. Misery loves company, and as discussed above, a man's sense of self-worth is validated by his success. To be a woman that has reached a high-level career wise or is bursting with ambition and on her way to something great, reminds a man what he could be...but isn't. Your success won't inspire certain men, it enrages them. How are you able to keep positive, to hustle, to push on, to not only climb, but reach the top? A weak man can never figure out your code to success, so his best option is to bring you down to his level.

How do you take away a woman's power? By making her feel guilty for having it. A man will slowly mind-fuck you, chipping away week by week, month by month, until your self-esteem is reduced to nothing. When you were dating, you were supposed to look for these signs, maybe they weren't there, maybe his life was on an upswing. The relationship him, however, may have fallen on hard times, and needs someone to take it out on. No matter if this was always in your boyfriend or a trait he's developing

347

based on a new situation that broke his spirits, it's unacceptable. You go out to dinner, and you reach for the check to be nice, "Okay, big money, I see how it is," said with a smirk is hostile. You are shopping for a new car, and at first he's happy and doesn't mind helping, then he's blowing you off as if he doesn't have time to go look. You graduate from school, and while he gets you flowers and a card, you can sense by his vibe that he's phoning it in emotionally. You come up with an idea for a business or want to change careers, and he greets you with 100 reasons it won't work, without ever giving you one reason it could. These are real life examples that I've seen, and women who don't understand what's going on turn the other cheek. You can judge people who stay in abusive relationships, brag about how no man could ever Ike Turner you, but few understand the subtle abuse happening every day which leads to that bigger abuse. If a man sees that you allow him to call you stupid, he will keep doing it. If he sees you shrink when he insults one of your physical features, he will keep pushing that button. If a man sees he can make you cry with his words, and then make you wet with his kiss, he will keep playing that game!

Spartans don't compete with anyone, man or woman. The day you see your boyfriend trying to overcompensate by spending money he doesn't have, trying to make you jealous with other women, or using bitch checks to eat at your confidence, let that become the day you go back to being single. Some problems are based on misunderstanding or miscommunication, those are solvable. A dark and nasty attitude towards you based on his own failures can only be resolved inside of that man. You can't fix a man; you can offer him a wrench, but he has to do the repairs. This may happen deep into a relationship when you're already in love and he's been the best boyfriend up to that point. You won't want to give up on him, you will want to talk it out, suggest therapy, or you may even take his side and come up with some asinine excuse for his actions that make it understandable. Do not revert to weak bitch behavior as if this man is irreplaceable. To show someone nothing but love, and have them reward you with hostility and resentment is unforgivable. A man that hates himself so much that he wants to take something strong and beautiful and turn her into something weak and sad isn't a man at all. It's always better to sleep alone than to sleep with the enemy.

Chapter 25:
He's Not a Victim – How to Stop
Boyfriend Manipulation

Placing blame is more effective than saying "sorry." As a relationship gets deeper, women tend to become weaker. Love creates trust, trust leads to vulnerability, vulnerability exposes you to manipulation. The point of dating like a Spartan was to sniff out manipulators who were after sex, trying to use you financially, or attempting to get comfortable with you with no intention of staying with you once he used you up. Another type of manipulation comes during the relationship stage, False Victimization. It will be used by men who love you, not to hurt you, but to get their way and maintain control. As discussed in the previous chapter, men can and will hide all forms of frustration and depression. There are others that won't hide their pain, but use it for sympathy or exploitation. Knowing that women rush in to save men, these males create false grenades for you to fall on. Boyfriend Manipulation preys on your emotions to hijack your brain and gain the upper hand throughout the relationship. You can't yell at him because you know how that hurts his feelings. You can't bring up his spoiled behavior because you know he has Mommy Issues. You can't bring up his financial situation because you know he feels discriminated against at work. You can't even talk about his weak sex game needing work, because his ex cheated on him, and that will put ideas in his head. These boyfriends may have started off great, but once they find out that you are willing to put up with their bullshit to spare their feelings or cater to a past trauma, you become a victim of their con game.

You may have dealt with a man who swore he would commit suicide if you left him. That's not a cause for panic, it's a common ploy. He probably used that on the last girl, because he knew that some women would rather suffer in a bad relationship then see a man hurt himself. No matter how sensitive you are to people going through depression, or if you know someone who really killed themselves, you have to see a con man for the piece of shit he is, not become his prisoner. Besides men who use their insecurities to keep your tit in their mouth, you may also meet guys who use your own insecurities as a smokescreen for their dirty deeds. This form of false victimization relies on him changing the subject of his mistake and placing blame on your attitude, behavior, or paranoia. Here's an example that a reader gave me permission to use:

<u>MISS DC & THE DICK OF DOOM</u>

"...a little more about me, I live in the DC area where I work for the school system. I have a very acquired sense of humor, history nerd, very socially active not as in clubbing lol, but as in social justice. I volunteer and organize on behalf of **** which is where I met my current boyfriend. His name is **** and it will be 16 months in March. We knew of each other for the first two then dated for the next three months, have been official since. Our passions and faith align, which is key for me and we are best friends. I know you hear that a lot but we really are. The problem is his past. Before I go into that I will say that I was previously married but for only a year lol sorry I should have said that at the top. I was young and stupid and he was old and full of shit. That was five years ago and **** is the first guy I have been with sexually and relationship wise since my divorce. Your article educated fool, was my come to Jesus moment lol. It introduced me to you and I wanted to be a Spartan so bad. There were other men I dated before but **** was the first one I actually went after and it lead to something that I think is special. Before you roll your eyes like why is this girl coming to me if things are so great. I will be honest. I messed it up, NC. I messed it up real bad and I can't afford to lose him. He has a girl who used to work at **** with him that has become an issue and I didn't handle it right."

[The girl was a platonic friend who her boyfriend had sex with once. Now this old girl has moved back to the area.]

"...helping her move in was not an issue. He did not ask my permission but he did discuss that he was helping a friend. I didn't know she was the friend until she calls him on facetime to thank him at 11pm at night. NC, you know that a woman does not facetime a man at night that's a magic hour, so off that I caught an attitude as if this bitch was trying to play me. He handled the situation properly, told her I was over and we were relaxing. She apologized and then asked could she say hello to the woman that stole his heart or some dumb shit like that. I was in my PJs, hair wrapped for sleep, I did not want to speak but he put me in front of her. Full face of makeup at 11pm I'm not exaggerating. From then I knew I had to watch her...two weeks ago I received a lunch invite from one of the donors, I consider her more of an associate than friend. I did not know if this was personal or professional. We begin to talk and she asks about **** and my boyfriend. I was caught by surprise. It didn't seem like gossip at the time, but she brought up that she had seen the two of them having lunch on 14th last week and then on Monday she passed them in the car around 6pm. On Monday he told me he had to help his friend out, again did not say her, and I did not go over to his apartment. The donor told **** left town before because she was carrying on with a married man.

I thanked her, took the rest of the day off of work, and I'm not going to lie yes I cried my eyes out. I asked **** to come over, but he was with his brother. This is the truth they wanted to include me in their event a day before but I declined. So I waited for him to call me to say goodnight. I couldn't sleep. I couldn't eat. I was a mess. I went to our pastor's youtube video to hear the word and calm down. That didn't work. I felt so stupid. I was even going to go to your website. Instead I tracked down **** mother's address from our database from when she was a member because I could not find her current address. Yes sir I drove to her mother's home this is now around ten. And I knock on the door.

The stepfather comes to the door and I ask if he knows where **** lives. I put on a calm voice, smiled, and he was about to give her up when the mom came asking what was going on. …about twenty minutes later **** shows up and I'm sitting on her mom's couch, cool and calm. She asks what's going on and I freaking explode. I could not tell you all the things I said but I accused her in front of her mom and her stepdad of having sex with **** being banished for sleeping around with every married man in DC and I wished death on her and eternal damnation lol. I was gone out of my head and didn't care.

The mom threatened to call the police but I assured her I was done. I only wanted **** to know she could have him. I knew **** was going to call me once he dropped his brother off and I would tell him then, but two minutes after I pull off, he is blowing up my phone. She called him. I ignore because I was so upset I know I would have crashed yelling at him. By the time I get home he's in my apartment already. He says I crossed the line. Her stepfather has cancer, and I had no right to disturb them. That they are only friends. I told him about the donor and stood my ground about him sneaking around with her. He pulled out his phone and showed me a text from the donor from a month earlier. This bitch was flirting with him via text and he was telling her off in that same text. She responded with something derogatory about me. **** went on to say that the donor was a snake in the grass and that's the only thing he has hid because he didn't want that to hurt my service work knowing we need her money. I felt like shit, NC. I got played by that bitch and allowed that devil to corrupt me. This was on Wednesday, we haven't spoken until this morning [**This email was sent on a Saturday**] and he told me that my trust issues from my husband lead to this, that I didn't fully love him, all I see is my ex, and that I need to get help. He is willing to stand by me so long as it doesn't happen again. I'm over my ex-husband, have been for years, I swear. Maybe there is something else wrong with me that would make me overreact? I don't want him to leave me? I want to get down deep and fix me. I could fill another email with all the things **** does for me and look how I behaved. Am I suppressing my marriage? Maybe something else? Do you think you can help me unblock this stuff?"

MASTER OF PUPPETS

Miss DC was bat shit crazy, that was my first thought. To track down another woman, when your man should be the person you confront is the ultimate weak bitch trait. She would rather face someone she has no emotional connection to than her boyfriend because she feared pushing him away with her anger, and I told her as much. However, his story sounded suspect and his reaction very manipulative. In the weeks that followed that email, I asked Miss DC to not distance herself from the donor, but to get closer. It turns out that the donor wasn't just flirting with Miss DC's boyfriend, she was sleeping with him for just as long as Miss DC had been official with him. The boyfriend distanced himself, as most do when side pussy loses its newness. This fallback lead to the donor stalking him, messaging him, and finally taking revenge by snitching to Miss DC about the other woman. The donor wasn't just gossiping she was trying to expose Miss DC's boo because he had a new side bitch. She told me these revelations but didn't want to confront her boyfriend in case it was a lie. If she brought more drama home, her boyfriend would leave her, and for a weak woman, love is enough to put up with disrespect. She didn't want to go forward with the truth, so she stopped emailing me.

Nearly a year later Miss DC returned telling me they broke up. Her boyfriend had been sleeping with his so-called friend and that female donor. Her boyfriend used that mother incident to make her feel ashamed enough to look the other way, which she did, then he became extremely sloppy to the point where he left evidence out in the open. Her last email to me was more of an apology about not listening. I'm never offended when a woman doesn't take my advice, it's not about me being right, it's about the truth they already know but are scared to confront. It wasn't Miss DC's intelligence; it was her fear that kept her guilt-ridden and a self-made prisoner to love. She knew that something was going on, but she allowed her want for love to cloud the evidence. Her boyfriend blamed her past relationship for her mentally being off, and she fell for it, choosing to question her sanity rather than his words. This man was able to make her think she had insecurities in order to get away with cheating, and she bought into his diagnoses above her own common sense.

I use her extreme to point to what may be your normal. In a relationship, disagreements happen; miscommunication happens. You two will become upset with one another, but you can't allow blame to be placed at your feet in such an obvious way. This starts with owning up to your own pettiness, so it can't be used as a ploy. Sometimes, you will be in the wrong, and he has the right to point this out. Know the difference between you being unreasonable and him playing puppet master. You wanted to spend time together, but he couldn't make it. So you caught an attitude as if he didn't care about the relationship. You told him to do you a favor, he forgot about it, and you overreacted as if it was purposeful. You didn't listen to something he said, he got upset, and you were overly defensive as if he didn't have the right to be pissed. You accused him of going behind your back when all you had was a feeling, not real evidence. He called out your paranoia, and you wouldn't own up to it. Most women go overboard when they feel as if something isn't going their way in the relationship, and often it will be imagined based on their past fear or current paranoia. You may be more secure in your emotions, but even you will fuck up. When you do, be woman enough to accept responsibility for your actions.

A Spartan does not carry insecurities into a relationship nor does she become so engulfed in love that she allows new insecurities to grow based on the fear of losing her man to another woman or losing her man to boredom. Those fears project distrust that causes arguments where a man will be on the defensive. Two people who are too stubborn to communicate will always invite drama into their relationship, and no matter how many times you make up, your relationship will grow weaker over time, not stronger. That shouldn't be in your character at this stage of your evolution. Stay the course and do not let negative thoughts take you back to that weak place where everyone is out to get you. Once you become woman enough to own up to your faults, you become immune to guilt trips. There can be no blame placed on your mental state once you erase second thoughts that you are acting out of irrational feelings.

SEEING THROUGH HIS ACT

If your boyfriend is crying about you not making time for him, but you know that you spend the majority of your free time with him, then his victim baiting won't work. Unlike a typical bitch that would race over and give in with, "I'm sorry babe, I didn't mean to be so busy," you can check him with receipts. "I've spent 4 hours a day over the last five days with you, and I stayed the night last Saturday, don't lay that shit on me." Do not let a man game you like a little boy game's his mother. Men want what they want when they want it; be smart enough to know that isn't love, it's control. The more you become caught up in being at his disposal the more he expects it, which translate to you ending up in a marriage where you can't breathe without him giving you the okay. Because you are so no-nonsense and forward, a man will try to use your strength against you. He will call you mean, say you're bossy, or make passive remarks about how you always have to be right. These are bitch checks. They aren't as brutal or vicious as those men who look to tear down women and abuse them, but they work in the same manner. As a Spartan, you will see through what men do, you know their motivation before they can even verbalize it, and this will lead to them trying to bring you down to the level of other women.

By putting thoughts in your mind that you are too strong, a man plants the seeds of loss. Your boyfriend will hint that you are in trouble of pushing him away by exercising control, which can cause you to let things slide, bite your tongue, or limit your personality to fit into his "be a nice girl" box. Take inventory of your personality, and prove that he's full of shit. Being mean is cursing him out for something small like hanging out an hour later than he planned or not taking the trash out. Being bossy is always making him do things or go places you want to go without compromise. Being a know-it-all is you constantly chiming in with an opinion, instead of having a two-sided discussion. You should know your personality at this point and how to co-exist with people in a way that's not narcissistic, abrasive, or condescending. When a man tries to check you with accusations, all you have to do is present facts.

This isn't an argument where you wag a finger in his face like, "Name one thing! Name one thing!" That's not how you prove your point.

You need to look at the situation, then prove your truth with evidence. Let's say he's calling you mean because he's sick, and you don't have time to come over and baby him. He ignores your call or says, "I'd do it for you, selfish ass." Remind him that while you know he's not feeling well; you have things you have to do first. If being responsible is mean in his world, then so be it. You aren't going to change your life for any man and he needs to know that now, not later.

Men are like bullies, you stand up to them once, you shut them down forever. You must be Spartan enough not to give a fuck about how he takes it. The fear that he will leave you, start talking to a woman who "gets" him, or any weak thought which pops into your head, is counterproductive to your mission. If a man wants to leave you because your personality is too strong or you won't kiss his ass and mommy him, then let him leave! You are a Spartan, the same way you found him, you can find one even better. By going through such a pussy of a man, you learn how to spot this breed even earlier during the screening stage. Men tend to blame women in an act of reverse psychology meant to make their lives easier. By pointing to you as having an attitude, being mean, or not seeing things from his viewpoint, it stops you from digging deeper into his behavior.

Is he a victim or is he like some dirty cop that gets caught, and has to reframe the evidence to make it seem like you were at fault? Know your behavior, know your flaws, and know the difference between you being in the wrong versus a man using your behavior as a motive for his dirt. A guy will blame cheating on the fact that you went out for a night with your friends. He will blame losing a job on you not being around to talk to him about his stress. He will even blame not calling you for a week on something you said that offended him. All of these things are meant to put you back in check, to let him get away with whatever sneaky shit he's been doing, and to send a message to you that this relationship is built on his sensitivity. Do not walk on eggshells for any man, do not cast doubt on your own sanity, and never surrender power to a manipulator.

Chapter 26:
Growing Apart - Threesomes, Breaks, & Other Mistakes

O nce you're in a relationship the mind shifts from getting a man, to keeping a man. What's supposed to be a time of enjoying each other, discovering new things, and moving into the realm of a lasting relationship, becomes panic. *He's going to get bored. He's going to cheat. He's going to get annoyed with me.* The fear of holding on to someone they can't physically control scares the fuck out of most women. In response, typical women create fairytale stories that make them sleep better at night. Do the things he likes and avoid asking him to go out of his way, and he won't grow bored. Give a man good sex, and he won't cheat. Don't nag and always provide a relaxed environment, and he won't get annoyed. Do you understand that there is no direct correlation to any of that shit? Your basic "how to make a man happy" blueprint crumbles under the truth that people are constantly growing and revamping what they want in life. Put a little boy in a room with all the toys he wanted for Christmas and he will crave the experience of something new by next month. It's the experience of life done different, not done at his command, that keeps a male's interests. A man will always grow apart from a woman who no longer challenges, teaches, or inspires him. To simply, *love him harder*, misses the point of what you both need to develop a strong partnership.

A woman should not be the game master that has to keep a relationship fresh. Yet, the misogynistic solution always comes back to female submission. Do you realize how often we men ask, "How do we keep our lady happy?" Never! How is it that men never have to consider ways to maintain your love, but you are consumed by how to maintain a man's love?

You read books, you go to lectures, you listen to podcasts, you ask other people—how do I keep him in love! That's not a Spartan mindset, that's pathetic. A man's only worry is when he fucks up, (and they all fuck up) and how to kiss ass and get back in her good graces. There is no extra drive to sustain a woman's love on a man's part, and it has nothing to do with who loves who more. Men know that you should never have to make someone happy to be with you; either they are or they aren't! This mentality has been working for centuries and men win with it daily. So why are women still in the business of trying so fucking hard to please a false master?

Unlearn the way you look at love. Your boyfriend does not need you to be his slave, his mother, or his jester. The person in the relationship with the most power is the one that tries the least. Unless this is a relationship you started after dating like a Spartan, then it's likely you are the one tap dancing for dick's approval. *What do you want to eat, bae? We can do whatever you feel like, bae. It's up to you, bae. I'm happy with whatever, bae.* You live like *I Dream of Jeannie,* and it's because you don't understand how to partner with a man, only to serve. Being a girlfriend, is not grunt work, it is not servitude, it is an equal alliance. Even if you like being domestic and are happy catering, understand what motivates you to take that role, and be sure it comes from a sincere place. For most, being a girlfriend is practice for being a wife. You do all the duties of a wife, he notices that effort, he knows that he will be taken care of, so he marries you. Ha! What an outdated formula that continues to fuck over ignorant women. This standard submission is tied to your quest to be chosen as a wife and it's time you reevaluated the lengths you should go for matrimony.

Little girls play house, grow up wanting to run a real house. Little girls play mom with their dolls, grow up wanting to be that mom to real dolls. How can you achieve those things at the ultimate level? You get married. A man is the gatekeeper to marriage. He has traditionally held the power of getting down on bended knee and proposing, and even in the 21st century, women buckle under the pressure of being chosen. If a man does not want you enough to ask for your hand, then you will remain that little girl simply playing that role. You don't want to live in a house with a man that is just a boyfriend. You don't want to co-parent with a man and be merely a baby's mama. The world is filled with women that can play those roles, but you want that real union. The pressure is on you to do whatever you can to open that gate, to make him see you as special, as deserving, as a WIFE. No matter how empowered you try to feel, you still think your happiness rests in the hands of a man. This is the root of why women try, while men are content to be.

A man doesn't have control, you give it to him by thinking in this fashion. When you place your power in the hands of a man to win his love, you will always fail. You end up the depressed woman who lives with the results of an unbalanced relationship or become that bitter woman who has to constantly start over because she didn't pay attention the first time. As I said in the beginning, your world will teach you the same lessons until you get it right. With all of this truth the universe is sending you, will you learn or will you keep playing dumb? There are three major things I want to address that will come up when your relationship hits a bump or two. The want to run away, and prove a point to your boyfriend. The want to overcompensate sexually, to keep him from other women. And finally, the want to sacrifice your power in order to hold on to a man who is no longer interested in a future with you. Fear of not ending up with what you wanted is at the core of these mistakes. At the relationship stage, fear's grip becomes the strongest, so you have to be at your hardest.

TAKING A BREAK VS. GIVING SPACE

Here's an example of checkers as opposed to chess. Your average couple goes through an issue that can't be handled in one sitting, or they continue to have the same exact problem over and over. This can range from not making time to see each other, a white lie about where someone was, not wanting to move in together, other people knowing too much of your business, loaning money, all the way to very serious things like infidelity, insulting someone in a way you can't take back, or the big one—not wanting to get married. A woman who's playing checkers will take one of these problems and try to solve it by "showing him I don't need him." To a non-Spartan this sounds very Spartan, but in reality, it's very Junior year of high school. Taking a break from your boyfriend is meant to give you time to regroup and figure out what you want. Here's where I can smell the bullshit seeping from your pores. No matter if you call it a "break" or actually break-up under the pretense of "for now..." you aren't walking away in a manner that evokes change or solves the issue. Unlike solid "it's over," breakups, breaks are half-ass declarations, not absolutes where you fully embrace being single again. You aren't showing a man you can do better, so he should do better, you're using a temporary separation as a bluff.

I've talked to women on breaks, and they aren't truly single. They tell me they're waiting for him to get his life together or taking time to figure out what they really want out of the commitment. Unlike a true single person, they have the safety net of, "I can go back," so these women never feel alone, just apart. Where's the challenge when a person is still available to you? Where's the motivation when your back isn't against the wall, just resting against one? Imagine an employee at an Amazon warehouse going to their boss and saying they need a break until they figure out if this job is for them. Not a vacation, not a sick day, they are going to walk away from the company until they are mentally ready to do the job or you treat them better. Amazon would fire his ass; no company is going to bow to ultimatums and indifference because that opens the door for a repeat of that same tactic. The break you are going on is an ultimatum meant to bring change, but will it work?

You taking a time out is the escalation of saying, "A good woman isn't going to wait around forever." When you bark at a man, he will apologize, promise to change and do better, then go back to the same behavior or excuses once things cool down. You can't negotiate with someone who doesn't respect your bite! The bark of "I'm not going to wait around," didn't work, so the only thing left to do is to show a man that you aren't playing by breaking up...but you don't want to actually break up—a break makes it real without being definite. By putting your boyfriend on a hard probation where you might be out dating other men and may never get back with him, should put the fear of God in him, but it doesn't, because he feels your lack of power.

I know four men that had babies while on break from their regularly scheduled girlfriends. Multiply that amount by five and that's how many guys I've known who have actively found new pussy while on break. "It's all good, I was on break when it happened," becomes the pill women must swallow when a man comes back with a pregnant woman or has to explain why a rival female is still hanging around trying to break them up after they get back together. Negative fallout from a break is rarely something a man has to deal with because women, as noted, don't give into the fact that they are fully single. They typically remain loyal to the man they are on break from. She may go on a date, make out with a guy, but the guilt that she still belongs to the man she considers her boyfriend remains. I had a very awkward sexual encounter with a woman on break, who took me to the edge, then pulled back with tears because she felt she was being unfaithful. On the other side, I had a good friend who went on break and had a girl pregnant by the end of that month. He was bursting at the seams to go raw in new pussy, and he let his excitement lead to conception. It's not about love, it's about sex—know the difference. **Most men see "break" as a pussy vacation, not a time to change their ways.** Your love will keep you loyal to a man who is technically not your man, but males aren't wired like that. People on break usually get back together within three months, both promise to love each other better and communicate more, then six months from then they go on another break usually related to some dirt that happened on the first break. It's a mess that you should always avoid.

If you still want to be with him, why go through with a charade? You can give a person space, or request that a person gives you space while still being committed to each other. The gimmick of a temporary breakup meant to crack the whip does not move you forward in an adult way. Here's what giving space should look like when trying to work through a solvable problem: Instead of hanging out each night, only see each other once a week. When you do meet up, it should not be to go on dates that rekindle the flame of romance. It should be real therapy or self-therapy. Go out to a public setting and talk openly about the issue for a solid two-three hours.

This means there is no chance it will lead to sex or uncontrollable arguing because you're right there in the middle of a coffee shop or something similar. It's not about laughing or saying "sorry" but hearing each other out. Pulling back to reevaluate the relationship is a smart strategy, but also ask yourself if any work is being done while separated. A man will tell you he's working on him, but is he? Women who push a man away only to take him back because he claims he changed are idiots. Think about this:

You want to take a dog off the leash, flag him away, and tell him to come back when he learns how to stop shitting on the carpet. A dog will come back with his head down, lick your face, but he will still shit on the carpet! You learn by talking, not by pushing that person away. If you love a person, you don't give them a break from their responsibilities. Being a boyfriend means he should stand in the pocket and do the work requested. Being a girlfriend means being emotionally strong enough to confront your anger, not drive it away until you calm down enough to forgive him. You two shouldn't be off on your own, you should be in each other's face trying to communicate on a real level. That means opening up about why the same mistakes keep happening and discussing rules you can set going forward. To give a man or yourself a golden ticket to go be a single person doesn't help, it creates further problems.

WILL HE CHEAT ON YOU?

You can't stop a man from cheating on you. It's that simple, but the majority of women don't want to believe that because it makes them nervous. Most girls like clean, simple, organized reasoning. Blueprint logic makes relationships formulaic and safe. Suck his dick, make him cum, tell him he's loved, and he will never look at another woman. That's how the world should work, right? Why would a man who is so well taken care of risk losing that just to cum in some girl he doesn't know, doesn't like, and won't remember? A man falling in love with someone new, that makes sense. With an emotional affair, you can reflect on what went wrong and how to prevent it, but for a man to randomly put his dick in some bitch just to scratch an itch you could have scratched is chaos. Isis attacks are more logical than men lusting after new pussy, and it worries you to death that nothing you can do will mean anything if a man gets an urge. The truth isn't meant to feel warm and protective. This icy feeling is why the truth doesn't win out over wishful thinking. You live in a world where other scared women tell you there is a rhyme and a reason for cheating which you can prevent. You live in a world where men who get caught with their hands in the cookie jar lie, "It's because I felt lonely only seeing you twice a week," or "I'm insecure about my manhood, don't leave me, help me."

There is always an incentive for a liar to keep lying even after being caught. For a Bill Clinton to walk up to a Hillary Clinton and say, "I just wanted my dick sucked, and she had that slutty look I like," does not save a marriage. The ability to apologize, blame it on some underlying issue, and promise to correct it, always gets a man a second chance! This is why there is so much misinformation about cheating, no one wants to talk about it in a real way. Therefore, if you sit in a group of ratchet women who only know what their cheating exes have told them, they will tell you that sucking his dick with a certain technique, dressing up, role playing, using toys, Kegel grips, or any of their basic ideas, will make a man stay faithful. It's garbage.

When you listen to survivalist tell you an earthquake is coming and you need to reinforce your home, you will become paranoid about earthquakes. When you listen to a bunch of birds' chirp about how to fuck, suck, and cater to a man's sex drive to keep him from stepping out, you will become paranoid about cheating. Instead of living your life, focusing on what's in front of you, and the joy of being in a relationship, it becomes all about protecting your investment from other women. His phone vibrates and he smiles at the text, could be another bitch—quick fuck him. He doesn't come over and wants to stay home for the night, could be another bitch—quick send him nudes. He didn't want to have sex last night or this morning, could be another bitch—quick amp up the freak level by sucking his balls while he sleeps. If you have to eat another girl's box in front of him, make sex tapes, and give your boyfriend hall passes to sample other women so you can keep his love, then he didn't love you in the first place. Has a man ever told you, "Do this or I'll fuck another chick?" If he did you would smack the taste out of your mouth for assuming that you would compete for love. Today's men don't have to tell women to do extra because women take it upon themselves to do it out of fear that he will grow bored.

My favorite New Yorker texted me a few months ago and she asked if I ever considered a threesome with my wife. What man wouldn't want a threesome in fantasy, but in reality, there are things you have to weigh. Mainly, who does it benefit and what are the repercussions? I know my wife better than the back of my hand, and no matter how many women she calls "cute," she's not about that life. A man will test the waters to see how bi-curious his woman is, but if it's not her cup of tea, it would be cruel to suggest she do something sexual she doesn't want to do.

My friend who was considering a threesome for her boyfriend said, "I didn't like the idea initially, but it's farfetched to believe you can keep a man satisfied for 20-50 years. You have to do something to add that excitement. As much as I'd like to think I'll never get cheated on, I know men get bored." I responded that a man's lust for new pussy doesn't stop once you invite threesomes. Trying to cure a man's lust for other women is like Bruce Banner trying to cure The Hulk, it's never going to happen.

Holding his hand while he gets his fix of something new, may bring some women the comfort that he's not going to do it behind her back, but again, a male's sex drive doesn't go by a woman's logic. Outside of the stereotype of him falling for the other woman, there's also the more normal reaction of, "If she's okay with me doing it with her, then me sliding off into something when she's not around won't hurt." Once that *what is cheating* line becomes blurred, you lose control of boundaries. At that point it may as well become an open relationship because telling a man to "wait until your birthday for new pussy," will not work. A man's want for other women, as discussed earlier in this book, isn't just about the physical act of thrusting inside of a new vagina. It's the hunt, the capture, and the challenge. To tell a man he can toss up some girl you found off Backpage, will be met with the same reaction as that Indominus Rex on *Jurassic World*; he doesn't want to be feed by you, he's a savage that will still find a way to get out and hunt.

In the case of my friend, she wouldn't mind experimenting with another woman. Therefore, I was all for her turning some girl into Ellen DeGeneres in pursuit of a nut, but I maintained that it should be for her benefit. If your sexual fantasy stays in the back of your head while he gets to play his out under the pretense of "I'm a man I need to be entertained," then where is the compromise? This is where all the progressive logic of threesomes, hall passes, and open relationships fall apart. If the true motivation (you know the true motivation if you're honest with yourself) is to keep him from growing bored, then it's not equal. Is your man worried about not satisfying you to the point where he will let another dude take a turn with you? Doubtful. Which goes back to the sad practice of women going to the extreme to keep a man satisfied, when extremes are not needed.

Would it have been better for Jackie to invite Marilyn Monroe into the bedroom at the White House? Should MLK have asked for a hall pass while he was on the road to be considerate of Coretta's feelings? In front of you or behind you, the emotional punch that comes from the person you love being inside someone else doesn't dull. Most men see getting pussy as just getting pussy, but women tend to see it as something meaningful. The solution isn't to change your view on sex to fit a male's view so it doesn't feel personal when he's hitting her from the back. You can't lie to yourself, it won't stick. No matter how often you two laugh about it after the ménage, the image will haunt you. If he's going to cheat, he's going to cheat. If your relationship fails, then it was meant to fail. A wild night can't save it.

This is about fear, not fun. The fear that you won't be enough to satisfy a man's appetite is so great you are willing to share. If he does it with you, it gives you some semblance of control. Nope! He's in control because you have admitted with clear actions that you will do anything to keep him while he simply has to show up and fuck two women. It's not about his birthday, anniversary, or a weekend in Vegas; it's about not being enough for your man and having to find out the hard way that he didn't exercise dick control. You don't want to find out in a way that embarrasses you, shames you, and turns you into just another girl with a man who's off the leash. Maybe your father cheated on your mother, maybe your ex cheated on you, maybe you were busting it open for a taken man, and you don't want to be on the other end of that. Your pride is tied to being a woman who can keep her man happy, and that's the problem. **You don't have to work this hard to keep your man happy—he is or he isn't.** Slinging dick, running the street, sneaking around, this is not a reflection of how unfulfilling you are, it's a reflection of how undisciplined he is!

To internalize a man's cheating as your own failure will erode your self-esteem, turn you bitter, and create trust issues. Where does that road lead you? Back to being another weakling scared of "what if" and scarred by paranoia that all men will cheat on her because the last man had ultimate power over her self-esteem. Never allow a stupid little man to break your spirit. Embrace the challenge that other women run from, don't let fear win by opening the door to your kingdom like, "Take him! Just let me watch." Be confident that you are more than enough to keep his attention.

PICKING AT SCABS

Forgiveness should be written in permanent ink. No matter how mad you become, don't dig up old dirt and shovel it on top of a new problem. Your man hurts you, and while caught up in the moment the only thing you can do to even the field is to remind him about the time XYZ happened. *Remember when you forgot my birthday? Remember that bitch I caught you texting? Remember that money I loaned you? Remember when I let you use my credit? Remember that night you got drunk and said*—stop it! If you are still with a man who has done wrong, that means you have forgiven him for that past wrong. Communication, working out problems, agreeing to new rules and boundaries, those are the tools used to hold love together when life tests you. What's the point of doing all of that work, just to unravel it during one heated argument? You can't blame it on your emotions. You own your emotions, you control what you say, and if you haven't mastered that by now, then go back to the first part of this book and keep resetting yourself until you let go of that weak bitch immaturity.

You can't rip open stitches and then say, "Sorry, I didn't mean it." You did mean it! People bring up old subjects that are still raw because they haven't made peace with them. Which begs the question, did you actually forgive or did you just accept? There's a difference. If you forgive someone, you embrace their actions, but you don't excuse them. Instead, you internalize and confront those mistakes, make peace with the reasons behind them that you were given, then let go without animosity or worry of a repeat. To accept as opposed to forgiving it, is to acknowledge a person's mistake, but leave the emotional hurt dangling like a sore spot you don't want to touch. You don't want to confront of reason because it pains you. You have to confront that hurt in order to forgive and heal or that would will fester. Be an adult, don't pick at scabs. If your boyfriend pulls this same act and throws your skeletons in your face, then the same rules apply. He's not over the hurt, and you need to call him out on it. Don't get into a screaming match about who did what. Repeat the steps listed in this chapter: Give each other space, communicate, and work towards a better solution. If old problems continue to create new arguments, then the well is too poisoned. It's time for a breakup...

Chapter 27:
How to Stop a Breakup

he's drifting away, and there is nothing you can think of to reverse the course of your relationship. Your boyfriend, love interest, partner, whoever he may be, no matter if he's a holdover from your pre-Spartan days or a result of your new life, how do you stop him from leaving you? The communication isn't working. The space you're giving each other just created more space. The talks keep going in circles. It's not working, but you aren't ready to risk the dick and lose him; he is a good man, and you are in love. You aren't stupid, though. You know he's getting tired of you. He isn't spelling it out, but the writing is on the wall, he's no longer happy. Ask yourself right now, are you happy? *I'm happy if he's happy*...isn't an answer, just proof you haven't graduated to Spartanhood. You can't even be honest about how you feel because your entire life is built around this man seeing you as special, staying with you, and you not ending up alone. You know you're soft, but you don't want to hear about how weak you are anymore, you want a fix. Your heart is breaking over this man. Physically you feel like shit and mentally you can't focus on anything but him. When you do pull it together and he leaves your mind, it only lasts for a bit...then you remember...and you're sucked back into sadness. You are about to lose your best friend, your soul mate, your future and you need a solution.

You want to Spartan Up, but this book came too late. To set things right with your man like a Spartan would require you to turn back time and do everything different. You can't re-meet him, re-date him, re-commit, and be this better version of you. So how do you fix it and stop a relationship that's already sinking? There is a medicine for your CPR relationship...

BLUE PILL

No matter if he fucked up or if you were the one in the wrong, you can keep your man and salvage your relationship. That solution? <u>Give in</u>. Whatever he wants, give it to him. Whatever he's done, forgive him. Whatever lie you caught him in, let it go. Whatever manipulation he's done to create that wedge, black it out. If he's grown tired of you and isn't putting in the effort, don't threaten him, show him that you are willing to compromise. If his attention has begun to split to other women, drop your anger and show him you are going to fight to bring back the spark. If you were being a brat or bully, caught up in your own baggage, and you broke his heart, get on your knees. Beg him to take you back by acknowledging your trust issues or past. Blame daddy, mommy, your exes, and then go find a therapist to show him you're trying for "us." He will give you another shot. If you want to keep a man, the solution is as simple as the things listed. Submit and do things his way. Give him your power and go back to being a placeholder. In a matter of months, all this stuff about being a Spartan will fade and you will be back in a mindset that makes life bearable, on autopilot. Just another peasant pretending to be a Queen. Just another weak bitch that barks at her man when he does wrong, but never bites. Another little girl trying to play house with a man who is still looking for her replacement.

You couldn't even make it to the mountaintop of Sparta, you made it to basecamp and turned back. You cried for change but chose to be like every other girl in the world; content, comfortable, typical. Take that easy road back down to normalcy where you hypnotize yourself to believe in fairytales again. No one has to know that you are weak. You can still walk around with false confidence, telling your fellow peasants what you will and won't do for love, give advice that you would never take, and play make believe on the internet as if you're happy. Those without power are no different than those that turn away from power. You belong in that flock of fraudulence that breathes lies and perpetrates through life. You never planned on changing. You saw what it took to get to the top and it scared you. Everything scares you, which is why it's better that you continue to settle like the coward you are. Give in and give up. Find solace in the field with the rest of the sheep because this crown is too heavy for your head.

RED PILL

If you knew the title of this chapter was a trick question, then you passed your final test. A Spartan would never ask, "how do I stop a breakup," that's the epitome of a typical weak bitch thought. A Queen doesn't hold on; she is held onto! What's a breakup to a Spartan? Death and Rebirth. Your game doesn't stop to mourn the loss of something that helped make you stronger, it pushes ahead to an even greater love. Your love life isn't a movie where the guy comes back and makes everything right in the end, it's the movie set where you wake the fuck up and realize you no longer need to follow that patronizing script. This book didn't come too late; this isn't about wishing you read this before your last relationship or years ago before your first mistake, it's about using it in the **now**. You are exactly where you need to be. If your relationship isn't working despite all of your efforts, then get the hint, it was never meant to work, it was a step on your ladder.

You may not want to lose him, but you have no choice. Your man isn't moving away from you, the universe is pushing him away. If you truly are a Spartan, then you recognize this is not a tragedy, it is your will. The fact that you two can no longer stay on the same page, no matter how hard you try, is all the proof you need to walk away. Even if you bent the rules of time, this boyfriend, your last boyfriend, the ones before him, none of them would have made it. If your eyes were this open and your confidence this solid, you would have attracted a much stronger man, but you didn't. You got the man who the old you manifested, needed, and deserved. This is the truth you don't want to stare in the eye, but you must. Your relationship doesn't need to be reset; it needs to be erased. You are your own salvation, and for the first time in this life, you should understand that you don't need a man's love to save you, complete you, or uplift you; yours is enough. The stronger you become, the stronger you will attract. This was never a love story; it was always meant to be a rise to power.

CORONATION

What's next? Conquest. Use your power by actually going out and doing these things. The old you would have read and re-read, and then found another book to read and re-read because she was indecisive. She wanted to think, think, and think some more as opportunity after opportunity passed her by. You don't need a PhD in this, you need to do it! Where do you start? At the beginning. I don't care what's going on in your life, if you are single, seeing someone, with someone, or stuck in-between one of those steps, you start at the beginning. Don't read about being a Spartan. Be a Spartan. Reset your mind, revamp your confidence, and change your world. This book is not to be cherry picked or flipped through; it has to be done in the ways laid out. If you are in the midst of a problem that you can't solve, a situation that is stressing you, or can't motivate yourself to get off your ass, start at the beginning. Do the work, Awaken the Spartan within, and let her conquer what you cannot. Every obstacle in life will fade away once success becomes the only goal allowed to enter your mind. To think you can't do something is the same as thinking you can do something, either way, you end up with results that reflect your beliefs. This is your world, Spartan. Believe in yourself like I believe in you.

<u>Every morning and every night remember to remember</u>

You deserve the affection that you kept trying to pour into others.
You deserve the same motivation that you tried to inspire in others.
You deserve the high of happy, without the low of sadness.
You deserve the joy of being spoiled, without the catch of having to repay.
You deserve the relaxation of trust, without the paranoia of betrayal.
You deserve to be confident, without the reminder to be humble.
You deserve to look at your reflection with eyes of awe, not judgment.
You deserve to be held forever, not for a night.
You deserve to be first, second, and third.
You deserve to have everything you want.
You deserve this power. It is who you are and who you will always be.

Men don't love women like you. They worship them.

Don't just read… Listen & Spartan Up!

Bonus Audio Book On Sale Now

CPSIA information can be obtained
at www.ICGtesting.com
Printed in the USA
LVHW03s0157140818
586832LV00015B/1579/P